P9-CKA-476

BUILDING
FOR THE
LAWN
AND
GARDEN

BUILDING
FOR THE
LAWN
and
GARDEN

A Step-by-Step Guide to Making Benches, Gates, Planters, Swings, Feeders, Tables, and More

JOHN KELSEY
AND
IAN J. KIRBY

Rodale Press, Inc.
Emmaus, Pennsylvania

OUR PURPOSE

*"We inspire and enable people to improve
their lives and the world around them."*

© 1997 by John Kelsey

Published in 1997 by Rodale Press, Inc.
by arrangement with John Kelsey

All rights reserved. No part of this publication may be
reproduced or transmitted in any form or by any means,
electronic or mechanical, including photocopy, record-
ing, or any other information storage and retrieval system, without the written permission of the publisher.

The authors and editors who compiled this book have
tried to make all of the contents as accurate and as correct as possible. Plans, illustrations, photographs, and
text have all been carefully checked and cross-checked.
However, due to the variability of local conditions, construction materials, personal skill, and so on, neither the
authors nor Rodale Press assumes any responsibility for
any injuries suffered or for damages or other losses
incurred that result from the material presented herein.
All instructions and plans should be carefully studied
and clearly understood before beginning construction.

Printed in the United States of America on acid-free ∞,
recycled ♻ paper

Library of Congress Cataloging-in-Publication Data

Kelsey, John (1946-)
    Building for the lawn and garden: a step-by-step guide to
making benches, gates, planters, swings, feeders, tables, and
more / John Kelsey and Ian Kirby
    384 p., 21.3 cm x 27.6 cm
    ISBN 0–87596–772–8 (alk. paper)
    1. Outdoor furniture. 2. Woodwork. 3. Garden ornaments
and furniture—Design and construction. I. Kirby, Ian J. II.
Title.
    TT197.5.09K45 1997
    684.1'8—dc21   96–54026

Distributed in the book trade by St. Martin's Press

2 4 6 8 10 9 7 5 3 1   hardcover

Building for the Lawn and Garden
Project Designer: Ian J. Kirby
Project Builder: Ian J. Kirby
Writer: John Kelsey
Step-by-Step Photography: John Kelsey
Drawings: John Kelsey
Book Design: Michael Mandarano
Page Layout: Michael Mandarano, Glee Barre
Copy Editors: Larry Green, Linda Whipkey
Production Associate: Morgan B. Kelsey
Indexer: Harriet Hodges

Rodale Press Home and Garden Books
Editor: Bob Moran
Cover Designer: Diane Ness Shaw
Cover Photographer: Mitch Mandel
Cover Photo Stylist: Marianne Grape Laubach
Copy Editor: Barbara McIntosh Webb

Vice President and Editorial Director: Margaret J. Lydic
Managing Editor, Woodworking Books: Kevin Ireland
Copy Director: Dolores Plikaitis
Art Director: Paula Jaworski
Associate Art Director: Mary Ellen Fanelli
Studio Manager: Leslie M. Keefe
Office Manager: Karen Earl-Braymer

Photo credits
Pages 10, 16, 32, 35, 42, 48, 56, 80, 94, 108, 134, 142, 160,
164, 168, 178, 192, 200, 206, 212, 215, 218, 222, 233, 244,
252, 282, 283, 324, 328, 330: Ted Spiegel
Pages 18, 29, 36, 72, 150, 288: Michael Mandarano
All others: John Kelsey

We're happy to hear from you.
If you have any questions or comments about the
editorial content of this book, please write to:
    Rodale Press, Inc.
    Book Readers' Service
    33 East Minor Street
    Emmaus, PA 18098
For more information about Rodale Press and the books and
magazines we publish, visit our World Wide Web site at:
http://www.woodforum.com

To my grandfather Roy Elm,
who could build anything.
—John Kelsey

To Robert V. Sparrow,
my gardening friend and guide.
—Ian J. Kirby

CONTENTS

Garden projects

Landscape projects

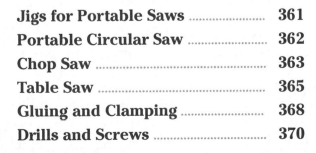

Index

INTRODUCTION

GOOD RESULTS, AND QUICK

This book shows you how to make sturdy, useful projects for your deck, patio, lawn, and garden. You'll find dozens of imaginative, good-looking designs that will enhance your family's outdoor life.

You can build handsome furniture and garden accessories with ordinary materials and simple tools, without a huge investment of time or money. These projects have been designed for busy householders who want fast results, for beginning woodworkers, and for household handy-persons who have neither an elaborate workshop nor a lot of equipment. You can get great results whether or not you're an experienced woodworker.

PRACTICAL, INTERESTING PROJECTS

You'll find picnic tables, deck furniture, barbecue gear, gardening tools and landscape enhancements. There's play equipment for kids, and work equipment for adults. There are big projects and quick projects. The common thread, however, is practical utility. Each of the 72 projects was originally designed and made because one of us had a real need for it. Every project has been redesigned and re-built especially for this book. We enjoyed having the opportunity to work bugs and kinks out of our designs, we simplified the techniques and construction methods, and we gave the designs a contemporary look.

ROBUST CONSTRUCTION

These projects are really strong and durable. They're held together with nails or screws plus water-resistant glue. They won't fall apart in the weather, nor under the stress of hard use. Most of them can be made with ordinary 1× and 2× lumber and other common materials you can find at the home center. A few were made with rough-sawn pine lumber from a small local sawmill, but you can substitute regular lumber if you like.

None of the projects uses chemically preserved wood. Along with our friends at Rodale Press, we believe the available treatments are neither environ-mentally wise nor personally safe, nor is there any real need for them. Trees are made of untreated wood and they don't come unstuck in the weather. Your wooden constructions, provided they can shed standing water, will survive for many, many years. And when they finally do give up, they'll sink gently and harmlessly into the earth.

WORK PLACE AND TOOLS

You need a place to work. You can work in the garage, in the basement, on the deck, in the family room or in a spare bedroom. You need a place to store your tools and materials, and you need a sturdy worktable with a flat surface. You could buy a workbench kit at the home center, or you can build a low worktable like the one you'll see in use throughout this book. There's a plan for it on page 348.

All of these projects can be built with a simple kit of basic tools. Bought new, these tools will cost about $250. Here's what you absolutely need:

8

Claw hammer
Square
Tape measure
Electric drill and bits
Handsaw
Six 12-inch clamps
Sharp pocket knife
Surform rasps
Screwdrivers, wrenches

The drill is the only power tool on the list. You'll use it for drilling pilot holes and for driving screws. As you get further into woodworking you'll find a few more tools helpful:

More clamps
Second electric drill
Electric router
Power saw

Clamps are extra hands—you can't do without them. With two drills, you can set one up for holes while leaving a screwdriver bit in the other. The router is mainly for rounding edges, so a small, inexpensive trim-router is all you need.

If you've already got a table saw, you're set. However, if you're shopping for your first power saw, consider a good jigsaw plus a sliding-arm chop saw instead of a cheap table saw. The critical saw maneuver is cutting wood to length with square ends. While it's handy to be able to saw wood lengthwise, it's usually possible to buy a width that's close enough.

How to use this book

Like kitchen-tested food recipes, these wood recipes have been shop-tested. The step-by-step instructions describe the procedures we actually followed, all the photos were taken in our own workshop, and all the measurements have been checked against our completed projects. Though many techniques are reviewed as they arise, you'll find a fuller discussion in the Techniques section starting on page 346.

Every project begins with a perspective drawing, a cutting list and a shopping list. The drawing shows which part goes where. The cutting list gives actual sizes. If the part is cut at an angle or shaped in some other way, the dimensions give the square-cut blank. The shopping list includes an allowance of about 20%, so you'll be able to work around knots and defects in the wood. The cost estimates are based on 1997 East Coast home center prices.

The goal of this book is to give you a collection of excellent shop-tested projects you can put right to work in your family's outdoor environment. If you follow the steps, and compare your construction with what's shown in the photos and drawings, your success is virtually guaranteed. Along the way, you'll learn a robust and straightforward construction method you can apply any time you want to make something. As a bonus, you might find that you enjoy woodworking as much as we do. If so, you've acquired a lifelong hobby that will bring you much pleasure and satisfaction.

FITNESS AND SAFETY

Woodworking is a healthy and enjoyable activity, suitable for people of all ages and sizes. With the help of modern power tools, you don't have to be big and muscular to work with wood. It's good exercise, it's fun, and it's safe, provided you follow a few common-sense safety rules.

—Wear hearing protection whenever you are working with noisy machines. Protective ear-muffs cost about $25; foam earplugs cost 25 cents. Both work.

—Wear eye protection whenever you hammer nails or use the table saw, chop saw or router. Suitable eye protection can be safety eyeglasses, plastic safety goggles, or a full face shield.

—Don't breathe solvent fumes. Apply paint or varnish outdoors, or if you must work indoors, open the windows and set up a fan to ensure cross-ventilation.

—Don't work when you are tired or drowsy. Researchers have found that most workshop accidents occur soon after lunch, when people naturally feel sluggish. Don't work when you are under the influence of drugs or alcohol, either.

—How to avoid cutting yourself: Don't ever propel a sharp cutting tool toward any part of your body. Any cutting edge is liable to slip. When a tool does slip, let it bang into wood or air, not flesh. Keep your holding hand on the handle side of the cutting tool, not on the blade side. Always keep your legs and your body out of the path of sharp edges and rotating cutters.

—Treat your muscles and joints the same way you would when exercising or participating in a sport. Do a warm-up stretch before you move a stack of heavy planks. If you wear a wrist brace to play tennis, wear it for woodworking. Take your time, and take a break before you get tired and sore. Your project will come out better, and you'll have more fun.

DECK AND PATIO PROJECTS

The deck and patio are the outdoor portions of the family living space. They're extensions of the home, the outdoor zone where we play, cook and eat, sit and talk. Here you need much of the same furniture as inside the house: tables and chairs for people, work spaces for food preparation, storage for everything.

Patio and deck projects give you the opportunity to make things that are both pleasant and useful, for your family's enjoyment. You can have a lot of fun tailoring projects to your own specifications, and you can get attractive results without a huge investment of time or money.

DUCKBOARD BENCH

Build it up like a many-layered cake

Here is a useful bench or coffee table for your deck or patio, with a heavyweight variation for the lawn. The duckboard construction allows the bench to shed rainwater, but the spacers keep the slats close enough together for sitting comfort. This construction also creates an interesting play of light and shadow, so the bench looks good in any outdoor setting.

To build the bench, you make one side frame, then use it as a template to add more rails, legs, slats and spacers. You stack up the bench like a many-layered cake. This method requires making the first side frame accurately. Then you can align everything else with it. This method allows the access you need as you work. If you were to build two side frames and then attempted to fill in between, you would come to a point where you couldn't insert screws where you needed them.

A bench made of standard 1× lumber, which is actually ¾ inch thick, is light enough to go along with your other deck and patio furniture. The bench shown has two wide rails at either side, with narrower slats in the center of the seat, for added visual interest. You can omit this detail simply by making the six slats out of the same 1×4 material as the four rails.

As an alternative, you could make the bench out of 2×4 lumber. The extra heft would make it more suitable for the lawn and landscape than for the deck. The 2×4 bench also would not have the variation in width between the rails and the slats. A workable size is 72 inches long and about 20 inches wide, which means you would make seven 72-inch rails, twelve legs, and eighteen spacers, all from nine standard 2×4 studs.

DUCKBOARD BENCH

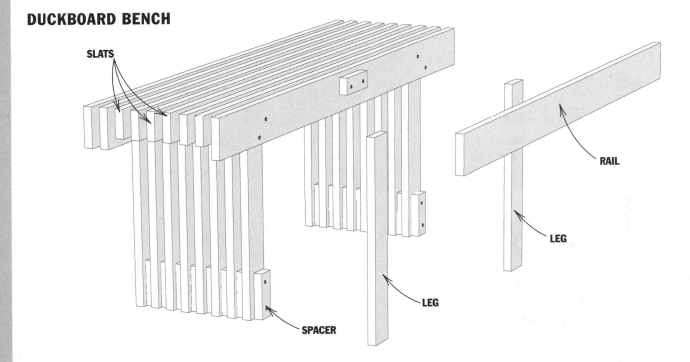

SLATS

RAIL

LEG

LEG

SPACER

Build up the bench like a many-layered cake. Glue and screw each set of two legs, one rail or slat, and three spacers, to the previous layer.

BENCH DETAIL

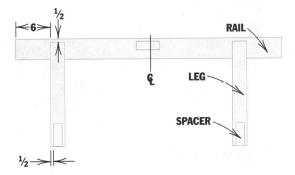

|←6→| ½

RAIL

Ȼ

LEG

SPACER

½

YOUR INVESTMENT
Time: One evening
Money: $30

SHOPPING LIST
16 feet 1×4 pine
60 feet 1×3 pine
10 feet 1×2 pine
#6 × 1¼-inch galvanized screws
#6 × 2-inch galvanized screws

PROJECT SPECS
The bench measures 46 inches long, 18½ inches high, and 14¼ inches wide.

CUTTING LIST

PART	QTY.	DIMENSIONS	NOTES
Rail	4	¾ × 3½ × 46	1×4
Slat	6	¾ × 2½ × 46	1×3
Leg	18	¾ × 2½ × 18	1×3
Spacer	24	¾ × 1½ × 4	1×2

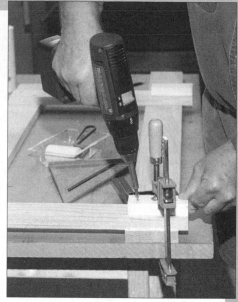

Make the first joint. The leg fits six inches from the end of the rail and a half-inch down, and the pieces meet at right angles. Use your measuring tools to set these distances (above). Drive one screw, then make sure the parts remain square before you drive the second screw (below).

Complete the leg frame. Glue and screw three spacers to the legs and rail. Drive two screws into each spacer. A scrap supports the legs' free end.

BUILDING THE BENCH

1 Saw all the wood. The bench is made from standard 1×2, 1×3, and 1×4 pine lumber. Choose the clearest wood you can find, and avoid wood with splintery edges. Saw all the wood to the lengths given in the cutting list. Precise lengths are not important, so long as all the rails and slats are the same length, and the legs all match, but square ends are important. Take the time to check and adjust your crosscutting set-up.

2 Make the first joint. Begin by gluing and screwing one leg to the face of one rail. The leg fits 6 inches in from the end of the rail, with its top set down ½ inch, as shown in the photo at left and the drawing on page 13. Use your square to draw layout lines. Roll glue on the leg, clamp the parts, drill pilot holes and drive one of the two 1¼-inch screws into the intersection. Then check that the two parts are truly square to one another, and nudge them into place if necessary, before you drive the second screw.

3 Complete the leg frame. Join the second leg to the other end of the rail, making a U-shaped assembly. Then complete the leg frame by gluing and screwing three spacers to the assembly, as shown in the photo above. One spacer is centered on the rail, but set down by ½ inch. The other two spacers fit flush with the bottom of the legs, centered from side to side. Spread glue on each spacer, clamp it and drive one 1¼-inch screw, then square it up before you drive the second screw.

4 Add the second rail. Glue and screw a second rail to the leg frame. Spread the glue and use your square to line this rail up with the first one, as shown in the photo at right. Clamp the rail in position while you drill pilot holes for two 2-inch screws in each joint. These screws are long enough to bite down through the leg or spacer and into the first rail. Drive one screw, then check the alignment of the parts before you drive the second screw.

5 Continue adding legs, slats and spacers. Now build up the bench, like a layer cake. Glue and screw two more legs to the assembly. Then add spacers and slats as shown in the photo at right. Follow the same method of spreading glue, clamping the parts, drilling pilot holes and driving screws. The key is to clamp each new part in the right place and to drive only one screw. Then check the alignment before you drive the second screw. Put two of the 2-inch screws in each intersection, and don't forget the glue. All the screws are important, so if you should break one off while driving it, pry the wood off, twist the screw out with pliers and replace it.

6 Complete the bench. When you come to the end of the slats, you'll be left with two rails, two legs and five spacers. Glue and screw a spacer to the center of the last slat, then glue and screw a rail to the assembly. Attach the remaining spacers to the bench, then glue and screw the last rail in place. The screw holes in the last rail will be visible.

Add the second rail. Spread glue on the legs and spacer where the second rail will fit (left). Use your square to align the rail, then clamp it in position (right).

Continue adding legs, slats and spacers. Build up the bench like a layer cake. Spread glue, align each new part, then clamp it, drill pilot holes, and screw it in place. A plastic square like the one shown helps align each new layer.

Complete the bench. The last rail has to be screwed to the outside of the assembly. These are the only visible screwheads in the bench (right).

7 Sand the bench. Wrap some 80-grit sandpaper around a block of wood and sand all the sharp corners off the wood. If you want to paint or stain the bench, now's the time, but you don't have to apply any finish. The wood will weather to a nice silver-gray all by itself.

BATTEN PLANTER

This tall box has style and function

Pansies and other cheery little flowers bring more pleasure when they're lifted off the ground and up to where you can see and touch them. This is the purpose of the simple batten planter. It's a quick project you can nail together in a short evening, but you do need to be able to saw wood to width.

The batten planter was designed to hold flats of such flowers as pansies or petunias. The platform can be lowered to house any plant in a clay pot or a plastic bucket. The planter is not, however, designed to be filled with earth. For that, you would need something stronger, like the box planter on page 32.

A batten is a strip of wood that reinforces a joint. In this planter, as in board-and-batten siding, the battens not only conceal the joints, but also give the design a strong vertical rhythm.

BUILDING THE PLANTER

1 **Crosscut the parts.** Saw four 23-inch lengths of 1×6 pine lumber for the legs and battens, and eight 19-inch lengths for the side panels. Try to work around knots, and keep the scrap for the plant platform.

2 **Rip the parts.** The parts are not all standard widths of lumber. With the tablesaw, rip (saw lengthwise) a 1¼-inch leg strip off each of the four 23-inch blanks. Measure the remaining width of wood and set the saw to split it in half, so you end up with four wide legs and four battens. Next, saw four of the 19-inch panel blanks to the narrow width of 4¾ inches, and keep the scrap for ledgers. Finally, crosscut the four battens to the same length as the side panels.

3 **Nail the four legs.** Use the 2-inch nails to join the four pairs of legs, as shown in the drawing. Strengthen the construction by angling the nails alternately left and right, dovetail-fashion, as shown on the facing page.

Assemble the planter. Dovetail nailing strengthens the construction. Tilt the nails alternately left and right.

4 **Nail the box corners.** Nail the four pairs of side panels together so that each corner consists of a wide 5½-inch panel and a narrow 4¾-inch panel, as shown in the drawing. Nail a leg assembly to the outside of each box corner.

5 **Assemble the planter.** Set two corner assemblies face down on top of a center batten. Join the two corner assemblies by nailing them to the batten, with 1½-inch nails. Join the other two corner assemblies in the same way. Complete the planter by fitting and nailing the resulting U-shaped halves together.

6 **Support the plants.** Choose your plants and decide how far down to place their support platform. Measure down another ¾ inch, and nail the ledger strips inside the planter, on two opposite faces. Finally, hold two pieces of scrap 1×6 across the top of the planter, mark them, and cut them so they will fit inside with about ¼ inch of clearance all around. There's no need to nail them to the ledgers.

7 **Finish the planter.** Pine weathers to a silvery grey. If you prefer, paint or stain the planter.

BATTEN PLANTER

Join the two-piece legs, then nail the side panels in pairs, to make box corners. Nail the leg assemblies to the box corners, then join everything together with the four battens.

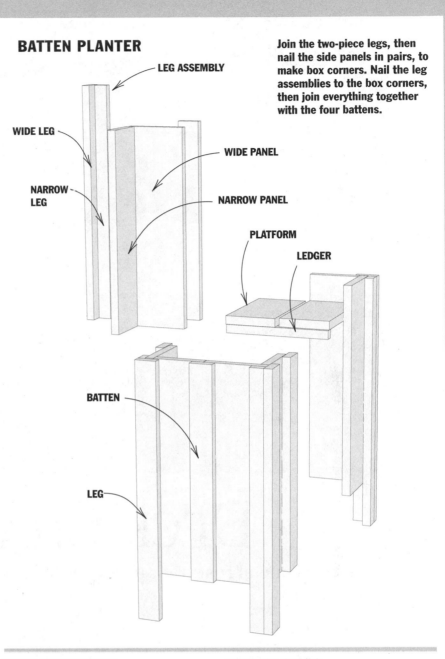

YOUR INVESTMENT
Time: One short evening
Money: $15

PROJECT SPECS
The batten planter is 19 inches high and 12½ inches square.

SHOPPING LIST
Three 8-foot lengths of 1×6 lumberyard pine
6d galvanized finishing nails
4d galvanized finishing nails

CUTTING LIST

PART	QTY.	DIMENSIONS	MATERIAL	NOTES
Wide panel	4	¾ × 5½ × 19	5/4 Pine	
Narrow panel	4	¾ × 4¾ × 19	5/4 Pine	
Batten	4	¾ × 2 × 19	5/4 Pine	
Wide leg	4	¾ × 2 × 23	5/4 Pine	
Narrow leg	4	¾ × 1¼ × 23	5/4 Pine	
Ledger	2	¾ × ¾ × 9¼	5/4 Pine	Cut to fit
Platform	2	¾ × 4½ × 9¼	5/4 Pine	Cut to fit

DECK CHAIR

Forget those metal rust traps, make these nifty wooden chairs instead

Every deck needs chairs, but most people make do with aluminum folders or plastic-coated steel ones from the home center. They sag or rust and chip, so every few years you have to buy some more. But it doesn't have to be that way, because here is a deck chair you can build yourself. It's a simple construction that relies on standard 1× and 2× lumber. The only tricky maneuver is cross-cutting some of the parts at a 10-degree angle, which you can do with any

kind of saw and the crosscut jig shown on page 361.

The chair is sized for a standard cushion, though you don't actually need any cushion because the wooden slats have just enough give to cradle your old bones comfortably.

The chair goes together quickly. It would only be a weekend project to make a suite of six of them. However, if you do decide to make a lot of chairs, start by completing one. This is because the exact length of the

seat spacer depends on the precise width of your lumber. Once you go through it once, you'll be able to cut a stack of spacers at the same setting.

The roundover profile on the edges of the back slats and seat slats is an optional detail. It does make the chair a little more comfortable, but if you don't have an electric router, you can get equivalent results by sanding the slats. Use 80-grit paper wrapped around a scrap of wood, as shown in the photo on page 21.

DECK CHAIR

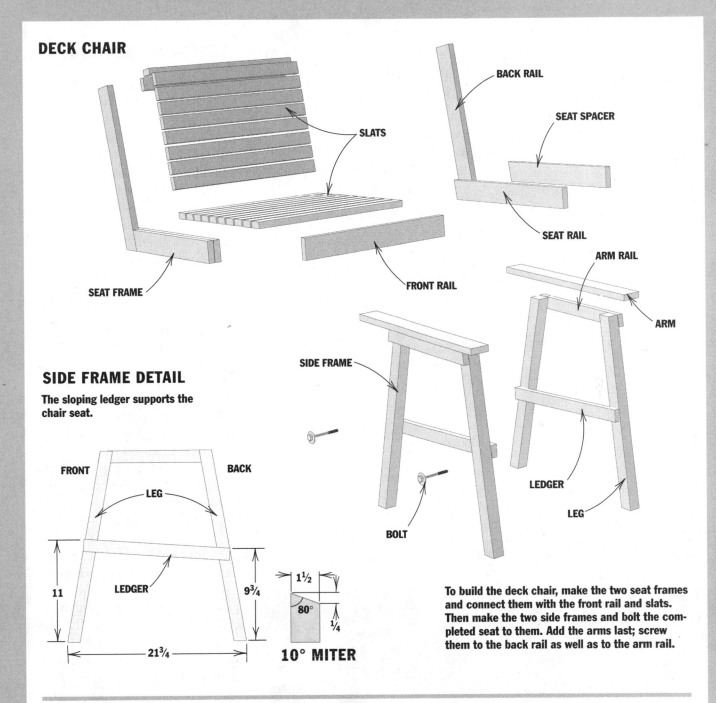

SLATS

BACK RAIL

SEAT SPACER

SEAT RAIL

FRONT RAIL

SEAT FRAME

ARM RAIL

ARM

SIDE FRAME

SIDE FRAME DETAIL

The sloping ledger supports the chair seat.

FRONT

BACK

LEG

LEDGER

11

$9\frac{3}{4}$

$21\frac{3}{4}$

$1\frac{1}{2}$

80°

$\frac{1}{4}$

10° MITER

BOLT

LEDGER

LEG

To build the deck chair, make the two seat frames and connect them with the front rail and slats. Then make the two side frames and bolt the completed seat to them. Add the arms last; screw them to the back rail as well as to the arm rail.

YOUR INVESTMENT

Time: One day
Money: $33

SHOPPING LIST

8 feet 2×2 pine
48 feet 1×2 pine
24 feet 1×3 pine
Four ¼ × 3½-inch galvanized hex-head machine bolts with nuts and washers
#6 × 2-inch galvanized screws
#6 × 1¼-inch galvanized screws
2-inch galvanized siding nails
2½-inch galvanized siding nails

PROJECT SPECS

The chair measures 30 inches high, 27 inches wide, and 22 inches front to back.

CUTTING LIST

PART	QTY.	DIMENSIONS	NOTES
Seat rail	2	¾ × 2½ × 20	1×3; miter one end 10°
Back rail	2	¾ × 2½ × 20	1×3; miter one end 10°
Seat spacer	2	¾ × 2½ × 17½	1×3; miter one end 10°
Front rail	1	¾ × 2½ × 20	1×3
Slat	20	¾ × 1½ × 20	1×2
Leg	4	1½ × 1½ × 24	2×2; miter both ends 10°
Arm rail	2	¾ × 1½ × 14¼	1×2; miter both ends 10°
Seat ledger	2	¾ × 1½ × 18	1×2
Arm	2	¾ × 2½ × 21	1×3

Join the first seat rail and back rail. Overlap the angled ends of the wood, use your square to make them flush, and draw a layout line (above). Glue and screw the rails together. Don't put a screw in the center of the joint because a bolt goes there (right).

DETAIL OF SEAT FRAME

To lay out a 10° miter on 2½-inch wide wood, measure an offset of 7/16 inch and connect that point to the opposite corner. On 1½-inch wood, the offset is ¼ inch.

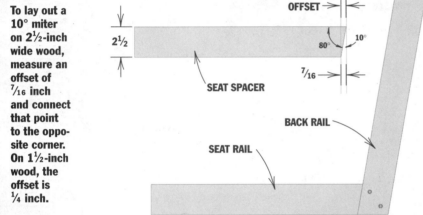

OFFSET

2½

80°   10°

7/16

SEAT SPACER

BACK RAIL

SEAT RAIL

Join the other seat rail and back rail. Set the second set of parts on top of the first and draw layout lines before drilling, gluing and screwing the parts together. The two seat frames are mirror images of one another.

BUILDING THE DECK CHAIR

1 Saw the wood. Cut all the parts to the lengths given in the cutting list. The seat rails, back rails, front rail and arms are all the same size, ¾ inch by 2½ inches by 20 inches, so saw a total of seven pieces to that dimension. The seat rails, back rails, and seat spacers have to be mitered 10 degrees, or sawn at an angle of 10 degrees off square, on one end; the four legs are sawn to the same 10-degree angle on both ends. Note that the leg miters must be parallel to one another.

2 Join the first seat rail and back rail. The seat rail and the back rail make an L-shaped frame that is splayed open by the miters sawn on the ends of the wood. This angle is what makes the seat comfortable. However, there's a right seat frame and a left frame, so make one of them and then use it as a guide for making the other, in Step 3. Overlap the angled ends of the two pieces of wood and draw a layout line where they will be joined together, as shown in the photo above left. Drill pilot holes for two screws, avoiding the center of the overlap because a bolt goes there later on. Spread glue, align the parts with care, and drive the two screws home.

3 Join the other seat rail and back rail. The second seat rail and back rail connect exactly the same way as the pair you just joined, except for their handedness. To work out the right frame and the left frame, set the parts up with spacer

blocks, as shown in the photograph below left. Draw the layout lines, drill the pilot holes and spread the glue as in the previous step, but drive only one of the two screws. Then put the two seat frames together and adjust the parts until the angles are the same. Then drive the second screw.

4 Add the seat spacers. The seat spacers butt against the back rails and are flush with the seat rails. Their purpose is to make the outside of the seat and back assembly into a flat plane, to which you can attach the chair's arms and legs. Since 1× pine varies somewhat in width, the length of the seat spacer has to be trimmed to fit. Set the spacer in place with its mitered end against the back rail. Its other end should come flush with the front of the seat rail. Mark the length, saw off the excess wood, then glue and screw the seat spacer to the seat rail, as shown in the photo above right. Drill pilot holes for the four 1¼-inch screws.

5 Profile the slats. The 1×2 slats connect the two sides of the chair, and form the sitting surfaces. This is a simple chair without body-shaped curves, but you can improve its friendliness by rounding the sharp corners off the slats. Use a ¼-inch roundover cutter in an electric router, as shown in the photo above right. If you don't have a router, you can achieve equivalent results by sanding with 80-grit paper wrapped around a block of wood. You don't have to remove much material to soften up the way the chair sits.

Add the seat spacers. Glue and screw the seat spacers to the seat rail.

Profile the slats. Use an electric router with a ¼-inch roundover cutter to remove the sharp edges of the slats (above). Instead of routing, you can sand the sharp corners off the wood (right).

6 Attach the front rail. The front rail connects the two seat frames. It establishes the width of the seat, stiffens the construction, and covers the end grain of the seat rails. Glue it, and nail it in place with the 2½-inch siding nails. Be sure to spread glue on the ends of the seat rails and seat spacers as well as on the face of the front rail. Start two nails near each end of the front rail, then stand the seat frame up on end as shown at right, so you can drive the nails home. Set the seat down on the worktable to make sure it's still flat, then stand it on end again to drive two more nails into each joint.

Attach the front rail. Glue and nail the front rail to the seat rail and seat spacer. Stand the seat frame on end to drive the nails home.

Space and nail the seat slats. Spread glue along the front rail and nail the slat in place with 2-inch siding nails. The narrow stick at the bottom left is the spacing gauge (above). Using the spacing gauge to locate the slats, glue and nail seat slats until you reach the back uprights (below).

Square the seat. Clamp the seat to the worktable and use a seat slat to gauge its width at the back, then measure the diagonals. Push the construction until the diagonals are equal.

7 Square the seat. The next step is to nail the slats to the front rails, but first make sure the construction is square. Clamp the seat frame to the worktable. Since the slats are the same length as the front rail, use one of them to gauge the width at the back of the seat. To verify that it is square, measure the diagonals as shown in the photo above. If they are not equal, loosen one clamp and push the diagonals equal. Then clamp the seat down tight.

8 Space and nail the seat slats. The seat slats and the back slats are exactly the same. Glue and nail the first slat to the front of the seat. Spread the glue right across the top of the front rail. Attach the slat with 2-inch siding nails. The remainder of the slats should be spaced ¼ inch apart. Find or make a wooden gauge of this thickness and use it to locate the next slat, as shown in the photos above right. Dab some glue on the

underside of the slat and attach it to the seat rails with two nails at each end. Continue to add slats until you reach the back.

9 Slat the back. Unclamp the construction and flip it over so you can continue gluing and nailing slats to the back rails. Start at the top of the back and work

Slat the back. Flip the construction so the back is on the worktable, and continue gluing and nailing the slats in place. Start at the top and work toward the seat.

Complete the back. Nail and glue a slat on top of the back rails and another on the back-side of the chair.

Join one arm rail to two legs. Align the arm rail at the top of the legs, with the angled cuts flush at the edges of the parts. Glue and screw the arm to one leg (left). Measure the outside width at the open side of the U shape. Adjust the width to 21¾ inches, then attach the arm rail to the other leg (below).

Add the seat ledger. Draw layout lines to locate the seat ledger on the legs, then glue and screw it in place. It goes on the opposite side from the arm rail.

toward the seat, spacing the slats with the ¼-inch gauge. However, don't fill in the entire back. For comfort, stop two slats, or about four inches, from the seat and leave the back open at this point.

10 Complete the back. To complete the back, glue and nail a slat on top of the back rails and another on the back side of the chair, as shown in the photo above. Now you're ready to move on to the structure of the chair legs and arms.

11 Join one arm rail to two legs. One arm rail and two legs make a U-shaped unit, which forms the side frame of the chair. Start by aligning the arm rail at the top of one of the legs so the angled cuts come flush with the edges of the parts. Draw a layout line, spread glue, clamp the parts together, drill pilot holes for a pair of 2-inch screws, and drive the screws. Now spread glue and clamp the other leg in position and measure the outside width at the open end of the U shape. Adjust the width to 21¾ inches before you screw the parts together, as shown in the photo at top right.

12 Add the seat ledger. The seat ledger completes the side frame. It will support the seat assembly. The seat ledger slopes downward towards the back.

Measure up from the bottom of the legs as shown on the drawing on page 19 to locate the seat ledger. Be sure the seat ledger goes on the opposite side of the

Make the second side frame. Glue and screw the remaining arm to the other two legs. Use the completed side frame to gauge the width (above). Clamp both side frames together, with the ledger in the middle. Transfer the location of the seat ledger from one frame to the other (below).

leg from the arm rail. Draw layout lines, then glue and screw the parts together with 2-inch screws through the ledger into the chair legs. This completes one side frame.

13 **Make the second side frame.** The second side frame should be exactly the same as the one you just completed, except one is right-handed and the other is left-handed. Begin by joining the arm rail to the two legs as you did in Step 11. Instead of measuring the width between the legs, use the completed side frame as a gauge, as shown in the photo at top left. Up to this point the two frames are the same. Now clamp the two frames together in the orientation they'll have in the completed chair, as shown in the photo below left, with the arm rails to the outside of the sandwich and the seat ledger trapped between the chair legs. This allows you to transfer the location of the seat ledger from one side frame to the other. Take the sandwich apart and complete the second side frame.

14 **Join the seat to the side frames.** The chair seat rests on the ledgers. It's held by two bolts in holes drilled through the legs and seat rails. Set the seat assembly on its side on the worktable and position the first side frame on it, as shown in the left photo on the facing page. The seat ledger fits tightly underneath the seat spacer, with its high end to the front of the chair. If the low end of the ledger is at the front, you've got the wrong side frame. Get the other one, or else turn the chair seat

Attach the arms. Clamp the arms to the arm rails and drive screws from the inside of the back rails.

Join the seat to the side frames. Set the seat assembly on its side and position a side frame on it. The seat ledger fits tightly under the seat spacer, with its high end toward the front. Align the low end of the ledger with the bottom corner of the back rail. Glue and bolt the parts together.

over. Align the low end of the seat ledger with the bottom of the back rail. Clamp the parts in position and drill a ¼-inch bolt hole through each leg, down through the back rail or seat spacer and seat rail. Unclamp the assembly so you can spread glue, then insert the bolts. The bolt head goes to the outside, with the nut under the chair seat. Put a washer under the bolt head and another washer under the nut. Tighten the bolt so the washers bite into the wood, as shown in the photo above. Turn the assembly over to bolt the other side frame to the chair seat.

15 **Make the arms.** The chair arms complete the structure of the chair, by tying the side frames into the back rails. A square connection at the back rail is important, but the rest of

the arm should be smooth and friendly to the touch. Draw a line 4 inches from one end of each arm, and round over all the corners and edges except for the two long edges within the 4-inch marks.

16 **Attach the arms.** Plant the arms on the arm rails so they are flush with the rear of the back rails. Mark where the arms cross the back rails, then remove them to drill pilot holes for two screws through each back rail. Spread glue where the parts cross one another. Clamp the arms to the arm rails, and drive 2½-inch screws through from inside the back, as shown in the photo at top right. Nail the arms to the arm rails with 2-inch siding nails.

17 **Finish the chair.** Go over the chair with the ¼-inch roundover

Finish the chair. Rout the corners off the bottom of the legs so they won't splinter when being dragged.

cutter in the router. Remove any sharp edge you think might cause discomfort. Also rout the corners off the bottom of the legs. This will make the chair easy to drag across your deck or patio. Paint the chair, or varnish it, or leave it unfinished to weather naturally.

DECK TABLES

Here's a simple and versatile design you can vary to suit your own needs

For real outdoor comfort, you need the same pieces of furniture as indoors. Where there are chairs, you also need tables. Here is a versatile design for a small table, which can be made in various heights and lengths.

Even though this is a simple construction, the results don't look simple. This makes it an interesting first project. You'll

learn the fundamental techniques of sawing a square end on the wood and also of sawing a miter (see page 356). You'll also learn about gluing and nailing, and clamping to a gauge to make identical assemblies.

The instructions include dimensions for two sizes of table. One is small and low, like a little bench, while the other is

taller and somewhat more robust, like an end table. The low table goes together with siding nails and glue. The end table goes together with screws and glue—its parts are included in the cutting list, and there's more detail about making it on page 29. You can see how straightforward it is to tailor this table design to your own purposes.

YOUR INVESTMENT

<u>Time:</u> Two tables in an evening
<u>Money:</u> Low table, $8; End table, $12

SHOPPING LIST

LOW TABLE
12 feet 1×6 pine
4 feet 1×4 pine
2½-inch galvanized siding nails

END TABLE
8 feet 1×8 pine
8 feet 1×6 pine
4 feet 2×4 stud
#6 × 2-inch galvanized screws
#8 × 2½-inch galvanized screws

PROJECT SPECS

The low table measures 16¾ inches high, 24 inches long, and 11½ inches wide. The end table measures 23¾ inches high, 24 inches long, and 15 inches wide.

LEG ASSEMBLY

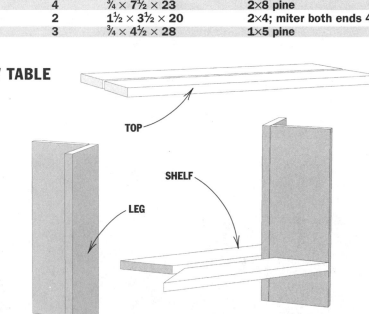

CUTTING LIST

PART	QTY.	DIMENSIONS	NOTES
LOW TABLE			
Leg	4	¾ × 5½ × 16	1×6 pine
Shelf	2	¾ × 3½ × 16	1×4; miter both ends 45°
Top	2	¾ × 5½ × 24	1×6 pine
END TABLE			
Leg	4	¾ × 7½ × 23	2×8 pine
Shelf	2	1½ × 3½ × 20	2×4; miter both ends 45°
Top	3	¾ × 4½ × 28	1×5 pine

LOW TABLE

TOP

SHELF

LEG

Make two wooden right angles and connect them with the mitered shelves. Then add the top. Tailor the dimensions to suit yourself.

BUILDING THE LOW TABLE

1 Saw the wood. The table parts come out of standard widths of pine lumber. If you've already been building projects around the house and yard, you've probably got a stack of salvageable short ends.

2 Assemble the legs. Each of the two leg assemblies is a wooden right-angle made by gluing and nailing two identical boards together. As shown in the photo at right, you can use one set of parts to prop up the ones you're working on. Spread glue on the edge of one board, and start three 2½-inch siding nails near the edge of the other.

Assemble the legs. Glue and nail two leg pieces together, forming a right angle (above). Scrape excess glue off the wood while it's still wet. Use a chisel or a putty knife (right).

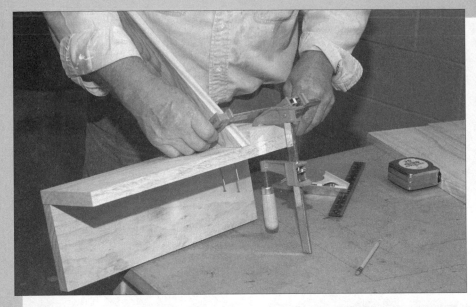

Join the shelves to one leg assembly. Clamp a gauge block to the leg, spread glue on the mitered end of the shelf, then clamp it to the gauge (left). Nail through the leg into the mitered end of the shelf (above).

Join the second leg assembly to the shelves. Spread glue on the miters and fit them around the second leg assembly. Nail the parts together.

Make the top. Align one top board across the table base. Its precise placement is up to you. Leave a gap between the top boards.

Line the pieces up as best you can, then drive one nail home. Check the alignment before you drive the other two nails. Assemble the other two leg pieces in exactly the same way.

3 Join the shelves to one leg assembly. The shelves connect the leg assemblies and stiffen the construction. To make a gauge for locating the shelves on the legs, find or cut a scrap of shelf material. Clamp it to one leg, as shown in the photo top left. The gauge establishes a temporary reference surface that's parallel to the ground. Roll glue onto the mitered end of the shelf, and clamp it to the

gauge, tight against the leg. The long point of the shelf miter comes flush with the outside corner of the leg. Now draw a layout line so you can drive three of the siding nails through the face of the leg and into the mitered end of the shelf. Glue and nail the other mitered shelf to the same leg assembly in the same way.

4 Join the second leg assembly to the shelves. The free ends of the mitered shelves make a vee-shape, into which you can plug the second leg assembly. Note, however, that by turning the second leg assembly upside down, you've

got a choice between two orientations, so choose the one shown in the drawing on page 27. Clamp the gauge across the leg, and spread glue on the two mitered shelf ends. Rest the shelves on the gauge and push the miters tight against the leg assembly, then clamp the shelves to the gauge. Now you can nail through the legs into the mitered ends of the shelf, as you did at the other end of the table.

5 Make the top. The tabletop consists of two boards nailed to the legs, with a gap in between them. Center the top boards on the legs, and decide on the width of gap you like. Then nail both boards down, with three nails into the end of each leg.

6 Finish the table. You can paint the table to match other outdoor furniture, or you can stain it to match your house, or you could varnish it to show off the wood. However, if you don't do anything, it will be OK. The wood soon will weather to a soft gray.

END TABLE

The end table is a larger and more robust version of the low table. Although its construction is the same, the parts are bigger, and the shelf is made of 2×4 instead of 1×4. This creates a broader shoulder of wood to resist racking stress. The addition of a third board to the table-top introduces an additional complication, which is discussed below.

Since glue and screws hold the end table together, you have to drill clearance holes. The purpose of a clearance hole is to make an easy path for the screw through the first piece of wood, plus a starting hole in the second piece. Even with clearance holes, you must hold the wood tightly together when you drive the screws, and it's best to clamp it.

When you screw a pair of leg pieces together, making a wooden right-angle, you can improve the alignment of the joint if you make it in stages. Spread the glue, align the parts, drill the first clearance hole and drive the first 2½-inch screw. Then check the alignment and adjust it if necessary before you drill clearance holes for the remaining two or three screws.

Screws also join the mitered 2×4 shelves to the leg assemblies. Use a gauge to position the shelf parts, as discussed in Steps 3 and 4 on the previous page. Trace the outline of the mitered shelf onto the leg pieces. Then drill each pilot hole twice, once from each side of the wood, instead of just from one side. This eliminates a little divot of wood, caused by the drill, that might otherwise interfere with a good connection. Drive four 2-inch screws into each miter, and don't forget the glue.

The top of the end table consists of three identical boards nailed to the legs. Because of the way you made the right-angle leg assemblies,

however, the table base is not a symmetrical construction. Draw a center line on the underside of the top center board. Then stand the table base upside-down on this board. You'll be able to see how to balance the base and top. Mark where the base meets the edges of the center board, so you can put the parts back in position right-side up. Nail or screw down through the center board into the ends of the legs. Now position the other two top boards alongside the center board, and attach them in the same way.

End table. The table has a space between its mitered shelves.

Use a gauge block to locate and support the 2x4 shelf.

Drill pilot holes for the screws. Drill from both sides of the wood.

Stand the table base upside-down on the top center board and balance its location. Draw layout lines so you can attach the top center board to the base.

CORNER PLANTER

Cut the angle without sawing bevels

The corner of the deck can be difficult space to use, but a corner planter takes care of it. The corner planter makes a home for a deck plant without intruding into the living space. The planter can be filled with earth or with a potted plant.

This corner planter is a simple 2×4 construction, planked with 1×6 pine boards and held together by galvanized spiral nails. It can be built without sawing any bevels, though you do have to cut the plywood bottom panel with a jigsaw.

BUILDING THE PLANTER

1 **Cut the wood.** Saw the posts, blocks and legs at the start of the project, but don't make the two front boards until Step 5. They'll have to be cut to fit.

2 **Make the legs.** Each leg consists of a block nailed to a post, as shown in the illustration on the facing page. The pieces are the same length, and flush along one edge. Fasten them together with four 2-inch spiral nails.

3 **Join the sides to the third post.** The third 2×3 post forms the back corner of the planter. Nail the sides to it, as shown in the bottom left photo. The corner detail is visually more interesting if you don't make the sides flush with the corner post. Offset them ⅜ inch in either direction.

4 **Nail the sides to the legs.** When you nail the sides to the legs, maintain the same ⅜-inch offset that you established when joining the sides to the third post, in Step 3.

Join the sides to the third post. Nail the 1×6 sides to the third post. Offset the sides ⅜ inch from the corner of the post.

Make the front. Cut the front pieces to fit the rabbets formed by the posts and blocks. Slide the front pieces in place, and nail them to the blocks.

CORNER PLANTER

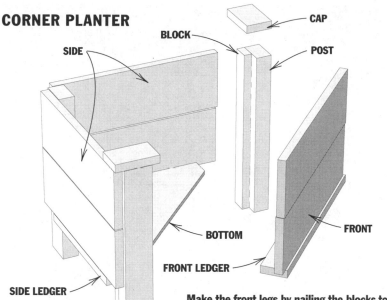

CAP

BLOCK

POST

SIDE

BOTTOM

FRONT

SIDE LEDGER

FRONT LEDGER

Make the front legs by nailing the blocks to two posts. Nail the sides to the third post, then nail to the two front legs. Fill in the front, fit the ledgers, and make the plywood bottom.

Fit the ledgers. Cut the ledgers to length, then nail them to the bottom of the sides and front.

Make the bottom. Trace the inside shape of the planter onto a piece of plywood, then jigsaw the shape and drop it into place.

YOUR INVESTMENT
<u>Time:</u> One evening
<u>Money:</u> $12

SHOPPING LIST
4 feet 2×3 pine
6 feet 1×2 pine
4 feet 1×3 pine
10 feet 1×6 pine
2-inch galvanized spiral nails

PROJECT SPECS
The planter is 16 inches high, 18 inches on a side, and 24 inches across the front.

CUTTING LIST

PART	QTY.	DIMENSIONS	NOTES
Post	3	$1\frac{1}{2} \times 2\frac{1}{2} \times 16$	2×3
Block	2	$\frac{3}{4} \times 1\frac{1}{2} \times 16$	1×2
Side	4	$\frac{3}{4} \times 5\frac{1}{2} \times 16$	1×6
Front	2	$\frac{3}{4} \times 5\frac{1}{2} \times 20$	1×6, cut to fit
Side ledger	2	$\frac{3}{4} \times 1\frac{1}{2} \times 13$	1×2, cut to fit
Front ledger	1	$\frac{3}{4} \times 2\frac{1}{2} \times 19$	1×3, cut to fit
Bottom	1	$\frac{1}{2} \times 18 \times 18$	CDX plywood
Cap	2	$\frac{3}{4} \times 2\frac{1}{2} \times 4$	1×3

5 Make the front. The front boards fit into the rabbets formed between the posts and blocks. Test-fit a piece of 1×2 to gauge the length of the two front boards. Cut them to length, slide them into the rabbets, then nail them in place as shown in the bottom right photo on the facing page. Use a nailset to drive the nail heads below the surface of the wood.

6 Fit the ledgers. The ledgers support the plywood bottom. Cut the 1×2 side ledgers to fit, and nail them to the bottom edge of the side pieces. Make the side ledgers flush on the outside. Cut the 1×3 front ledger to a snug fit between the legs and align its front corners with the leg corners, as shown in the top photo. Nail it to the bottom edge of the front.

7 Make the bottom. Turn the planter upside-down on the sheet of ⅜-inch plywood, trace its inside shape, and jigsaw it out. Drop the plywood onto the ledgers.

8 Cap the legs. The cap pieces are optional, but if you like them, nail them to the top of the front legs. Add some rocks and soil to the planter, and plant.

BOX PLANTER

Here's a log cabin you can fill with earth

When you want to fill a deck planter with heavy earth, you need a sturdy box with reinforced corners. This handsome box planter goes together with 2-inch nails, and it's an easy one-evening project. Besides the ability to nail, you need only one skill: sawing wood to length.

The planter sits above the deck on a plinth, which bears all the weight. The plinth improves how the planter looks, and it also makes space for getting a good grip when you want to move your plants around.

The planter shown in the photo was made of 2-inch-wide strips of rough-sawn pine lumber, which measures about an inch thick. You can substitute regular 1×3 or 5/4 × 3 pine from the home center with no change in the cutting list. The only part that would be affected, the corner block, starts out extra long so it can be cut to length toward the end of the project.

We left our planter with no finish, and in time it will weather to a pretty silver-gray. You could paint yours, or stain it, to suit the siding on your house.

BUILDING THE PLANTER

1 Saw the parts. The planter box is made of 20 side rails, which alternate long-short, log-cabin fashion. Saw the 10 long side rails to their final length of 18 inches. Cut the 10 short side

BOX PLANTER

Build the box planter by nailing long side rails to corner blocks. Then fill in the spaces with short side rails. The ledgers connect the planter box to its base.

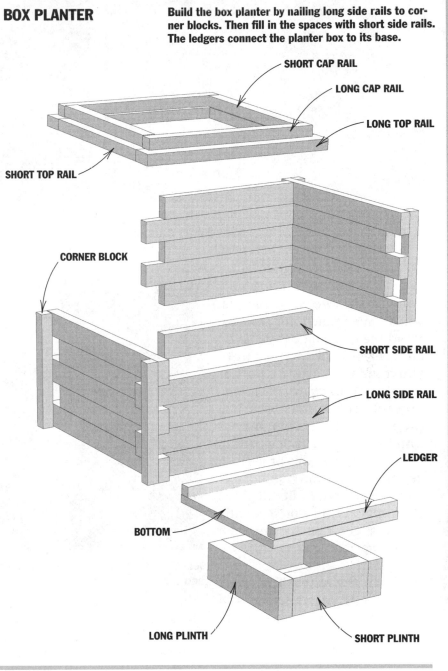

- SHORT CAP RAIL
- LONG CAP RAIL
- LONG TOP RAIL
- SHORT TOP RAIL
- CORNER BLOCK
- SHORT SIDE RAIL
- LONG SIDE RAIL
- LEDGER
- BOTTOM
- LONG PLINTH
- SHORT PLINTH

Build a side panel. Nail three long rails to each pair of corner blocks, using another rail to space the parts you are nailing.

rails to 15 inches. They'll be marked and trimmed to final length as you go along. Make the top rails, cap rails, and corner blocks now, too.

2 Build a side panel. One pair of side panels goes short-long-short, while the other pair goes long-short-long. Make a long-short-long panel by nailing three long rails across two corner blocks, leaving spaces for the two short rails. Gauge the spaces with a short rail, as shown in the photo above. Make a second side panel in exactly the same way.

YOUR INVESTMENT
<u>Time:</u> **One evening**
<u>Money:</u> **$15**

SHOPPING LIST
32 feet 1×2 rough-sawn pine
4 feet 2×4
13½-inch square of ¾-inch plywood
2-inch galvanized finishing nails
2½-inch galvanized nails
3-inch galvanized nails

PROJECT SPECS
The box planter is 12 inches high, 18 inches wide, and 18 inches deep.

CUTTING LIST

PARTS	QTY.	DIMENSIONS	NOTES
Long side rail	10	1 × 2 × 18	
Short side rail	10	1 × 2 × 15	Cut to fit
Corner block	4	1 × 1 × 12	Trim length at end
Long top rail	2	1 × 2 × 18	
Short top rail	2	1 × 2 × 14	Cut to fit
Long cap rail	2	1 × 1¼ × 16¼	
Short cap rail	2	1 × 1¼ × 14	Cut to fit
Ledger	2	1 × 1 × 14	Cut to fit
Long plinth	2	1½ × 3½ × 11⅛	2×4
Short plinth	2	1½ × 3½ × 8⅛	2×4
Bottom	1	¾ × 13½ × 13½	Plywood

Frame the box. Join the two side panels by nailing long rails into the spaces. Leave the corner blocks extra long until you get the whole planter together.

Fill in the sides. Trim the short rails so they're a tight fit, tap them in place, then nail through the long side pieces into their ends.

3 Frame the box. If you connect these two side panels, you'll have framed out the box. Stand the two side panels up on end, as shown in the photo above. Make sure the corner blocks face outward. Fit a long side rail into the first space. Nail the rail to the corner blocks with two 2-inch finishing nails in each end. Repeat this process to use up all the long side rails. The pieces should fit snugly in their spaces, but not so tightly that you can't easily tap each one into place.

4 Fill in the sides. The short side rails fit into the spaces in the box. They butt tightly against the long side rails, so they need to be trimmed to fit. Hold each rail in place to mark its length, then saw it on the mark. Drive two nails through the long side rail and into the end grain of the short side rail, and so on around the box, until the sides are completely filled in.

5 Complete the top. The top rails and cap rails give a visual finish to the planter. Like the side rails, there are long and short top rails and cap rails. Fit

Join the box and plinth. Drop the plinth and plywood bottom onto the ledgers, and screw the parts together.

the long top rails, then trim the short top rails to fit in between them. Nail these rails in place. Mark and saw the narrower cap rails to frame the box opening, and nail them in place as well.

6 Make the plinth. The plinth, which lifts the box, is made from 2×4 lumber. Crosscut four plinth pieces to the lengths given in the cutting list, and spike them together with 3-inch nails. Drive two nails through the face of the long plinth into the end grain of the short plinth

at each corner. Center the plywood bottom on the plinth and attach it with the 2½-inch nails.

7 Join the box and plinth. The two ledgers connect the planter box to the plywood bottom and to the plinth. Nail the ledgers inside the box, at the top edge of the bottom rail. With the planter upside down on the bench, drop the plywood bottom onto the ledgers and screw the assembly together, as shown above. Your new planter is ready for soil and tomatoes.

PLANT HANGER

Wooden triangle is quick to make

The plastic hangers that come with potted plants look cheesy at best. Sure, everybody plans to repot the fuschias into something nice, with a ropy macramé hanger, but somehow the season flies by before anyone gets around to it. Here's a wooden plant hanger you can get around to making, because it takes hardly any time at all.

The hanger is nothing more than three square sticks of wood, interlaced over-under-over, and held together with a nail or screw through each intersection. A loop of twine around each intersection suspends the device. The size and strength of the nails or screws doesn't mat-ter because they don't bear any weight—they're just locators.

For a 10-inch plant pot, make the sticks 20 inches long and drive the nails or screws 16 inches apart. For an 8-inch pot, make 16-inch sticks and drive the screws 12 inches apart. For other sizes, you can do the geometry if you want, or else you can pin two corners together and fit the sticks around the pot to mark the third intersection.

Cut three pieces of twine twice as long as you want the pot to descend, plus a foot. Double each piece of twine to find its center, then wrap the twine around an intersection of the sticks and knot it, leaving the long ends to dangle. Finally, set the plant in the hanger, bring all six long ends together, and lift the hanger by the twine. Fiddle the twine ends until the plant hangs level, then tie them together with an overhand knot.

YOUR INVESTMENT

Time: 20 minutes
Money: 20 cents

SHOPPING LIST

2 feet 1×4 pine
Ball of twine

PROJECT SPECS

Hangs one 10-inch plant pot.

CUTTING LIST

Part	Qty.	Dimensions	Notes
Rail	3	¾ × ¾ × 20	Fits 10-inch pot

PLANT HANGER

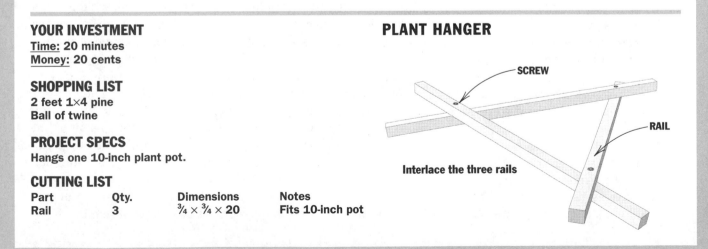

SCREW

RAIL

Interlace the three rails

BARBECUE CART

Load this beauty with food and roll it from the barbecue or kitchen to your outdoor guests

When you entertain out-doors, you have to truck the dishes and victuals from the kitchen and barbecue to the guests. This wheeled cart makes it easy. Like a tea trolley, it has two wheels at one end and a robust handle at the other, so you can lift the handle end and trundle away. It holds a lot of stuff, yet it's narrow enough to cruise through doorways. The cart also has a second handle at the wheels end, so two people can lift the whole thing up or down a step, or across a deep threshold.

The cart has two spacious levels, both of which extend out over the wheels, so there's a lot of space to load with dishes, food and drink. The top is table height, so that once you're seated with your guests, it becomes a serving sideboard. Both the top and the shelf have a gallery, or railing, which keeps the goodies from sliding off as you roll across uneven ground.

The rubber wheels, from the home center, are lawn mower replacement parts. They've got ball-bearing hubs for easy rolling. They're inexpensive, but if you have an old mower head-ing for the trash, you could sal-vage its wheels for zero cost. Cut the handles from a standard closet pole, new or used.

BARBECUE CART

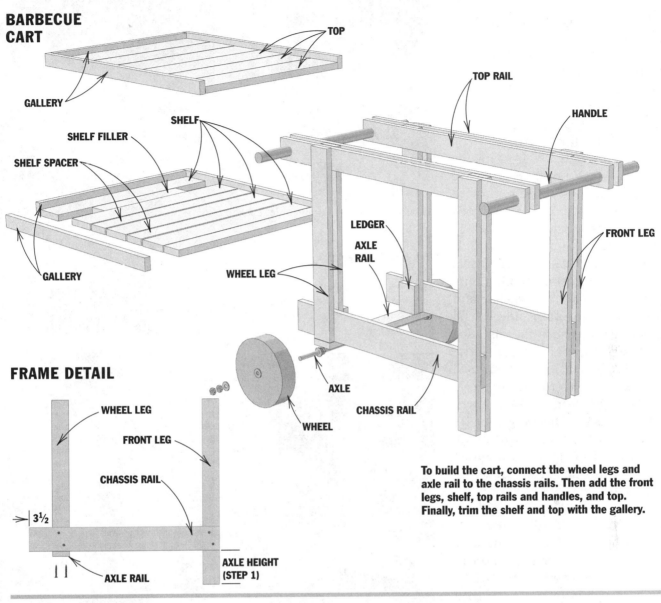

TOP

GALLERY

SHELF FILLER

SHELF SPACER

SHELF

GALLERY

TOP RAIL

HANDLE

LEDGER

AXLE RAIL

WHEEL LEG

FRONT LEG

AXLE

CHASSIS RAIL

WHEEL

FRAME DETAIL

WHEEL LEG

FRONT LEG

CHASSIS RAIL

$3^{1}/_{2}$

AXLE RAIL

AXLE HEIGHT (STEP 1)

To build the cart, connect the wheel legs and axle rail to the chassis rails. Then add the front legs, shelf, top rails and handles, and top. Finally, trim the shelf and top with the gallery.

YOUR INVESTMENT

<u>Time:</u> One day
<u>Money:</u> Wood, $28; wheels, $16

SHOPPING LIST

16 feet 1×2 pine
32 feet 1×3 pine
16 feet 1×4 pine
12 feet 1×5 pine
Two ½-inch U-bolts
#6 × 1¼-inch galvanized screws
#6 × 2-inch galvanized screws
2-inch galvanized siding nails
½ × 24-inch threaded rod
Two 8-inch lawn mower replacement
  wheels

PROJECT SPECS

The cart is 36 inches long, 24 inches
wide and 29 inches high.

CUTTING LIST

PART	QTY.	DIMENSIONS	NOTES
Axle rail	1	¾ × 2½ × 18	1×3; trim to fit
Chassis rail	2	¾ × 3½ × 28	1×4
Wheel leg	4	¾ × 2½ × 22¼	1×3
Front leg	4	¾ × 2½ × 27¼	1×3
Ledger	2	¾ × 2½ × 3½	1×3
Shelf	4	¾ × 3½ × 22	1×4
Shelf spacer	3	¾ × 2½ × 22	1×3
Shelf filler	1	¾ × 2½ × 13	1×3; trim to fit
Top rail	4	¾ × 2½ × 36	1×3
Handle	2	1¼ dia. × 24	Closet pole
Top	6	¾ × 4½ × 20	1×5
Gallery	1	¾ × 1½ × 160	1×2; cut to fit

BUILDING THE CART

1 Start with the wheels and axle. The diameter of the wheels affects the length of the wheel legs as well as the height where the front legs join the chassis rails. Standard lawn mower wheels are 8 inches in diameter with a ½-inch bore, but if you're using salvaged wheels, they're probably a different size and you'll have to adjust. The axle is a 24-inch length of ½-inch threaded rod. Mount the wheels on the axle as shown in the photos at right, with a washer and two nuts on either side of the bearings. Measure the distance between the nuts to verify the length of the axle rail, then trim the axle rail to fit. Set the axle rail on the axle, make it level, and measure the height of its top surface, as shown in the photo at top right. With 8-inch wheels, this height will be about 5 inches.

2 Saw the wood. Once you know the height of your axle rail, you can saw the wood to length. The length of the wheel legs is the length of the front legs minus the height of the axle rail. Saw everything except the 1×2 gallery. Cut those pieces to fit after you get the rest of the cart together.

3 Join the wheel legs and chassis rails. Begin the construction by joining a wheel leg to each chassis rail, as shown in the photo at bottom left. The leg is inset 3½ inches from the end of the rail, which you can gauge with a combination square or with a scrap of 1×4 wood. The end of the leg fits flush with the

Start with the wheels and axle. Lock each wheel on the threaded rod with a washer and two nuts on either side. Jam the nuts tightly against one another (above). Trim the axle rail and set it on the axle between the jammed nuts. Use the combination square to measure the height of the axle rail (right).

Join the wheel legs and chassis rails. Glue and screw the wheel leg to the chassis rail. Inset the leg 3½ inches from the end of the rail.

Add the axle rail. Drive screws through the axle rail to connect the two assemblies of wheel legs and chassis rails.

bottom of the rail. When you get the parts in position, draw a layout line, spread glue, and clamp them to the worktable. Drill pilot holes and drive three 1¼-inch screws through the leg and into the rail. Join the other leg and rail the same way, but be sure you end up with two mirror-image assemblies.

4 Add the axle rail. The axle rail connects the two leg-rail assemblies. Clamp the chassis rail to the worktable and hold the axle rail in place so you can see where to spread the glue. Drill two pilot holes through the rail and into the end of the wheels leg, as shown in the photo above. Drive 2-inch

screws, then drill and drive two more screws into the bottom edge of the chassis rail. Turn the assembly over so you can glue and screw the other wheel leg and rail to the other end of the axle rail.

5 Add the second pair of wheel legs. The remaining two wheel legs sandwich the chassis rails and stiffen up the construction. Spread glue on the mating surfaces and clamp them in place before you drill pilot holes and drive the 2-inch screws. Screw through the legs into the chassis rails, and also screw into the ends of the legs from beneath the axle rail.

6 Attach the ledgers. The cart's bottom shelf will rest on the chassis rails, except at the wheel legs, where two small ledgers hold it up. Glue and screw the ledgers to the inside of the wheel legs, tight against the axle rail, as shown in the photo at top right.

7 Join the front legs. The four front legs sandwich the free ends of the chassis rails. They cross the chassis rails at the same height as the axle rail, which you measured in Step 1. With a combination square set to this height, transfer the measurement to the front legs. Roll glue onto the first leg and set it in position under the chassis rail, as shown in the center photo. Make sure the assembly is square and flush, clamp the leg and screw it in place with four of the 1¼-inch screws. Join the second front leg to the other side of the same chassis rail, then flip the assembly over on

Add the second pair of wheel legs. Glue and screw the remaining pair of wheel legs to the inside of the chassis rails.

Attach the ledgers. The ledgers, which will help support the cart's shelf, sit on the axle rail and are glued and screwed to the wheel legs.

Join the front legs. Glue and clamp the first of the four front legs to the free end of the chassis rail, and screw it in place. Attach the other three front legs in the same way.

the worktable in order to attach the other two front legs.

8 Bolt the axle to the axle rail. Two U-bolts connect the axle to the axle rail. What home centers sell as ½-inch U-bolts actually have an opening 1 inch wide, but they do the job nevertheless. These bolts come with metal connecting plates and nuts, which you can see in the photo

Bolt the axle to the axle rail. Clamp the axle to the axle rail, and tap the U-bolt into the wood to mark where to drill. Keep the bolts far enough inboard to clear the ledgers.

below left. Turn the cart upside-down on the floor and clamp the axle to its rail. Tap the U-bolt into the wood to locate the holes, as shown in the bottom photo on the previous page. Be sure the bolts clear the ledgers. Drill the holes and install the bolts to lock the axle in place.

Make the shelf. Trim the shelf filler to fit between the wheel legs and nail it to the ledgers. The U-bolt connecting plate has to clear the ledger on the axle rail (above). Use a framing square to keep the shelf boards in line while you nail (right).

TOP RAIL DETAIL

9 Make the shelf. The shelf consists of alternating wide and narrow boards nailed to the chassis rails. Start by trimming the shelf filler to a neat fit between the wheel legs, and nail it to the ledgers there. Use two 2-inch siding nails at each end of the board, and be sure to center

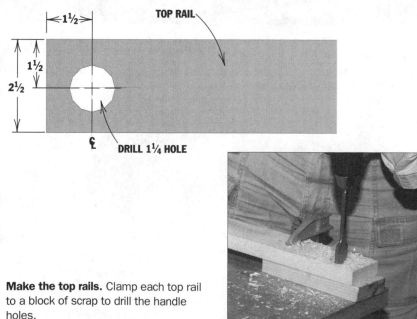

Make the top rails. Clamp each top rail to a block of scrap to drill the handle holes.

it from side to side. Next, nail a wide shelf to the projecting ends of the chassis rails, outside the wheel legs. Nail a narrow shelf spacer tight against the front legs of the cart. Finally, arrange the remaining shelves and spacers along the chassis rails. Use a framing square to align the shelf boards as you nail them down, as shown in the photo at left.

10 Make the top rails. The four top rails connect the legs, support the top shelf, and anchor the handles. Lay out and drill the holes for the handles before you attach the top rails to the cart. While the 1¼-inch holes could be centered in the width of the top rails, the construction will be stronger if they are offset toward the bottom. This requires you to examine your rails wood and decide which edges to put uppermost. Lay out the hole centers 1½ inches from the top edge of the rails, and 1½ inches in from each end. Lay out with care, because if one hole is a little off, it will be difficult to insert the handles. Drill the holes with a spade bit and use a backup block, as shown in the photo below left.

11 Mount the top rails and handles. Two of the top rails fit in between the legs, with the other two on the inside of the legs. Attach the rails between the legs first, leaving the inside pair loose until after you install the handles. Center the rails from end to end and make a layout line. Spread glue, clamp the rails in place, and screw them to the legs with two 2-inch screws driven into each joint from the inside surface. Now thread the

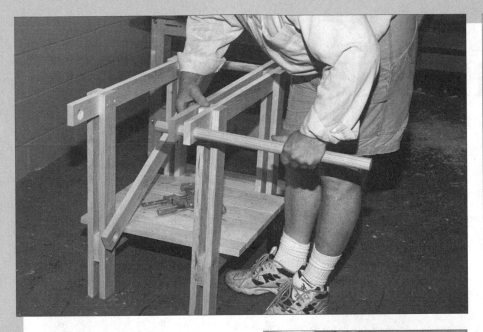

Mount the top rails and handles.
Thread the handles through the holes in all four top rails. The inside rails are not yet connected to the legs (left). Anchor the handles with screws underneath the top rails (above).

handles through the holes in all four top rails, as shown above. This is where things get tight if you drilled the holes inaccurately, and you might have to rasp the last hole a little oversize. Glue and screw the second pair of top rails to the inside of the legs. Finally, center the handles from side to side and drive 1¼-inch screws through the bottom of each top rail into the handles, as shown at top right.

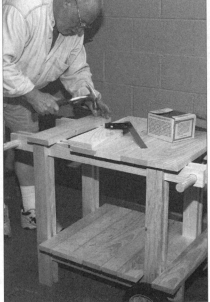

12 Make the top. The top consists of six identical boards fastened to the top rails with 2-inch siding nails. The boards are centered from side to side, and they fit closely together, but they are not centered from one end of the cart to the other. You need more clearance at the handle end, so start nailing there, aligning the first top board with the front legs. For a neat pattern of nailheads, drive two nails into the inside top rail, and one into the outside top rail, as shown in the photo at center right.

13 Make the gallery. The gallery, or railing, keeps dinner

Make the top. Set all six top boards in position, then start nailing at the front, or handle end, of the cart (left). Arrange the nailheads in a neat triangular pattern (above).

from sliding off the cart as you wheel across bumpy ground. It consists of pieces of 1×2 nailed to three sides of the top and shelf. You don't need the gallery at the handle end of the cart because that's the end you push. Its absence there makes it easy to sweep up crumbs and other culinary debris.

14 Finish the cart. You'll want to wipe the cart clean, so it's a good candidate for gloss varnish or enamel paint.

Make the gallery. Fit, cut and nail lengths of 1×2 to make a gallery along the sides and wheels end of the shelf and top.

BARBECUE STATION

This handsome summer kitchen makes deck cooking a real picnic

Barbecuing on the deck requires all the same assortment of tools and supplies as you use in your indoor cooking area. You also need barbecue tools and coals, a couple of kinds of hamburger buns, ketchup, and mustard, and don't forget some hot dogs for the kids. Before long, your outdoor cooking area will be a real mess.

Our barbecue station solves the problem. It cozies up right next to your grill, giving you a generous work counter for mixing, chopping, and serving, right at the height you need. The low shelf parks pots and serving dishes, extra rolls, and a bag of charcoal. The shelf's front extension is handy for platters, but if you think you might bang your knees, you can trim it flush. The high shelf is for spices and sauces and other small stuff.

The barbecue station can stay out in the weather all summer long, and if your deck has an overhanging roof, you could even leave it stocked with tools and accessories. It's very light and easy to move.

The barbecue station has an extremely useful and versatile structure, one you can adapt any time you need to make a lightweight table or counter. For the simplest counter, make the back legs the same length as the front legs, and make the shelf the same size as the top. All the frame joints are made the same way, with two or three #6 × 2-inch galvanized construction screws. Use galvanized finishing nails to hold the work surface and shelves in place.

Make the first joint. Use a scrap of work-surface material to set the top end rail down ¾ inch from the top of the front leg, and square a layout line across.

BUILDING THE BARBECUE STATION

1 Cut all the wood. Saw the front and back legs from regular 2×4 studs. Cut them to length first, then saw the 2×4, lengthwise, right down the middle. All the rest of the parts come out of standard 1×6 pine lumber, which actually measures 5½ inches wide by ¾ inch thick. You can saw two of the wide rails, or three of the narrow rails, out of one width of 1×6.

2 Make the first joint. Each end frame consists of a tall back leg and a shorter front leg, connected by two identical end rails. The first joint to make is the one between the top end rail and the top of the front leg. Locate the top end rail on the front leg: The end of the rail comes flush with the outside surface of the leg, but the top of the rail is set down ¾ inch, that is, the thickness of the table top. Gauge the ¾-inch offset with a scrap of wood, use your combination square to align the pieces, and draw layout lines on the leg. Drill two pilot holes for screws in both ends of all four end rails. Spread glue between the layout lines, clamp the parts together, and drive one of the two 2-inch screws. Then recheck that the top rail is still square with the leg before you drive the second screw. Drive the screw heads

BARBECUE STATION

TOP SHELF

TOP RAIL

WORK TOP CENTER

WORK TOP OUTSIDE

TOP RAIL

END SHELF MIDDLE

SHELF SUPPORT

END RAIL

CENTER SHELF MIDDLE

CENTER SHELF EDGE

SHELF SUPPORT

END SHELF EDGE

BOTTOM RAIL

FRONT LEG

BACK LEG

END FRAME

Make the end frames first, then connect them with the long rails. Nail the work surface and shelves on last.

YOUR INVESTMENT

<u>Time:</u> One day
<u>Money:</u> $30

SHOPPING LIST

16 feet 2×4
40 feet 1×6 pine
#6 × 2-inch galvanized screws
1½-inch galvanized finishing nails
1¼-inch galvanized finishing nails

PROJECT SPECS

The barbecue station is 48 inches long and 19½ inches deep. The work surface is 34 inches high.

CUTTING LIST

PART	QTY.	DIMENSIONS	NOTES
Front leg	2	$1\frac{1}{2} \times 1\frac{1}{2} \times 34$	Rip from 2×4
Back leg	2	$1\frac{1}{2} \times 1\frac{1}{2} \times 47$	Rip from 2×4
End rail	4	$\frac{3}{4} \times 2\frac{11}{16} \times 19\frac{1}{2}$	
Top rail	4	$\frac{3}{4} \times 1\frac{3}{4} \times 38\frac{1}{2}$	
Bottom rail	2	$\frac{3}{4} \times 2\frac{11}{16} \times 38\frac{1}{2}$	
Top shelf	1	$\frac{3}{4} \times 5\frac{1}{2} \times 48$	
Work top outside	2	$\frac{3}{4} \times 5\frac{1}{2} \times 40\frac{1}{8}$	
Work top center	1	$\frac{3}{4} \times 5\frac{1}{2} \times 42\frac{1}{8}$	
Center shelf edge	2	$\frac{3}{4} \times 5\frac{1}{2} \times 22$	
Center shelf middle	1	$\frac{3}{4} \times 5\frac{1}{2} \times 23$	
End shelf edge	4	$\frac{3}{4} \times 5\frac{1}{2} \times 17\frac{1}{2}$	
End shelf middle	2	$\frac{3}{4} \times 5\frac{1}{2} \times 18\frac{1}{2}$	
Shelf support	2	$\frac{3}{4} \times 1\frac{3}{4} \times 14$	

Complete the end frames. With two rails attached to the front leg, transfer the layout lines to the rear leg (above). Then glue and screw the frame together. Measure the diagonal to check for squareness (bottom right). If the frame is off, push it to square before the glue sets (top right).

down into the surface of the wood. Follow this same sequence for all the joints in the barbecue station: Locate the joint, spread glue, clamp if possible, drive one screw, check for square, and drive the second screw.

3 Complete the end frames. The top edge of the bottom end rail is 18 inches off the floor. Measure up from the bottom of the leg, draw layout lines, and screw the bottom rail to the leg the same way you attached the top rail. Now place the long rear leg alongside the front leg and transfer the rail heights from one to the other. Glue and screw the rear leg to the two end rails. Measure the diagonals to verify that the frame is square and if it is off, adjust it before the glue sets, as shown top right. Transfer the layout

lines to the other pair of legs and assemble the other end frame in the same way. The frames can go right-handed or left-handed, so make sure that the second frame is a mirror-image of the first.

4 Prepare the long rails. The two top rails and the two bot-

tom rails connect the two end frames. The top rails are narrower than the bottom rails, which improves your access to the storage shelf. These long rails fit tight between the end rails and tight against the inside faces of the legs. Drill two pilot holes for screws near both ends of all four long rails.

Connect the end frames. Stand the two frames upright on the bench to position the long top and bottom rails. Clamp one of the rails in place (above). Drill pilot holes and drive the first screw through the cross rail and into the end grain of the long rail (below). Unclamp, then drive two more screws through the face of the long rail and into the leg.

5 Connect the end frames. Stand the end frames up on edge on the workbench, as shown in the photograph above, line up the rails, and draw layout lines. Smear glue on one leg where the top rail will fit, clamp the rail in place, and drive a screw through the end rail and into the end grain of the top rail. Remove the clamp and drive the remaining two screws through the face of the top rail and into the leg. Screw and glue the bottom rail to the leg, and repeat the process on the other legs to complete the frame of the barbecue station.

6 Attach the shelf rails. The two shelf rails are the same size as the top rails. Screw them to the top of the rear legs, one on the front and one on the back.

7 Fit the work surface. The work surface consists of three long boards. The outer two fit flush with the end rails, while the center one overhangs an inch at each end. There's no structural

Fit the work surface. Spread glue on the top of the long rail, clamp the outside work-surface board in place, and nail it down (left). Clamp and nail the other two work-surface boards in the same way (right).

Make the shelves. Glue and nail the shelves to the table rails. Begin nailing at the center of the bottom shelf, and work out toward both ends.

reason for this; it just looks better. Spread glue atop the front rail and the end rails, and position the first board. Fasten it to the rails with 2-inch finishing nails. Space the nails about 6 inches apart. Attach the other two long boards to complete the work surface.

8 Make the shelves. The top shelf is a 48-inch board that extends beyond the width of the work surface. It's fastened to the shelf rails with glue and 2-inch finishing nails. The bottom shelf consists of nine shorter pieces of wood, patterned together as shown in the illustrations. This not only makes the table look more interesting and enlarges the useful surface, but it also uses up short ends of wood. Start by gluing and nailing the center board across the front and back bottom rails. The two boards adjacent to it will support the end shelves, so you need to glue and nail shelf supports to their outside edges. Use 1¼-inch finishing nails. Nail the remaining shelf pieces in place with two or three nails in each. If you prefer, you can make the bottom shelf out of three long boards, same as the work surface.

9 Finish the table. Sand off the sharp edges. This detail makes the edges hand-friendly. If you intend to paint the barbecue station, it'll also help keep the paint from crawling.

CHAISE LONGUE

Classic long chair tilts up and down, and rolls away

The chaise longue is a deck and poolside classic. On our version the back lies flat for snoozing in the shade and lifts up for reading or talking. When you want the chaise to go elsewhere, lift the foot end and roll it away on the semi-concealed wheels. "Chaise longue," by the way, is French for "long chair," not "lounge chair."

You must purchase your lounge cushion before you can make the long chair. To keep the fabric bag from flopping around, the inside dimensions of the frame should end up about the same size as the cushion itself. The cushion shown measures 74 inches long by 23½ inches wide, with its hinge point at 29 inches, and the cutting list is built around this size. If your cushion is a different size, you'll need to adjust the lengths of the parts. The widths and thicknesses won't change, nor will the leg dimensions.

The chaise is made with standard widths of planed pine lumber, mostly 1×4 and 1×2. The legs come out of wider pieces, and the support blocks are sawn from a 2×4. The outer frame of the chaise has mitered corners and rounded-over edges. You can rout the edges, or rasp and sand them smooth.

As with most of the constructions shown in this book, the mating parts should be clamped to the worktable and each subassembly should be checked for squareness, before anything gets screwed together. This is the only way to achieve strong and accurate results with ordinary pine lumber.

The back of the chaise longue lifts up and lies flat (left).

The prop holds the back at the height you want. The wheel rail, beneath the head of the chaise (right), allows you to pick up the foot end and wheel it away.

CHAISE LONGUE

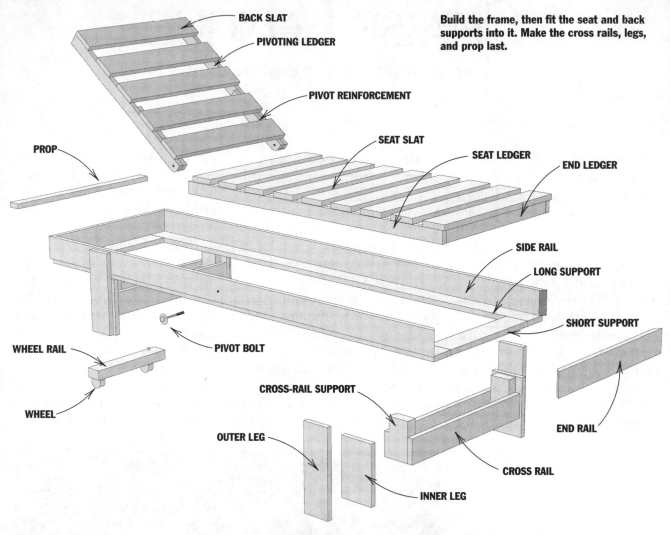

BACK SLAT

PIVOTING LEDGER

PIVOT REINFORCEMENT

PROP

SEAT SLAT

SEAT LEDGER

END LEDGER

SIDE RAIL

LONG SUPPORT

SHORT SUPPORT

WHEEL RAIL

PIVOT BOLT

CROSS-RAIL SUPPORT

END RAIL

OUTER LEG

WHEEL

CROSS RAIL

INNER LEG

Build the frame, then fit the seat and back supports into it. Make the cross rails, legs, and prop last.

YOUR INVESTMENT

<u>Time:</u> One weekend
<u>Money:</u> $50 for wood, $75 for the cushion, $5 for hardware

SHOPPING LIST

80 feet 1×4 pine
8 feet 1×6 pine
4 feet 2×4
Scrap of ¾-inch hardwood plywood
#6 × 2¼-inch trim-head screws
#6 × 1¼-inch galvanized screws
#6 × 2-inch galvanized screws
Two ⁵⁄₁₆ × 3 hex-head bolts with nuts and washers
Two 2-inch white plastic furniture casters

PROJECT SPECS

The chaise shown is 75½ inches long, 24½ inches wide, and 13 inches high. Adjust dimensions to suit the cushion you purchase.

CUTTING LIST

PART	QTY.	DIMENSIONS	NOTES
Side rail	2	¾ × 3½ × 75½	1×4; miter both ends
End rail	2	¾ × 3½ × 24½	1×4; miter both ends
Long support	2	¾ × 3½ × 74¾	1×4
Short support	2	¾ × 3½ × 18	1×4; trim length to fit
Seat ledger	2	¾ × 1½ × 45	1×2
End ledger	1	¾ × 1½ × 22	1×2; trim length to fit
Pivoting ledger	2	¾ × 1½ × 27¾	1×2
Pivot reinforcement	2	¾ × 1½ × 12	Maple or birch plywood
Back slat	5	¾ × 3½ × 22⅜	1×4
Seat slat	9	¾ × 3½ × 23	Trim length to fit
Prop	1	¾ × 1½ × 26	1×2
Prop stop	6	⅜ dia. × 2	Dowel rod
Inner leg	4	¾ × 5 × 8½	1×6
Outer leg	4	¾ × 4 × 12½	1×5
Cross-rail support	4	1½ × 3 × 5⅝	Saw from 2×4
Cross rail	4	¾ × 3½ × 23	Trim length to fit
Wheel rail	1	1½ × 2½ × 14	Saw from 2×4

BUILDING THE CHAISE

1 Prepare all the material. Cut all the parts to length and width as given in the cutting list, and miter both ends of the side and end rails. If your cushion is a different size from ours, be sure to adjust the lengths of the parts accordingly. The cross-rail supports and the wheel rail come out of a standard 2×4 sawn to 3 inches wide. Saw a narrow strip off both edges of the 2×4, to eliminate both of the manufacturer's rounded edges.

2 Make the first joint. Clamp a mitered side rail up on edge on the worktable, making sure it's square to the surface. Bring a mitered end rail up to the long rail and clamp it in place. Use the square to verify that the two pieces do form a right angle, as shown in the top and right photos. Also with the square, transfer the inside faces of the wood to the outside of the miter and draw layout lines. For maximum strength, the screws should enter the wood on this layout line, but on a shallow angle into the wood, as shown in the bottom photo. Drill a pilot hole and drive the first screw. If you can find them, use 2¼-inch trim-head screws, which have a smaller head than regular screws. Drive the head just under the surface of the wood, but stop before you pull the miter out of line. Drive the second screw into the adjacent face of the miter, then drive another screw into each face, for a total of four screws per joint. Join the other three corners of the frame in the same way.

Make the first joint. Clamp a side rail up on edge on your worktable. Bring the mitered end rail up to it. Make sure the pieces fit squarely together (above and left). Draw a layout line and drive two screws through the joint from each direction (below right). Drive the screws on the angle indicated by the pencil (bottom).

Round the frame corners. Mount a ⅜-inch round-over cutter in the router and run it around the frame edges, including the mitered corner. Leave the bottom inside edges square. Instead of routing, you can rasp and sand the corners off.

Make the legs. Use a small paint roller to spread glue on the face of the outer leg, then screw it to the inner leg.

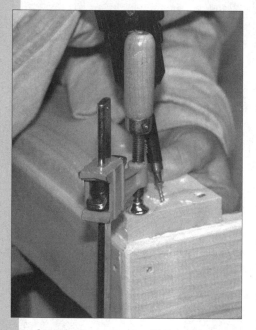

Attach the supports. Glue and screw the long supports to the frame. Check that the frame is square before drilling pilot holes and driving the two screws across the end of the support.

3 Round the frame corners. Once you attach the bottom supports you won't be able to get at all of the edges of the frame, so round them over now. Clamp the frame to the worktable. Mount a ⅜-inch roundover cutter with a ball-bearing pilot in the router and trace around all the corners, inside and out. Round the outside of the miter as well. Turn the frame over to do the outside bottom corner, but don't round the bottom inside of the frame. This is where the supports attach, in the next step.

4 Attach the supports. The long supports are glued and screwed to the bottom of the chaise frame, just inside the roundover margin. Spread glue on the bottom edge of the frame, clamp the first long support in place, and screw it to the frame with 2-inch screws spaced about 12 inches apart. Since the edges of the support will be rounded over, set the screws ⅝ inch back from the corner of the wood and angle them into the meat of the frame. When you get to the end of the support, measure the diagonals to be sure the frame is still square, and if it is not, pull it into square. Then drill pilot holes and drive two screws across the width of the support strip, into

the end rails of the frame, as shown in the photo left. Attach the other long support, and the two short supports, in the same way. Then round over the outside edges of all four supports, the same way you did in Step 3.

5 Make the legs. Each leg consists of an inner piece and an outer piece, glued and screwed together as shown in the illustration. Before you join the parts, round over all four corners on one face of the outer leg pieces, plus the two long corners on one face of the inner leg pieces. Dry-assemble two leg pieces to draw a layout line, then spread glue and screw the parts together, using six of the 1¼-inch screws. Join the other three legs in the same way. Finally, round over the bottom corners of each assembled leg.

6 Attach the legs to the frame. The legs sit 10 inches from either end of the chaise frame and are held there with glue and screws. Set a square to this distance to locate each leg, and

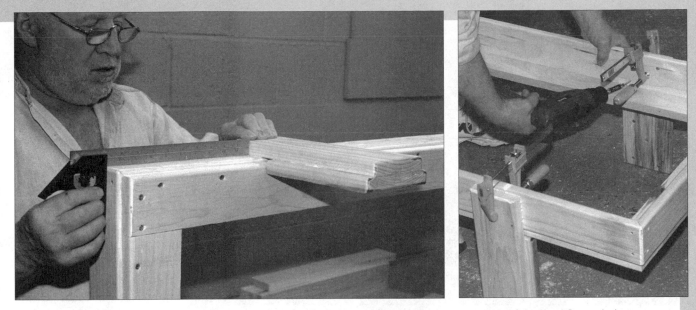

Attach the legs to the frame. Locate the legs on the frame with a combination square set to 10 inches. Spread glue, clamp the pieces in place, then drive screws from inside the frame.

draw layout lines. Then spread glue on the leg parts and clamp them in place. Make sure the inner leg pieces butt up tight against the bottom support strips. Drive four 1¼-inch screws through the side rail and into each leg. Drive all the screws from the inside of the frame, so their heads don't show.

7 Make the cross rails. The cross rails and the cross-rail supports ensure that the legs won't snap off when unruly teenagers drag the chaise sideways across an uneven patio. The cross rails at the head of the chaise also create a secure attachment for the wheels, which calm adults will use to move the chaise. The length given for the supports works with standard 2-inch furniture casters. If you substitute different wheels, you'll have to adjust the length of the supports to suit. The wheels should clear the ground by ⅛ inch to ¼ inch. Center the support blocks on the inside faces of the legs, then drill pilot holes and glue and

Make the cross rails. Glue and screw the cross-rail supports inside the legs (above). Trim the four cross rails so they fit tightly between the legs. Attach the wheel rail to the cross rail under the head of the chaise, then glue and screw all the cross rails to their support blocks (left).

Make the pivoting ledgers. Glue and screw the plywood pivot reinforcement to the pivoting ledger. The curve is for tilting clearance.

screw them in place, using three 2½-inch screws for each block. Drive the screws from the inside, through the support blocks into the legs. Glue and screw the wheel rail to the face of the cross rail that will go underneath the head end of the chaise, using four of the 2-inch screws. Finally, glue and screw all four cross rails onto their support blocks, flush with the supports' bottom ends.

Attach the seat ledgers to the chaise frame. Set the tilting back frame inside the chaise and make sure the seat ledgers allow ½ inch of clearance. Glue, clamp, and screw the ledgers to the chaise frame.

PIVOTING LEDGER DETAIL

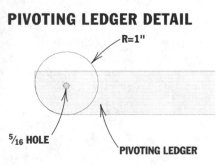

R=1"

5/16 HOLE

PIVOTING LEDGER

8 Make the pivoting ledgers. The back frame tilts up and lies flat. It has to be an easy fit inside the chaise frame. Begin by making the two pivoting ledgers. Lay out the clearance radius and drill the 5/16-inch pivot holes. Cut the clearance radius on one end of each ledger. You can remove the waste with a belt sander or disk sander, with a jig saw or band saw, with a sharp chisel or a rasp, or just gnaw it off. Make the two plywood pivot reinforcements to match the shape of the ledgers, as shown above, and glue and screw them onto the ledgers. Drill the pivot bolt hole through the plywood.

9 Assemble the tilting back frame. Use the chaise as a jig for assembling the back frame. Set the first pivot ledger inside the chaise frame, and fasten one of the back slats to its square end, using glue and two of the trim-head screws. Screw the other end of the back slat to the square end of the other pivot ledger in the same way. Screw and glue the second back slat to the pivot end of the ledgers. It's offset 1½ inches from the end of the ledgers. Set the tilting frame in position inside the chaise frame. The pivot action requires ⅛ inch of clearance to the end of the frame, so insert a shim to ensure the clearance. Transfer the location of the pivot bolt holes, and drill the 5/16-inch holes through the chaise side rails.

10 Attach the seat ledgers to the chaise frame. The seat ledgers fit tightly against the bottom support strips and tightly against the end of the chaise frame. Spread glue on the ledgers and clamp them in position. There should be a gap of ½ inch between the seat ledgers and the tilting back frame. Drive 1¼-inch screws through the ledgers into the chaise frame. Finally, glue and screw the end ledger to the chaise frame. It fits tightly between the seat ledgers.

11 Fasten the seat slats to the ledgers. Begin at the foot of the chaise. Spread glue on the top of the end ledger, fit the slat in place, and screw it down tight. Use two trim-head screws in each end. Fit the seat slat nearest the pivoting back frame next. Leave clearance of ¼ inch to the end of the seat ledger. Space the

Fasten the seat slats to the ledgers. Set the seat slats in place and space them evenly apart, then glue and screw them to the ledgers.

Install the prop. The first prop stop should hold the seat back nearly vertical. The remaining stops should be the prop's width apart (top). A $7/16$-inch hole in the prop permits intermediate settings (above).

remaining seven seat slats evenly along the ledgers. Glue and screw all the slats in place. Fit the remaining three back slats in the same way.

12 Install the prop. The prop that retains the tilting back is a simple stick of wood with its edges rounded over. The prop stops against $3/8$-inch dowels drilled into the long sides of the chaise frame. Begin by installing the pivot bolts and washers, then lift the back into its most upright position, a few inches from vertical. Set the prop across the rails and against the tilting back, and mark where the prop rests on the long chaise rails. This locates the edge of the first pair of dowel holes. Drill the holes $1\frac{1}{2}$ inches deep into the chaise rails. Cut two 2-inch lengths of $3/8$-inch dowel and glue them into the holes. Now set the prop tight behind the dowels,

and mark and drill the next pair of holes. You'll find that three sets of dowels are enough, because at lower angles friction keeps the prop in place. To make the prop stop at intermediate positions, drill a pair of $7/16$-inch holes through the prop.

13 Mount the wheels. The mounted wheels should clear the floor by about $1/8$ inch. When you pick up the other end of the chaise, the wheels will contact the floor, allowing you to roll it wherever it wants to go. Drill two $1/2$-inch holes through the wheel rail, an inch in from the front edge and 12 inches apart. Tap the sleeves of the furniture casters into the holes.

14 Test the chaise. Toss the cushion onto the slats, check out how the back pivots to various comfortable angles, lie down, and take the nap you've earned.

Mount the wheels. Drill holes in the wheel rail for the 2-inch furniture casters. They should clear the floor by a fat $1/8$ inch, allowing you to pick up the other end of the chaise to wheel it off.

15 Finish the chaise. Sand the wood with 80-grit and 120-grit sandpaper. Then prime it and paint it. Don't forget to paint the parts that come into view when you tilt the back.

Umbrella Table

Here's how to make shade while the sun shines

Nothing says summer like an umbrella table with a tray of chilled drinks on it. It makes welcome shade in any climate, and you can always fold the umbrella when you want the full sun.

The design problem is creating enough understructure to support the umbrella, while still leaving some knee room. This handsome table uses a pinwheel construction to accomplish both goals.

The spokes of a pinwheel don't radiate from a common center. Instead, they chase one another around a center space, in this case, a space the size of your umbrella pole. Most sun umbrellas have a 1½-inch pole. Don't guess, however. Measure your umbrella before you construct the table. This dimension also determines the thickness of the legs and the center supports. In the interest of lightness, we made these parts square in section. As an alternative, you could make them of 3-inch-wide wood. This is the width that remains when you saw the rounded edges off a standard 2×4.

Glue and #6 × 2-inch galvanized construction screws are what hold the table structure together. The tabletop is made from ¾-inch pine. It is fastened to the frame with 2-inch galvanized finishing nails. In a high-wind region, there is no way to keep an umbrella table from lifting off the deck, short of nailing it down, so do just that. Drive a nail at an angle through each table leg into the deck itself.

Not only can you choose to make the table legs wider but you also could make all of the parts from thicker wood than the ¾-inch 1×3s and 1×4s shown here.

Make the top pinwheel. Clamp the four long top rails to the umbrella gauge (above). Drill pilot holes, and drive a single screw through the face of each rail into the end of the rail it meets. Remove the clamps and gauge, and turn the assembly over to drive the second screw into each joint (right).

You could substitute 5/4 pine, which finishes around 1⅛ inch thick, without changing any other dimensions. This is because everything follows from the lengths of the parts. The pieces can be wider or thicker without affecting the construction.

BUILDING THE UMBRELLA TABLE

1 Saw the parts. Saw all the wood for the table structure before you begin to build. There are a lot of parts and, confusingly, they are all of similar size, so group them and give each group an identifying mark to help you keep track. You can saw the wood for the tabletop at the same time, or you can leave it to cut to fit at the end. But while you are working at the saw, make a square stick of wood the same dimension as your umbrella pole. It will be the gauge piece around which you assemble the table framework.

2 Make the top pinwheel. The core of the table structure is a pair of pinwheels. Start by clamping the four top rails to the umbrella gauge piece, as shown in the top photo. Check for square, then drill pilot holes and drive one screw through the face of each top rail and into the end grain of the next rail around the pinwheel. Remove the clamps and turn the assembly over on the worktable. Drill pilot holes and drive a second screw through each joint. For the strongest joints, angle the screws. Join the four bottom rails into a second pinwheel in exactly the same way.

UMBRELLA TABLE

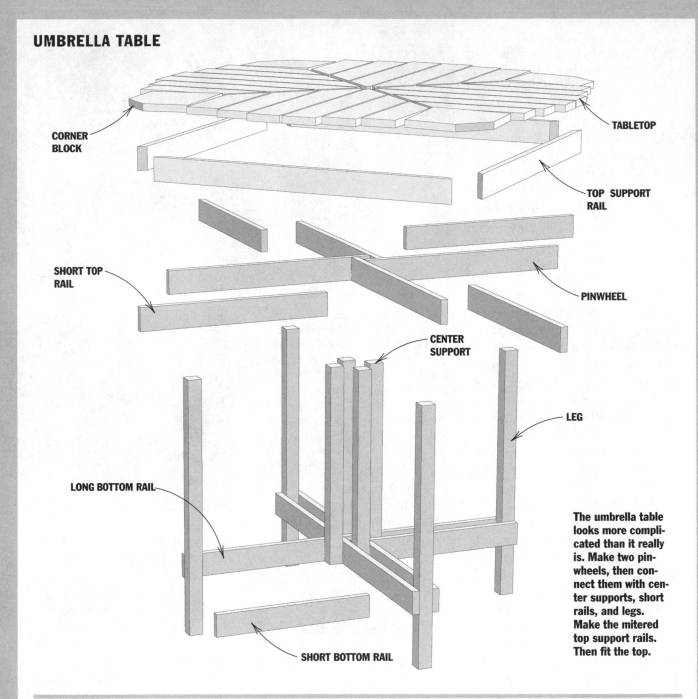

CORNER BLOCK

TABLETOP

TOP SUPPORT RAIL

SHORT TOP RAIL

PINWHEEL

CENTER SUPPORT

LEG

LONG BOTTOM RAIL

The umbrella table looks more complicated than it really is. Make two pinwheels, then connect them with center supports, short rails, and legs. Make the mitered top support rails. Then fit the top.

SHORT BOTTOM RAIL

YOUR INVESTMENT

Time: One weekend
Money: $60

SHOPPING LIST

40 feet 1×3 pine
40 feet 1×4 pine
10 feet 2×4
4 feet 1×12
#6 × 2-inch galvanized screws
2-inch galvanized finishing nails

PROJECT SPECS

The table is 29 inches high. The top is 48 inches across.

CUTTING LIST

PART	QTY.	DIMENSIONS	NOTES
Long top rail	4	$\frac{3}{4} \times 2\frac{1}{2} \times 23$	1×3
Long bottom rail	4	$\frac{3}{4} \times 2\frac{1}{2} \times 20$	1×3
Center support	4	$1\frac{1}{2} \times 1\frac{1}{2} \times 22$	Cut from 2×4
Short bottom rail	4	$\frac{3}{4} \times 2\frac{1}{2} \times 17\frac{3}{4}$	1×3
Leg	4	$1\frac{1}{2} \times 1\frac{1}{2} \times 28$	1×2
Short top rail	4	$\frac{3}{4} \times 2\frac{1}{2} \times 20\frac{3}{4}$	1×3
Top support rail	4	$\frac{3}{4} \times 2\frac{1}{2} \times 32$	Miter both ends
TABLETOP			
Corner block	4	$\frac{3}{4} \times 11\frac{3}{8} \times 9\frac{1}{2}$	Mitered as shown
Short tabletop	8	$\frac{3}{4} \times 3\frac{1}{2} \times 13$	Miter one end
Long tabletop	8	$\frac{3}{4} \times 3\frac{1}{2} \times 17\frac{1}{2}$	Miter one end
Center tabletop	8	$\frac{3}{4} \times 3\frac{1}{2} \times 22\frac{1}{4}$	Double miter

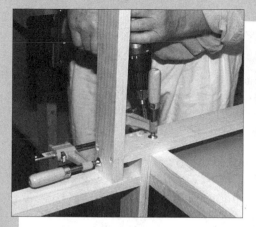

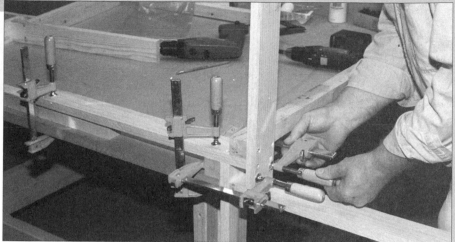

3 Add the center supports.
The four center supports connect the two pinwheels, as shown in the illustration below, but as a first step just join them onto the top wheel. Begin with one center support. Set it on the edge of the worktable, then position the pinwheel on it, as shown in the top left photo. Draw layout lines so you can spread glue on the mating surfaces, then clamp the assembly together. Drill pilot holes. Drive two screws through the face of the rail and into the center support. Drive a third screw into the support from inside the pinwheel center. Bury the screw head in the wood. Join the other three center supports to the wheel in the same way.

4 Connect the pinwheels. The second pinwheel should plug right onto the free end of the four center supports. If the pinwheel seems as if it can't possibly fit, it's upside-down. When you get it right, draw layout lines so you can spread glue, then clamp the whole assembly together. It will take eight clamps to bring all the mating surfaces tightly together. Measure the distance between each pair of top and bottom rails to make sure the two pinwheels are parallel to one

Add the center supports. Glue and clamp the pinwheel to the first center support, so you can drill pilot holes and screw the parts together (left). Rotate the assembly to add center supports. Support the free end of the top rail with a block of scrap, as at left in the photo above.

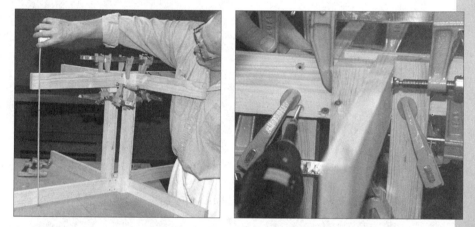

Connect the pinwheels. Spread glue, plug the two assemblies together, and clamp them. Measure the height at the ends of the rails to make sure the two pinwheels are parallel (left). Drill pilot holes and screw through the rails into the center supports (right).

PINWHEEL CONNECTION

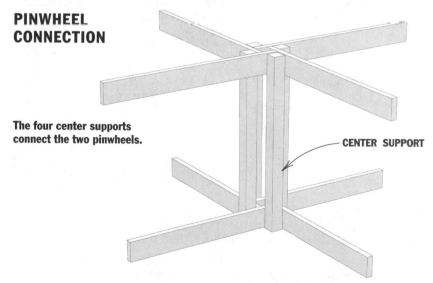

The four center supports connect the two pinwheels.

CENTER SUPPORT

LEGS AND RAILS

Glue and screw the legs and the short rails to the pinwheel assembly.

SHORT TOP RAIL

LEG

SHORT BOTTOM RAIL

another. Drill pilot holes and drive two screws through each joint. Always drive the screws through the rail and into the wood of the center support.

5 Add the legs and rails. Glue, clamp, and screw a leg to the assembled pinwheels, then remove the clamps to glue and screw the short rails in place. The illustration at left shows how these parts fit together. You can make the joints tight and accurate, but only if you take the time to draw layout lines, spread glue, and clamp. Drill pilot holes and drive two screws through each joint, then unclamp the assembly in order to drive another pair of screws into the joint from the other side. Rotate the table base on the worktable to add the remaining three legs and all the rest of the rails.

6 Miter the top support rails. The four top support rails not only support the tabletop boards but they also tie the table base tightly together. Start by mitering one end of each support rail at 45°. Stand the assembled base upright on the floor. Hold the rails in position to mark and cut the remaining miters.

7 Connect the mitered rails. The mitered rails should fit tightly between the arms of the leg-and-rail assemblies. Spread glue on the face of the miters, then clamp the first support rail in position. Drill pilot holes for two galvanized screws in each end, and drive the screws home. Start the screws about an inch back from the ends of the rails, so they bite through the full thickness of the wood.

Connect the mitered rails. Clamp each mitered top support rail against the top rails. The clamps won't slip if you position them as shown here. Glue and screw the support rails in place. Set the screws an inch back from the end of the rails.

Lay out the top. Tack-nail the ½-inch spacer gauge strips to the table base. Make sure the strips are square to each other and to the top support rails.

Fit the top boards. Starting with the center boards and working one section at a time, fit the tabletop together (left). Space the boards with the narrow gauge strips and nail them to the table structure (right).

8 Lay out the top. The tabletop is a herringbone pattern of 1×4 boards. The corners are filled in with five-sided corner blocks sawn from a 1×12 board. Start at the center of each section, and work out toward the corner blocks. To begin, saw two pairs of spacer gauge strips. One pair is ½ inch thick, and the other is ¼ inch thick. Tack-nail the thick gauge strips to the table frame, as in the bottom photo at left.

9 Fit the top boards. Crosscut all the top boards to the lengths given in the cutting list, and miter them all. Nip ½ inch off the point of the eight center boards, so they'll clear the umbrella opening. Set two center boards against the gauge strips. Butt the miters together. Nail the center boards to the table structure with the 2-inch finishing nails. Work toward the corners, spacing the boards with the ¼-inch gauge strips and nailing them to the structure. Fill in the other three sections in the same way.

TOP LAYOUT

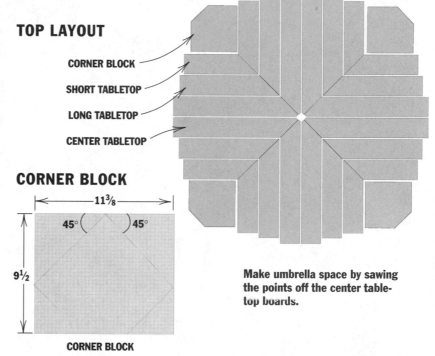

CORNER BLOCK
SHORT TABLETOP
LONG TABLETOP
CENTER TABLETOP

CORNER BLOCK

11⅜

45° 45°

9½

CORNER BLOCK

Make umbrella space by sawing the points off the center table-top boards.

10 Fit the corner blocks. The corner blocks have five sides, but they're made by cutting a series of miters, as shown in the drawing above. Begin by cross-cutting four 9½-inch lengths off the 1×12 board. Draw a center-line and saw a miter both ways from this center point. Finally, make square cuts from the ends of the miters. The corner blocks should neatly fill the corner spaces. Nail them to the frame.

11 Finish the table. To make your umbrella table friendly to the touch, sand a small flat on all the exposed edges. Sand all the surfaces as well, with 80-grit and 120-grit paper. Now you can paint the table, varnish it, or leave it alone to weather.

PORCH SWING

Gentle rocker is love-seat width and hangs from chains

No front porch can be considered complete without a hanging swing. This porch swing is the perfect place for watching the world pass by, and it's just wide enough to do so with a friend. When the swing is at rest, the arms are level. If you're gentle, you can rock the swing without having to hang onto your lemonade.

The swing is made from standard 1× pine lumber, which measures about ¾ inch thick, plus one 2×4 stud. To make the swing, you need to be able to saw an accurate crosscut, which you can do with a handsaw, a chop saw, or a table saw. There are three angled cuts, but you don't need to rip, or saw parts lengthwise. The seat and back are curved. You draw the curves by flexing and tracing a thin piece of wood, then cut them out with a jigsaw.

The seat slats and the back slats are attached to the swing's structure with 2½-inch siding nails. These special nails are designed for hanging clapboard siding on houses. They're long and thin, with a relatively small head. The point is dubbed off, so they're less likely to split the wood. The shaft is grooved up to an inch from the head, so the nail locks into the structure. And they're galvanized to resist rust.

Traditionally, the porch swing is a love seat, just wide enough for two. This one follows tradition, though you can make your swing wider if you like. Chains suspend the swing from the beams of the porch. The three-point connection to the support chains is important. Without it, the seat can pivot and dump you out. Though you often see swings hung with rope, chain is better because it does not stretch or wear.

BUILDING THE SWING

1 Cut all the parts. Saw all the wood to length at once, before you begin constructing the swing. This is the most efficient way to work.

2 Curve the seat rails. The swing seat gets its shape from the curve sawn into the three curved seat rails. The curve is

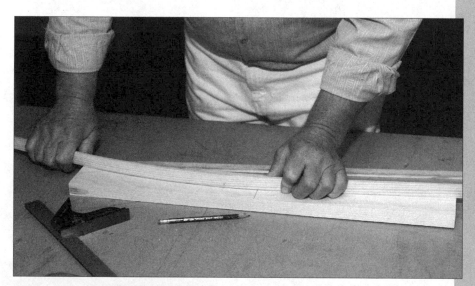

Curve the seat rails. Mark the center and end points of the curve. Flex a thin stick of wood between these points, and trace its shape (above). Saw the curves with a jigsaw. Clamp the wood to the worktable, with the layout line overhanging the edge (left).

PORCH SWING

Build the L-shaped seat frames and connect them with the rear rail. Add the front rail and seat slats. Make the back as a separate unit, then attach it to the back uprights. The arms and seat beams go on last.

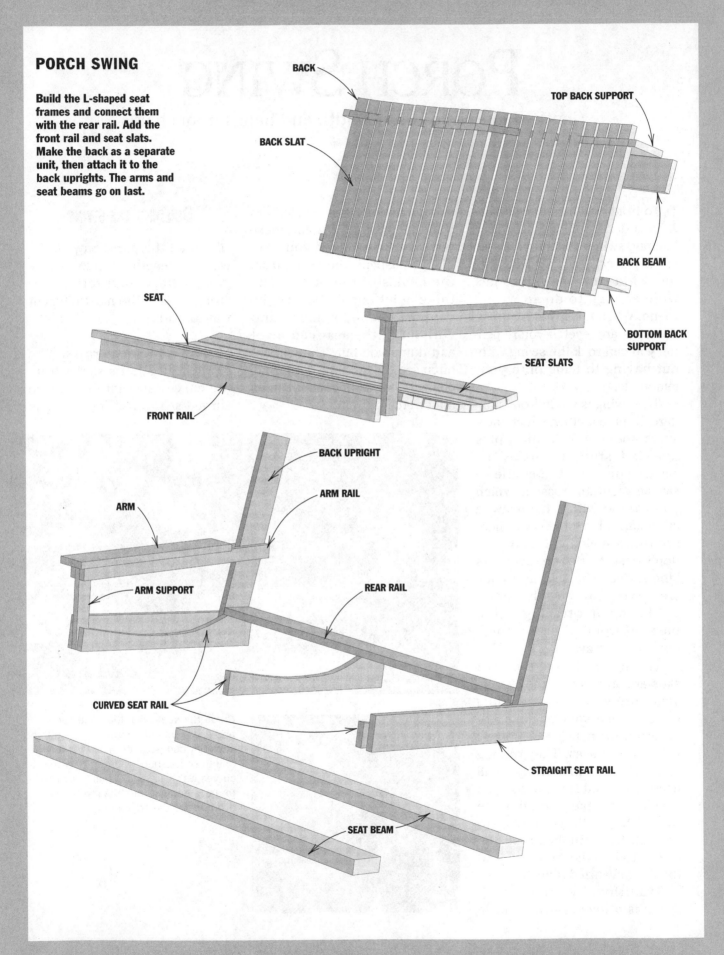

BACK

TOP BACK SUPPORT

BACK SLAT

BACK BEAM

SEAT

BOTTOM BACK SUPPORT

SEAT SLATS

FRONT RAIL

BACK UPRIGHT

ARM RAIL

ARM

ARM SUPPORT

REAR RAIL

CURVED SEAT RAIL

STRAIGHT SEAT RAIL

SEAT BEAM

approximate. You can lay it out freehand, as in the drawing at right, or you can draw it by flexing and tracing a thin stick of wood. Begin by marking the curve's end-points A and C, and the center B, as shown in the drawing. Then hold the stick on A and B and bend it with your thumbs so it makes a nice shape. Enlist a friend to help you draw the curved line along the edge of the stick. Draw the curve from B to C in the same way, fudging the shape smooth at point B. Saw the curve with the jigsaw. Trace around this first curved rail to lay out and saw two more just like it.

3 Angle the back uprights. The slope of the back comes from a small angle sawn at the bottom of the back uprights. The angle is about 7½°, which you can lay out by measuring 7/16 inch from the corner of the wood, as shown in the illustrations at right. Saw the angle on both back uprights, using the chop saw or a handsaw.

SEAT AND BACK DETAIL

Draw the seat curve by bending a thin stick between points A, B, and C.

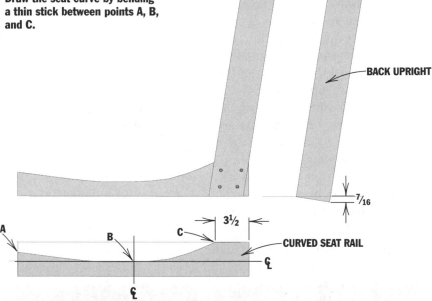

BACK UPRIGHT

7/16

3½

A

B

C

CURVED SEAT RAIL

Angle the back uprights. Measure 7/16 inch up from the corner of the wood and draw a line to the opposite corner. Saw on this line.

YOUR INVESTMENT

<u>Time:</u> One weekend
<u>Money:</u> $50

SHOPPING LIST

8 feet 2×4 stud
95 feet 1×2 pine
4 feet 1×3 pine
36 feet 1×4 pine
6 feet 1×5 pine
2½-inch galvanized siding nails
#6 × 1¼-inch galvanized screws
#6 × 2-inch galvanized screws
Six 3/8 × 4-inch eye bolts, with nuts and washers
Six spring-loaded snap links
24 feet 1-inch chain

PROJECT SPECS

The porch swing is 48 inches long, 24 inches front to back, and 24 inches high.
It requires a sturdy overhead support.

CUTTING LIST

PART	QTY.	DIMENSIONS	NOTES
Curved seat rail	3	¾ × 3½ × 24	1×4; saw curve
Back upright	2	¾ × 3½ × 24	1×4; miter one end 7½°
Straight seat rail	2	¾ × 3½ × 24	1×4
Rear rail	1	¾ × 3½ × 41½	1×4
Seat slat	11	¾ × 1½ × 43	1×2
Front rail	1	¾ × 2½ × 40	1×3
Arm support	2	¾ × 1½ × 9	1×2
Arm rail	4	¾ × 1½ × 26½	1×2; cut to fit
Arm	2	¾ × 3½ × 21	1×4
Bottom back support	1	¾ × 3½ × 44	1×4; saw curve
Top back support	1	¾ × 4½ × 44	1×5; saw curve
Back slat	23	¾ × 1½ × 18	1×2
Back beam	1	¾ × 3½ × 48	1×4
Seat beam	2	1½ × 3½ × 48	2×4

4 Make the first joint. The seat begins to take shape when you join the back upright and the curved seat rail. Set the curved seat rail flat on the back upright. The angled end of the upright sits flush with the bottom of the rail, and the top corner of the rail meets the back edge of the upright. These relationships are shown on the drawing on the previous page and in the photo below. Pencil a layout line, spread glue on one of the parts, and clamp the two parts together. Drive four of the 1¼-inch screws into the joint. When you join the other back upright and curved seat rail, make sure you end up with a right-handed part and a left-handed one.

5 Add the straight seat rail. The straight seat rails are companions to the curved seat rails, and complete the seat frames. They're attached to the outside of the back uprights. The straight seat rails align exactly with the curved seat rails. Spread glue and use a spacer block to help you clamp each rail in place while you drive four of the 1¼-inch screws. At this point you should have two L-shaped seat frames, as shown in the photo at bottom right.

6 Connect the seat frames. The rear rail connects the two seat frames, creating the skeleton of the porch swing. Sit the two seat frames on the worktable and fit the rear rail between them, as shown below. The rear rail sits on the flat at the back of the curved seat rails, and butts tightly against the two back uprights. Spread glue where the parts meet, drill pilot holes, and drive three 2-inch screws into

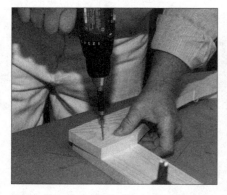

Make the first joint. Spread glue, press or clamp the two parts tightly together, and drive four screws into the joint (above). The two L-shapes should be identical, except for their handedness. Clamp the second assembly on top of the first one in order to align the parts before fastening them (right).

Add the straight seat rail. The straight seat rail lines up with the curved one, but on the opposite side of the back upright. Use a scrap of wood as a spacer at the front end of the seat frame (left).

Connect the seat frames. Stand the seat frames upright on the worktable and connect them with the rear rail. Drive the screws diagonally into the back upright and seat rails (right).

each joint. Angle the pilot holes so the screws go down through the curved seat rail and into the back upright.

7 Assemble the front beam. The first seat slat helps stiffen the construction by being glued and nailed to the front rail, forming the front beam. Spread glue on the top edge of the front rail, and plant the seat slat on it, flush with the face of the front rail. Center the slat from end to end. Nail the slat to the rail with the 2½-inch siding nails. Use a ¼-inch roundover cutter in the router to smooth the sharp front corner off this beam assembly.

8 Join the front beam to the seat rails. The front rail fits between the curved seat rails, but it must be inset 1¼ inches at the front, to make room for the arm supports. Measure 1¼ inches back from the ends of the curved seat rails, spread glue, and position the parts. Then attach the first slat to the curved seat rail with 2½-inch siding nails. Ensure the connection with a 2-inch screw angled through the bottom corner of the curved seat rail into the end of the front rail.

9 Fit the third curved seat rail. The third curved seat rail supports the center of the seat. However, it must be trimmed to fit behind the front rail. Hold the curved rail in position and measure how far it protrudes beyond the rear rail. Transfer this measurement to the front end of the rail. This is how much wood has to be sawn off. As shown in the photo below, lay out the angle of the saw cut by clamping two scraps

Assemble the front beam. Center the first seat slat from end to end on the top edge of the front rail. Glue and nail these pieces together.

Join the front beam to the seat rails. Leave a 1¼ inch space in front of the front rail for the arm support. Glue and nail the first seat slat to the curved seat rails.

Fit the third curved seat rail. The third rail fits behind the front beam. Mock up the front beam with a couple of pieces of scrap. This shows you where to saw the rail so it will fit snugly against the front rail.

Install the third seat rail. Nail the first seat slat to the third seat rail, then drive screws through the front rail and rear rail into the third seat rail.

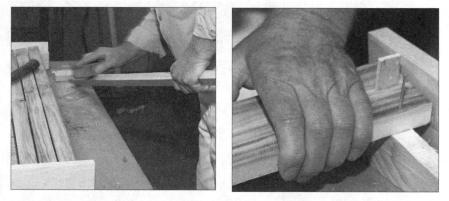

Fill in the seat. Lay the seat slats in place and choose their top surfaces. Sand the sharp top edges off with 80-grit paper wrapped around a block (left). Use a thin scrap of wood to space the slats (right). Glue and nail them to the curved seat rails.

BOTTOM BACK SUPPORT

Draw the curve by bending a thin stick so it touches points A, B and C. Saw the shape, then trace it onto the top back support.

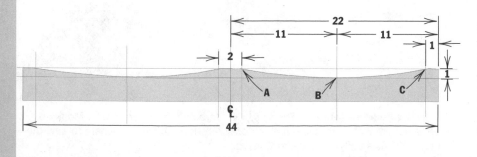

together to represent the first slat and front rail, and use them as a gauge. Saw the curved seat rail to length on this layout line.

10 Install the third seat rail. The third curved seat rail should now fit neatly against the front rail, and up against the rear rail. Spread glue, and hold it in place with a single siding nail through the top of the first slat. Then drive two 2-inch screws through the front rail and into the end of the seat rail, as shown at left. Finally, drill pilot holes and drive three screws through the rear rail into the curved seat rail.

11 Fill in the seat. The seat slats will be nailed to the curved seat rails, but first, lay them all in position and choose their top surfaces. Now sand the sharp corners off the top edges of all of the slats, using 80-grit sandpaper. To space the slats, use two spacers of scrap wood about $3/16$ inch thick. Dab some glue on the curved seat rails, plant the slat against the spacers, and nail it down with $2\frac{1}{2}$-inch siding nails. When you reach the back of the seat, there'll be a gap of about an inch to the rear rail. Round over the front edge of the rear rail, by routing or sanding, and don't worry about the gap.

12 Make the back supports. The back supports echo the curve of the seat, and you lay out their curves in the same way, either freehand or by flexing and tracing a thin stick of wood. Start with the bottom back support, which is an inch narrower than the top one. As shown on the drawing at left, mark the end points and the

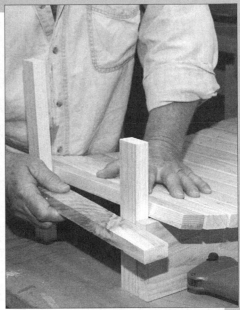

Complete the back. March the back slats across the curved back supports. When you get to the edges, insert a couple of scraps to reserve space for the arm rails.

Attach two center slats. Block the bottom back support up on scraps of wood, then glue and nail a back slat at the center of each curve in the back supports.

midpoints of the two curves. Flex the stick so it touches all three points of one curve, enlist your friend to draw the line, and repeat for the second curve. Once you've jigsawn the bottom back support, trace its shape onto the top back support and saw it as well.

13 Attach two center slats. The 23 back slats march across the back supports, just like the seat slats, but the first thing to do is attach a slat in the center of each curve. Start by sanding the sharp corners off the all of the back slats. Next, set the two back supports up on edge on the worktable. One is wider than the other, so put a piece of wood under the narrow one to block it up. Mark the midpoints of the curves and place slats on these marks, as shown in the photo above. Separate the back supports so the slats overhang by 2 inches at the top and bottom.

Use the 2½-inch siding nails to attach the two center slats.

14 Complete the back. To make sure the back is square, measure the diagonals. If they are not equal, push the back into square and clamp it to the worktable. Next, add the two end slats, but they don't go at the very ends of the back supports. There has to be room for the arm support, so leave a space the thickness of a piece of scrap wood, as shown in the photo at top right. Now fill in the spaces with the remaining back slats, driving two siding nails into each back support. Space the slats evenly.

15 Mount the back beam. The back beam supports the back assembly and connects it to the back uprights. The back beam fits under the top back support, centered from end to end, with a half-inch overhang, as shown at bottom right. To position the

Mount the back beam. Clamp the back beam near the edge of the worktable, then hang the completed back on it. Center the top back support from end to end, with a ½-inch overhang toward the rear. Glue and nail it in place.

parts, clamp the back beam to the edge of the worktable, and set the top back support on it. Spread glue and nail the parts together with the siding nails.

Connect the back to the seat. Clamp a scrap support block to each back upright, six inches down from the top. The support block positions the back assembly while you screw it to the back uprights (left). Remove the scrap block to screw through the back upright into the bottom back support (above).

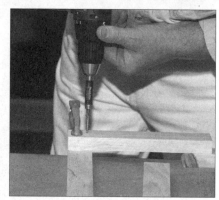

Assemble the arm structure. Screw the arm support to the arm rails. These parts make a right angle.

16 Connect the back to the seat. You're finally ready to connect the back to the seat, and the first step is to clamp a scrap support block to each back upright. It goes about 6 inches down from the top of the back upright—check the precise distance by measuring the distance from the top of the back slats to the bottom of the back beam. Now you can rest the back beam on the clamped scraps. Mark where the surfaces mate, and spread glue there. Drill clearance holes through the back uprights and drive $2\frac{1}{2}$-inch screws into the ends of the top back support. These screws pull the back supports together, so it's important to drive them first. Then screw through the back beam into the back upright, and also through the back upright into the end of the bottom back beam, as shown in the photo above.

17 Dub off the corners. Before you attach the arms in the next step, go over the whole swing with 80-grit sandpaper and remove all the sharp edges and corners.

18 Assemble the arm structure. The arm structures consist of an arm support sandwiched between two arm rails. The arm itself fits on top of the arm rails, in the next steps. The arm support and arm rails go together at right angles, held with glue and $1\frac{5}{8}$-inch screws, as shown in the photo at left.

19 Join the arm structure to the swing. The arm support fits between the seat rails, and the arm rails fit around the back uprights. Position the top surface of the arm rails $11\frac{1}{2}$ inches up from the bottom of the back uprights, and push the arm support as far back as it will go. The arm rails will project about an inch beyond the back uprights, as shown in the top left photo on the next page. Get the pieces in the right place, then take them apart to spread glue. Drill pilot holes and screw them together with $2\frac{1}{2}$-inch screws.

20 Attach the arms. The arms, at last, sit on top of the arm rails. Each arm projects 1 inch at the front, and overhangs $\frac{1}{4}$ inch to the outside. This puts about

Join the arm structure to the swing. The top of the arm rail is 11½ inches high at the rear of the back upright, and tight against the front beam at the front of the seat.

Attach the arms. Glue, clamp and nail the arms to the arm supports.

an inch of overhang to the inside of the swing. If you were to center the arm on the arm supports, it would interfere with the chain suspension. Sand off all the sharp corners and edges, then attach the arms with glue and siding nails.

21 Attach the seat beams. The suspension chains support the seat beams, which support the swing. That's why the beams are 2×4 material, instead of 1×. Position the front seat beam tight against the edge of the front rail, centered from end to end. Drill clearance holes, and screw it to the seat rails with the 2½-inch screws. Position the back seat beam as far back as possible. Screw it to the rails as well.

22 Install the eye bolts. The swing and the people sitting on it depend upon sturdy eye bolts firmly connected to the seat beams. You must use eye bolts with washers and nuts, not screw-thread eyes that twist

Attach the seat beams. Turn the seat upside-down on the work table to attach the sturdy seat beams to the seat rails.

Install the eye bolts. Drill holes for the eye bolts near the ends of the seat beams and back beam. Put a washer on the eye side as well as on the nut side.

directly into the wood. Drill ⅜-inch holes in the ends of both seat beams. Fit a washer between the eye and the wood, and a second washer under the nut. Tighten the nuts with a wrench. To keep the swing from tipping, install a third pair of eye bolts in the ends of the back beam. These will be connected to the main support chains by chain snap-links, as shown in the photo on page 62.

23 Hang the swing. Chain snap links are standard hardware items. They make a quick connection between the suspension chain and the eye bolts. Now you have a choice: You can connect the suspension chains somewhere above the swing in a Y-shape, or you can carry both chains right up to the overhead support. The overhead support must tie securely into the structure of the building.

WINDOW BOXES

They bring the garden right up to the house

I t's easy to love a window box, because it brings the garden up close to your window view. Window boxes look great from outside the house as well as from the inside.

These days you'll see as many window boxes on the deck as under a window. They can hang from a railing, or sit on it, as easily as from a windowsill.

This project shows you how to make a window box for either situation, windowsill or deck railing.

The problem with window boxes is size. They have to be big enough for the plants to last all day on one watering, but they're often so big that the weight of soil and water pulls them apart in just a season or

two. This project offers two solutions: Make a small box, or make a box with front legs.

The small box is designed to hang from a deck railing. The dimensions given in the cutting list work best with a 2×4 railing. If your deck or balcony has a wide 2×6 railing, or a narrow metal railing, you can change the width of the top plate to suit. The small box is very plain. To make it blend right into your house, you can paint it, or side it with clapboard or shakes and stain or paint them to match.

The box with legs can be attached to a wall, a windowsill, or a deck railing. Its back rail can rest on the windowsill or railing, or it can lean against the wall of the building. A couple of screws through the back rail will secure it in place. The box with legs has a wide slot across the front and ends, and also in its bottom—it's designed to be filled with sphagnum moss, for plants that like to poke through. If you intend to use soil instead of sphagnum, make one of the bottom boards an inch wider than specified, and make the top and bottom front and ends out of the same 2½-inch wood.

Window boxes generally should be painted, both for longevity and for unobtrusiveness. This means you don't have to worry about nailheads and screw holes, because you can fill them with putty before you paint.

BUILDING THE SMALL WINDOW BOX

1 **Saw the wood.** Cut the sides and bottom pieces to the dimensions given in the cutting list. Don't cut the trim and spacers until you've nailed the box together. Then saw those pieces to fit.

2 **Make the box sides.** Make two identical assemblies that are L-shaped in cross section by gluing and nailing the box sides to the bottom boards. Stand the bottom board on edge on the

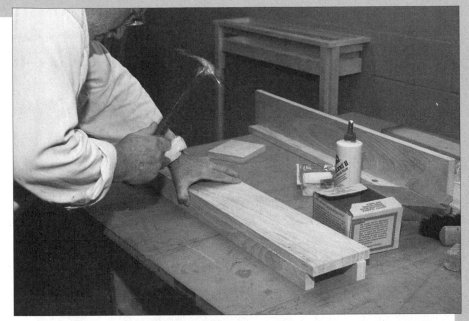

Make the box sides. Glue and nail each side piece to a bottom piece. Nail through the side into the edge of the bottom.

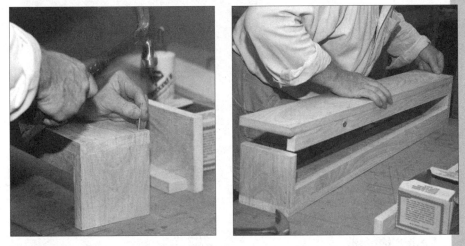

Attach the ends. Glue and nail one side-bottom assembly to the box ends. The grain of the end pieces runs in the same direction as in the sides (left). Glue and nail the other side-bottom assembly to the box ends (right).

worktable, roll glue on its edge, and plant the side board on it. Center the side board from end to end. Nail through the side board into the edge of the bottom board with 2-inch siding nails, as shown in the top photo.

3 **Attach the ends.** The grain of the end pieces runs in the same direction as in the side pieces. In effect, the wood grain wraps all around the window box. Begin by nailing one end piece to one of the side-bottom assemblies, as shown in the photo above left. Nail the other end piece to the same side-bottom assembly. Then glue and nail the other side-bottom assembly to the box, as shown in the photo above right. You'll have made a complete trough with a wide slot in the bottom, which will be filled in by the third bottom piece in Step 5.

SMALL WINDOW BOX

Glue and nail a bottom piece to each box side, then nail the sides and bottom to the ends. Attach the top plate and trim the box. Screw the spacers to the third bottom board and drop it in place.

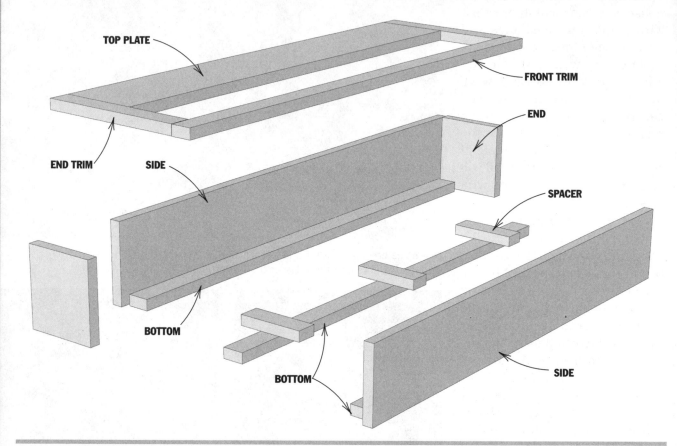

TOP PLATE

FRONT TRIM

END

END TRIM

SIDE

SPACER

BOTTOM

BOTTOM

SIDE

YOUR INVESTMENT

<u>Time:</u> One evening per window box
<u>Money:</u> Small window box, $10; Window box with legs, $12

SHOPPING LIST

SMALL WINDOW BOX
16 feet 1×2 pine
12 feet 1×6 pine
2-inch galvanized siding nails
2½-inch galvanized siding nails

WINDOW BOX WITH LEGS
24 feet 1×2 pine
16 feet 1×3 pine
4 feet 1×6 pine
#6 × 1¼-inch galvanized screws
#6 × 2-inch galvanized screws
2-inch galvanized siding nails
Two-part wood putty

PROJECT SPECS

The small window box is 38 inches wide, 6½ inches front to back, and 6 inches deep.
The window box with legs is 40 inches wide, 9 inches front to back, and 6½ inches deep.

CUTTING LIST

PART	QTY.	DIMENSIONS	NOTES
SMALL WINDOW BOX			
Side	2	¾ × 5½ × 36	1×6
Bottom	3	¾ × 1½ × 34½	1×2
End	2	¾ × 5½ × 5	1×6
Top plate	1	¾ × 5½ × 34½	1×6
Top trim	1	¾ × 1½ × 37½	1×2
End trim	2	¾ × 1½ × 12	1×2; cut to fit
Spacer	3	¾ × 1½ × 4¾	1×2; cut to fit
WINDOW BOX WITH LEGS			
Leg	4	¾ × 1½ × 42	1×2; cut to fit
Ledger	4	¾ × 1½ × 4	1×2
Back plate	1	¾ × 5½ × 36	1×6
Back rail	1	¾ × 2½ × 37	1×3; trim to ft
Lower end	2	¾ × 2½ × 7	1×3
Lower front	1	¾ × 2½ × 36	1×3
Upper end	2	¾ × 1½ × 7	1×2
Upper front	1	¾ × 1½ × 36	1×2
Bottom	2	¾ × 2½ × 36	1×3
Front trim	1	¾ × 1½ × 40	1×2; trim to fit
End trim	2	¾ × 1½ × 9	1×2; trim to fit

Attach the top plate and trim the box. Glue and nail the front trim to the front edge of the window box, and the top plate to its back edge of the box. The offsets accommodate the end trim (above). Mark the end trim to length, and saw it (top right). Stand the window box on end so you can nail through the width of the end trim into the top plate (right).

4 Attach the top plate and trim the box. The top plate connects the window box to your deck railing. It's glued and nailed to one side of the box, which therefore becomes the back. Center the top plate from end to end, and make it flush with the inside of the window box, as shown in the top left photo.

The front trim piece runs along the front edge of the box. It extends beyond the box ends far enough to cover the end trim, as you can see in the top left photo. Glue and nail the front trim to the window box. Then cut the end trim to length, and glue and nail it in place as well. Stand the assembled box up on end to nail through the width of the end trim into the end of the top plate, as shown in the top right photo. Use 2½-inch siding nails.

5 Fit the third bottom piece. Excess water drains out through the bottom of the box. The box

Fit the third bottom piece. Glue and screw the spacers to the third bottom piece. Center them from side to side. Drop the bottom piece into the box. Its loose fit allows excess water to drain.

ends are wide enough so the third bottom piece is a loose fit in its slot. Trim it ½ inch short so there's drainage at the ends as well. Next, trim the three spacers so their length is an easy fit across the width of the box. Glue and screw the spacers to the bottom piece, as shown in the lower left photo. The spacing isn't critical, but the spacers do

need to be centered from side to side. Now you can drop the bottom piece into the box.

6 Finish and mount the box. The box sides are very plain. You can decorate them to match the walls of your house, with siding, clapboard or shakes. Window boxes last longer if they're painted or stained.

BUILDING THE WINDOW BOX WITH LEGS

1 **Cut all the wood.** The length of the legs depends on the height of your window. Measure from the ground up to where you want to see the top edge of the box, and subtract $\frac{3}{4}$ inch. The remainder of the pieces come from the cutting list.

2 **Assemble the legs.** Each of the two leg assemblies consists of two legs connected by two ledgers. The ledgers fit $5\frac{1}{2}$ inches from either end of the legs. Glue and screw the ledgers onto one of the legs, using $1\frac{1}{4}$-inch screws, as shown in the photo below. Then glue and screw the second leg to the

Assemble the legs. Glue and screw the ledgers $5\frac{1}{2}$ inches from the ends of the leg (above). Use a square to align the ends of the legs, then glue and screw the second leg piece to the ledgers (below).

WINDOW BOX WITH LEGS

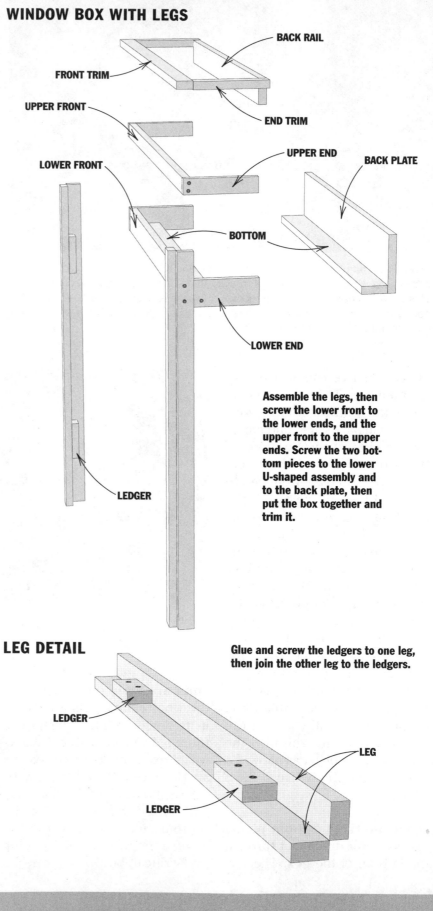

BACK RAIL

FRONT TRIM

END TRIM

UPPER FRONT

UPPER END

BACK PLATE

LOWER FRONT

BOTTOM

LOWER END

LEDGER

Assemble the legs, then screw the lower front to the lower ends, and the upper front to the upper ends. Screw the two bottom pieces to the lower U-shaped assembly and to the back plate, then put the box together and trim it.

LEG DETAIL

Glue and screw the ledgers to one leg, then join the other leg to the ledgers.

LEDGER

LEG

LEDGER

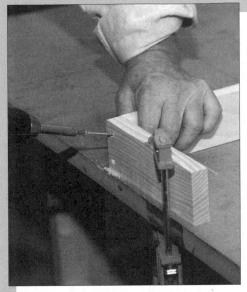

Make the U shapes. Clamp the lower end piece to the worktable and bring the lower front up it. Drill and screw through the end piece and into the end grain of the front piece.

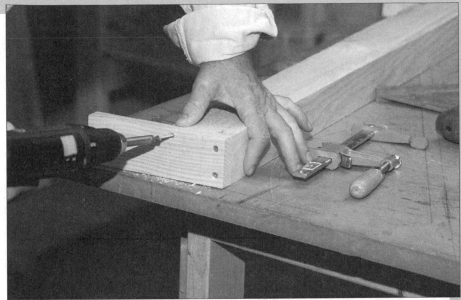

Attach the bottom. Screw one of the bottom pieces to the lower U-shaped assembly (above). Screw the other bottom piece to the back plate (below left).

ledgers, but not to the first leg. Assemble the other two legs and ledgers in exactly the same way. Since the box is going to be painted, don't worry about concealing any screw holes. You'll fill them in Step 9 below.

3 Make the U shapes. The box itself consists of a back plate and two U-shaped assemblies, the upper and lower fronts and their ends. Because this window box has an open slot in the front for the plants to poke through, each U-shape is made with different widths of wood. If you didn't want the opening, you could make them both the same. Begin by clamping the lower end piece to the worktable, as shown in the top left photo, and bring the lower front piece up to it. Drill two clearance holes and screw through the lower end piece into the end grain of the front piece, using the 2-inch screws. Attach the second lower end piece to the other end of the lower front piece in the same

Join the box. Connect the free ends of the lower U-shaped assembly to the back plate and box bottom. There will be a drainage gap about an inch wide between the two bottom pieces.

way. Then make the second U-shape, using the two upper ends and the upper front.

4 Attach the bottom. There are two bottom pieces. Screw one of them to the lower U-shape, and the other to the back plate, as shown in the top right and bottom left photos. Use 2-inch screws. In the next step, you'll bring both of these subassem-

blies together and the window box will appear.

5 Join the box. Now you can plug the lower U-shaped assembly onto the back plate of the window box. Screw through the lower end pieces into the back plate, and also into the box bottom. There will be a drainage slot about an inch wide between the two bottom pieces.

Attach the legs. Fit the ledger against the bottom of the box, and screw the legs in place.

Attach the upper U-shape. Screw the upper U-shaped assembly to the back plate.

Trim the box. Cut and fit the trim pieces, and nail them in place.

Prepare the box for paint. Use a pocket knife or putty knife to butter the screw holes with two-part wood filler. When it sets, sand it smooth.

6 Attach the upper U-shape. Complete the box by screwing the upper U-shape to the back plate. It fits flush with the top of the back plate, creating the wide slot in the front and ends of the box. Drive two of the 2-inch screws through the upper box ends, into the end grain of the back plate. The front of the upper U-shape will be supported by the legs in the next step.

7 Attach the legs. The window box rests on the ledgers inside the legs. When you put it in place, you'll see where to screw through the legs into the box itself, as shown in the top right photo. Be sure to put a couple of screws into the upper U-shape, as well as into the lower one.

8 Trim the box. The trim consists of a front piece, two side pieces, and the back rail. Cut the front trim piece to the outside width of the box and legs and nail it in place with 2-inch siding nails. Cut the two end trim pieces so they butt up to the front trim and cover the top edge of the box plus the thickness of the back rail, as shown in the lower left photo. Nail them in place. Finally, cut the back rail to fit between the end trim pieces and nail it too.

9 Prepare the box for paint. Since the window box will live outdoors, you can't fill the screw holes with spackle or some other indoor compound. You have to use a durable two-part wood filler, which is very similar to auto-body plastic. Mix the filler in small batches. It sets up quickly, and hot weather accelerates it. Putty the holes with a knife, as shown in the bottom right photo. When the putty sets, sand it flush with the wood, and sand all the sharp corners off at the same time. Now the box is ready to paint and fill with plants.

WINDOW SHELF

This handy folder creates a pass-through when you need it

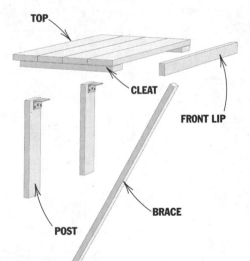

WINDOW SHELF

Connect the four-board top with the cleats, then screw the hinges to the posts and to the top. Screw the posts onto the outside wall of the house.

YOUR INVESTMENT

Time: One evening
Money: $12

SHOPPING LIST

16 feet 1×4 pine
6 feet 1×2 pine
#6 × 1¼-inch galvanized screws
#8 × 2½ inch galvanized screws
Pair 1 × 2½-inch galvanized fixed-pin utility hinges

PROJECT SPECS

The window shelf is 30 inches long and 14 inches deep, and any height you like.

TOP

CLEAT

FRONT LIP

BRACE

POST

CUTTING LIST

PART	QTY.	DIMENSIONS	NOTES
Top	4	¾ × 3½ × 30	1×4
Front lip	1	¾ × 1½ × 30	1×2
Cleat	2	¾ × 3½ × 13	1×4
Post	2	¾ × 3½ × 13	1×4
Brace	1	¾ × 1½ × 36	1×2

Well, the kitchen is inside the house and the barbecue is outside, and you need one hand for the screen door, plus two hands for a tray full of dishes and drinks, and it's no wonder nobody wants to eat on the deck. It's too much hassle.

The window shelf converts the kitchen window into a pass-through. You can have the shelf up on the wall in a couple of hours.

BUILDING THE SHELF

1 **Cut the wood.** The wood is all standard 1×4 and 1×2 lumber. Trim the brace after you've mounted the shelf on the wall.

2 **Make the front lip.** Roll glue on the edge of one top board and screw the front lip to it.

3 **Complete the top.** Glue and screw the two cleats to the 1×4s of the shelf top, leaving small spaces between the boards.

4 **Hinge the top.** Screw a hinge to each of the two posts. Screw the other leaf of each hinge to the underside of the shelf.

5 **Mount the shelf.** For clearance, clamp the shelf underneath the windowsill with the brace sandwiched in between. Screw the cleats to the wall.

6 **Trim the brace.** The brace lodges between the shelf's front lip and the corner of the wall and deck. Hold the shelf up level so you can mark and saw its length. When you fold the shelf, stow the brace in the clearance under the windowsill.

OPEN SHED

This versatile house organizes the clutter on your deck

Out on our deck there was a little stack of split logs for the fireplace, and a sodden sack of barbecue coals. The barbecue itself not only got a bellyful of rain water, it also collected stray spatulas and tongs. It all added up to an annoying quantity of clutter. Not only that, the fire-

wood, the coals, and the barbecue tools would all be better off if they could be stored out of the weather.

The little shed solved these common household problems. It is a useful and versatile structure you can park on your deck or against the side of the house

or garage. The version shown has two compartments, a wide one with a floor, for firewood or folding lawn furniture, and a narrow one with no floor, for the barbecue. One of the compartments must have a front rail and a floor for structural reasons, but it doesn't matter which one,

FRAME DETAIL

This cross-section of the structural frame shows how the center frame differs from the two end frames. The doubled front uprights brace the eave and dress up the construction.

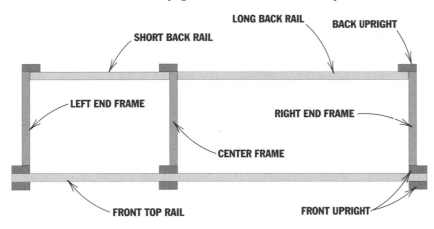

LONG BACK RAIL — BACK UPRIGHT — SHORT BACK RAIL — LEFT END FRAME — RIGHT END FRAME — CENTER FRAME — FRONT TOP RAIL — FRONT UPRIGHT

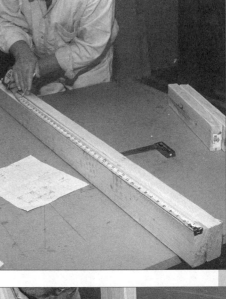

Lay out the frames. Measure 10 inches and 42 inches up from the bottom of the front and back uprights to locate the top edges of the cross rails (top). Square the measurements across the edges of the wood. Then stand each cross rail in position on the uprights and draw around it (above).

so you can tailor your shed to the clutter you want to accommodate.

The little shed is almost 7 feet wide, 5 feet high at the ridge, and 32 inches deep. It is made out of standard 2×4 and 1×2 lumber, with two sheets of T1-11 siding for the roof and back. The narrow compartment fits a standard kettle-style grill, while the wide one matches the width of a sheet of T1-11 siding. We made the bottom shelf and the end panels out of solid lumber because we had some knotty planks and short ends to use up. If you make these parts out of T1-11, you'll need to buy a third sheet. Screws and glue join the structure together—screws generally have more holding power than nails.

Even though the shed has a pitched roof and an eave, everything except the four barge boards is a square piece of wood, without angles to saw. And although you could complete the shed in the workshop, it's heavy to move and it probably won't fit through the doorway, so it's better to build it in the garage or outdoors.

BUILDING THE SHED

1 Saw the uprights and rails. The structure of the firewood shed consists of three rectangular frames, made from standard 2×4s. Note that there are two sets of three front uprights. One set of three makes the frames in the next step. Reserve the other set for completing the front of the shed, in Step 15. You can get one 60-inch front upright and two 18-inch cross rails out of one 8-foot stud. Saw the front and back rails now too.

2 Lay out the frames. Each of the three frames consists of a front and back upright and two cross rails. The two end frames are the same, except for their handedness: In cross-section, they're Z-shaped, one right-handed and the other left-handed. The center frame is different: In the cross-sectional view, it's U-shaped. You can see these differences on the drawing above, but the only way to get it right is to work carefully. Make each joint with three 3-inch screws and no glue, so you can always disassemble a frame if

you get it together the wrong way around. Start by laying out the top edges of the cross rails on all six uprights, by squaring lines 10 inches and 42 inches up from the floor. Working one frame at a time, balance the parts the way you want them to go together, and draw a line around the ends of the cross rails on the inside faces of the uprights, as shown in the photos above.

OPEN SHED

Build the shed's 2×4 framework, then erect the rafters and ridge. The frame is glued and screwed together. The siding and roof are nailed to the frame.

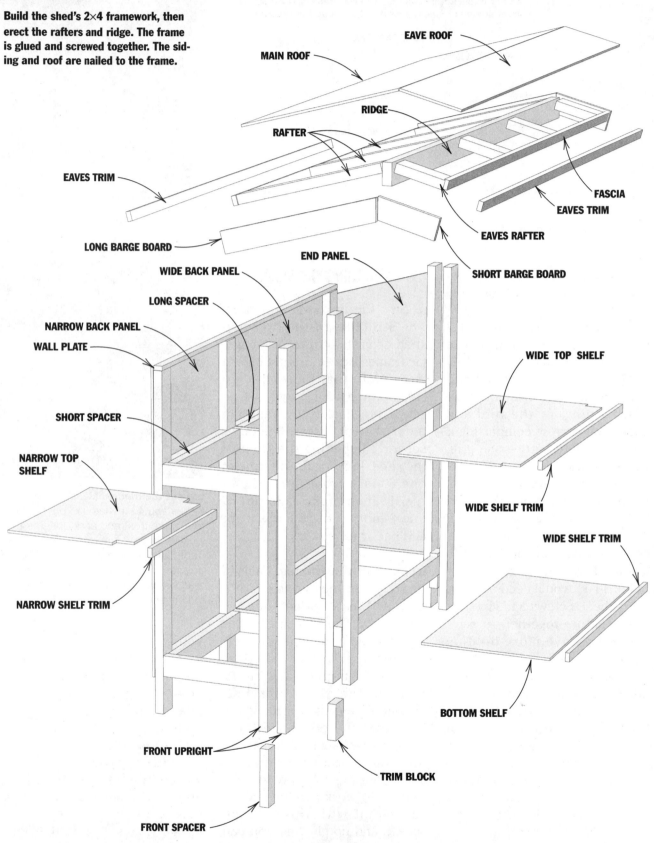

MAIN ROOF

EAVE ROOF

RIDGE

RAFTER

EAVES TRIM

FASCIA

EAVES TRIM

EAVES RAFTER

LONG BARGE BOARD

END PANEL

SHORT BARGE BOARD

WIDE BACK PANEL

LONG SPACER

NARROW BACK PANEL

WALL PLATE

WIDE TOP SHELF

SHORT SPACER

NARROW TOP SHELF

WIDE SHELF TRIM

WIDE SHELF TRIM

NARROW SHELF TRIM

BOTTOM SHELF

FRONT UPRIGHT

TRIM BLOCK

FRONT SPACER

FRAME DETAIL

To construct the shed frame, make the two end frames and the center frame, then connect them with the front and back rails. The cross-sectional view on page 81 shows how the end frames and center frame differ from one another.

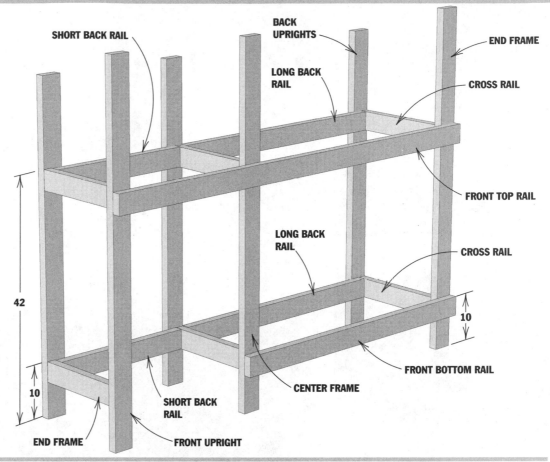

SHORT BACK RAIL

BACK UPRIGHTS

END FRAME

LONG BACK RAIL

CROSS RAIL

FRONT TOP RAIL

LONG BACK RAIL

CROSS RAIL

FRONT BOTTOM RAIL

CENTER FRAME

SHORT BACK RAIL

END FRAME

FRONT UPRIGHT

42

10

10

YOUR INVESTMENT

<u>Time:</u> A long weekend
<u>Money:</u> $100

SHOPPING LIST

14 2×4 studs
66 feet 1×2 pine
8 feet 1×4 pine
3 sheets T1-11 plywood
#8 × 3-inch galvanized screws
#6 × 2½-inch galvanized screws
#6 × 2-inch galvanized screws
2-inch galvanized siding nails
2-inch galvanized spiral nails
2½-inch galvanized spiral nails
1½-inch galvanized roofing nails

PROJECT SPECS

The open shed is 80 inches wide, 62 inches high at the ridge, and 32 inches from front to back.

CUTTING LIST

PART	QTY.	DIMENSIONS	NOTES
Front upright	6	$1\frac{1}{2} \times 3\frac{1}{2} \times 60$	2×4
Back upright	3	$1\frac{1}{2} \times 3\frac{1}{2} \times 54$	2×4
Cross rail	6	$1\frac{1}{2} \times 3\frac{1}{2} \times 18$	2×4
Front top rail	1	$1\frac{1}{2} \times 3\frac{1}{2} \times 80$	2×4
Front bottom rail	1	$1\frac{1}{2} \times 3\frac{1}{2} \times 51\frac{1}{4}$	2×4
Short back rail	2	$1\frac{1}{2} \times 3\frac{1}{2} \times 26\frac{3}{4}$	2×4
Long back rail	2	$1\frac{1}{2} \times 3\frac{1}{2} \times 44\frac{3}{4}$	2×4
Wall plate	1	$\frac{3}{4} \times 1\frac{1}{2} \times 76$	1×2
Wide back panel	1	$\frac{3}{8} \times 48 \times 48$	T1-11 siding
Narrow back panel	1	$\frac{3}{8} \times 28 \times 48$	T1-11 siding
Short spacer	2	$\frac{3}{4} \times 1\frac{1}{2} \times 22\frac{3}{4}$	1×2
Long spacer	2	$\frac{3}{4} \times 1\frac{1}{2} \times 42\frac{3}{4}$	1×2
Front spacer	1	$1\frac{1}{2} \times 2\frac{1}{2} \times 10$	Cut from 2×4
Rafter	4	$1\frac{1}{2} \times 3\frac{1}{2} \times 24$	2×4
Ridge	1	$1\frac{1}{2} \times 3\frac{1}{2} \times 80$	2×4
Eave rafter	4	$1\frac{1}{2} \times 3\frac{1}{2} \times 7\frac{7}{8}$	2×4
Front and back fascia	2	$\frac{3}{4} \times 1\frac{1}{2} \times 80$	1×2
Long barge board	2	$\frac{3}{4} \times 3\frac{1}{2} \times 26$	1×4
Short barge board	2	$\frac{3}{4} \times 3\frac{1}{2} \times 10$	1×4
Main Roof	1	$\frac{3}{8} \times 26 \times 80$	T1-11 pieced together
Eave roof	1	$\frac{3}{8} \times 10 \times 80$	T1-11 pieced together
Wide top shelf	1	$\frac{3}{8} \times 47 \times 20\frac{7}{8}$	T1-11 siding
Narrow top shelf	1	$\frac{3}{8} \times 29 \times 20\frac{7}{8}$	T1-11 siding
Wide shelf trim	2	$\frac{3}{4} \times 1\frac{1}{2} \times 46$	1×2; Trim to fit
Narrow shelf trim	1	$\frac{3}{4} \times 1\frac{1}{2} \times 26$	1×2; Trim to fit
Eaves trim	2	$\frac{3}{4} \times 1\frac{1}{2} \times 82$	1×2; Trim to fit
Trim block	2	$1\frac{1}{2} \times 3\frac{1}{2} \times 6\frac{1}{2}$	2×4
End panel	2	$\frac{3}{8} \times 20 \times 54$	T1-11 or scrap lumber
Center divider	1	$\frac{3}{8} \times 16\frac{1}{2} \times 36$	T1-11 or scrap lumber
Bottom shelf	1	$\frac{3}{8} \times 22\frac{1}{2} \times 44\frac{3}{4}$	T1-11 or scrap lumber

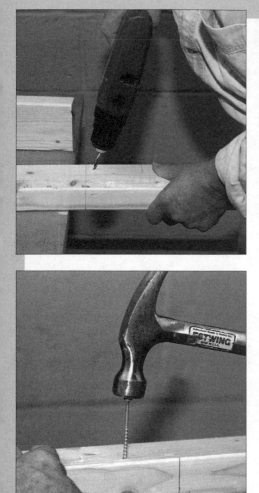

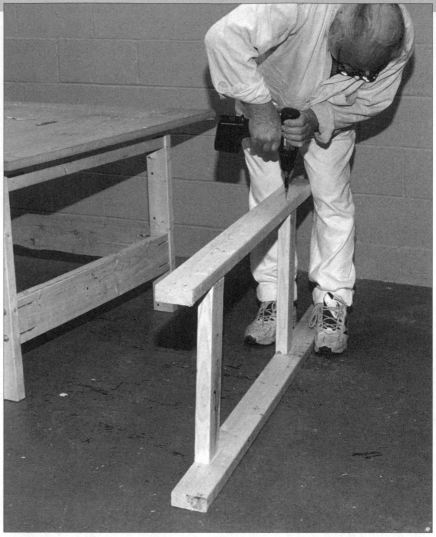

Join the frames. Drill clearance holes through the uprights, inside the layout lines. Angle the two end holes to increase the strength of the joint (top left). Hold the parts in position and tap the center screw to start it. It will slip through the clearance hole and bite into the end of the rail (left). Brace the parts with your knees while you drive the screws. Note the Z-shaped profile of this end-frame (above).

3 Join the frames. The 3-inch screws bite nicely into the end grain of the cross rails, but to make a really strong joint, you have to drill clearance holes through the uprights. A clearance hole should be just a hair smaller than the outside diameter of the threads: For #8 screws, drill $\frac{3}{16}$-inch holes. Use three screws per joint. Drill the center hole straight, but angle the other two holes, as shown in the top photo, so the screws don't go in parallel to one another. To make each joint, hold the parts in position, and tap the center screw into the wood with the hammer. This locates it while you screw it in.

Check to make sure the cross rail is square and straight, and adjust it if it is not, then drive the other two screws.

4 Join the bottom front rail. The bottom front rail establishes the width of the wide compartment. Stand the center frame and the end frame up on edge, with their back uprights flat on the worktable or the shop floor. Spread glue on the face of the front uprights, where

the rail will fit. Clamp the rail in place and drive one screw through each end. These screws will hold the parts in position while you use a framing square to make the rail square to the upright, as shown at the top of the next page. Then measure the distance between the uprights, at both the bottom and the top. Adjust the parts until these distances are equal. Drill clearance holes and drive three more screws into each joint.

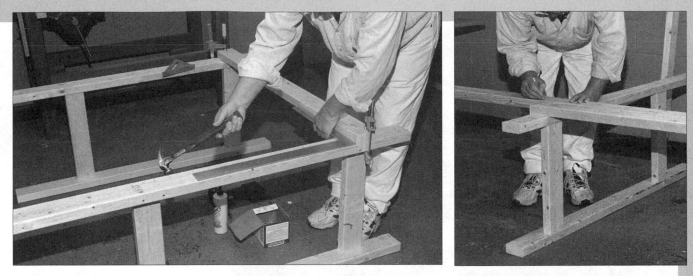

Join the bottom front rail. Glue and clamp the bottom front rail across the center frame and end frame. Drive one screw in each joint to hold it while you check the construction with a framing square, and tap it into place with the hammer. Then drive three more screws in each joint.

5 Join the top front rail. The top front rail will tie all three frames together. Hold it up to the bottom front rail and make a layout line to position the center frame. Glue and screw the rail to the front uprights of the center frame and the one end frame, the same way you attached the bottom front rail.

Join the top front rail. To locate the center frame, transfer the length of the bottom front rail to the top front rail (top right). Glue and screw the bottom front rail across the center and end frames (above).

6 Connect the other end frame. The other end frame connects to the free end of the top front rail. To position the frame, stand it in place, and drop the two short back rails into place on the back uprights. Push the assembly together, using the loose short back rails as a gauge. Then glue and screw the end frame to the top front rail, as shown at bottom right. Stand the construction upright and you'll begin to see the shed.

7 Join the short back rails. The short and long back rails

Connect the other end frame. Glue, clamp and screw the other end frame to the free end of the top front rail. Use the short back rails, visible by the craftsman's sneakers, to gauge the width of the assembly.

Add the long back rails. To join the long back rail to the center frame, drive the screws on an angle through the cross rail (above and below).

Join the short back rails. Glue and clamp the short back rails between the back uprights and screw it to the cross rails. Then remove the clamps and screw it to the back uprights as well.

span the distance between the frames and complete the wall structure of the shed. Start by clamping the short back rails to the back uprights, in line with the cross rails in the end frames. Once you see where each back rail goes, unclamp it so you can

spread some glue in there, and clamp it up again. Then drill clearance holes through the cross rails for three screws into each end of the short back rails. The clearance holes allow the screws to pull the pieces tightly together. Now remove the

clamps and drive three more screws through the back rails and into the back uprights.

8 Add the long back rails. Spread glue and clamp one end of each long back rail to the back upright at the end of the frame. Screw through the cross rail into the end of the long back rail, and also screw through the face of the long back rail into the back upright. At the center frame, the end of the long back rail lines up with the short back rail, so you can't screw straight into it. You have to drive the screws on a diagonal, toenail fashion, as shown in the photos above.

Make the center divider. Saw the center divider to size and nail it to the center cross rails while the access is easy.

9 Make the center divider. The center divider keeps the firewood from banging into the barbecue. It can be made out of plywood or T1-11 siding, but it's also a fine place for using up knotty and twisted wood, as you can see in the photo above. The available opening is 16½ inches wide and the boards or plywood should be 36 inches long. Use 2-inch spiral nails to attach them to the cross rails, from inside the narrow compartment.

10 Make the back. The back of the wide compartment is a 48-inch square of T1-11 plywood siding. The T1-11 siding is awkward to handle and saw in full 4×8 sheets, but you can do it with a portable circular saw, handsaw or jigsaw, as shown in the photo at right. In order to anchor the T1-11, nail the wall plate across the top of the back uprights, using 2½-inch spiral

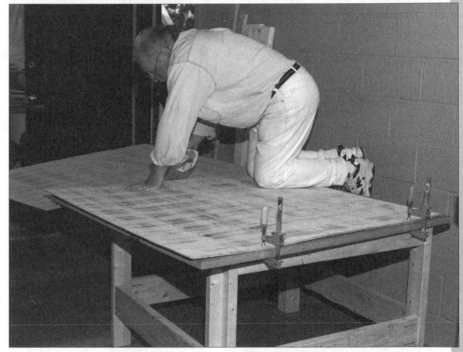

Make the back. Nail the wall plate across the tops of the back uprights (top). T1-11 siding is awkward to handle, but if you clamp it to the worktable, you can saw it with a handsaw, jigsaw, or portable circular saw (above). Nail the panels of siding to the back of the shed frame (right).

nails. Then nail the T1-11 to the back uprights, using 1½-inch roofing nails spaced 6 inches to 9 inches apart. These nails have a large head, so the thin plywood sheet isn't likely to pull off them. Finally, nail the siding to the edge of the wall plate.

11 Insert the spacers. The back of the shed is anchored to the uprights and wall plate, but the panels still are not adequately supported. They need to be nailed to something along their bottom edges as well as in the middle. The long and short spacers, which fit between the

back rails and the siding, do this job. Insert each spacer so its top surface is flush with the top surface of the rail, and screw through the rail to hold it in place, as shown in the photo below left. Then nail through the back panels into the spacers.

12 Make the top shelves. Saw the top shelves from the T1-11 offcuts. They're straight along the back, but the front edges have to be notched to fit around

the front uprights. Saw the pieces of siding to length and width to match the inside of your shed. To lay out the notch, set the shelf in place against the back uprights and mark where it rests on the front uprights, as shown below. The other notch dimension is the distance between uprights, which you measure. Saw the notches with a handsaw, drop the shelves in place, and nail them to the rails with the 1½-inch roofing nails.

Insert the spacers. Fit the long and short spacers between the back rails and the siding, and screw them to the back rails. Then nail the siding to the spacers.

Make the top shelves. Set the top shelves in place against the back uprights, in order to lay out notches for the front uprights (right). Saw the notches (above).

13 Raise the rafters. Unlike conventional construction, the rafters lie flat on their faces, instead of standing up on edge. This makes it possible to continue to screw the shed together. The rafter span, from front upright to wall plate, is so short that resistance to bending is not an issue. Three of the rafters line up with the front uprights. The fourth rafter, which goes in after the ridge in the next step, breaks up the wide roof span. Set the rafters in position. Use the speed-square to align their bottom front corners with the faces of the front uprights, as shown in the photo below. Drill clearance holes and screw down through the rafters into the ends of the front uprights. Then drill and screw through the low end of each rafter into the wall plate and back uprights. Use the 3-inch galvanized screws.

14 Make the ridge. The ridge is a 2×4 which, like the top front rail, spans the full width of the structure. Clamp it roughly in position, then use a square to line it up with the top of the rafters, as shown in the bottom left photo. Screw it to the front uprights as well as to the rafters. Now fit the fourth rafter into the middle of the wide compartment. Screw it to the ridge and to the wall plate, as shown at bottom right.

Raise the rafters. Align the ends of the rafters with the face of the front uprights (left). Screw the rafters to the front uprights and also to the wall plate and back uprights (above).

Make the ridge. Clamp the ridge in position, then align its top corner with the top of the rafters. Screw the ridge to the front uprights and to the rafters (above). With the ridge in place, screw the last rafter across the compartment (right).

Double the front uprights. Screw the second set of front uprights to the ridge and front rails. Insert the front spacer in the gap between the two front uprights at the left of the photo.

Fit the back fascia. Align the back fascia with the top of the rafters and screw it to their ends.

Make the barge boards. Clamp the long barge board to the outside rafter, with its top corner aligned on a vertical centerline drawn on the end of the ridge. Transfer the centerline to the bottom edge of the long barge board (left). Draw a line from the top corner to the transferred mark. This is the angle at which to saw all four barge boards (right).

15 **Double the front uprights.** The second set of three front uprights goes onto the structure now. These pieces help the look of the construction, and also support the eave. Screw them to the ridge and to the front rails, with one 3-inch screw in each intersection. Since the front bottom rail doesn't continue across the narrow compartment, you can't attach the upright there, until you make the front spacer and fit it between the two front uprights.

16 **Fit the back fascia.** The back fascia creates a nailing surface for the edge of the roof, and also tidies the construction. Attach it to the ends of the rafters with a single 2½-inch screw into each rafter.

17 **Make the barge boards.** The barge boards define the end of the roof and conceal the edge of the roofing. The long barge boards also position the short barge boards, and therefore the eave. The wood has to be cut at an angle, which you find by direct layout, not by measuring. Start by drawing a vertical centerline on the end of the ridge. Saw the two long barge boards to the square dimension given in the cutting list. Line the first one up with the rafter, its top corner on the ridge centerline. Mark it and saw it so the cut end falls on the centerline, as shown in the photo at left. Trace this angle from the first long barge board onto the second one and also onto the two short ones, so you can saw them all.

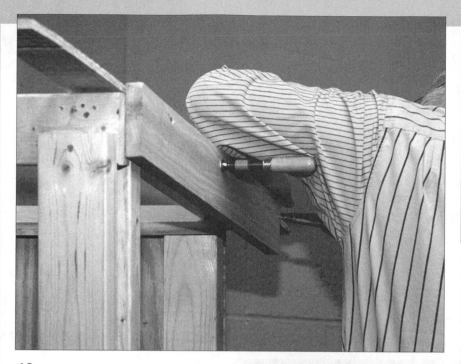

Attach the barge boards. Position the long barge board so it overlaps the edge of a scrap of T1-11 siding. Screw it to the rafter (left). Butt the short barge board up to the long one, and screw it to the front upright and ridge (above).

18 **Attach the barge boards.** The long barge boards will cover the edges of the plywood roof at both ends of the shed. Use a scrap of the T1-11 as a gauge to position the barge boards, as shown above. Screw the long barge boards to the sides of the rafters. The short barge boards butt up to the long ones, as shown in the photo at top right. The points of the angled cuts should meet. Screw the short barge boards to the ridge and front uprights.

19 **Make the eave rafters.** The four eave rafters support the eave at the front of the shed. The end ones are screwed to the short barge boards and also to the ridge. The center ones don't go in until the next step. Use the scrap of T1-11 siding to position the eave rafters against the ridge and short barge boards, as shown at right. Drill clearance holes and screw through the barge boards into the rafters, then through the ridge into the rafters, then through the rafters into the front uprights.

Make the eave rafters. Clamp the outside eave rafter to the barge board, but set it down by the thickness of the T1-11 scrap. Screw the eave rafter to the barge board, and also to the ridge and front upright.

Fit the front fascia. Screw the front fascia to the ends of the outside eave rafters (above). Fit the remaining two eave rafters between the front fascia and the ridge, and screw them in place (right).

Roof the shed. Nail the T1-11 siding onto the rafters, ridge and fascia (above). Shove a 2x6 prop under the center of the eave to support it while you nail the siding to it (right).

20 Fit the front fascia. Like the back fascia, the front fascia creates a nailing surface for the edge of the roof. It also supports the remaining two eave rafters. Screw the front fascia to the ends of the outside eave rafters. As insurance, you can also drive a screw through the barge board into the end of the fascia. Then fit the last two eave rafters between the ridge and the fascia, and screw them in place.

21 Roof the shed. The roof is made of ⅜-inch T1-11 siding, same as the shed's back and top shelf. You have to piece it together from whatever siding you have. Since the 10-inch front eave is more likely to be visible than the back roof, start roofing at the front. And since the center of the eave is not directly supported, saw a 2×4 or 2×6

prop, as shown in the photo at left, to resist the stress of nailing. Make the prop a fat ⅛ inch longer than the distance from the fascia to the ground. Fit the roofing tight to the barge boards and flush with the front face of the fascia. Nail into the ridge, rafters and fascia, with the 1¼-inch roofing nails. Space them a hand-span apart. Roof the main part of the shed in the same way. Get the best fit you can at the ridge, but don't worry about it—the ridge cap will cover any gaps.

22 Cap the ridge. You could make your own ridge cap from two lengths of 1×2, but that would require sawing a long bevel on one edge. Your alternative is to buy a standard aluminum ridge cap from the home center. Either way, nail it over the gap in your roofing, using the 2-inch siding nails.

23 Trim the top shelves and eave. Strips of 1×2 trim not only cover the visible edges of the T1-11 siding, they also create an interesting pattern of shadows. The dimensions in the cutting list are about an inch longer than you need, so you can mark and saw each strip of trim to a neat fit. Attach the eave trim with 2-inch siding nails, but use 2-inch spiral nails for the shelf trim.

24 **Make the bottom shelf.** The bottom shelf can be made of T1-11 siding, but if you have short ends of wood around, it's a good way to use them up, as shown in the photo at right. Fit the boards loosely together and attach them to the front and back rails with the siding nails.

25 **Panel the ends.** If you are using lumber for the ends, you'll be able to tuck square boards up behind the barge boards. If you are using T1-11 siding, you'll have to lay out and cut an angle to match the slope of the roof. Nail the end panels to the uprights and cross rails, using the 2-inch siding nails.

26 **Fit the trim blocks.** The two trim blocks help support the bottom front rail, and they complete the trim on the front of the shed. Tap them into position so a half-inch of each block projects beyond the front uprights, and drive two screws into each of them.

27 **Finish the shed.** The shed will stand out, unless you finish it with paint or stain to match your house. However, if you never do get around to applying a finish, the siding and the wood eventually will weather to a uniform silver-gray, though they may appear blotchy for the first couple of years.

Trim the top shelves and eaves. Nail the eaves trim over the edges of the T1-11 roofing (left). Trim the top shelves (above).

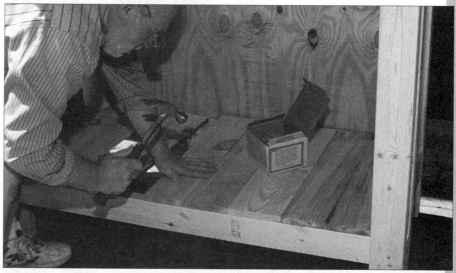

Make the bottom shelf. You can use a piece of siding, or short ends of wood to make the bottom shelf. Nail the shelving to the bottom rails.

Panel the ends. Make the shed ends out of solid lumber or else of T1-11 siding, whichever you prefer.

Fit the trim blocks. The trim blocks fit between the front uprights, beneath the bottom front rail.

LAWN PROJECTS

The lawn is play space, where adults entertain and children romp. It's multipurpose space, but in a way it is also temporary: today's lawn party becomes tomorrow's badminton court, and the site of Sunday's picnic. We move the furnishings around the lawn, as the family moves from one activity to the next.

Lawn projects must be built to withstand the weather, but they generally don't have to harmonize with the trim on the house. The lawn is free space that you can make over to suit what you like for today and whatever you might need for tomorrow.

SKIRT BENCH

Simple bench has strong visual lines

Here is a robust bench you can use for garden seating or for an outdoor coffee table. It's made out of 2×4 and 1×6 lumber, held together with screws and glue. The long rails, or skirts, support the seat and tie the two ends together, which is how the bench gets its name.

Structurally the skirt bench is very simple and strong. There are no angled cuts or tricky fits. This makes it a good project for beginners, and a quick project for experienced builders. If you are a beginner, this project will show you how to use your measuring tools to align parts

and make them square.

The simplicity of the bench also gives you a chance to experiment with the visual aspects of the design. We made the end slat thicker and longer than the other seat slats, in order to create a harmonious visual termination, a good-looking way of coming to the end of

the seat. This is a common strategy in architecture. If you look at the eaves of houses, or the skirt boards around the perimeter of a deck, you'll see the same thing.

Similarly, the two-piece leg construction has a visual function instead of a structural one. The bench legs would be more than strong enough if they were one piece of 2×4. But the second piece bulks up the legs, making them look strong. How a piece of furniture looks, even subliminally, affects how people feel about it, and whether they feel comfortable enough to risk sitting down. Furniture that looks unstable sends out a warning, regardless of whether or not it actually is stable.

SKIRT BENCH

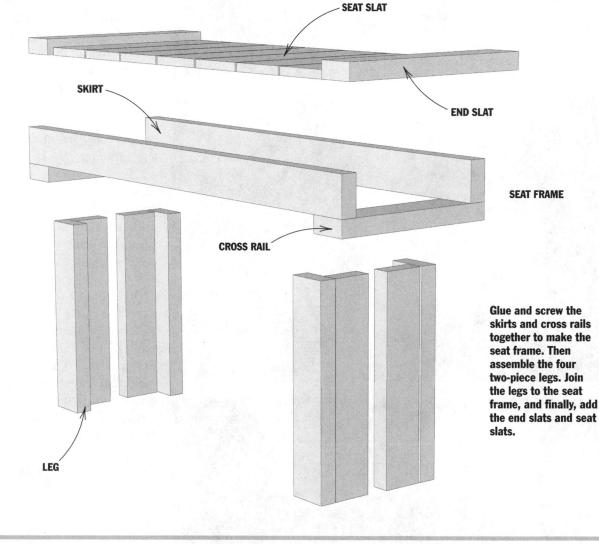

Glue and screw the skirts and cross rails together to make the seat frame. Then assemble the four two-piece legs. Join the legs to the seat frame, and finally, add the end slats and seat slats.

SHOPPING LIST
Four 8-foot 2×4
Two 8-foot 1×6 pine
#8 × 2½-inch galvanized screws
2½-inch siding nails

PROJECT SPECS
The bench is 4 feet long, 19 inches high, and 18 inches deep.

YOUR INVESTMENT
Time: One evening
Money: $18

CUTTING LIST

PART	QTY.	DIMENSIONS	NOTES
Skirt	2	1½ × 3½ × 47	2×4
Cross rail	2	1½ × 3½ × 15	2×4
Leg	8	1½ × 3½ × 18	2×4
End slat	2	1½ × 3½ × 18	2×4
Seat slat	7	¾ × 5½ × 17	1×6

Connect the skirts with the cross rails. Use your speed square to align and true up the joint (above). Spread glue (right), clamp the parts together (below), and drive the screws (bottom).

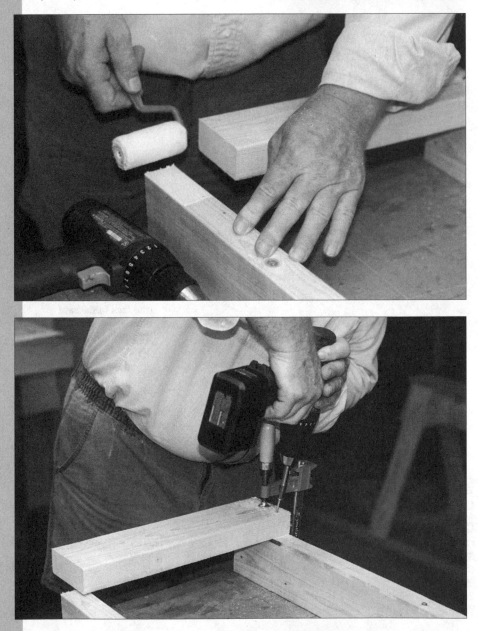

BUILDING THE SKIRT BENCH

1 Cut the wood. It's generally efficient to saw all the wood to finished length at one time, except for any pieces that might have to be trimmed to fit the construction as it goes along. In this project, the only piece to trim is the width of the last seat slat, in Step 7 below. Choose your 2×4s with care—you want the straightest material you can find. Twisted and bowed wood will give you trouble when you assemble the bench. Note that the eight leg pieces and two end slats are all the same length, 18 inches.

2 Connect the skirts with the cross rails. The two cross rails and the two skirts make a rectangular seat frame. Glue and screw the cross rails to the skirts, as shown in the photos at left. Start with one corner. Hold the parts in position, draw a layout line, spread glue on the edge of the rail, and clamp the first corner together. Then drill two clearance holes through the cross rail. Drill the holes on an angle relative to one another; they'll hold better this way. Drive two of the 2½-inch screws through the cross rail and into the skirt. Make the other three corners of the seat frame in the same way.

3 Make the legs. The bench legs are two-piece assemblies, like angle iron. This is an enormously strong and versatile construction. Drill three clearance holes through the face of one of the legs, on a line about ¾ inch from the edge. Roll glue onto the edge of the other leg piece. Align

Make the legs. Drill clearance holes through one of the leg pieces (left). Roll glue on the edge of the other leg piece. Screw the two pieces together (above), making an L-shape like the ones shown in the foreground at left.

and clamp the two pieces together. Make the connection with three of the 2½-inch screws. Join the other three legs in the same way.

4 Join the legs to the seat frame. The legs fit inside the seat frame, with the parts oriented as shown in the drawing on page 97. Join the parts with the seat frame upside-down on the worktable; that is, with the cross rails upward. Join one leg assembly at a time, connecting the narrow face to the skirt before connecting the wide face to the cross rails. All the 2½-inch screws go through from the inside of each leg, into the skirt and cross rail. Set the first leg assembly in position and draw layout lines where the parts intersect. Spread glue within the layout lines, then clamp the leg assembly in place. Use your speed square to make sure the leg is vertical. Drill clearance holes and drive three screws through the leg into the skirt. Then reclamp the leg tight against the cross rail, drill

Join the legs to the seat frame. Use your speed square to get the leg vertical inside the seat frame (above), then clamp it in place. Screw through the leg into the skirt (below). Turn the assembly up on end to screw into the cross rail (right).

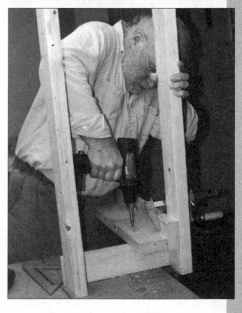

Sand the seat frame and legs. Sand the sharp corners off the wood before you add the bench top, while everything is easy to get at (above). Round-over the bottom edges of the legs, so they don't splinter.

clearance holes and drive two more screws. Join the other three legs in the same way.

5 Sand the seat frame and legs. It's possible to get at everything without the seat slats being in the way, so now's the time to clean up the wood. Use 100-grit sandpaper to sand all the sharp corners off the legs and rails, and sand the visible faces of the wood as well. Sand the seat slats too. Turn the bench upside-down to rout the bottom edges of the legs with a roundover cutter, so they won't splinter when the bench gets dragged across a patio. You'll have to decide whether to round over any other parts of the bench. We decided to retain the crispness of square corners, and quit routing after rounding just the long corners off the end slats.

Attach the end slats. Use your combination square as a gauge to center the end slat on the skirts (above) and to set its end overhang (below left). Then clamp it in place and screw it down (below right).

6 Attach the end slats. The two end slats terminate the bench seat. They are thicker than the seat slats and 1 inch longer, so they overhang each skirt by 1½ inches. They overhang the ends of the skirts by ½ inch. Use a combination square to center each end slat and to gauge its overhang, as shown in the photos at left below. Then drill clearance holes for two screws at either end of each end slat, and fasten them to the skirts with 2½-inch screws.

7 Fit the seat slats. There's no way to guarantee the width of 1× pine boards, unless you saw them to width yourself. Therefore, nail the seat slats to the skirts from both ends of the bench, then fit the center slat or slats into whatever space remains. Use a couple of regular nails as spacers, and attach each slat with two 2½-inch siding nails at each end. When you come to the center slat, you

Fit the seat slats. Nail the seat slats to the skirts. Use a couple of loose nails to gauge the space between the slats.

might get lucky, but you'll probably have to saw its width, as in the top left drawing below.

8 Finish the bench. The shapes of the bench skirt and legs are strong, and paint will emphasize this. Mix two-part wood putty and

fill all the screw heads. The putty dries quickly, so let it dry, then scrub it level with 100-grit sandpaper. Prime the wood and paint it the color you like. These benches look especially nice with a painted understructure, and no finish on the slats.

ALTERNATIVES Once you've made the base of the skirt bench, you can handle the top in any number of ways. If you decide to run the boards lengthwise, however, skip the end slats and add a support rail between the midpoints of the skirts.

PARK BENCH

Seat and back slope comfortably, with no angles to cut

The classic park bench has a wooden seat and back, set into one-piece ends made of wrought iron or reinforced concrete. This is an economical and durable civic construction, yet one that permits a surprising amount of comfort. Who doesn't enjoy a rest, or a little snooze, on a park bench?

This park bench, which is made entirely of 2×4 lumber, relies on glued-and-screwed end assemblies. All the pieces are simple rectangular lengths of 2×4. The design achieves the seat and back slopes necessary for comfort without sawing any angles, as you'll see in the illustrations and in the steps that follow.

The critical maneuver is making sure you construct mirror-imaged end assemblies. One is right-handed and the other is left-handed. Therefore, make the end assemblies in stages, so you can compare them as you go. You'll see this method in the construction photos.

The bench shown is 60 inches long. You could shorten it to 48 inches, or lengthen it to about 72 inches, without having to make any structural changes. A longer bench would benefit from a second pair of cross rails, plus a brace inside each back leg.

Some of the edges have been rounded over with a router, and some have been left square, to retain the classic park bench look. You can rout as many edges as you like, though if you want to give your router a real workout, consider the loveseat on page 114.

BUILDING THE PARK BENCH

1 Choose and saw the wood. You can saw all of the 2×4 lumber to length at the beginning of the project, except for the stretcher. It has to be trimmed to length after the rest of the bench has been assembled. Try to choose clean wood, working around knots and defects. Make sure none of your seat and back slats have pitch pockets.

2 Join the sloper to the back leg. The sloper gives the back slats the tilt they need for comfort. The angle comes from the size and arrangement of the square-cut pieces, not from a protractor. The drawing below shows how the sloper fits diagonally on the back leg. If you match up the sloper's top front corner with the top front corner of the back leg, and allow the sloper's bottom back corner to touch the front edge of the leg, you've got it right. Draw a layout line, spread glue, clamp the parts

PARK BENCH

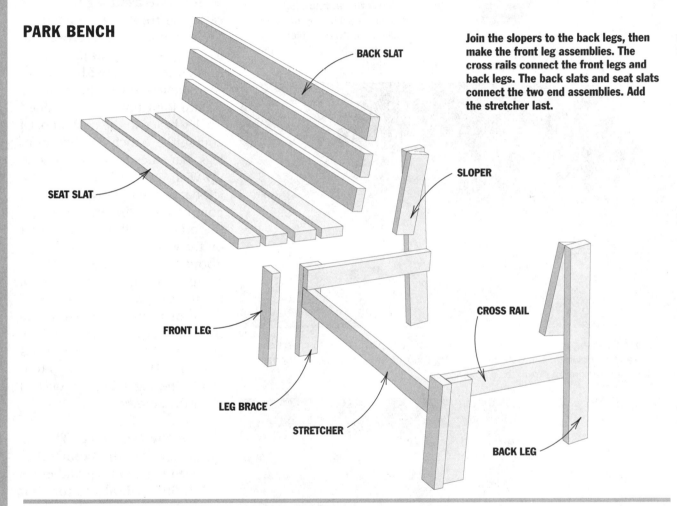

BACK SLAT

SEAT SLAT

SLOPER

FRONT LEG

CROSS RAIL

LEG BRACE

STRETCHER

BACK LEG

Join the slopers to the back legs, then make the front leg assemblies. The cross rails connect the front legs and back legs. The back slats and seat slats connect the two end assemblies. Add the stretcher last.

YOUR INVESTMENT
Time: One afternoon
Money: $15

SHOPPING LIST
Six 8-foot 2×4 studs
#8 × 2½-inch galvanized screws
#8 × 3-inch galvanized screw

PROJECT SPECS
The park bench is 60 inches long, 32 inches high, and 28 inches wide at the ground.

CUTTING LIST

PART	QTY.	DIMENSIONS	NOTES
Back leg	2	1½ × 3½ × 32	2×4
Sloper	2	1½ × 3½ × 14	2×4
Front leg	2	1½ × 3½ × 16½	2×4
Cross rail	2	1½ × 3½ × 24	2×4
Leg brace	2	1½ × 3½ × 16	2×4
Back slat	3	1½ × 3½ × 60	2×4
Seat slat	4	1½ × 3½ × 60	2×4
Stretcher	1	1½ × 3½ × 46	2×4; cut to fit

Join the sloper to the back leg. Fit the sloper diagonally at the top of the back leg and roll glue onto both pieces (above). Clamp them together to drive the screws (left).

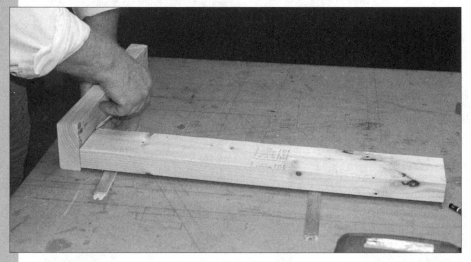

Join one front leg and cross rail. Prop the cross rail up on sticks to create the inset, and mark where it meets the front leg (above). Drive the screws toenail fashion, for maximum strength (below).

together, drill clearance holes for four 2½-inch screws and drive the screws down tight. Join the other sloper and back leg in the same way, but be sure you get a right-handed and a left-handed assembly. You can see this relationship in the large photo on the facing page.

3 **Join one front leg and cross rail.** The front leg connects to the end grain of the cross rail, making a right angle. Even though it's made with three of the 3-inch screws, this is not a secure joint until you've added the leg brace in the next step. Of course the bench has two front legs, but since it's critical to end up with a right-handed and a left-handed assembly, it's best to complete one before beginning the other. Lay the cross rail flat on the worktable and block it up about ³⁄₁₆ inch on a couple of scraps of wood. Align the top of the front leg with the top edge of the cross rail as shown in the photo at left, draw a layout line, and drill three clearance holes through the front leg. Then clamp the parts in position and drive the screws.

4 **Add the leg brace.** The leg brace secures the connection between the front leg and cross rail. It fits flush at the top, but it's inset by ½ inch at the bottom. This inset allows the seat of the bench to slope toward the back. Roll glue onto the edge of the brace that fits against the front leg, and also glue where it fits against the cross rail. Clamp the brace to the leg, drill clearance holes, and drive two of the 2½-inch screws into it through the front face of the leg. Then

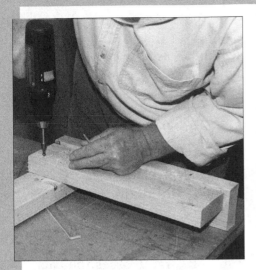

Add the leg brace. Glue and screw the leg brace to the back of the front leg, as well as to the cross rail. Note the ½-inch offset at the bottom of the brace.

END FRAME DETAIL

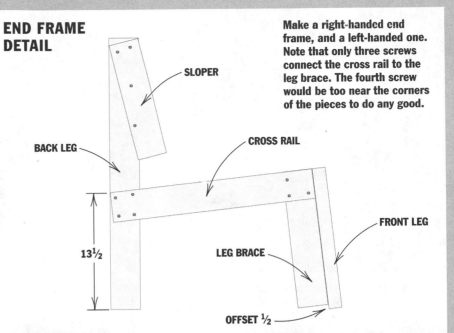

Make a right-handed end frame, and a left-handed one. Note that only three screws connect the cross rail to the leg brace. The fourth screw would be too near the corners of the pieces to do any good.

SLOPER

BACK LEG

CROSS RAIL

FRONT LEG

LEG BRACE

13½

OFFSET ½

Make the second front leg assembly. The second leg assembly matches the first, except one is right-handed and the other is left-handed.

Join the front and back legs. With the back leg square to the 2×4 that represents the ground, the top of the cross rail is 13½ inches high (above). The cross rail and sloper are on the same side of the leg (right).

drill and drive three more screws through the cross rail into the brace. Position these screws as shown in the illustration at top right.

5 Make the second front leg assembly. To make the other leg assembly, follow the same sequence as in Steps 3 and 4. However, keep the completed leg assembly close by and make

sure you end up with a right-handed assembly and a left-handed one, as shown above.

6 Join the front and back legs. The cross rail connects the front leg assembly to the back leg and

The top back slat connects the end assemblies. Clamp the back legs to the worktable to center and attach the top back slat.

Complete the back. Glue and screw the bottom back slat to the sloper.

Make the seat. Center the front seat slat from side to side, overhanging the front leg by 1 inch. Space the other three slats about ¾ inch apart.

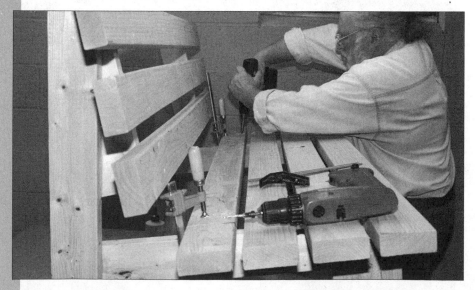

sloper. Set the parts up on the worktable as shown in the center photo on the previous page. Clamp one of the seat slats to the edge of the table to represent the ground. Now if you make the back leg vertical, and allow the front leg and brace to both touch the "ground," you'll have created the backward slope of the bench seat. You can verify the slope by direct measurement: Verify that the top of the rail crosses the back leg 13½ inches up from the ground. Draw a layout line, spread glue, drill four clearance holes and drive the 2½-inch screws. Join the other end of the bench in the same way, using the first one as a guide to make sure you end up with mirror-image assemblies.

7 The top back slat connects the end assemblies. Set the two end assemblies up on the worktable. Clamp the back legs to the table, 48 inches apart from outside to outside, as shown in the photo above left. If you don't have a big worktable (page 348), you'll have to set up on the floor or on the edge of your deck. Center the top back slat from side to side, and make it flush with the top of the sloper and back leg. Glue and screw the top back slat to the sloper with the 2½-inch screws.

8 Complete the back. Center, glue and screw the bottom back slat to the sloper, followed by the middle back slat. The bottom slat overlaps the end of the sloper by about ¼ inch. Center the middle slat in the space between the top and bottom slats.

Add the stretcher. Fit the stretcher into the socket formed by the front leg, leg brace and cross rail. Screw it to the front leg (above). Screw into the stretcher through the leg brace (right).

9 Make the seat. To attach the seat slats, turn the bench upright. The front seat slat, which is centered from side to side, overhangs the front leg by 1 inch. Drill clearance holes and drive four of the 3-inch screws down through the front seat slat and into each front leg assembly. Space the remaining three seat slats ¾ inch apart. Drill and drive two 3-inch screws through each end of each slat and into the cross rail below.

10 Add the stretcher. The stretcher is a cut-to-fit length of 2×4 that connects the front legs, underneath the seat and cross rail. If you turn the bench upside-down on the worktable, you'll see how it drops neatly into place. Mark and cut the stretcher to length, spread glue where it overlaps the front legs and cross rails, and drive two 2½-inch screws from each direction.

Finish the bench. Rout or rasp the corners off the bottom of the legs, for easy dragging. Also round the front edge of the seat, and the top edge of the back.

11 Finish the bench. Forest-green paint is the traditional park-bench finish. To prepare for finishing, fit a roundover cutter in the router and smooth off selected edges. Round the bottom of the legs, to prevent splintering during dragging across the patio. Round the front edge of the seat, and the top of the back. Unless you want a mushy appearance, don't round the ends of the slats. Sand the sharpness off them with 100-grit paper, but leave them crisp. Fill the screw heads with two-part wood putty, and sand all the flat surfaces smooth, and you're ready to prime and paint.

PICNIC TABLE

A hearty board for the whole family, yet it wheels away
with the greatest of ease

Does anyone not have fond memories of whiling away summer afternoons around a picnic table in the park? With this kind of table you can carve your initials into the top and jump off the benches, spill cans of soda and chop garlic, and it all rolls right off. You can also spread a checkered cloth and

have the whole family over for a barbecue, because a 6-foot-long table easily seats six people, or eight if some of them are children. And the table shown here can be built any length you like, up to 12 feet.

These days you can buy a picnic table at the home center. It'll probably cost you $200, and

it won't be made with any care. If you make your own table you'll spend less than half the money, plus you'll be able to choose the wood and detail the table to suit yourself. You can work around big knots and pitch pockets, you can select top boards that more or less match, and you can avoid splintery

PICNIC TABLE

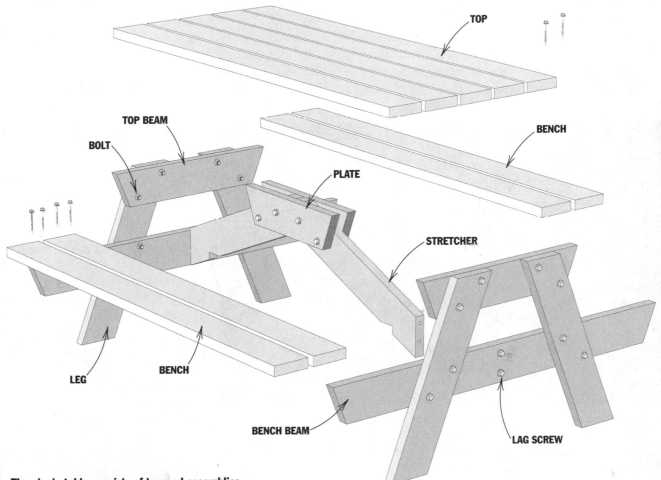

The picnic table consists of two end assemblies connected by the stretcher assembly, benches, and top. All the mitered parts are sawn at the same angle, 22½°, but the leg miters are parallel to one another, while the beam miters are cut in opposite directions.

YOUR INVESTMENT

Time: **One day**
Money: **$55 for wood, $35 for hardware**

PROJECT SPECS

The table with benches is 70 inches long, 60 inches wide, and 29 inches high.

SHOPPING LIST

Eight 12-foot 2×6 planks
Sixteen ⅜ × 3½-inch hex-head bolts with nuts and washers
Two ½ × 7-inch hex-head bolts with nuts and washers
Four ⅜ × 5-inch hex-head bolts with nuts and washers
Forty ¼ × 3½-inch lag screws with washers

CUTTING LIST

PART	QTY.	DIMENSIONS	NOTES
Bench	4	1½ × 5⅝ × 70	2×6
Top	5	1½ × 5⅝ × 70	2×6
Leg	4	1½ × 5⅝ × 29	2×6, miter both ends 22½°, parallel
Top beam	2	1½ × 5⅝ × 28	2×6, miter both ends 22½°, opposite
Bench beam	2	1½ × 5⅝ × 59	2×6, miter both ends 22½°, opposite
Stretcher	2	1½ × 5⅝ × 33⅜	2×6, miter both ends 22½°, parallel
Plate	2	1½ × 5⅝ × 22	2×6, miter both ends 22½°, opposite

benches. You'll end up with a useful table your family will really enjoy—an indestructible kind of heirloom.

The table will, however, be heavy. It will take two strong men to move it—unless you also make the table truck shown on page 113. Then you can lift one end and roll it away.

This picnic table is made of 2×6 construction lumber, bolted together. It pays to take the time to choose the cleanest material you can. You don't have to find knot-free wood, but do try to avoid splintered edges and long splits. For a 6-foot table, you'll need eight 12-foot planks.

If you want to make an extra-long table, just cut longer benches, top boards and plates. The legs and support beams remain unchanged. For an 8-foot table, buy seven 16-foot planks; for a 10-foot table, buy eight 16-foot planks.

Set up one end. Clamp the top beam to the legs and clamp two scraps at the height of the bench beam, as shown in the drawing below. Square center lines across the top beam and bench beam in order to align them from side to side.

END ASSEMBLY

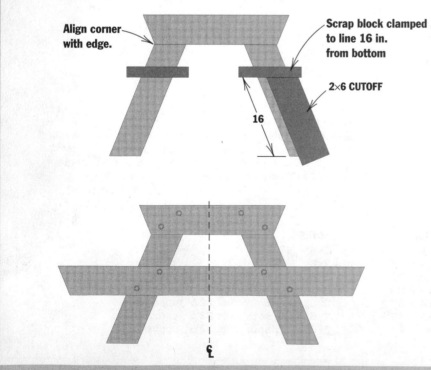

Align corner with edge.

Scrap block clamped to line 16 in. from bottom

2×6 CUTOFF

16

BUILDING THE PICNIC TABLE

1 Crosscut the planks. Construction lumber is heavy, so you can use a helper. It is easiest to work on a chopsaw or a radial-arm saw, but you can get good results with a portable circular saw, too. Crosscut five of the 2×6 planks in half for the top and benches. When you trim the ends, you'll end up with nine boards about 70 inches long and one extra piece of wood.

2 Saw the angled parts. All of the angled parts are sawn at the same miter setting, 22½ degrees. You can get four legs out of one plank, two bench beams out of a second plank, and the two top beams and two stretchers out of a third plank. The half-plank left over from sawing the benches and top is more than enough for the plates.

3 Set up one end. A table end consists of two legs, a top beam and a bench beam. The strategy is to clamp these parts together, then drill bolt holes. The miters determine the location of the parts. Start by laying both legs flat on the worktable. Set the top beam in position across the legs. The short points of the miters line up with the outside edges of the legs. Locate the bench beam by measuring up 16 inches, then draw lines parallel to the ground. The easiest way to do this is with a mitered 2×6 offcut, as shown in the illustrations on the facing page. Clamp scraps of wood on these lines, and set the bench beam on the scrap blocks. Square a centerline across the top beam and the bench beam so you can align them end to end. Clamp everything together.

4 Join the legs and beams. The connectors are ⅜-inch galvanized hex-head bolts, with a washer under each head and another washer under the nut. Two bolts go through each joint, separated for maximum triangulation, as shown in the drawing at left. Use scraps of 2×6 to block the assembly up off the worktable. Drill two ⅜-inch holes through both parts of each joint. Tap the bolts into the holes with a hammer, and tighten the nuts down with a socket wrench. You should be able to hear the washers bite into the wood.

5 Join the stretchers. The angled stretchers brace the tabletop to the bench beams. They're held in place with bolts and lag screws, which might seem like overkill until the first time you drag the table across an uneven deck or patio. In this step you'll join an angled stretcher to each of the end assemblies, then in the next step you'll connect the stretchers with the two plates.

Begin by drilling a ½-inch hole through the center of the bench beam, 2 inches up from the beam's bottom edge. Then lay out the notch and bolt hole in the stretcher, as shown in the drawing below. Note that the hole is square to the mitered end of the stretcher. Saw the notch first, then clamp the stretcher flat on the worktable to drill the hole. Bolt the stretcher to the bench beam. Drill pilot holes and install the 3½-inch lag screw. Join the other stretcher and bench beam in the same way.

Join the legs and beams. With the end assembly clamped together and propped up on scraps, drill through both parts at once. The bolts will be a tight fit, so tap them home with a hammer.

Join the stretchers. Grab the stretcher in a vise to saw the notch (left). Clamp the stretcher flat on the bench to drill the bolt hole (right).

STRETCHER DETAIL

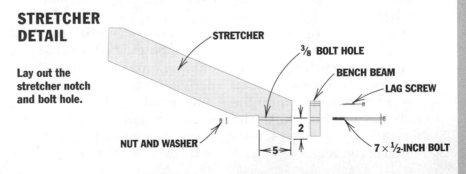

Lay out the stretcher notch and bolt hole.

STRETCHER

⅜ BOLT HOLE

BENCH BEAM

LAG SCREW

NUT AND WASHER

2

5

7 × ½-INCH BOLT

Connect the table ends. Clamp a length of scrap lumber to the two stretchers, and bring their miters together. Clamp the plates to the stretcher joint and drill for bolts (left). Saw the protruding miter points off the stretchers (above).

6 Connect the table ends. The stretchers, joined to each other by the two plates, connect the two ends of the picnic table. Bring the mitered ends of the stretchers together and clamp them to a length of scrap lumber to hold them in position; you can see this piece of scrap below the plates in the photo above. To align the plates with the top beams, stand two of the top boards across the top beams, and bring the plates up to them. Clamp the plates to the stretchers. Now you can drill through the plates and stretchers for four $\frac{3}{8}$-inch bolts. Finally, saw or rasp the protruding miter points off the stretchers, creating a level support for the tabletop.

7 Attach the benches and top. Lag screws, two through each end of every board, connect the bench and top boards to the table frame. Four more screws go through the center top board

Attach the benches and top. Set the top and bench boards in position to lay out holes for lag screws. Drill countersink holes for the bolt heads and washers.

into the stretcher plates. Lay out all the holes. Drill the $\frac{3}{4}$-inch countersink holes first. Then drill $\frac{1}{4}$-inch clearance holes through all the boards. Set the boards in position on the table frame to transfer the locations of these holes. Then remove the boards in order to drill $\frac{1}{8}$-inch pilot holes into the table frame. Drive all the lag screws home.

8 Finish the table. The best finish for a picnic table is no finish. Let the weather take care of it. The next best is paint.

TABLE TRUCK

Without a table truck, you'd need two strong men to move a heavy picnic table across the lawn. This handy contraption allows one person to move a heavy table unaided. It jacks under the bench beam at one end, then you lift the other end and roll the table away. With two trucks, one person could move the heaviest picnic table without any lifting at all.

The table truck consists of short lengths of 2×4 glued and screwed together, with a pair of ⅜-inch hex-head bolts in the center. The bolts resist the stress of jacking up the table. The longest part is 18 inches, so you might be able to get everything out of scrap. If not, you'll need 12 feet of 2×4.

Set the two rear pillars on the worktable and lay two beams across them. Drill clearance holes, spread glue, and drive four 2½-inch screws into each intersection.

Turn the assembly over, center the front pillar on it, drill bolt holes, and start the ⅜-inch bolts. Create clearance by slipping an extra washer onto each bolt between the beams and pillar.

Saw a ½-inch deep groove lengthwise in the face of the axle beam for the 24-inch threaded rod. Saw the groove so the threaded rod fits tightly in it. Now fit the axle and screw the axle beam to the ends of all three pillars.

The handles and tongue give you leverage for jacking up the table. Glue and screw the handles to the tongue, then screw the assembly to the front pillar.

To mount the wheels, tighten a nut and washer onto each end of the axle. Add a washer, then the wheel, then another washer, and finally a pair of nuts.

Rock the table truck under one end of the table, then lift the other end and roll.

TABLE TRUCK

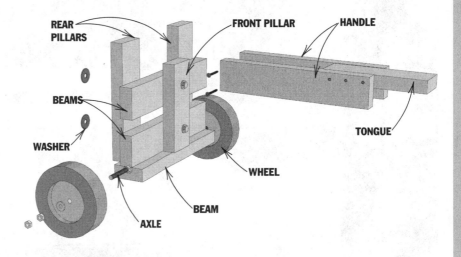

YOUR INVESTMENT
Time: One evening
Money: $20

SHOPPING LIST
12 feet 2×4
Two 8-inch replacement lawn mower wheels
One 24-inch × ½-inch threaded rod
Six ½-inch nuts and washers
Two ⅜ × 3½-inch bolts with nuts and washers

CUTTING LIST

PART	QTY.	DIMENSIONS	NOTES
Beam	3	1½ × 3½ × 18	2×4
Rear pillar	2	1½ × 3½ × 14	2×4
Front pillar	1	1½ × 3½ × 10½	2×4
Handle	2	1½ × 3½ × 18	2×4
Tongue	1	1½ × 3½ × 12	2×4

GARDEN LOVESEAT

Lattice back and fluted edges enliven this delight

Garden furniture doesn't all have to be rustic. It's delightful to meander down a path and happen upon a traditional garden loveseat, tucked beneath a tree or into a flower bed.

You could pay several hundred dollars for a traditional loveseat with a herringbone back. Today's catalog version probably would be made of teak, even though the original English loveseat was either painted softwood or unpainted oak or softwood, like the one shown here.

The delicate shadows come from routing a fluted profile into the edges of the wood. The flutes catch the light in quite a different way from the usual roundover. However, if you prefer the look of beveled or rounded edges, of course you can do that instead.

This is a big project with a lot of pieces of wood, so give it a week of evenings or a full weekend. There are no tricky cuts or difficult joints. The only non-rectangular pieces are the curved seat rails, which you shape with a jigsaw. There are a number of aesthetic and technical decisions to make along the way, as discussed in the steps that follow.

The loveseat shown here is painted a deep vermilion. The paint enhances the fluting and the trim. It also hides defects and discolorations in the wood, and it allows the loveseat to be joined together entirely with screws, because you can putty over the screwheads. If you want to varnish your loveseat, you can color the wood putty to match your wood, or you can buy wooden plugs to glue over the screwheads. In that case, attach the seat with finishing nails in Step 9.

BUILDING THE LOVESEAT

1 Cut all the wood. If you plan to varnish your loveseat, choose the wood with extreme care. Pay attention to color as well as texture. If you intend to paint the loveseat, you don't have to worry about the color of the wood. In either case, however, it's important to avoid knots and pitch pockets, because they are liable to bleed through your finish, marring the elegance of this project. All the structural wood can be cut to length at the start of this project. The back's herringbone grille and the trim pieces, however, must be cut to fit.

2 Flute the legs. The loveseat gets its elegant appearance from the fluted profile routed into the edges of the parts. You have to flute the 2×4 legs before beginning construction, because you won't be able to get at them later on. Clamp the leg to the worktable and track the router around all the edges you can reach, as shown in the photo at left. Remove the clamp to rout the edge it was blocking, then flip the wood over to rout the other side. It's up to you whether you rout the flute profile into all the trim stock at the start of the project, or whether you cut to fit and rout as you go along, or a bit of both.

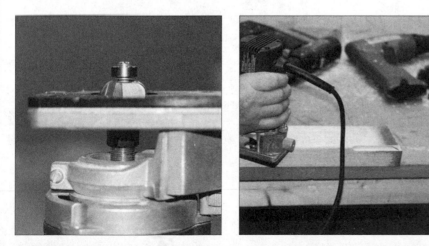

Flute the legs. Mount a fluting cutter in the trim router (left). Rout along all the edges of the 2x4 legs (right).

GARDEN LOVESEAT

To build the loveseat, begin with the end frames. Then make the curved seat rails, attach the front rail, and the seat slats. Trim the bench ends. Make and install the back frame and its herringbone grille as a separate assembly.

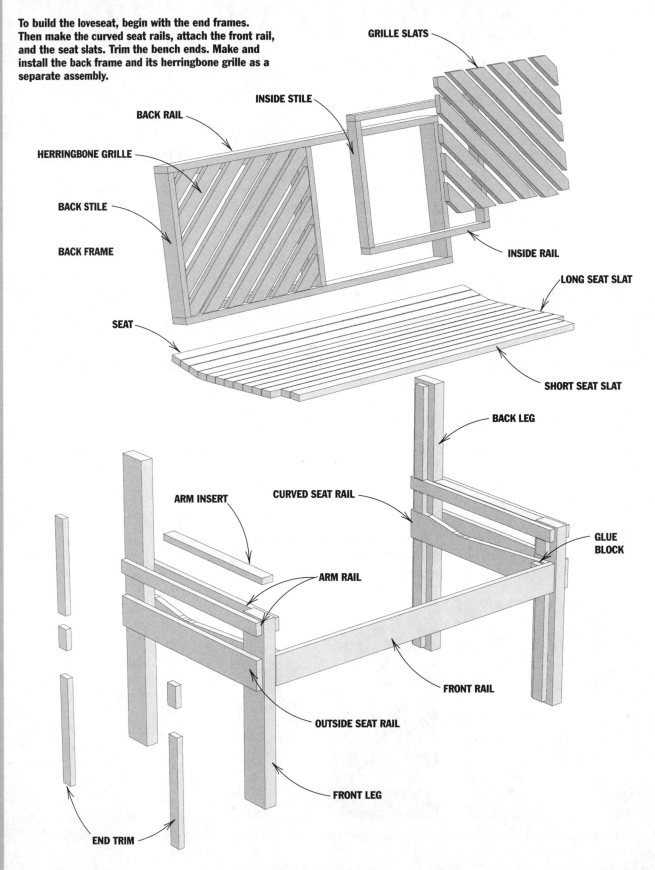

GRILLE SLATS

INSIDE STILE

BACK RAIL

HERRINGBONE GRILLE

BACK STILE

BACK FRAME

INSIDE RAIL

LONG SEAT SLAT

SEAT

SHORT SEAT SLAT

BACK LEG

CURVED SEAT RAIL

ARM INSERT

GLUE BLOCK

ARM RAIL

FRONT RAIL

OUTSIDE SEAT RAIL

FRONT LEG

END TRIM

END ASSEMBLY AND TRIM DETAIL

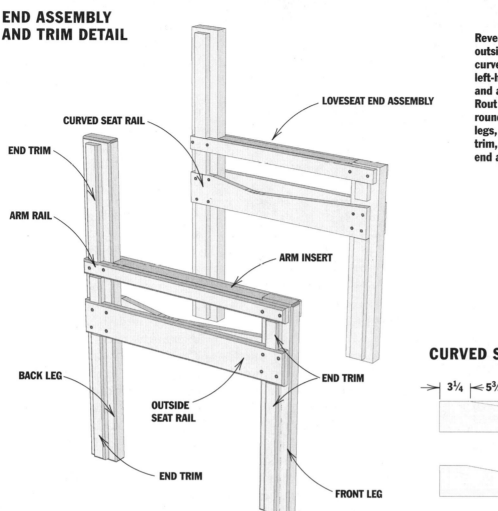

CURVED SEAT RAIL

END TRIM

ARM RAIL

BACK LEG

END TRIM

LOVESEAT END ASSEMBLY

ARM INSERT

END TRIM

OUTSIDE SEAT RAIL

FRONT LEG

Reverse the position of the outside seat rail and the curved seat rail to create a left-handed end assembly and a right-handed one. Rout the chamfer, flute or roundover profile around the legs, outside seat rails, and trim, as shown on the left end assembly.

CURVED SEAT RAIL

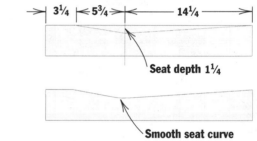

$3\frac{1}{4}$ $5\frac{3}{4}$ $14\frac{1}{4}$

Seat depth $1\frac{1}{4}$

Smooth seat curve

YOUR INVESTMENT

<u>Time:</u> All weekend
<u>Money:</u> $40

SHOPPING LIST

12 feet 2×4 pine or fir
128 feet 1×2 pine
16 feet 1×3 pine
16 feet 1×4 pine
#6 × 1¼-inch galvanized screws
#6 × 1⅝-inch galvanized screws
#6 × 2-inch galvanized screws
#6 × 2½-inch galvanized screws
#8 × 3-inch galvanized screws
1½-inch galvanized finishing nails
2-inch galvanized finishing nails

PROJECT SPECS

The loveseat is 46½ inches wide, 36 inches high, and 25 inches deep.

CUTTING LIST

PART	QTY.	DIMENSIONS	NOTES
SEAT			
Back leg	2	$1\frac{1}{2} \times 3\frac{1}{2} \times 34$	2×4
Front leg	2	$1\frac{1}{2} \times 3\frac{1}{2} \times 22$	2×4
Curved seat rail	2	$\frac{3}{4} \times 3\frac{1}{2} \times 23\frac{1}{4}$	1×4
Outside seat rail	2	$\frac{3}{4} \times 3\frac{1}{2} \times 24$	1×4
Arm rail	4	$\frac{3}{4} \times 1\frac{1}{2} \times 24$	1×2
Arm insert	2	$\frac{3}{4} \times 1\frac{1}{2} \times 18$	1×2; trim to fit
Front rail	1	$\frac{3}{4} \times 3\frac{1}{2} \times 41\frac{1}{2}$	1×4
Glue block	3	$\frac{3}{4} \times 1\frac{1}{2} \times 3$	1×2 scrap
Short seat slat	2	$\frac{3}{4} \times 1\frac{1}{2} \times 41\frac{1}{2}$	1×2
Long seat slat	10	$\frac{3}{4} \times 1\frac{1}{2} \times 44\frac{3}{8}$	1×2
Seat brace	1	$\frac{3}{4} \times 2\frac{1}{2} \times 14$	optional
BACK FRAME			
Back rail	2	$\frac{3}{4} \times 2\frac{1}{2} \times 40$	1×3
Back stile	3	$\frac{3}{4} \times 2\frac{1}{2} \times 16$	1×3
Inside rail	4	$\frac{3}{4} \times 1\frac{1}{2} \times 18\frac{7}{8}$	1×2
Inside stile	4	$\frac{3}{4} \times 1\frac{1}{2} \times 14\frac{1}{2}$	1×2
TRIM			
Grille slats		$\frac{3}{4} \times 1\frac{1}{2} \times 30$ feet	1×2; cut to fit
End trim		$\frac{3}{4} \times 1\frac{1}{2} \times 18$ feet	1×2; cut to fit
Back trim		$\frac{3}{4} \times 1\frac{1}{2} \times 39$	1×2

Join back legs and outside seat rails. The top of the rail crosses the back leg 17½ inches up from the ground. The rail stops ⅛ inch inside the margin of the flute.

Join front legs and outside seat rails. Glue and screw the free end of the rail to the front leg. The board in the foreground represents the floor.

squareness and position. Now drill four clearance holes through the outside seat rail and drive the 2-inch screws into the leg. Join the other back leg and outside seat rail in the same way, but make sure you get one of them right-handed and the other left-handed, as shown in the drawing on the previous page.

4 Join front legs and outside seat rails. Now add the front legs to the two end assemblies. They go on the same side of the outside seat rails as the back legs, preserving the opposite handedness of the two ends. The front legs are vertical, so the tops of the outside seat rails fall 17½ inches up from the ground, same as on the back legs. Set the ends of the rails ⅛ inch inside the margins of the fluting. Glue, clamp and screw as in the previous step.

5 Add the arm rails. The arm rails fit on either side of the legs, parallel to the outside seat rail. Before you attach them, rout the flute into the short corners of the top of the legs, as shown in the photo below. Then align the

3 Join back legs and outside seat rails. The back leg and the outside seat rail make a T shape, with the top of the rail 17½ inches up from the bottom of the leg. The end of the rail should fall ⅛ inch inside the margin of the flute routed into the leg, as shown in the photo above. This creates a delicate shadow line. Position the parts, draw a layout line, spread glue, and clamp them in place. Use your measuring tools to verify

Add the arm rails. Flute the short corners of the front legs (below). Align the two arm rails, then glue and screw them to the legs (left).

first arm rail as in the previous step: ⅛ inch inset from the margin of the fluting at the top of the front leg and square to both legs. Glue and screw the arm rail to the legs, with two screws at either end. Turn the end assembly over to attach the second arm rail to its other side, then add the arm rails to the other end assembly in the same way.

6 Make the curved seat rail. The curved seat rail makes the loveseat comfortable, but there's nothing critical about the curve. To lay it out, mark the end points and center point as shown in the drawing on the previous page. Connect the two end points to the center point, making a shallow triangle. Then work your pencil freehand to draw a nice smooth curve at the apex of the triangle. Jigsaw one of the curved seat rails, then trace is shape onto the other one and saw it too.

7 Join the curved seat rails. The curved seat rail fits inside the end assembly, in line with the outside seat rail. Use your square to align the bottom of the two rails. The curved rail comes ⅛ inch from the edge of the flute in the back leg, but falls 1 inch behind the flute in the front leg. This space is for the front rail, in Step 8. Draw a layout line and spread glue, clamp the rail in place, drill four clearance holes at each end, and screw the rail to the legs. Use the 2-inch screws. Join the other curved seat rail to the other end assembly in the same way.

8 Attach the front rail. The front rail connects the two end

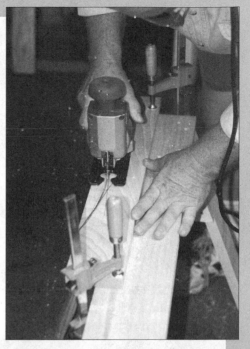

Make the curved seat rail. Mark the center of the seat and draw two straight lines. Then doodle the curve (above). Jigsaw the curve (right).

Join the curved seat rails. Glue and screw the curved seat rail to the legs. The 1-inch inset, beneath the thumb, is for the front rail.

Attach the front rail. Glue and screw the front rail to the end of the curved seat rail (left). Glue and screw a glue block inside this corner joint (right).

Make the seat. Use a thin stick of wood to space the seat slats and screw them to the curved seat rail.

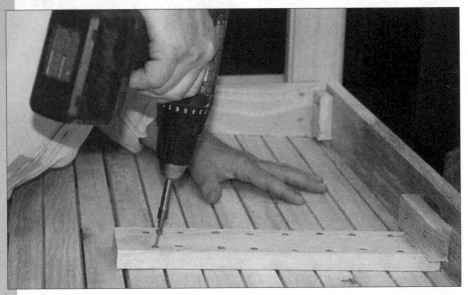

Reinforce the seat. To take the bounce out of the seat, glue and screw a brace and glue block underneath it. The brace is optional.

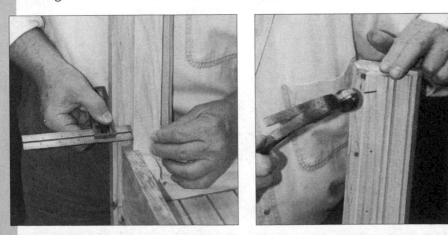

Trim the loveseat ends. The combination square helps center the trim pieces on the legs (left). Flute the inside trim before gluing and nailing it in place (right).

assemblies. It fits tight against the ends of the curved seat rail, as shown in the bottom photos on the previous page. Spread glue, drill clearance holes and drive two of the 2½-inch screws through the face of the front rail into the end of each curved seat rail. Insure the joints by screwing a glue block inside each corner. Screw it to the front rail as well as to the curved seat rail.

9 **Make the seat.** Because of the way the curved seat rail passes the front leg, there are two short seat slats at the front of the seat, followed by ten long seat slats. Set the slats in position and select their top faces. With 100-grit sandpaper, dub off the long top edges of all the slats. The first seat slat fits flush with the face of the front rail. Glue and screw the first seat slat to the top of the front rail, using seven of the 1⅝-inch screws. Use a thin stick of wood to space the next slat, then glue and screw it to the curved seat rail, with a 1⅝-inch screw at each end. Space and attach the remainder of the seat slats in the same way, as shown above left.

10 **Reinforce the seat.** Sit down on the loveseat and decide whether you like the amount of give in the seat slats, or not. It's not going to break, so you don't have to do anything, but if you want to eliminate all the bounce, glue and screw a brace underneath, as shown in the middle photo at left.

11 **Trim the loveseat ends.** The trim pieces, which are all vertical, complete the loveseat ends. Every bare length of 2×4 leg

Install the arm inserts. Roll glue between the arm rails, then tap the arm insert down level (left). Clamp it and nail it (above).

Flute the trim. Stand the bench up on end to rout all around the trim pieces.

needs a piece of trim on both sides. Flute the inside trim pieces before you glue and nail them to the 2×4 legs because you won't have router access afterward. The outside trim can go on fluted or not because access is not a problem. Use a combination square to center the trim on the legs. Set the square to half the difference in width between the two pieces, as shown in the bottom left photo on the facing page. Roll glue on each trim piece, hold or clamp it in place, and fasten it with at least two 1½-inch finishing nails. Now set the nailheads below the surface of the wood.

12 Install the arm inserts. Fit the arm inserts between the arm rails and the legs. You might have to saw or rasp them to width to match the thickness of your 2×4 legs. Once you see where the arm inserts go, spread glue on both surfaces, and tap them down flush with the top of the arm rails, as shown above. Clamp across the arms as shown in the photo at top right, and

guarantee the connection with a few of the 1½-inch finishing nails.

13 Flute the trim. Now rout all the square edges off the trim pieces. Go over both loveseat ends, inside and out, as shown in the photo at right.

14 Make the back frame. The back frame contains the herringbone grille. Make it by gluing and screwing the two back rails to

Make the back frame. Glue and screw the five frame pieces together. To keep the frame flat, work flat on the worktable.

Make the inside frame. Lightly clamp the inside frame pieces to the back frame. Adjust them until a piece of trim wood, alongside the hammer handle, comes level with the bottom of the frame flutes (above). Glue and screw the inside frame to the back frame (right).

the three stiles. Start at one corner. Spread glue on the end of a stile, clamp the rail and stile to the worktable in an L-shape, drill clearance holes for two screws through the rail piece, and drive the 2½-inch screws home. Join the second stile to the other end of the rail in the same way, then connect the second rail to the free ends of the two stiles. Insert the center stile and glue it and screw it to the rails. Finally, run the fluting cutter around the top edge of the back frame, inside and out. Don't flute the short outside corner of the frame, unless you can safely miss the screws there.

Make the herringbone grille. Saw a point on one end of the corner slat (above). Mark the length and cut the piece to fit (right). Glue and nail the slats to the inside frame, and set the nailheads (below).

15 **Make the inside frame.** The inside rails and stiles support the herringbone grille. They are glued and screwed inside the back frame. Since there's considerable variation in the width of 1×2 wood, you'll have to adjust their placement by eye. Hold an inside rail in place and set a piece of 1×2 on top of it, as

shown in the top left photo on the facing page. The edge of the 1×2 should align flush with the bottom of the routed flute in the back frame. When you see where the rail has to go, spread glue on it, clamp it, and screw it to the back frame from the outside with 1¼-inch screws. Screw the rest of the inside rails and stiles in place in the same way.

16 Make the herringbone grille. The herringbone grille is a network of 1×2 slats with fluted edges, nailed into the back frame. All the slats are mitered at 45 degrees. There's no way around making the grille by cut-to-fit, but you can be systematic about it. The general method, shown in the bottom three photos on the facing page, is to miter one end of a slat, hold it in place to mark and saw the other end, flute the long edges, spread a little glue, and nail it down with a 2-inch galvanized finishing nail in each end. Start with the four center slats, which run diagonally from the center bottom and outside top corners of the frame. They have a 45-degree point on the bottom end, so cut that first. Once you get past the corners, both ends of the slats are ordinary miters, and the spacing between slats is up to you—in the loveseat shown, it's a uniform ¾ inch, the thickness of the slat.

17 Install the back. Fit the back frame between the back legs of the loveseat. It has to slope, and the slope has to remain within the embrace of the back legs. But exactly how it slopes is up to you. Clamp the back frame in place, take a good look, and

Install the back. Level the back frame by measuring from both ends of the seat (above). Experiment with the tilt, and when it suits you, screw the back frame to the back legs (right).

have a sit. Adjust it until you like it. On our loveseat, there's a gap the width of a seat slat between the seat and back. The back frame itself is screwed diagonally onto the trim piece inside the back leg. The back edge of the frame comes forward to the intersection of arm rail and inside back-leg trim; the front edge of the frame tips back and lines up with the front edge of the same trim piece.

18 Trim the top of the back. There's room for a piece of fluted trim along the top of the back frame. Cut it and flute it and glue it and nail it, or screw it, or flute it after it's attached, as suits you.

19 Finish the loveseat. Go over the whole loveseat with 100-grit sandpaper. Make the wood smooth and knock off any woolly

bits left by the router, but don't scrub the clean edges off the routed trim. Fill the screwheads with two-part wood putty. Now the loveseat is ready to prime and to paint.

TEA TIME FOR TOTS

Little suite of chairs and table gives the kids a place to dine or play

Small children need small furniture, and if you spend a lot of time out on your lawn or deck, they will too. This suite of two chairs and a table can be used at mealtime, but it also gives the kids a place to play at having tea, to set up games, and to color or draw. You'll probably bring the suite into the family room for winter play.

All the pieces of wood are rectangular, with no angles to saw anywhere. The construction is completely straightforward glue-and-screw, like most of the pieces in this book. The finished suite can be painted in gay colors, or it can be left to weather.

The design of the chairs and table looks quite interesting as shown, but if you wish to pretty it up you could decorate the sides and back panels as shown on page 129. While you could knock off all the corners and edges with a roundover cutter in your router, doing so would diminish the impact of the design. You can make the wood plenty safe and friendly to the touch with a careful sanding, using 100-grit paper.

CHILD'S CHAIR

CHAIR SIDE

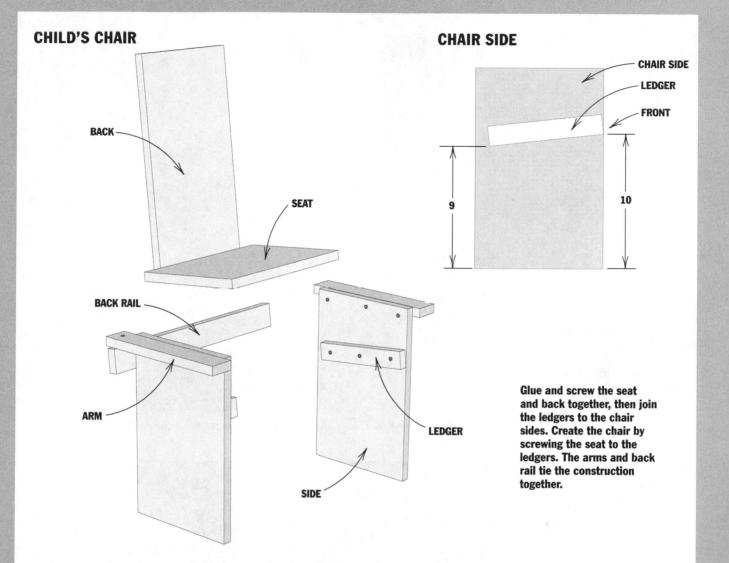

BACK

SEAT

BACK RAIL

ARM

SIDE

CHAIR SIDE

LEDGER

FRONT

9

10

LEDGER

Glue and screw the seat and back together, then join the ledgers to the chair sides. Create the chair by screwing the seat to the ledgers. The arms and back rail tie the construction together.

BUILDING THE CHILD'S CHAIR

1 Cut the wood. The chair sides, seat and back are ordinary 1×10 pine lumber, which actually measures about 9½ inches wide. The ledgers, arms and rails are pine 1×2. Saw all the parts except the arms and back rail to finished length. Trim the back rail to length before you screw it to the chair in Step 6, then trim the arms flush with the rail in Step 7. Try to avoid including knots in any of the chair parts; if you can't avoid them entirely, organize the knots into the chair sides instead of the seat and back.

YOUR INVESTMENT

<u>Time:</u> **One afternoon**
<u>Money:</u> **One chair, $8; One table, $10**

PROJECT SPECS

**The chair is 27 inches high, 18 inches wide, and 12 inches deep.
The table is 19 inches square and 16 inches high.**

CUTTING LIST

PART	QTY.	DIMENSIONS	NOTES
CHAIR			
Seat	1	¾ × 9½ × 13	1×10 pine
Back	1	¾ × 9½ × 18	1×10 pine
Side	2	¾ × 9½ × 15	1×10 pine
Ledger	2	¾ × 1½ × 8 ½	1×2 pine
Arm	2	¾ × 1½ × 13	1×2; trim to fit
Back rail	1	¾ × 1½ × 19	1×2; trim to fit
TABLE			
Leg	4	¾ × 9½ × 15½	1×10 pine
Top	2	¾ × 9½ × 19	1×10 pine

SHOPPING LIST

CHAIR
6 feet 1×10 pine
6 feet 1×2 pine

TABLE
10 feet 1×10 pine

HARDWARE FOR BOTH
#6 × 1¼-inch galvanized screws
#6 × 2-inch galvanized screws

Join the seat and back. Center the chair back on the edge of the seat, then glue and screw the parts together.

Make the ledgers. Align the ledger so its bottom front corner is flush with the edge of the chair side.

2 Join the seat and back. Draw a centerline on one end of the back, and a centerline on one edge of the seat. Spread glue on the edge of the seat, align the two center marks, and screw through the back and into the edge of the seat with five of the 2-inch screws, as shown in the photo above.

3 Make the ledgers. The ledgers support the seat. They're simple strips of 1×2 glued and screwed to the sides. Draw layout lines on the sides to locate the top of the ledgers, with the front of the line 10 inches up from the floor, and the back of the line 9 inches up. With the top of the ledger on the layout line, its bottom front corner comes flush with the edge of the chair side, as shown in the photo above right. Spread glue, drill clearance holes, and drive three 1¼-inch

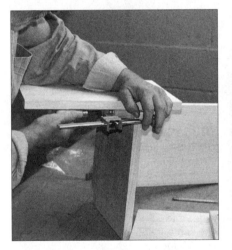

Connect the seat and sides. Clamp the chair seat to the ledger (above), then screw through the side into the seat, and also through the seat into the ledger (right).

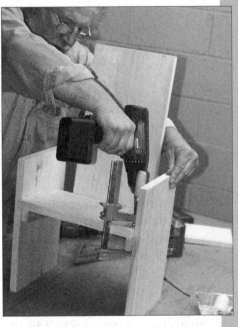

screws through each ledger into the side.

4 Connect the seat and sides. The chair seat rests upon the ledgers. The back of the seat sits flush with the back end of the

ledgers. Set the seat in position on one of the ledgers and line it up so you can see where to spread glue. Spread the glue, then clamp the seat to the ledgers, as shown in the photo at left. Drill clearance holes and screw through the side into the edge of the seat, using two of the 2-inch screws. Then remove the clamps and screw down through the seat into the ledgers, with the same size screws. Connect the second chair side to the seat in the same way.

5 Join the arms to the sides. The arms are pieces of 1×2 attached edge-on to the sides, then tied into the back by the back rail. The offset at the front of the arm is ¾ inch, or the thickness of a piece of scrap, as shown in the photo at right. Spread glue, clamp each arm in place, drill pilot holes and drive three of the 2-inch screws through the chair sides and into each arm.

6 Add the back rail. The back rail connects the chair arms and supports the back. Hold it in place to mark and saw it to length. Spread glue on the rail, bring it up under the arms, and clamp it flat onto the chair back. Drive three of the 1¼-inch screws through the rail into the chair back. Then drive one 2-inch screw down through each arm into the top of the back rail, as shown in the center photo.

7 Finish the chair. Saw the back end of the arms flush with the back rail. Wrap a piece of 100-grit sandpaper around a block of wood and sand all the sharp edges and corners off the chair. Work over the whole chair, including the bottom of the sides. If you intend to paint the chair, fill in the screw heads with two-part wood putty, let it dry, and sand it flush.

Join the arms to the sides. Use a piece of scrap to gauge the offset between the chair side and arm. Screw through the side into the arm.

Add the back rail. Screw the back rail to the chair back, then anchor it to the arms.

Finish the chair. Saw the extra wood off the back ends of the arms (left). Sand the sharp corners off the wood, making it friendly to the touch (right).

BUILDING THE CHILD'S TABLE

1 Saw the wood. All the parts of the table come out of regular 1×10 pine lumber. Choose the clearest wood for the tabletop.

2 Make the wooden right-angles. The pinwheel base consists of two identical right-angles of wood. Spread glue on the edge of one leg piece, then set a second piece in position on it. Align the edges carefully, as shown in the photo at near right. Then drill clearance holes and make the connection with three 2-inch screws. Make the second L-shape in the same way.

3 Make the pinwheel base. Fit the two wooden right-angles together as shown in far right photo. Draw a layout line, spread glue, then drill clearance holes for 2-inch screws. Drive two screws from each direction.

4 Join the tabletop and base. The two-board tabletop sits on the base at 45 degrees, as shown in the photos below. Position the wood, then connect the parts with two 2-inch screws into each piece of the pinwheel.

5 Finish the table. Sand all the sharp corners off the wood, using a piece of 100-grit sandpaper wrapped around a block of wood. If you want to paint the table, putty the screwheads with two-part wood filler. When the filler dries, sand it flush with the tabletop. Prime the wood before you apply the color coat.

CHILD'S TABLE

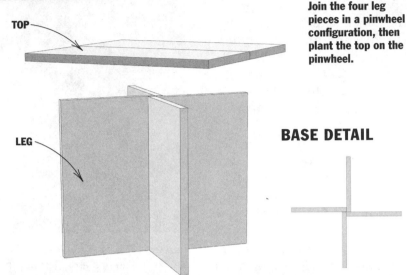

TOP

LEG

Join the four leg pieces in a pinwheel configuration, then plant the top on the pinwheel.

BASE DETAIL

Make the wooden right angles. Prop the leg pieces in position, align them so you can draw a layout line, then glue and screw them together.

Make the pinwheel base. Fit the two wooden right angles together pinwheel fashion, then glue and screw the joint.

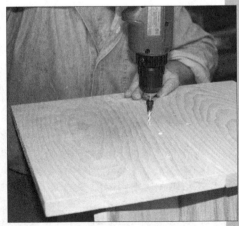

Join the tabletop and base. Make a centerline on the edge of the tabletop and align it with the center of the pinwheel (left). Screw the tabletop to the base (right).

ALTERNATIVES

You can dress up the child's table and chairs in any number of ways. The round suite needs a larger tabletop than the square version, 22 inches instead of 19 inches.

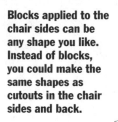

Blocks applied to the chair sides can be any shape you like. Instead of blocks, you could make the same shapes as cutouts in the chair sides and back.

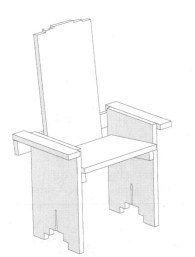

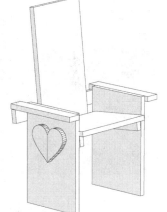

Jigsawn shapes lend architectural character to the chairs, as do trim strips.

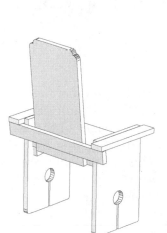

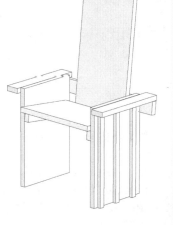

HAMMOCK TRIPOD

Ingenious contraption slings your slumberous web in the middle of a field

A hammock is a wonderful thing, provided you've got two convenient trees. If not, you're out of luck—until you make a hammock tripod. This ingenious structure liberates your summer naptime from where the trees happen to grow. With one of them you can sling your hammock from a single tree. If you make two tripods, you can swing in the middle of the lawn without regard to whether there are any trees.

Each hammock tripod consists of three 2×4 studs joined together by a single sturdy bolt and anchored to the ground with a pair of wooden stakes. Tripods are forgiving. They're stable on uneven ground, and they can even make good use of twisted lumber. These tripods also fold into compact bundles for easy storage.

You must take care to stake your hammock tripods to the ground, or nail them to a deck. Though it doesn't take a lot of anchoring to keep a tripod from being pulled over, its own weight is not enough. Like any outdoor construction, the weather and active children will take their toll. It's the responsibility of the maker to keep an eye on the structure, and make sure it remains stable and correctly staked to the ground.

HAMMOCK TRIPOD

Attach the bolt blocks to the post, drill the bolt holes in the post and legs, and assemble the tripod. Attach the eye bolt, stop block and stake block. Stake the hammock tripod on the lawn, with an 8-foot spread between the two legs, and 12 feet from the legs back to the post. Hang the hammock, and take a nice nap.

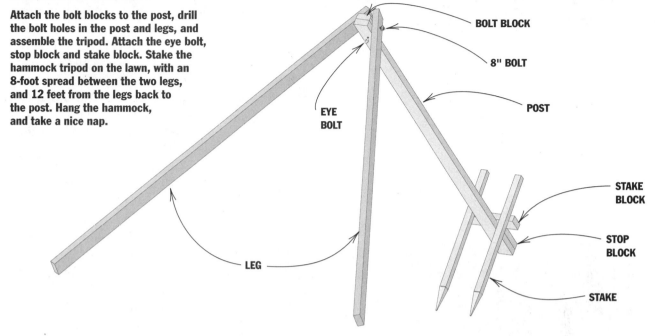

BOLT BLOCK

8" BOLT

POST

EYE BOLT

STAKE BLOCK

STOP BLOCK

LEG

STAKE

YOUR INVESTMENT

<u>Time:</u> All day
<u>Money:</u> $15

SHOPPING LIST

Four 8-foot 2 × 4 studs
One $\frac{1}{2}$ × 8-inch galvanized bolt
One 1 × 3-inch eye bolt
#8 × 3-inch galvanized screws

PROJECT SPECS

On the ground, the hammock tripod makes a triangle that's 12 feet long and 8 feet wide. The eye bolt is 5 feet above the ground.

CUTTING LIST (ONE TRIPOD)

PART	QTY.	DIMENSIONS	NOTES
Post	1	$1\frac{1}{2}$ × $3\frac{1}{2}$ × 96	2 × 4
Bolt block	1	$1\frac{1}{2}$ × $3\frac{1}{2}$ × 6 $\frac{1}{2}$	2 × 4
Leg	2	$1\frac{1}{2}$ × $3\frac{1}{2}$ × 96	2 × 4
Stake block	1	$1\frac{1}{2}$ × $3\frac{1}{2}$ × 12	2 × 4
Stop block	1	$1\frac{1}{2}$ × $3\frac{1}{2}$ × 9	2 × 4
Stake	2	$1\frac{1}{2}$ × $1\frac{1}{2}$ × 36	2 × 2

BUILDING THE HAMMOCK TRIPOD

1 Choose the wood. If you are buying 2×4 studs, choose knot-free pieces, but don't worry about twisted wood. This is one of the few projects where twisted wood doesn't matter.

2 Join the bolt block to the post. The bolt block reinforces the post where the main bolt passes through it. The block fits flush with the end of the post. Spread glue on the block, clamp it in place, drill clearance holes for four screws, and drive the 3-inch screws through the block and into the post, as shown in the photo at right.

3 Drill the bolt hole. The hole for the $\frac{1}{2}$-inch bolt passes through the center of the seam between the bolt block and the post. Clamp the post to the bench as shown in the photo at the top of the next page. Sight the drill to make sure it is vertical from the end as well as from the side. Drill completely through the post and block.

Join the bolt blocks to the post. Glue and screw the bolt block flush with the end of the post.

Drill the bolt hole. Clamp the post to the bench and sight the drill for vertical from the end and from the side. Drill directly through the seam between the post and post block.

Bevel the bolt block. Rasp the corners off the bolt block. This is what allows the tripod legs to splay.

Bolt the tripod together. Bolt the two legs to the post with the 8-inch bolt. Then drill a hole and install the eye bolt just below the post block. The eye itself goes opposite the bolt block, as on the tripod at left.

Add the stake block. Glue and screw the stake block and stop block to the bottom end of the post, on the same side of the post as the bolt block.

Make the stakes. Jigsaw a four-sided point on the end of the stakes. Eyeball the shape and saw from the point toward the body of the stake.

4 Drill the legs. The legs get their splayed angle from an over-sized bolt hole of $\frac{13}{16}$ inch diameter. The hole is centered on the width of the leg, 4 inches from the end. Clamp the leg to the worktable to drill the hole, but stop when the drill bit just breaks through. To prevent splintering, turn the leg over and complete the hole from the other side. Drill the other leg in the same way.

5 Bevel the bolt block. In order to spread the legs of the tripod, you'll need to bevel the top corners off the bolt block. Use a Surform rasp, as shown in the photo above right. The amount of the bevel is not critical; go about half-way down the thickness of the block and $\frac{1}{4}$ inch in from its edge.

6 Bolt the tripod together. Equip the 8-inch bolt with a washer under the head and another beneath the nuts. Run the bolt through the holes in the legs and post, with a leg on either side of the post. Tighten the two nuts together at the end of the bolt, but don't tighten the nuts against the three pieces of wood. You need plenty of play for the tripod to open up. While you're at it, drill a hole in the post for the eye bolt just below the bolt block. Tighten the eye bolt so the eye itself is on the opposite side of the post from the bolt block, as shown in the photo at center left.

7 Add the stake block. The stake block and stop block create a stable anchor at the ground end of the post. These blocks go on the same side of the post as the bolt block, that is, opposite the eye of the eye bolt. Screw the stop block flush with the end of the post, using six of the 3-inch screws. Butt the stake block against it and screw it to the post.

8 **Make the stakes.** The wooden stakes are sharpened lengths of 2×2, which you can saw from 2×4 scrap. Jigsaw the point, as shown at bottom left.

9 **Install the hammock tripod.** The distance between tripods, or from tripod to tree, depends on the length of your hammock. You might have to experiment to get it right. The details of the installation depend upon your precise situation. In general, you spread the tripod, drive the corners of the legs so they bite into the ground, then drive the stakes alongside the stake block as discussed in the next step. Spread the legs 6 feet to 8 feet apart, or as far apart as the bolt allows. The legs and post of the spread tripod make an angle of at least 90 degrees, and are about 12 feet apart.

10 **Stake the tripod.** Anchor the tripod by driving a pair of wooden stakes alongside the stake block, as shown in the photo at center right. Then guarantee the installation by screwing each stake to the stake block with two of the 3-inch screws.

11 **Install the hammock.** Fasten your hammock to the tree at one end, and to the tripod at the other, or sling it between two tripods. The empty hammock should pull almost level, as shown at right.

Install the hammock tripod. Spread the legs of the tripod and drive their corners into the ground (left). Seat them firmly with a tap on the top end (right).

Stake the tripod. Drive the stakes alongside the post and stake block (left). Then screw the stakes to the tripod (right).

Install the hammock. Unroll your hammock and fasten it to the tree and tripod, or between two tripods, as shown here. Stretch the hammock almost level.

ADIRONDACK CHAIR

Here's a summer delight you can build in a long evening

The Adirondack chair is a great example of carpenter ingenuity. It's surprisingly comfortable, and perfect for sitting out on a summer evening. You can kick back, sip a long drink, and forget all about the high price of car repairs or whatever else might ail you.

The level arm with the angled seat and back make the Adirondack chair look complicated to build, but it is not. The important angles come from direct linear measurement, with no need for protractors or bevel gauges. The seat rail and the back leg are the same sloping piece of wood. The whole thing comes out of standard lumber with a few easy angle cuts. Just follow the dimensions given in the drawings, and your chair will come out right.

While it's possible to set up the angled cuts on the chop saw, it's easier, quicker and safer to handsaw them, as shown in the steps that follow. However, you do need to have a sharp saw—your old tree-pruning saw won't do the job. If you shop for a saw, look for a short blade with long, shark-style teeth, as shown on page 137. Stanley and Sandvik both make a short tool-box saw that's right for this kind of work.

In the Adirondacks, they make these chairs out of white

An Adirondack ottoman (page 142) completes your outdoor living room.

Join the front legs. Roll glue on the front leg brace, and nail the front leg to it. Make sure the ends and edges are flush.

cedar. Down here on the flat land, cedar can be somewhat expensive, so we use regular lumberyard 1× pine, which we paint. For a rich alternative, make the chair in redwood. Then decide whether to varnish it, which means renewing the varnish annually, or to leave it unfinished.

Plane or sand the sharp edges and corners off all the pieces of wood, either before you start assembling the chair or as you go along. This makes the chair more comfortable, and it also makes it easier to paint.

BUILDING THE CHAIR

1 Crosscut all the wood. All the parts come from standard widths of 1× lumberyard pine, which is ¾ inch thick. Crosscut all the parts to the finished lengths given on the next page before you fit anything together. Cut two extra pieces of scrap to the same length as the front legs (20 inches). You'll use them as props in Step 12.

2 Join the front legs. Glue and nail the front leg brace to the front leg, to make a composite leg that is L-shaped in cross section. Roll glue onto the edge of the brace. Set the front leg in position on it, making sure the edges and ends are flush. Nail

ADIRONDACK CHAIR

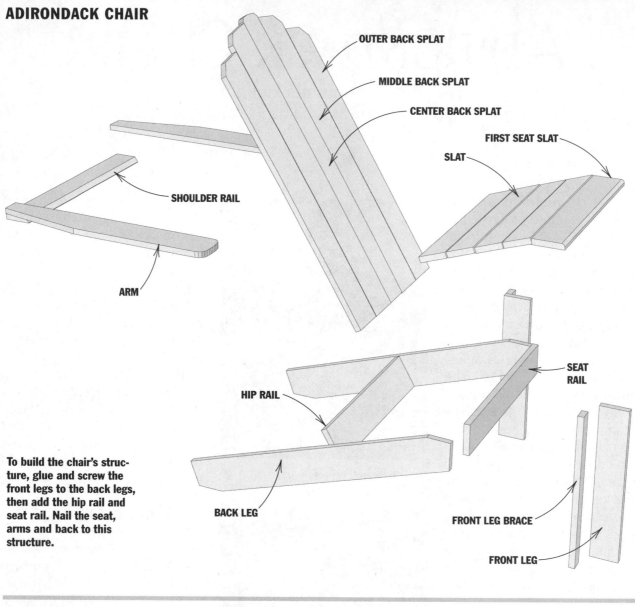

OUTER BACK SPLAT

MIDDLE BACK SPLAT

CENTER BACK SPLAT

FIRST SEAT SLAT

SLAT

SHOULDER RAIL

ARM

SEAT RAIL

HIP RAIL

BACK LEG

FRONT LEG BRACE

FRONT LEG

To build the chair's structure, glue and screw the front legs to the back legs, then add the hip rail and seat rail. Nail the seat, arms and back to this structure.

YOUR INVESTMENT

<u>Time:</u> One day
<u>Money:</u> $35

SHOPPING LIST

4 feet 1×2 pine
20 feet 1×4 pine
36 feet 1×5 pine
3-inch galvanized spiral deck nails
2-inch galvanized spiral deck nails
#6 × 2-inch galvanized screws
#6 × 1¼-inch galvanized screws

PROJECT SPECS

The chair is 38 inches high, 37 inches front to back, and 31 inches wide at the arms.

CUTTING LIST

PART	QTY.	DIMENSIONS	NOTES
Front leg	2	¾ × 3½ × 20	
Front leg brace	2	¾ × 1½ × 20	
Back leg	2	¾ × 4½ × 37	
Hip rail	1	¾ × 4½ × 22	
Seat slat	4	¾ × 3½ × 23¾	
Seat rail	1	¾ × 4 × 23½	Round one edge
First seat slat	1	¾ × 4 × 23½	Optional bevel on one edge
Arm	2	¾ × 4½ × 31	
Shoulder rail	1	¾ × 3½ × 26¼	Optional bevel on one edge
Outside back splat	2	¾ × 4½ × 36½	
Middle back splat	2	¾ × 4½ × 39¾	
Center back splat	1	¾ × 3½ × 40	

BACK LEG LAYOUT

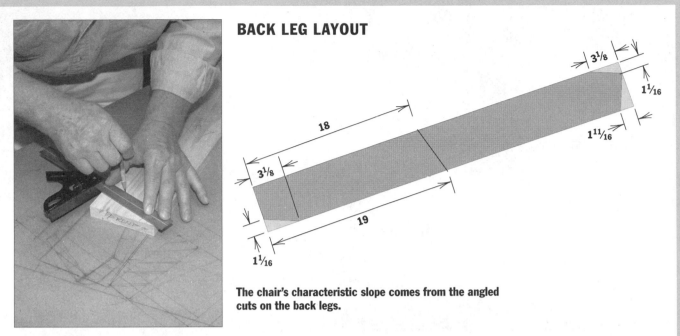

The chair's characteristic slope comes from the angled cuts on the back legs.

Lay out the back legs. Draw the angled cuts from the measurements given in the drawing. It may help you to make a full-size layout of the chair side, like the design drawing that's visible on the surface of the worktable.

each composite leg together with five 2-inch spiral deck nails.

3 Lay out the back legs. The two back legs are identical, so it's best to lay out both of them at the same time. Mark the front and back ends of the wood. Measure 19 inches from the back bottom corner and 18 inches from the back top corner. Connect these points and extend the lines all the way around the wood. These lines will locate the hip rail. Lay out the angled cuts at the back and front of the back legs, as shown in the drawing above. These cuts establish the slope of the back leg and seat.

4 Saw the back legs. Saw the angled cuts with a jigsaw or with a handsaw. With the jigsaw, be sure you are using a blade for cutting wood. With a sharp handsaw in soft pine, the weight of the saw does the work—all you do is steer. If you lean on

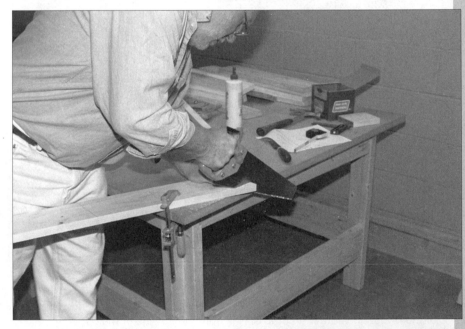

Saw the back legs. To make the angled cuts, clamp the wood to the worktable (above). Clamp both legs together in the vise to saw both at once (right).

the saw, you'll make a rough cut with a lot of splinters. Clamp the wood to the worktable, or grab it in a vise, so you can concentrate on sawing straight instead of on holding things still.

Join the back legs to the front legs. Clamp the front leg to the back leg. The top of the back leg should be 16 inches above the table, while the front leg should be square to the table and inset 1 inch from the end of the back leg (left). Glue and screw the front leg to the back leg (above).

Nail the hip rail. Use scrap blocks to clamp the hip rail to the back leg, in front of the layout lines drawn in Step 3. Nail from the outside of the back leg.

6 **Nail the hip rail.** The hip rail, which is 22 inches long, is the structural center of the chair. Its length establishes the chair's overall width as well as the size of the seat and back parts. Clamp a block of scrap to the back side of the layout line you drew in Step 3. Then clamp the hip rail to the block of scrap, as shown at left. Drive three 3-inch spiral nails through the face of the back leg, into the end of the hip rail. Clamp the other leg assembly to the other end of the hip rail, and drive three more nails.

5 **Join the back legs to the front legs.** Set the parts in position on the worktable, as shown in the top photo, with the top of the back leg 16 inches up the front leg assembly. The front leg fits an inch behind the front end of the back leg. Draw layout lines on both parts. Roll glue onto the faces of the back legs, inside these layout lines. Clamp the parts together, drill pilot holes and screw through the back leg into the front leg. Drive 2-inch screws into the front leg brace and 1¼-inch screws into the leg itself. Be sure you end up with a right side and a left side—the two should mirror one another.

7 **Add the seat rail.** The seat rail spans the front of the chair, underneath the front edge of the seat. It's nailed into the ends of the back legs with 3-inch spiral nails. These nails are close to the end of the rail, so drill pilot holes to prevent splitting. To keep the chair from skidding around while you nail, clamp a stop board to the worktable, as shown in the photo at the top of the next page.

8 Shape the seat slats. The first seat slat, which is level, has a rounded front edge so it doesn't cut into your legs. Shape it with a ⅜-inch round-over cutter in the router, or rasp it with a Surform. The next slat makes the transition from level to the slope beneath your thighs. As an option, you can bevel its front edge. This narrows the gap toward the first slat. You can saw the bevel at 20 degrees on the table saw, or you can rasp it to a line ¼-inch off one edge of the wood.

9 Nail the seat. The first seat slat sits flat on top of the seat rail, with its front edge over-hanging by about 1/16 inch. Spread glue on the top edge of the seat rail. Nail the first seat slat to the back leg and to the seat rail, using the 2-inch spiral deck nails. Glue and nail the next slat with its beveled edge toward the front slat, leaving a small gap between the two slats. Now clamp a piece of scrap to the hip rail in the position the back splats will occupy, to act as a stop and to reserve the thickness of the splats. Fit a seat slat tight against the scrap and nail it in place. Arrange the remaining two seat slats in the space that's left, and nail them down.

10 Shape the arms. The arms have round ends and taper toward the back. Clamp the arms together face to face to lay out the taper shown in the drawing. Saw the taper with the jigsaw. Choose a suitable template to lay out the rounded end, such as a coffee can or a soda cup, as shown in the photo above right. Saw the curve with

Add the seat rail. The seat rail stabilizes the chair frame. The stop board at the far edge of the worktable keeps the assembly from skidding around while you drill pilot holes and nail the rail in place.

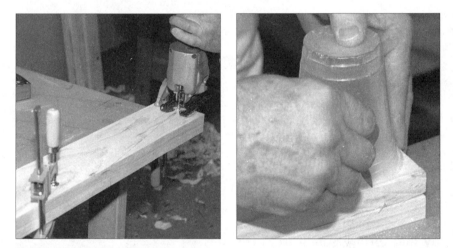

Shape the arms. Clamp the arms to the worktable and saw the taper with the jigsaw. The taper is 12 inches long and half as wide as the arm blank (above left). Draw the arm radius around a suitable cup or can (above right).

ARM LAYOUT

The shoulder rail supports the arm slats. Its beveled edge makes a neat fit with the back splats, but the bevel isn't structurally necessary.

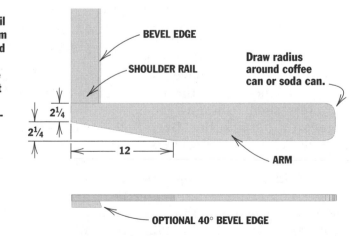

BEVEL EDGE

SHOULDER RAIL

Draw radius around coffee can or soda can.

2¼

2¼

12

ARM

OPTIONAL 40° BEVEL EDGE

Connect the arms. Clamp the arms face down on the worktable, position the shoulder rail and screw the assembly together.

Fit the arms. Support the arm assembly with two 20-inch scrap props. To position the arms back to front, clamp back splats to the bottom rail and bring the shoulder rail up to them (above). When you like the position of the arms, drive 3-inch spiral nails down into the front legs (below).

the jigsaw, starting from the end and cutting toward the side. Sand or rasp the wood smooth.

11 Connect the arms. The shoulder rail connects the chair arms and supports the back splats. It will make a neat fit if you bevel one edge at 40 degrees, which you can lay out by measuring ½ inch from the corner of the wood. You can saw this bevel on the table saw, you can saw it with the jigsaw, you can plane it or you can omit it, because it is not structural. Clamp one arm face down on the worktable. Set the shoulder rail on it, with the bevel down and facing toward the front, as shown in the photo above left. Drive a 1¼-inch screw through the intersection, then square the pieces to one another. Drive three more screws. Repeat these steps to join the other arm to the shoulder rail, making a U-shape. The distance between the arms equals the hip rail, or 22 inches, and a bit wider is OK.

12 Fit the arms. Make two 20-inch props out of scrap to hold the chair arms in position while you nail them to the legs. Clamp the props to the back legs just behind the hip rail. Clamp two back splats to the hip rail. Set the arm subassembly in position and bring it forward until the two back splats rest against the edge of the shoulder rail. Center the arm assembly from side to side. When it looks exactly right, drive three 3-inch spiral nails down through the top of each arm and into the front legs.

13 Compose the back. You can make the back splats any shape you like. Lay the five boards together on the worktable. Draw the shape you want on the center board and the two boards on one side of it. Then clamp the boards together in matching pairs in order to cut the shapes with the jigsaw, the same way you made the arms.

14 Attach the back. Turn the chair upside down on the worktable. Slide one of the outside back splats into position. Spread glue and screw it to the hip rail, from underneath the seat. Use three 1¼-inch screws. Attach the other outside back splat in the same way. Next, draw a centerline on the shoulder rail in order to center the center splat. Finally, clamp the two middle splats in place and center them in their spaces. Screw them to the hip rail.

15 Anchor the back. You need some support before you can anchor the back splats, so re-clamp the two props in position under the chair's arms. Drive two 3-inch spiral nails through each back leg into the edges of the outside back splats. Tuck a straightedge up under the chair arms and draw a layout line across the back. Drive two of the 2-inch spiral nails through each splat into the shoulder rail. Drive the nails ⅜ inch below the layout line, horizontal to the chair back. They should go straight into the edge of the shoulder rail. Now you can have a test sit.

Compose the back. Lay the five back boards together on the worktable, and draw the back shape. It can be any shape you like.

Attach the back. Turn the chair upside down in order to attach the back splats. Glue and screw them to the inside face of the hip rail (left).

Anchor the back. Draw a layout line and nail through the back splats into the shoulder rail. Drive the nails horizontally (below).

ADIRONDACK OTTOMAN
The essential accessory for every mountain lodge

Every Adirondack chair needs a companion footstool. It transforms the rustic seat into a veritable Barcalounger. Just add a crystalline mountain lake plus a dollop of mosquito repellent, and you're on vacation.

BUILDING THE OTTOMAN

1 Cut the parts. The ottoman comes out of the same standard 1×4s and 1×5s as the Adiron-

Join the legs and rails. Glue and screw a long leg and a short leg to each long rail, making a pair of U-shapes.

dack chair on page 134. Cross-cut all the parts to length.

2 Make the long rails. Lay out the 1×5 long rails, as shown in the drawing at right. Saw the angles with the handsaw, on the chopsaw or table saw, or with the jigsaw. The ottoman is rustic, and precision is not critical.

3 Join the legs and rails. Glue and screw a long leg and a short leg to each long rail, making a pair of U-shapes, one right-handed and the other left-handed. Use four of the 1¼-inch screws per intersection.

4 Join the hip rail. The hip rail connects the short legs. It fits against the inside edge of the short legs and butts against the long rails. Glue and nail the hip rail in place. Nail through the hip rail into the edge of the leg, and also nail through the long rail into the hip rail. Use 2-inch galvanized spiral nails.

5 Nail the first slat. The first slat rests on the long legs and on the flat at the top of the long rail, as shown in the drawing. Drive a pair of 3-inch spiral nails through the slat and into the end grain of each long leg.

6 Nail the front rail. Round-over the front edge of the front rail by sanding, rasping or routing. Nail the front rail onto the long legs of the ottoman with 2-inch spiral nails. The front rail should come up flush with the top surface of the first slat, and it should cover the ends of the long rails.

7 Nail the slats. Sand the sharp corners off the remaining slats and nail them to the long rails. Leave a gap of ¹⁄₁₆ inch to ⅛ inch from one slat to the next. Drive three 2-inch spiral nails through each end of each slat. Round-over the overhanging edge of the last slat.

8 Finish the ottoman. Paint the ottoman to match your Adirondack chair. Want two ottomans? It's quick and easy to make another. And another.

ADIRONDACK OTTOMAN

Glue and screw the legs to the long rail, add the hip rail and front rail, then nail the seat to this understructure.

LONG RAIL

Lay out and saw the angles. Make two long rails.

YOUR INVESTMENT
Time: One evening
Money: $14

SHOPPING LIST
20 feet 1×4 pine
4 feet 1×5 pine
2-inch and 3-inch galvanized spiral deck nails
#6 × 1¼-inch galvanized screws

PROJECT SPECS
The ottoman is 15 inches high, 18 inches front to back, and 21 inches wide.

CUTTING LIST

PART	QTY.	DIMENSIONS	NOTES
Long leg	2	¾ × 3½ × 13½	
Short leg	2	¾ × 3½ × 11	
Long rail	2	¾ × 4½ × 18	
Hip rail	1	¾ × 3½ × 19½	
Front rail	1	¾ × 3½ × 21	Round-over one edge
Slat	5	¾ × 3½ × 21	Sand sharp edges

LAWN TABLE

Handy enough for dinner or drinks, it's nice enough to take inside

When you entertain out-doors, you need little tables for drinks, snacks and buffet meals. This little table is good-looking, sturdy and versatile. It's attractive enough to come indoors for the winter.

The table has been designed to fit alongside a chair, or in front of it. It's light and easy to move. There are no tricky cuts or difficult gluing maneuvers, so it's quick to make. You can make two or three in hardly more time than the first one takes.

If you do get into making multiple tables, you'll be able to tighten up on the shopping list. The table looks best when it's made of clear wood, so the shopping list has been inflated by a full 20%, to allow you to work around knots. If you can find clear wood, you can reduce the quantities accordingly.

The shelf is a nice detail and it does help the table structurally, but it would be strong enough without it, so you can leave it off if you like. In that case, put the lower four leg blocks at the very bottom of the legs. They'll look better.

LAWN TABLE

Join pairs of leg pieces with blocks, add the caps, then connect the leg assemblies with the short and long rails. Make the shelf, then nail the table top to the rails.

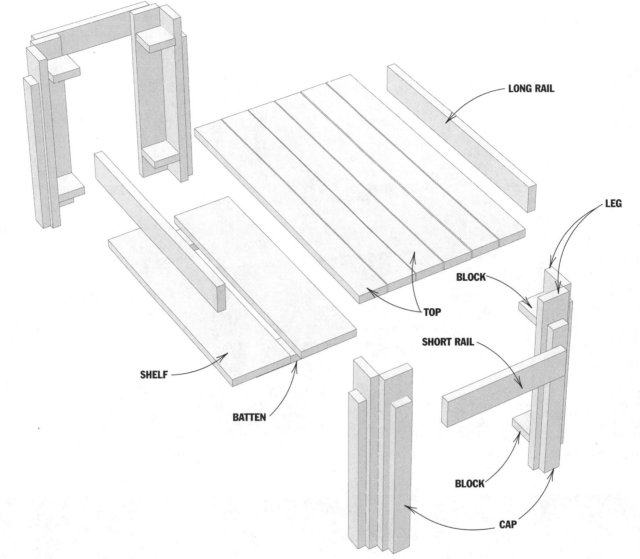

LONG RAIL

LEG

BLOCK

TOP

SHORT RAIL

SHELF

BATTEN

BLOCK

CAP

YOUR INVESTMENT
Time: One evening
Money: $18

SHOPPING LIST
12 feet 1×2 pine
40 feet 1×3 pine
6 feet 1×6 pine
#6 × 1¼-inch galvanized screws
2-inch galvanized siding nails

PROJECT SPECS
The lawn table is 26 inches long, 16 inches wide, and 18¼ inches high.

CUTTING LIST

PART	QTY.	DIMENSIONS	NOTES
Leg	8	$\frac{3}{4} \times 2\frac{1}{2} \times 17\frac{1}{2}$	1×3
Cap	8	$\frac{3}{4} \times 1\frac{1}{2} \times 15$	1×2
Block	8	$\frac{3}{4} \times 2\frac{1}{2} \times 2\frac{1}{2}$	1×3
Short rail	2	$\frac{3}{4} \times 2\frac{1}{2} \times 11$	1×3
Long rail	2	$\frac{3}{4} \times 2\frac{1}{2} \times 21$	1×3
Shelf	2	$\frac{3}{4} \times 5\frac{1}{2} \times 22$	1×6
Batten	2	$\frac{3}{4} \times 2\frac{1}{2} \times 7$	1×3
Top	6	$\frac{3}{4} \times 2\frac{1}{2} \times 26$	1×3

BUILDING THE TABLE

1 Cut all the wood. All the saw cuts are made at right angles, but two of the lengths are critical. They are the lengths of the eight cap pieces and of the twelve little blocks, which both depend on the width of your 1×3 pine. The length of the cap, plus the width of the 1×3 rails, has to equal the length of the leg. The length of the block equals the width of the 1×3.

2 Block the legs. Two leg pieces joined corner to corner make up each right-angle leg. They're held together by a pair of blocks inside each leg. Begin by gluing and screwing two blocks to the inside face of four of the leg pieces. In the next step, you'll add the other leg piece. The blocks fit their own length in from either end of the leg pieces. Roll glue on the edge of a block, position it as shown in the photo at left, and drill a clearance hole through the face of the leg. Then drive a single 2-inch screw through the leg and into the block. Join the other blocks and legs in the same way.

3 Add the second leg pieces. To complete a right-angle leg, roll glue onto the edge of both blocks and position the second leg piece. Drill a clearance hole through the face of the leg piece into each block and drive the 2-inch screws, as shown in the photo at below. Complete the other three legs in the same way.

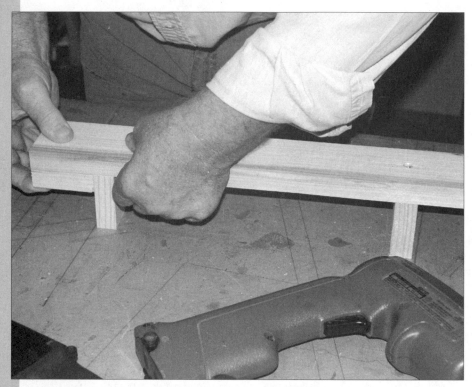

Block the legs. Gauge the block placement with another block. Glue and screw two blocks to each of four leg pieces.

Add the second leg pieces. Roll glue onto the edge of the blocks, but not on the leg piece (above). Screw the second leg piece to the blocks (right).

Cap the legs. Set a combination square to ½ inch to center the caps on the legs. The offset at the left end of the leg in the photo is for a rail (above). Glue the caps to the legs, then drive screws from the inside (right).

4 Cap the legs. The caps fit on the outside of the leg pieces. They support the rails, and cover the screw heads. The caps fit flush with one end of the legs, leaving space for the rails at the other end. The caps are an inch narrower than the legs, so you can center them with a combination square set to ½ inch, as shown in the photo above. Roll glue on the face of the cap, position it on the leg, and clamp it in place. Then fasten it with three of the 1¼-inch screws, driven from inside the leg. Because of the clamp, you can get away without clearance holes. Cap both faces of all four leg assemblies in the same way.

5 Join the short rails. The short rails connect the leg assemblies in pairs, forming the ends of the table. The short rails fit tight on top of the caps, aligned with the caps' outside edges. Hold the first short rail and leg together and draw a layout line. Spread glue, then clamp the short rail in place, as shown

Join the short rails. Glue and clamp a short rail to the leg and screw the parts together (above). Add the second leg to the free end of the rail and tap the parts into line (right).

in the photo above. Drill clearance holes to prevent the wood from splitting, and drive three of the 1¼-inch screws into the short rail through the back of the leg. Join the second leg assembly to the other end of the short rail. Make the other end of the table in the same way.

Join the end assemblies. Glue, clamp, and screw the long rails between the end assemblies.

Make the shelf. Use blocks of scrap to center the battens on the shelf boards, and to maintain a uniform space between them.

6 Join the end assemblies. Now you have two table ends. Complete the table base by connecting the ends with the long rails. Screw the long rails to the legs in the same way as you joined the short rails in the previous step, as shown in the photo above.

7 Make the shelf. Make and install the shelf before you make the table top. The two battens connect the two shelf boards. Use scraps of wood to position the battens on the underside of the shelf, as shown in the photo at top right. A ¾-inch space separates the two shelf boards, with the battens centered from side to side and inset ¾ inch at the ends. Fasten the battens to the top boards with 1¼-inch screws.

8 Install the shelf. Drop the shelf onto the bottom blocks inside the legs. Clamp the shelf to the blocks and drive a 1¼-inch screw through each block into the shelf.

9 Center the table top. The six top boards overhang the base by ¼ inch all around. Mark the center of the short rails, and

Complete the table top. Then attach the edge boards, and fill in the spaces in between.

begin installing the top at the center. Place a board on either side of the center marks, with a gap of about ⅛ inch. Set a combination square to ¼ inch to equalize the overhang at either end. Attach the two center boards with two 2½-inch siding nails at each end.

10 Complete the table top. Use the combination square to align the outer boards of the top with the table base, nail them in

place, and fill in the remaining space. Space the siding nails with care, so their heads make a regular pattern.

11 Prepare the table for finishing. Wrap 100-grit sandpaper around a block of wood and knock the sharp corners off the table. Go over all of its edges, but don't sand so much that you destroy the crispness of the design. Sanding brings any inaccuracies into line.

TABLE STAKE

Quick project uses up scrap, dresses up garden parties

You're planning a garden party and how can people have a good time when they must juggle drinks along with plates of chicken wings?

These little stake tables can do the trick.

Each stake makes a little table at whatever height you want. They're made entirely out of scrap, so they couldn't be simpler or quicker to make. You can keep them for next time, or toss them away and make more.

The basic stake is a pine 1×2, anywhere between 18 and 30 inches long. The shelf is any square piece of scrap wood. It's glued and screwed or nailed to the stake. You can leave the shelves square, or else jigsaw them into circles or ovals.

MAKING THE STAKES

1 Gather the scrap wood. You'll probably have to saw some of it out of larger offcuts. Saw squares for the shelves.

2 Sharpen the stakes. Use the jigsaw to whittle a point on the stakes. Draw the point freehand, about a hand-span long. Saw the two sides of the stake, then saw one face of it.

3 Make the shelf. Square a line across the face of the stake, a couple of inches down from the top end. Drill two clearance holes through the stake. Smear some glue on it. Drive the screws through the stake into the edge of the shelf, pulling it tight.

4 Install the furniture. Once you decide where to plant the stake, tap it about six inches into the ground with your hammer.

Sharpen the stakes. Draw a layout line and jigsaw the point on the stakes. Saw toward the point

Make the shelf. Glue and screw the stake to the edge of the shelf.

DRINK STAKE

Sharpen the stake, then attach the shelf to it.

SHELF

STAKE

YOUR INVESTMENT
Time: 10 minutes
Money: 10 cents

SHOPPING LIST
#6 × 2-inch galvanized screws

CUTTING LIST

PART	QTY.	DIMENSIONS	NOTES
Stake	1	¾ × 1½ × 28	From scrap
Shelf	1	¾ × 5½ × 5½	From scrap

GLIDER SWING

Gentle loveseat rocks within its own low frame

Porch and lawn swings tend to be large and ungainly contraptions, but not this little jewel. It's a simple bench slung from a low frame. It doesn't swing a long way, but the motion is soft and gentle—just about perfect for watching meteor showers on a starry August evening.

Even though the action is gentle, a glider swing puts a great deal of stress on its framework, so strong joints are important. The basic joints in this glider's frame are made with

#8 × 3-inch galvanized screws, driven into the second piece of wood through clearance holes in the first piece of wood. The difference between a clearance hole and a pilot hole is, the clearance hole is big enough to clear the full diameter of the screw's threads, whereas the pilot hole is only as big as the central shaft of the screw. A clearance hole allows the screw to pull the second piece of wood tight to the first. For #8 screws, drill $3/32$-inch pilot holes, but $3/16$-inch clearance holes.

Even though the glider's seat and back make a comfortable angle, all the wood is sawn square. There are round-ended slots in the front seat slat and the center back slat, to make room for the arm assembly, and there's a heart-shaped cutout in the back. All these cutouts are made with a jigsaw and a drill-mounted holesaw.

The glider swing should feel soft and friendly, so the edges of the wood have been sanded smooth and some of them have been rounded over with a $3/8$-inch router cutter. This detail is cosmetic, not structural. If you don't have a router, you can sand all of the edges instead.

BUILDING THE GLIDER

1 Saw all the wood. All the parts of the glider swing come from regular 1× and 2× lumber. Cut all the parts to length before you begin to assemble the project. Try to avoid knots that have a black ring of bark, because they're liable to loosen and fall out.

2 Join the legs to the bottom cross rails. The ends of the swing have to be stable, sturdy frames because they must support the seat and also withstand the variable stresses of gliding. They're made out of 2×4s, held together with 3-inch screws, for which you must drill clearance holes. Locate the legs on the bottom cross rail as shown in the photos at top right. They're flush with the edge of the cross rail, and set in six inches from the ends. Mark where the two legs go, drill the $\frac{3}{16}$-inch clearance holes, and drive the screws. Join the second bottom cross rail to the other two legs in the same way. Leave the top cross rails aside for now, because otherwise they'll be in your way.

3 The long rails connect the end frames. The long rails, which connect the two end frames, have to withstand a lot of stress, so the screw joints must be strong, and glue will be a help here too. Set the first long rail on one of the bottom cross rails and center it with a square set to 1 inch, as shown above. Draw a line where the rail will fit,

Join the legs to the bottom cross rails. The legs sit flush with the edge of the bottom cross rail, 6 inches in from the ends. Drill three $\frac{3}{16}$-inch clearance holes for #8 screws (left). Drive the screws through the bottom cross rail and into the legs (below).

The long rails connect the end frames. Plant the long rail on the bottom cross rail and center it with a square set to 1 inch. Draw layout lines (above left). Drill $\frac{3}{16}$-inch clearance holes through the leg and bottom cross rail (above right). Screw the parts together. Stand the assembly upright on the floor to screw through the bottom cross rails (below).

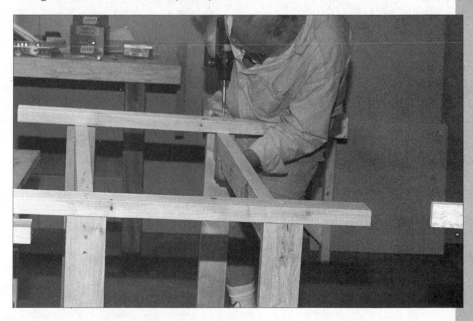

GLIDER FRAME

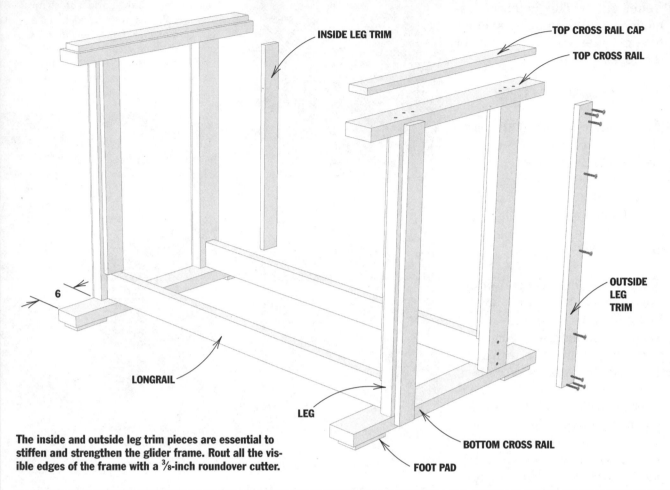

INSIDE LEG TRIM

TOP CROSS RAIL CAP

TOP CROSS RAIL

OUTSIDE LEG TRIM

6

LONGRAIL

LEG

BOTTOM CROSS RAIL

FOOT PAD

The inside and outside leg trim pieces are essential to stiffen and strengthen the glider frame. Rout all the visible edges of the frame with a $\frac{3}{8}$-inch roundover cutter.

YOUR INVESTMENT

<u>Time:</u> One weekend
<u>Money:</u> Wood, $60; hardware, $20

SHOPPING LIST

40 feet 2×4 lumber
8 feet 1×2 pine
40 feet 1×3 pine
32 feet 1×4 pine
4 feet 1×5 pine
24 feet 1×6 pine
#8 × 3-inch galvanized screws
#6 × 1¼-inch galvanized screws
#6 × 1⅝-inch galvanized screws
#6 × 2-inch galvanized screws
2-inch galvanized siding nails
Eight ⁵⁄₁₆ × 3-inch ring bolts with
   nuts and washers
Four 24-inch pieces of 1-inch chain
Four spring-loaded snap links

PROJECT SPECS

The glider swing is 54 inches wide, 34 inches high, and 37 inches front to back. It needs 6 inches of swinging clearance front and back.

CUTTING LIST

PART	QTY.	DIMENSIONS	NOTES
Leg	4	$1\frac{1}{2} \times 3\frac{1}{2} \times 32$	2×4
Bottom cross rail	2	$1\frac{1}{2} \times 3\frac{1}{2} \times 33$	2×4
Long rail	2	$1\frac{1}{2} \times 3\frac{1}{2} \times 50$	2×4
Top cross rail	2	$1\frac{1}{2} \times 3\frac{1}{2} \times 30$	2×4
Outside leg trim	4	$\frac{3}{4} \times 2\frac{1}{2} \times 34$	1×3
Inside leg trim	4	$\frac{3}{4} \times 2\frac{1}{2} \times 29$	1×3, cut to fit
Top cross-rail cap	2	$\frac{3}{4} \times 2\frac{1}{2} \times 29$	Counterbore
Foot pad	4	$\frac{3}{4} \times 2\frac{1}{2} \times 5$	1×3
Seat rail	4	$\frac{3}{4} \times 3\frac{1}{2} \times 24$	1×4
Seat back	2	$\frac{3}{4} \times 3\frac{1}{2} \times 24$	1×4
Arm rail	4	$\frac{3}{4} \times 1\frac{1}{2} \times 27$	1×2
Arm support	2	$\frac{3}{4} \times 1\frac{1}{2} \times 9$	1×2
Arm cap	2	$\frac{3}{4} \times 2\frac{1}{2} \times 20$	1×3
Back slat	3	$\frac{3}{4} \times 5\frac{1}{2} \times 43$	1×6
Back filler slat	1	$\frac{3}{4} \times 3\frac{1}{2} \times 43$	1×4
Back cap	1	$\frac{3}{4} \times 4\frac{1}{2} \times 43$	1×5
Fascia	1	$\frac{3}{4} \times 3\frac{1}{2} \times 43$	1×4
Seat slat	3	$\frac{3}{4} \times 5\frac{1}{2} \times 43$	1×6
Seat filler slat	1	$\frac{3}{4} \times 3\frac{1}{2} \times 43$	1×4
Beam	2	$1\frac{1}{2} \times 3\frac{1}{2} \times 45\frac{1}{2}$	2×4

GLIDER SEAT

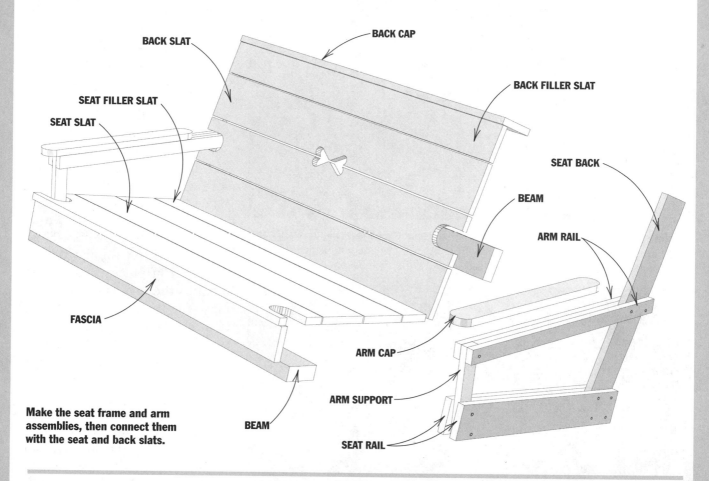

BACK SLAT

BACK CAP

BACK FILLER SLAT

SEAT FILLER SLAT

SEAT SLAT

SEAT BACK

BEAM

ARM RAIL

FASCIA

ARM CAP

ARM SUPPORT

SEAT RAIL

BEAM

Make the seat frame and arm assemblies, then connect them with the seat and back slats.

take it off, drill clearance holes, and spread glue. Then replace the long rail and drive the screws through from the outside of the legs, as well as up through the bottom of the cross rails. Connect the second long rail to the adjacent leg and cross rail, then screw both long rails to the other leg subassembly.

4 Add the top cross rails. The top cross rails complete the structure of the glider's end frames. They fit parallel to the bottom cross rails, centered from end to end: The offset should be $4\frac{1}{2}$ inches from the legs. Drill pilot holes through the top cross rails and screw them to the legs, with the 3-inch screws.

Add the top cross rails. Set a square to $4\frac{1}{2}$ inches to center the top cross rails on the legs. Drill clearance holes and screw them in place.

5 Round over all the edges. Mount a $\frac{3}{8}$-inch roundover cutter in the router, and round over all the edges you can reach, on every part of the glider frame. In some of the corners, the router

Round over all the edges. Run the router all around the edges of the frame assembly. The router shown is a small laminate trimmer.

base will bang into the parts, leaving the roundover incomplete, or stopped. A stopped bevel is a traditional detail, and the stopped roundover is today's equivalent.

Trim the legs. Saw the inside leg trim so it's a tight fit between the long rail and the top cross rail. In the left foreground you can see how the outside leg trim overlaps the top cross rail, and how the screws stiffen the assembly.

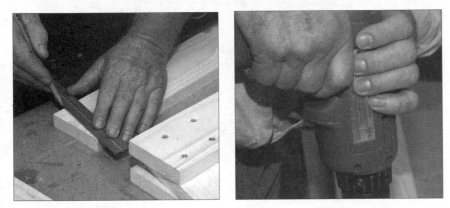

Make the seat frames. Measure ¾ inch from the corner of the seat rail and draw a line. The seat back fits on this line. Spread glue on the mating surfaces, clamp the parts to the worktable, and drill pilot holes for the screws.

DETAIL OF SEAT FRAME AND ARMS

Find the back angle by measuring ¾ inch from the back corner of the seat rail.

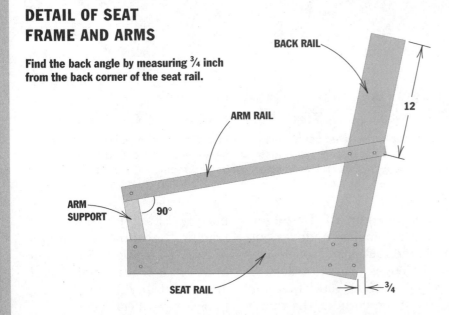

6 Trim the legs. The eight pieces of leg trim, four inside and four outside, stiffen the frame and help guarantee the joints between the legs and top cross rails. Saw the inside leg trim pieces so they're a tight fit between the long rails and top cross rails. Round the edges on one face of each piece of trim, and drill pilot holes for 1⅝-inch screws: Three holes in each inside leg trim, and nine in each outside leg trim, as shown in the drawing on page 152. Then roll glue all over the flat side of the leg trim pieces, and screw them to the legs and top cross rails. The top of the outside leg trim meets the margin of the roundover on the top cross rails, as shown in the photo at left above.

7 Make the foot pads. The four foot pads lift the glider frame above irregularities in the patio or lawn, and also above the damp. Nail them onto the bottom cross rails without any glue, so when they eventually do rot, you can replace them. This completes the structure of the glider frame.

8 Make the seat frames. Each seat frame consists of a seat back and two seat rails. All three pieces are the same size and although they're joined at an angle, they're sawn square. You find the angle by direct measurement, not with a protractor. Measure ¾ inch over from one corner of the seat rail, and draw a line to the other corner. The seat back fits on this line, as shown in the drawing and in the photo at center left. Draw layout lines where the parts fit to-

Make the arms. The arm rails sandwich the arm support, making a right angle. Glue and screw the joint together.

Join the arms to the seat frames. Fit the arm support between the seat rails and adjust the assembly so the arm rails extend ½ inch beyond the seat back. Glue and screw the parts together.

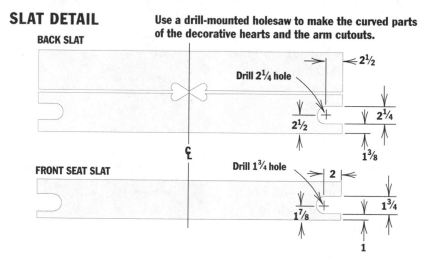

Make slots in the center back slat. Drill the round end of the slot with a 2¼-inch holesaw (left). Cut the straight part of the slot with the jigsaw (right).

gether, spread glue, and clamp the assembly to the worktable. Drill pilot holes and drive four 1¼-inch screws into the joint. Glue and screw the other seat rail to the other side of the seat back, using four 2-inch screws.

9 Make the arms. Each arm is an L-shape consisting of an arm support and two arm rails. These parts join at a right angle, as shown in the drawing at left. Spread glue on the arm support and one arm rail, and connect them with a 1¼-inch screw. Turn the assembly over to glue and screw the second arm rail in place. Make the other arm in the same way. Arm caps will complete the arms, in Step 17.

10 Join the arms to the seat frames. The arm support fits between the two seat rails, and the two arm rails fit around the seat back. The bottom of the arm rails crosses the mid-point of the seat back, that is, 12 inches down from the back's top end. Adjust the arm support until it's completely enclosed by the seat rails, with the arm rails extending about ½ inch beyond the seat back, as shown in the drawing at left. Make the two subassemblies

of arm and seat frame identical, then glue and screw the parts together. There are three thicknesses of wood, enough for the 2-inch screws.

SLAT DETAIL

Use a drill-mounted holesaw to make the curved parts of the decorative hearts and the arm cutouts.

BACK SLAT

Drill 2¼ hole

2½

2½

2¼

1⅜

℄

FRONT SEAT SLAT

Drill 1¾ hole

2

1⅞

1¾

1

11 Make slots in the center back slat. The center back slat has a slot at each end, so it will fit around the arms. As shown in the drawing above, the slot is

Cut out the hearts. Draw around the holesaw to lay out the hearts. Drill and saw the half-heart shapes, and sand their edges smooth.

Nail the back slats to the frame. Clamp one slat to the seat rails as a gauge, and measure the width at the top of the seat back to make sure the frames are parallel (above). Start by nailing the center back slat around the arm rails, then nail the other back slats in place. Bring the back cap forward about ⅛ inch, then nail it to the back filler slat and the ends of the seat backs (below).

3⅛ inches deep and 2¼ inches wide, centered on the width of the slat. Make the ends of the slots with a 2¼-inch holesaw, then saw the sides with the jigsaw. If you don't have a holesaw, you could cut the slots entirely with the jigsaw, but the curve is tight so you would have to make clearance cuts to release the waste wood in stages.

12 Cut out the hearts. The heart-shaped cutout is traditional for a love seat, but of course it is optional. The hearts shown, which are half in one back slat and half in the other, were cut with a 1½-inch holesaw and the jigsaw. Draw around the holesaw blade to lay out the hearts, making each lobe just a hair less than a complete circle. Leave about ¼ inch of untouched wood between the

points of the hearts. Drill the holes, make the straight cuts, then sand the shapes smooth and fair with 100-grit sandpaper.

13 Nail the back slats to the frame. The three back slats fit

flush with the outside faces of the seat rails and arm rails. Before you start nailing, sand the sharp corners off all of the back slats; if you sand the seat slats now too, you won't have to remember to do it later. Clamp one of the back slats to the seat rails as a gauge. Measure to make sure the seat frames are parallel. Spread glue on the seat backs, and nail the back slats in place. Use 2-inch siding nails. Once you get two slats nailed down, unclamp the gauge and nail it in place. The back filler slat fits level with the top of the seat backs. The back cap covers the ends of the seat backs and the edge of the back filler slat. Bring the cap forward $\frac{1}{8}$ inch, to create a shadow.

14 **Slot the first seat slat.** The first seat slat, which comes over the edge of the front fascia, has slots that fit around the arm supports. Lay out and saw the slots the same as the slots in the center back slat, using a $1\frac{3}{4}$-inch holesaw. The slots end $2\frac{3}{8}$ inches inside the seat slat. There's an inch of wood between the slot and the front edge of the slat, as shown in the drawing on page 153. Set one end of the first slat around the arm support, then spring the arms apart to slip the other end into place. Don't fasten it yet.

15 **Attach the fascia.** The fascia stiffens the seat and conceals the ends of the seat rails. Glue and screw the front fascia to the front ends of the seat rails. Use 2-inch screws. Now slide the first seat slat forward so it overhangs the fascia by $\frac{1}{8}$ inch, then glue and nail the first seat slat to the fascia and to the seat rails, using the 2-inch siding nails.

16 **Complete the seat.** Glue and nail the remaining two seat slats, and the seat filler slat, to

Slot the first seat slat. Drill and saw the slots in the ends of the first seat slat, then spring the frame apart so you can pop it into place.

Attach the fascia. Glue and screw the fascia to the ends of the seat rails. Then glue and nail the front seat slat to it.

Cap the arms. Draw around the holesaw to lay out the semicircular end on the arm caps. Cut it with the jigsaw.

the seat rails. Leave a gap of about $\frac{1}{2}$ inch between the seat and back slats. The gap permits rainwater and stray pocket change to drip off the seat.

17 **Cap the arms.** The arm caps make the glider arms comfort-

able and friendly. They're jigsawn round at both ends, with curves that match the cutouts in the seat and back slats. Use the large holesaw or a coffee cup as a template for drawing the round shape, cut it out with the jigsaw, and sand the edges

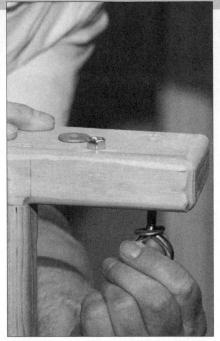

Mount the hardware. Drill $5/16$-inch holes near the ends of the top cross rails. Place a washer next to the eye and a second washer underneath the nut. Mount the ring bolts on the seat and back beams the same way.

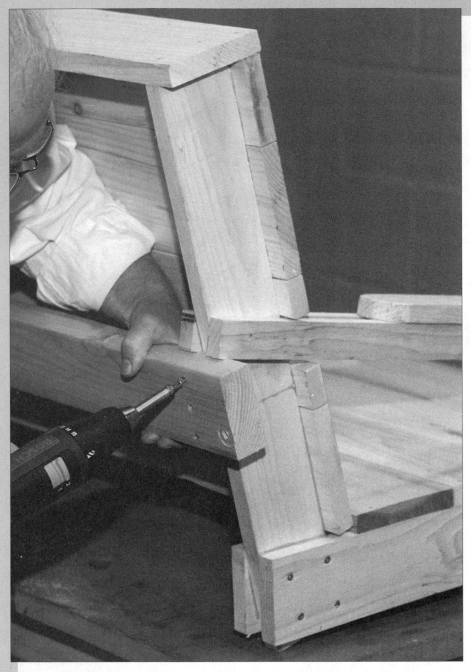

Make the beams. Screw the back beam tight under the arm rails. The large hole near the bottom end of the beam is for the ring bolt and chain.

smooth. Then nail the arm caps onto the arm supports with the siding nails.

18 Make the beams. The seat beam and back beam are identical. Screw the seat beam to the seat rails under the front edge of the glider seat, and the back beam to the seat back just below the arm rails. Drill clear-

ance holes and use three of the 3-inch screws at each end of each beam.

19 Mount the hardware. The glider seat hangs from four short chains, which in turn are suspended from four eye bolts drilled through the top cross rails of the frame. Drill $5/16$-inch holes for the eye bolts and

install them with a wrench. Use two washers, one next to the eye and the second under the nut. Mount the other four eye bolts in the ends of the seat beams, close to the ends of the beams. The eye bolt in the back seat beam points toward the front of the seat.

20 Counterbore the top cross rail caps. The caps on the top cross rails both conceal the ring bolts and complete the look of the glider frame. Round over the top corners of the caps, and counterbore two 1-inch holes to fit over the ring bolts and nuts. To locate the counterbores, set the cap in place on the top cross rail and tap it onto the ends of the ring bolts. The resulting indentations show you where to drill. The diameter of the counterbore doesn't matter, so long

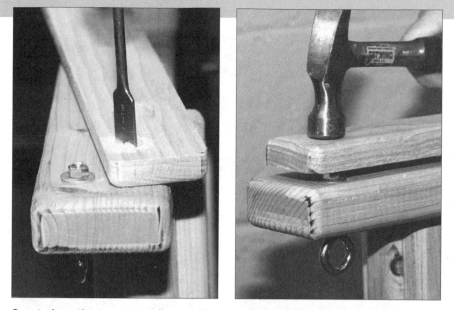

Counterbore the top cross-rail caps. The counterbores allow the rail caps to fit down flat over the eye bolts. To locate the counterbores, tap the cap onto the eye bolts.

Hang the swing. Spring-loaded snap links connect the 1-inch chain to the eye bolts. These snap links are standard hardware items (above). Maneuver the glider seat into the frame, then block it up so the arms are level. Snap the chains onto the eye bolts (below).

as it is larger than ¾ inch. If you can, use a Forstner bit or a spade bit with a short point, so the pilot doesn't come through the top side. Otherwise, there'll be a small hole on the top. Screw the caps onto the top cross rails, without glue. This way, if you ever want to get at the ring bolts, you'll be able to pop the cap.

21 **Hang the swing.** Spring-loaded snap links allow you to connect the suspension chains to the ring bolts. Snap a link onto each ring bolt, then hang the four lengths of chain from the glider frame. Lift the seat into position in the frame and block it up high enough to allow you to connect the chains. Now you can adjust the length of each chain link by link, until the swing hangs the way you want it. The best position is with the arms level, but the height is up to you. Make sure that any extra links of chain don't interfere with the suspension. If just one piece of chain doesn't hang perfectly straight, the glider won't glide.

22 **Finish the swing.** The glider swing shown has a painted frame, with an oiled seat. The oil resists water and brings out the wood colors.

PLANT POST

A skyhook for baskets of flowers

Hanging baskets of impatiens, fuschias or begonias are delightful, but what if there's nowhere to hook them? This plant post is a freestanding column you can nail to your deck or stake in the garden. It has eight hooks from which to hang your favorite flowering plants.

The post's construction creates interesting patterns of shadows that change as the sun moves. The base and top construction looks like intricate wooden joints, but it's just simple pieces of wood glued and nailed together. The key is always to bridge two short pieces of wood with a long piece.

We built our post out of 1-inch rough-sawn pine lumber. You can substitute regular 1× (¾-inch) pine, or 5/4 pine, if you prefer, as long as all your wood is the same thickness.

BUILDING THE POST

1 Cut all the parts. Rough-sawn 1×6 pine measures close to 6 inches wide, but 1×6 pine from the home center, which has been planed smooth, measures about 5½ inches wide. Rough or smooth, by carefully sawing lengthwise, you can get a wide flat piece and a narrow

PLANT POST

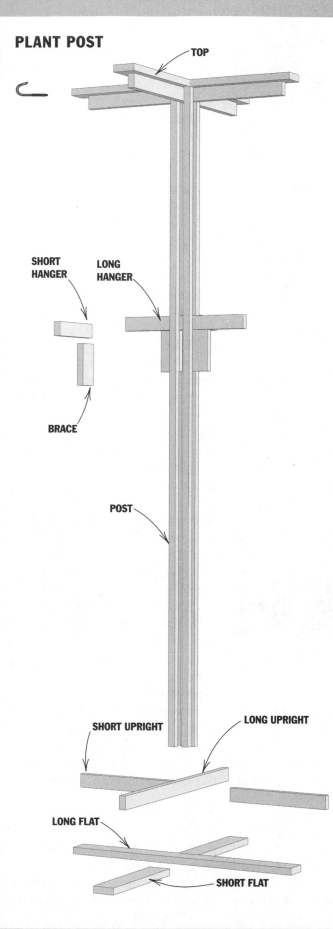

TOP

SHORT HANGER

LONG HANGER

BRACE

POST

SHORT UPRIGHT

LONG UPRIGHT

LONG FLAT

SHORT FLAT

The plant post's cross-shaped top and base are identical. The long flat piece crosses the long upright piece, with the short pieces nailed and glued to this cross.

DETAIL OF BASE AND TOP

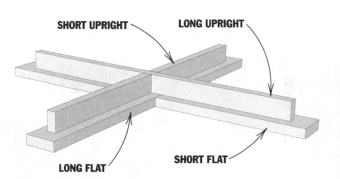

SHORT UPRIGHT

LONG UPRIGHT

LONG FLAT

SHORT FLAT

YOUR INVESTMENT

<u>Time:</u> One afternoon or evening
<u>Money:</u> $15

SHOPPING LIST

24 feet 1×6 rough-sawn pine
2½-inch galvanized spiral nails
3-inch galvanized spiral nails
Eight #6 × 3-inch steel hooks

PROJECT SPECS

The plant post stands 8 feet high and its base is a 36-inch cross.

CUTTING LIST

PART	QTY.	DIMENSIONS
Post	4	$1 \times 1 \times 96$
Long flat	2	$1 \times 3\frac{3}{16} \times 36$
Long upright	2	$1 \times 2 \times 32$
Short flat	4	$1 \times 3\frac{3}{16} \times 16\frac{1}{2}$
Short upright	4	$1 \times 2 \times 15\frac{1}{2}$
Long hanger	1	$1 \times 2 \times 19\frac{1}{2}$
Short hanger	2	$1 \times 2 \times 9\frac{1}{16}$
Brace	4	$1 \times 3 \times 6$

Make half the base. Glue, clamp and nail the first short upright piece to the long flat piece. The short piece is inset $1\frac{7}{8}$ inches from the end (above). Reserve a space the thickness of a piece of scrap, and join the other short upright to the base assembly (right).

Complete the base. Glue and nail the long upright into the gap, then join the short flat pieces to the base. Spread the glue with a small paint roller.

upright piece from each length of 1×6 material. The four vertical posts are also sawn out of one 8-foot length of 1×6 lumber. This way they'll all come out exactly the same length.

2 Make half the base. The joints in the cross-shaped base are created by the way you assemble the parts, not by cutting notches or slots. Spread

glue on the edge of one short upright piece, and position it on a long flat piece. Center the upright piece from side to side, but set it $1\frac{7}{8}$ inches back from the end of the flat piece. Clamp the two pieces together, then nail through the long flat into the short upright. Use $2\frac{1}{2}$-inch nails. Glue and nail the second short upright piece to the long flat in the same way, but insert a

scrap spacer to create a gap the precise thickness of the wood, as shown in the top right photo.

3 Complete the base. Fit the long upright into the gap you created with the piece of scrap. It should be a tight fit. Center it and check it for square, and twist it into line if necessary, then lock it in place with a pair of $2\frac{1}{2}$-inch nails through the bottom of the long flat piece. Now glue and nail the two short flat pieces onto the assembly. This completes the base.

4 Make the top. The top of the plant post is the same as the base. Glue and nail two long pieces and four short ones together in exactly the same way. Now examine the two cross-shaped assemblies. If one has a flatter bottom side than the other, declare it the base.

5 Join the base and posts. Lay two of the posts across the worktable and plug the base assembly onto them. See where glue should go, and spread the glue. Hold the parts together with spacer blocks and clamps, and check for square as shown in the top left photo on the facing page. Drill a pilot hole and drive a 3-inch spiral nail through the base into the end grain of each post. Nail the posts to the base's upright pieces. Nail the other two vertical posts to the base assembly in the same way.

6 Join the top to the posts. The top assembly plugs directly onto the four posts. Put the parts together dry to see where to spread glue, then take them apart in order to spread it.

Clamp up, check for square, and nail as in Step 5.

7 Nail the long hanger. The hangers and braces fit into the slots between the posts. Slide the long hanger down to 32 inches from the top and center it from side to side. Nail it to one post, then check for square before nailing it to the other. Glue and nail two braces between the posts, tight under the long hanger.

8 Nail the short hangers. The two short hangers and the two remaining braces fill the remaining spaces between the posts. Spread glue on the braces and hangers before you tap them into place, then nail them tight.

9 Add hooks and plants. Drill $\frac{3}{16}$-inch pilot holes for the hooks in the ends of the top flat pieces and hanger pieces. Twist the #6 hooks into the wood. Now add plants. To keep the post from blowing over, nail the base to the deck, but leave the nailheads sticking up so it's easy to move.

Join base and posts. Clamp two posts to the worktable, then clamp the base assembly to them. Check for square (above). Nail the base to the posts (top right). Blocks of scrap help clamp the second pair of posts to the base. Drill pilot holes and nail through the flat base pieces into the ends of the posts (right).

Nail the short hangers. Fit the last two braces between the posts, then add the short hangers. Nail them to the posts.

SANDBOX

A colorful awning shades the tots from the sun

Small children love a sandbox, and so do mothers of small children. This sandbox has a simple awning, made from a checkered tablecloth, to shelter the tots from the summer sun.

The sandbox is a sturdy, forgiving construction, which you can tailor to suit yourself. The one shown has 5-foot sides, which is large enough for a bunch of kids. It will contain one-third of a cubic yard of sand, or nine 85-pound sacks.

To make the sandbox, you need to be able to crosscut and also to saw a 45° miter. The box in the photos is made from rough-sawn 1×6 pine lumber. You could make it out of construction 2×6 lumber, smooth-planed 1×6 pine lumber, or regular 5/4 × 6 pine. Use the material that is easiest and cheapest for you to obtain.

To install the sandbox, choose a level spot and dig out the turf to suppress weeds. If you want to add a weed barrier, use landscaping plastic, which won't retain water.

The awning has brass eyelets in the corners so it can be tied to nails in the ends of the awning poles. This makes the awning easy to string up and take down. Fabric shops and home centers sell kits for installing metal eyelets in cloth.

SANDBOX

Screw the sides and pole braces together, then join the construction by adding the corner seats.

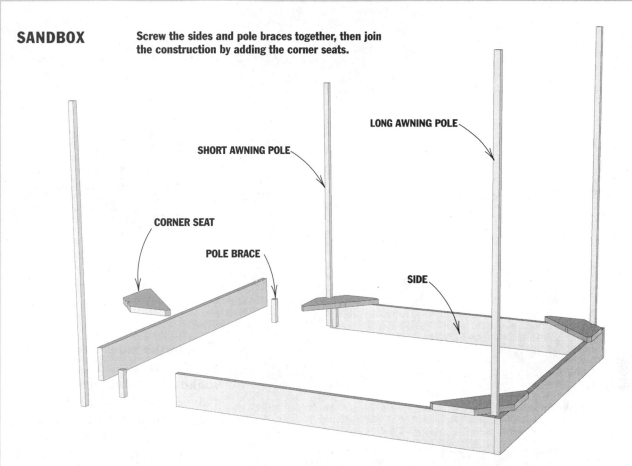

LONG AWNING POLE

SHORT AWNING POLE

CORNER SEAT

POLE BRACE

SIDE

SANDBOX CORNER SEATS

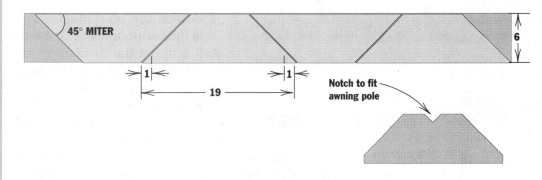

45° MITER

1

19

1

6

Notch to fit awning pole

Saw the corner seats by mitering a 6-foot plank of wood. Cut off the corners and make the notch with a handsaw.

YOUR INVESTMENT

<u>Time:</u> Sunday afternoon
<u>Money:</u> Wood, $20; Tablecloth, $10; Eyelet kit, $7

SHOPPING LIST

48 feet 1×6 rough-sawn pine
#6 × 1⅝-inch galvanized screws
#8 × 2½-inch galvanized screws
#8 × 3-inch galvanized screws
Cotton tablecloth
⅜-inch brass eyelet kit

PROJECT SPECS

The finished sandbox is a 62-inch square, 6 inches deep.

CUTTING LIST

PART	QTY.	DIMENSIONS	NOTES
Side	4	1 × 6 × 60	
Corner seat	4	1 × 7 × 19	Mitered 45°
Pole brace	8	1 × 1 × 5	
Long awning pole	2	1 × 1 × 64	
Short awning pole	2	1 × 1 × 52	

Saw all the parts. Draw around a piece of scrap to lay out the awning-pole notch in the corner seat (left). Saw the notches with a handsaw. Precision is not important (above).

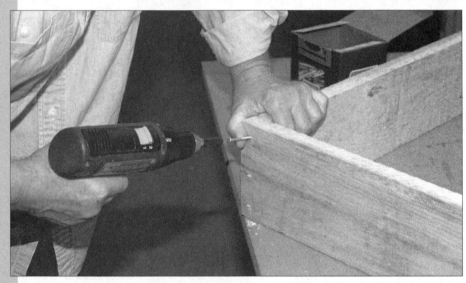

Join the sides in pairs. Drill clearance holes and drive 3-inch screws through the face of one side, into the end grain of the other.

Attach the pole braces. Screw the pole braces into the two completed corners of the box. Space them with a scrap of awning pole material.

BUILDING THE SANDBOX

1 Saw all the parts. Make all four sides the same length. We made the four awning poles by sawing a 6-foot plank of 1×6 lumber lengthwise, but you can purchase regular 2×2s instead. Lay out the four corner seats on a 5-foot board, as shown in the drawing on page 165, miter them at 45 degrees, and saw off the corners. Draw the pole notches around a pole scrap, and saw them out with a hand-saw. The precise depth of the notch is not critical.

2 Join the sides in pairs. The sandbox is big and awkward, so make it in two manageable halves. You'll join the halves in Step 6. Drill $\frac{3}{16}$-inch clearance holes for three 3-inch screws. Screw each pair of sides together.

3 Attach the pole braces. The pole braces permit you to insert and remove the awning poles. It's easiest to install the pole braces before the corner seats. Hold a scrap of the pole material in the corner of the sandbox and screw a pole brace to each side of it, allowing just a small amount of clearance. Use glue with the $1\frac{5}{8}$-inch screws.

4 Round-over the seats. The corner seats anchor the awning, and also make the sandbox friendly to the kids. But there can't be any sharp corners, so rout around the wood with a $\frac{3}{8}$-inch roundover cutter, or else round the corners with a wood rasp or Surform plane. Round the top edges of the box sides, too, and sand any roughness.

5 **Attach the seat.** Screwing the corner seats to the sandbox sides makes the sandbox strong. Insert the scrap of pole material in the corner of the sandbox, and fit the seat notch against it. Drill pilot holes for three 2½-inch screws down into each sandbox side. You'll end up with two complete box corners.

6 **Join the half-boxes.** While you could squat on the floor to join the two halves of the sandbox, it's easier to work at bench height. Balance one half of the sandbox on your worktable and clamp three scrap props to it. The props make it into a free-standing piece, as shown at right. Now lift the other half of the box onto the worktable and bring the two assemblies together. Drill clearance holes and join the two halves with the 3-inch screws, three in each joint. Add pole braces and corner seats. This completes the sandbox itself.

7 **Put eyelets in the awning.** Four ropes connect the awning to the poles. The ropes thread through brass eyelets in the corners of the awning. The awning shown was made from a rectangular tablecloth; it can be round or square. Set the eyelets as instructed by the eyelet kit.

8 **Mount the awning.** Tie a loop of twine in each eyelet. Drive a nail in the end of each awning pole. Insert the poles in the corners of the sandbox and decide whether you prefer the two long poles on the same side or diagonally opposite one another. Tie the twine loops to the nails. Add sand and small children.

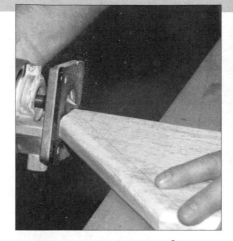

Round-over the seats. With a ⅜-inch roundover cutter in the router, remove the sharp corners and edges from the corner seats.

Attach the seat. Fit a scrap of awning pole into the sandbox corner, and fit the seat against it. Screw the seat to the sandbox sides.

Join the half boxes. Balance half of the sandbox on the worktable to clamp three props to it, then stand it to one side. Lift the other half onto the worktable and bring the two halves together. This is a good way to manage large projects.

Put eyelets in the awning. To set an eyelet, assemble it on the disk-shaped anvil, set the cylindrical tool on it, and strike it with your hammer (left). Loop twine through the eyelets (below).

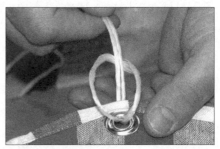

PLAY HOUSE

A castle, a ship, a fort, a place to exercise the young imagination

Little children love a play house. It can be a castle or a hideaway, a fort or a ship. They'll climb on it and inside it, they'll hide behind it and fill it with toys, and given a chance they'll keel over for a nap inside. A robust play house is both an escape from the adult-scale world and a gateway for the young imagination. In England, a substantial play house with door and window openings is called a Wendy house in homage to the Peter Pan story.

This play house has a doorway, a clerestory roof, and as many windows as you like.

There are four important design considerations: size, strength, access, and deconstruction.

The play house should be big enough to accommodate children up to the age of 8 or 9. After that, they lose interest in make-believe play. Most manufactured play houses are too small. They're fine for very young children, but the 6-year-olds and 8-year-olds find they can no longer stand up inside.

The three-piece corner system shown in this project makes a very strong connection. Two of the pieces are permanently glued and screwed to one of the plywood panels, with the third piece glued and screwed to the other panel. You lock each corner with screws but no glue, which allows you to take the joint apart and assemble it again. You could design an equivalent joint with bolts and nuts, but you would have a tough time aligning the holes when reassembling. Screws avoid this difficulty.

Adults should be able to reach inside the play house, even if they can't easily wriggle through the doorway. The adult-sized opening is the front window. Depending on the age and general rowdiness of your children, you could decide to make this opening even larger than the one shown, so you can crawl right in after the scamps. There is a second window in the back wall, and naturally you can make additional openings in the other walls of the play house.

Unless you plan to build the play house on the little deck (page 283) or on a semi-permanent foundation in the backyard, it's helpful to be able to take it apart and move it or store it. Taking it apart requires removing quite a few screws, and it will consume several hours, but it is possible to do. You may want the play house to be outside for the summer, then relocated to the family room for the winter. And ultimately, you may want to bundle it up and pass it along to another young family, sell it, or squirrel it away for your grandchildren.

BUILDING THE PLAY HOUSE

1 Start with the plywood. Home centers sell plywood cut into 48-inch squares and 24-inch by 48-inch rectangles, for virtually no price premium over full sheets. These pieces are much easier to move and manage than the four 4×8 sheets you would otherwise need. This house requires three 4×4 wall panels and nine 2×4 panels, four for the walls and five for the roof. When you get the plywood into the workshop, begin by mocking up the walls of the play house, as shown in the photo below.

Standing the wall panels in position will orient you. One of the three 4×4 panels forms the wide end, one forms the front, and one forms the wide section of the long back wall. The four 2×4 panels become the narrow end, the door panel, the return wall, and the narrow section of the back wall.

2 Saw the roof line. The slope of the roof comes from sawing triangles of plywood off the return wall and the wide end wall. In Steps 13 and 14, these triangles will be reattached to the narrow end wall and to the back of the wide end wall, creating the clerestory. Start with the 24-inch return wall. Lay out the diagonal cut by measuring 9 inches down from one corner of the sheet, as shown in the top photo on page 171. Cut the wood with the handsaw, jigsaw

Start with the plywood. Lean the plywood panels in position in a corner of the workshop to see how the play house will go together.

PLAY HOUSE

Make and trim each of the seven wall panels as a separate unit, complete with window openings, corner strips and corner angles. Fasten the walls together, then attach the ridge and rafters and assemble the roof panels.

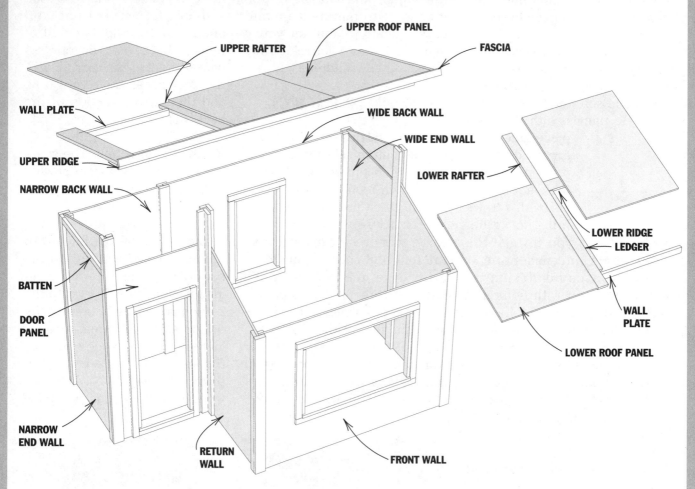

YOUR INVESTMENT

<u>Time:</u> Two weekends
<u>Money:</u> $150

SHOPPING LIST

4 sheets ½ × 48 × 96 CDX plywood
144 feet 1×2 pine
64 feet 1×3 pine
16 feet 1×5 pine
#6 × 1-inch galvanized screws
#6 × 1¼-inch galvanized screws
#6 × 1⅝-inch galvanized screws
#6 × 2-inch galvanized screws
2½-inch galvanized siding nails

PROJECT SPECS

The play house measures 77 inches long and 59 inches wide at the eaves, and is 60 inches high at the ridge.

CUTTING LIST

PART	QTY.	DIMENSIONS	NOTES
Wide wall panel	3	½ × 48 × 48	CDX plywood
Narrow wall panel	4	½ × 24 × 48	CDX plywood
Narrow corner strip	4	¾ × 1½ × 40	
Narrow corner strip	4	¾ × 1½ × 48	
Narrow corner strip	4	¾ × 1½ × 57	
Wide corner strip	2	¾ × 2½ × 40	
Wide corner strip	4	¾ × 2½ × 48	
Wide corner strip	3	¾ × 2½ × 57	
Ridge pole	2	¾ × 2½ × 57	
Trim		¾ × 1½ × 72 feet	Cut to fit
Sill		¾ × 2½ × 54	Cut to fit
Batten	2	¾ × 1½ × 21	
Upper ridge	1	¾ × 2½ × 72	
Lower ridge	1	¾ × 2½ × 48	
Wall plate		¾ × 1½ × 96	Cut to fit
Upper rafter	4	¾ × 4½ × 36	
Lower rafter	1	¾ × 2½ × 42	
Ledger	2	¾ × 2½ × 22	Cut to fit
Lower roof panel	2	½ × 24 × 28¼	CDX plywood
Upper roof panel	3	½ × 24 × 36	CDX plywood
Fascia	1	¾ × 1½ × 78	Trim to fit

or portable circular saw. Now use the offcut to lay out the same cut on one side of the 48-inch panel at the other end of the play house. Finally, saw a 9-inch strip off the top edge of the front wall. The results of this trimming are shown in the photo at center right.

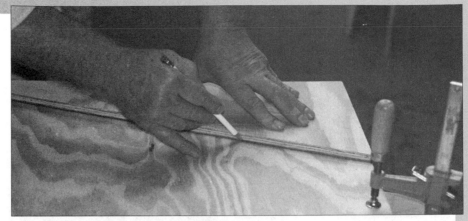

3 **Make the trim, casings and sills.** The trim, casing and sill pieces must be cut to fit the openings you decide to saw in the walls of the play house. The play house as shown has a door and two windows, plus the clerestory openings along the roof. The bill of materials includes enough material to trim and case these openings. If you make more openings, you will need more 1×2 and 1×3 lumber.

4 **Make the corner angles.** Each corner joint needs a right-angle made up of a wide corner strip and a narrow one, glued and screwed together as shown in the photo at bottom right. Roll glue on the edge of the narrow strip and plant the wide strip on it, using a scrap of the 1×2 wood for support. Drill clearance holes and join the two pieces of wood with four of the 2-inch screws. Sand the sharp edges off the wood. Make three 57-inch corner angles, two 48-inch ones, and two 40-inch ones.

5 **Make the door panel.** The door panel goes directly under the ridge of the house. It needs a 57-inch corner angle on one edge, and a 57-inch corner strip on the other edge. These pieces extend above the top of the panel and act as ridge poles to support the ridge itself. The

Saw the roof line. Measure 9 inches down from the front corner of the return wall and saw off the triangle (top). Trace the triangle onto the wide end wall and saw it off as well. Reattaching the plywood triangles to the two end walls creates the clerestory windows (above).

Make the corner angles. Each corner angle consists of a wide corner strip and a narrow one (right). Make up all the corner angles at once.

Make the door panel. Roll glue on the corner strip and fit it flush with the edge of the plywood. Drill and countersink clearance holes, then drive 1-inch screws into the corner strip.

DOOR PANEL

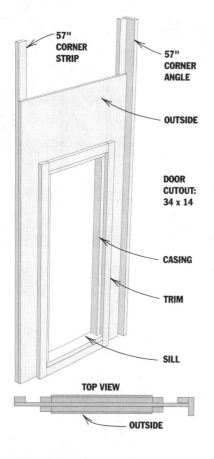

- 57" CORNER STRIP
- 57" CORNER ANGLE
- OUTSIDE
- DOOR CUTOUT: 34 x 14
- CASING
- TRIM
- SILL
- TOP VIEW
- OUTSIDE

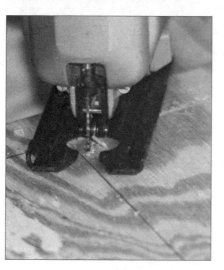

Make the door opening. Brace the toe of the jigsaw on the plywood and firmly lower the reciprocating blade into the wood (above). Saw straight into the corner (left), then back up and saw a curve around the corner (below left). Finally, square up by reversing the saw in the kerf and sawing back into the corner (below right).

panel has an inside and an outside, and therefore a right and a left edge, as shown in the drawing above. Glue and screw the corner angle and the corner strip to the door panel. The wide side of the corner angle lies on the edge of the plywood, with the 1½-inch piece flat on the face. When you see how each piece of wood goes, make a layout line, then drill and countersink clearance holes through the plywood. Roll glue on the inside of the corner angle or corner strip, fit it in place, and drive 1-inch screws to hold it, as shown in the photo at top left.

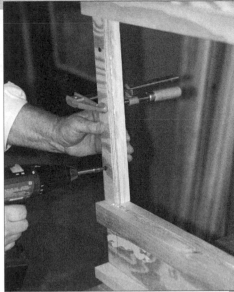

6 Make the door opening. The door opening measures 34 inches high and 14 inches wide. It's centered on the door panel, 1½ inches up from the bottom edge. Lay out and saw the door opening. You can drill a hole to start the jigsaw, or you can ease it into the cut as shown in the top photo on the facing page. To make square corners, saw straight into the corner, back up and turn the corner on a curved path, then saw back into the corner. This maneuver is shown in the bottom three photos on the facing page.

7 Trim the door opening. The door trim covers the rough edges of the plywood and also stiffens the panel. It's attached to the face of the plywood by a cut-and-fit process. Begin by trimming the long sides of the opening with pieces that extend from the bottom edge of the panel to 1½ inches beyond the opening at the top. Use scraps of the trim material to gauge the overlap, then make four identical trim pieces. Glue and screw them alongside the door open-

ing, on both sides of the plywood, using the longest screws you can fit. The top and bottom trim fits between the attached pieces of side trim, so mark and cut each of the four pieces to length, then glue and screw them in place, as shown in the photos above and at right.

8 Case the door opening. The casing fits inside the door opening, covering the edge of the plywood. It consists of a sill made of 1×3, with a header and side casings made of narrower 1×2 material, same as the trim. The casing is glued and nailed in place with the 2½-inch siding nails. Begin by measuring, cutting and attaching the sill and header, as shown at right. Then complete the opening by fitting the two side casings. Center them on the thickness of the trim pieces. This completes the door panel.

9 Make the front wall. The front of the play house is the panel that was trimmed down to 39 inches in Step 2. It's got a narrow corner strip at either side,

Trim the door opening. Glue, clamp and screw 1×2 trim flush with the edges of the opening (above left). Screw the first piece through the plywood, then screw through the second piece into the plywood (top right). Mark and saw the top trim to fit between the side trim (above).

Case the door opening. Glue and nail the casing inside the opening, covering the plywood edge.

WIDE BACK WALL

TOP VIEW

WINDOW CUTOUT: 24 x 12

48" WIDE CORNER STRIP

48" NARROW CORNER STRIP

OUTSIDE

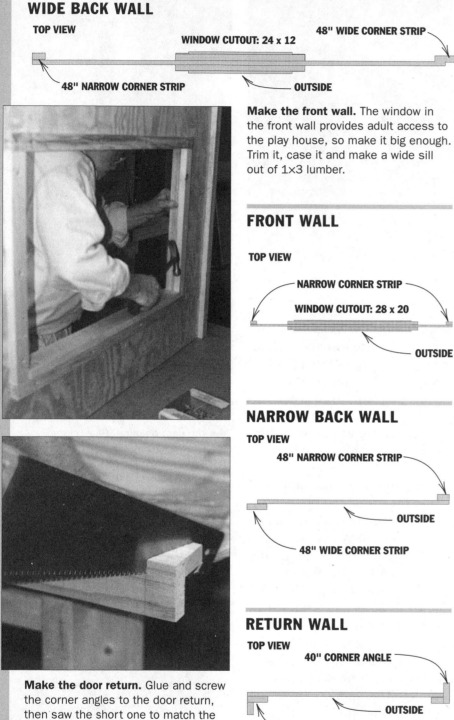

Make the door return. Glue and screw the corner angles to the door return, then saw the short one to match the slope of the roof.

Make the front wall. The window in the front wall provides adult access to the play house, so make it big enough. Trim it, case it and make a wide sill out of 1×3 lumber.

FRONT WALL

TOP VIEW

NARROW CORNER STRIP

WINDOW CUTOUT: 28 x 20

OUTSIDE

NARROW BACK WALL

TOP VIEW

48" NARROW CORNER STRIP

OUTSIDE

48" WIDE CORNER STRIP

RETURN WALL

TOP VIEW

40" CORNER ANGLE

OUTSIDE

57" CORNER ANGLE

and a centered 20-inch by 28-inch window opening. Glue and screw the corner strips to the back face of the plywood, flush with the edges of the sheet. Saw the window opening the same way you made the door opening in Step 6. Trim and case the window opening the same way you finished the door panel in Steps 7 and 8. Sand the sharp corners off the 1×3 sill.

10 **Make the wide back wall.** The wide back wall has a tall and narrow window opening, which is sawn, trimmed and cased the same as the door opening and the window in the front wall. The wide back wall has a narrow corner strip at one edge, and a wide corner strip at the other edge. The wide corner strip, which makes the connection with the narrow back wall, extends off the plywood by half its width. Glue and screw both corner strips to the inside face of the wide back wall.

11 **Make the narrow back wall.** The narrow back wall is an untrimmed piece of 24-inch × 48-inch plywood. It has a narrow corner strip glued and screwed along one long edge, with a wide corner strip along the other. The wide corner strip goes on the opposite face of the plywood from the narrow corner strip, so it can complete the connection with the wide back wall.

12 **Make the return wall.** The return wall has a 40-inch corner angle attached to its short edge, and a 57-inch corner angle attached to its long edge. Orient the corner strips as shown in the drawing at left. Then trim the 40-inch corner angle to follow the sloped edge of the plywood, as shown in the bottom left photo.

13 **Make the narrow end wall.** The narrow end wall has a 57-inch corner angle along one long edge, with a 48-inch corner angle on the other. The 57-inch corner angle becomes the ridge pole at one end the play house. The narrow end wall has to be extended by the plywood triangle sawn off the return wall in Step 2. Glue and screw the corner angles to the wall, then fit the plywood triangle, as shown in the photo at right. Attach the triangle with a 1×2 batten, glued and screwed.

14 **Make the wide end wall.** The wide end wall has two ridge posts glued and screwed to its center, one on each face of the plywood, as shown in the photo below. These 57-inch pieces of 1×3 are the same size as the wide corner strips. The wide end wall has a corner angle attached at each edge, as shown in the drawing at right. Trim the 40-inch corner angle to follow the slope sawn into the plywood. Finally, join the plywood triangle sawn from one part of the wide end wall to the other part of the same wall, as shown in the bottom right photo. Screw the plywood to a glued batten, same as in Step 13.

Make the narrow end wall. Glue and screw the two corner angles to the narrow end wall, then fit the plywood triangle atop the wall. Use a straight edge to align it with the corner angle, then attach it to the wall with a 1×2 batten.

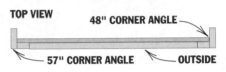

NARROW END WALL

TOP VIEW
48" CORNER ANGLE
57" CORNER ANGLE
OUTSIDE

WIDE END WALL

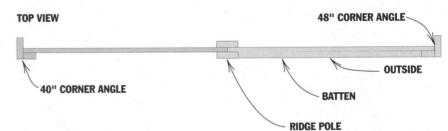

TOP VIEW
48" CORNER ANGLE
OUTSIDE
40" CORNER ANGLE
BATTEN
RIDGE POLE

Make the wide end wall. Attach two ridge poles to the center of the end wall, one on either face of the plywood (left). Slide the plywood triangle into the slot between the ridge poles, align it, and attach it with a 1×2 batten (above).

Assemble the walls. Hold the walls in place with clamps, then screw the corners together (left).

Raise the upper ridge. Clamp the upper ridge to the ridge poles and screw it in place (above).

Make the lower ridge. Fit the lower ridge against the ridge poles and screw into it through the plywood walls.

Make the wall plates. Fit the 1×2 wall plates between the corner angles on the front and back walls. Screw them to the plywood from the inside.

15 Assemble the walls. Fit the walls together as shown in the top left photo, and anchor them with screws through each corner angle. You'll probably need a helper to push each joint tight as you drive the 1¼-inch screws. If you are building the play house in your workshop, drive no more than two or three screws through each corner angle, so you can disassemble it in order to move the play house to its final location.

16 Raise the upper ridge. The upper ridge is a 6-foot 1×3 that spans the three ridge poles. Clamp it to the back side of the ridge poles, and fasten it with two or three of the 1⅝-inch screws at each intersection.

17 Make the lower ridge. The lower ridge is a 4-foot 1×3 that bridges the sloping eaves of the lower roof. Fit it in place as shown in the lower left photo, and screw into the lower ridge

through the plywood panels.

18 Make the wall plates. The wall plates stiffen the plywood walls and create attachment points for the lower roof. They are lengths of 1×2 screwed to the outside face of the front and back walls, as shown in the photo above.

19 Fit the upper rafters. There are four upper rafters, made of 1×5 wood and installed face-up instead of edge-up. Wood of this width both stiffens the roof and allows making the roof of 24-inch plywood panels. The upper rafters are 36 inches long, with a 5-inch overhang at either end, as shown in the bottom photo at right. Attach each rafter to the wall plate and the ridge with two 2-inch screws at each joint.

20 **Make the lower rafter and ledgers.** The lower rafter is 42 inches long. Its top end touches the upper rafter, as shown in the photo at top right. Screw it to the wall plate and to the lower ridge, then drive a couple of screws into it through the upper rafter. The ledgers, lengths of 1×3 screwed to the underside of the lower rafter, create a rabbet that will support the roof plywood. Trim them to fit in between the lower ridge and the front wall, and screw them to the rafters.

21 **Fit the lower roof.** Drop the two lower roof panels onto the ledgers. They'll rest on the top edges of the plywood walls, as shown in the center photos. You'll have to notch one corner of the roof to fit around the center ridge pole.

22 **Fit the upper roof.** Center the three upper roof panels on the rafters and screw them in place. Use the 1-inch screws. Drive six screws into each long edge, as shown at right.

23 **Attach the fascia.** The fascia tidies the front edge of the roof. Screw it to the ends of the rafters with a couple of 2-inch screws in each rafter. Trim it to length after it's in place.

24 **Finish the play house.** You may need to disassemble the play house to move it to its final location, but you'll be able to do so because the assembly joints were all made without glue. Reassemble the house where it will rest, with five or six screws at each corner angle. To make a rudimentary foundation, set a row of bricks under the walls. Protect the playhouse from the weather by painting or staining the wood. We used a second color to pick out the trim pieces and corner angles, as shown in the photo on page 168.

Make the lower rafter and ledgers. Screw the lower rafter to the lower ridge, and to the front wall plate. Attach the ledgers to its underside.

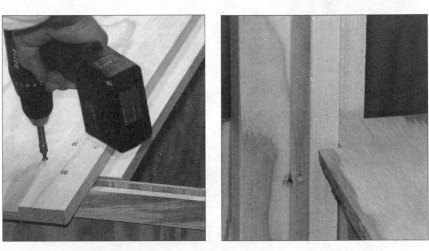

Fit the lower roof. Butt the lower roof panels to the lower rafter (left). Lay out and saw a notch so the left-hand panel fits around the ridge pole (right).

Fit the upper roof. Drop the upper roof onto the rafters. Center the panels and screw them in place.

GARDEN PROJECTS

The garden is a work zone, and gardeners need tools. You might be surprised by how much of your gardening accoutrements you can build for yourself. You can make fences and gates, compost boxes and cold frames, plant stands and potting benches. Some gardening tools have to be complex constructions, like tool sheds and heavy-duty carts, but with a little ingenuity and perseverance, you can construct these items as well.

The best thing about home-built gardening equipment is no compromises. You can make things to suit your own needs and tastes, in sizes that are comfortable for you. It's in this way that making your own equipment can really enhance your gardening experience.

GARDEN FENCE

Tailor the decorative slats to suit your own taste

Here is an attractive garden fence you can make yourself. It features a modular system of posts and fence panels. You can tailor the decorative details to suit your own taste, without changing the structure of the fence.

A garden fence is a big project, but you get a lot of help from the metal post stakes that have recently shown up at the home centers. These welded steel devices allow you to set a sturdy post wherever you need one, without the hard work of digging post holes and planting posts in them. They also hold the post off the damp ground and allow it to drain, so it won't rot and you don't need to work with pressure-treated wood.

As an alternative to making the whole fence, you can also get a lot of help from manufactured fence panels. While there is a great variety of fence panels at the home center, there's a shortage of interesting designs. So one way to approach a fence project is to make your own posts, then fill in with the home center's panels. The project on

FENCE PANEL

Glue up the stile pieces, forming a wide rabbet. Fasten the rails to the rabbet, then screw the decorative slats to the rails. The slat widths and spacing are up to you.

POST

Construct the post around the 4x4 stub, then add the cap, trim and retainers.

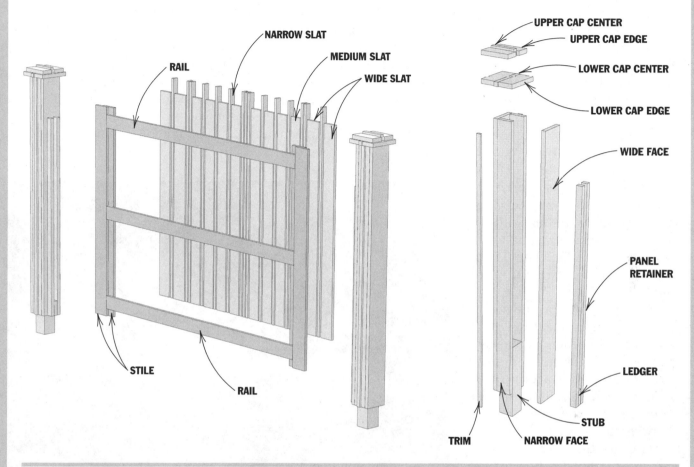

YOUR INVESTMENT

<u>Time:</u> **All weekend**
<u>Money:</u> **Post, $22; Metal stake, $15; Fence panel, $70**

SHOPPING LIST

POST
2 feet 4×4 fir
16 feet 1×2 pine
16 feet 1×4 pine
16 feet 1×6 pine
#8 × 3-inch galvanized spiral nails
2½-inch galvanized siding nails

FENCE PANEL
70 feet 1×2 pine
60 feet 1×4 pine
50 feet 1×5 pine
#6 × 1¼-inch galvanized screws

PROJECT SPECS

The top of the installed fence post is 6 feet high. Each fence panel is 6 feet wide and 5 feet high.

CUTTING LIST

PART	QTY.	DIMENSIONS	NOTES
FENCE PANEL			
Rail	3	¾ × 3½ × 72	1×4
Stile	4	¾ × 4½ × 56	1×5
Narrow slat	12	¾ × 1½ × 60	1×2
Medium slat	6	¾ × 3½2 × 56	1×4
Wide slat	6	¾ × 4½ × 56	1×5
POST			
Stub	1	3⅝ × 3⅝ × 18	4×4
Narrow face	2	1 × 3⅝ × 65	1×4
Wide face	2	1 × 5⅝ × 65	1×6
Lower cap center	1	1 × 1 × 8½	
Lower cap edge	2	1 × 3½ × 8	1×4
Upper cap center	1	1 × 1½ × 6	1×2
Upper cap edge	2	1 × 3 × 7	1×4
Trim	2	½ × 1 × 65	
Panel retainer	2	1 × 1½ × 54	1×2
Ledger	1	1 × 1½ × 4	1×2

these pages includes both a post and a fence panel, so you can go either way. There's a matching gate on page 188.

A two-part post is the key to using the metal post stake. A short stub of 4×4 fits the cup in the metal stake. The decorative outer post is a hollow construction built right around the stub. The post shown is made of rough-sawn pine. You can substitute smooth pine boards from the home center.

The fence panels consist of a rail-and-stile framework, glued and screwed together, with the decorative slats attached to the horizontal rails. The fence panel is made of regular pine lumber.

Two panel retainer strips and a ledger connect the vertical stiles of the fence panels to the posts. This method gives the fence panel a couple of inches in which to float, in case your posts aren't quite vertical or perfectly spaced.

The modular fence panels can be made to a height and width that suits your situation, and the slats can be spaced to meet your privacy needs. Though 8-foot wide panels are standard in the fencing business, the 6-footers detailed in this project are easier to manage. You can tailor the height as well, but be sure to check the local building code because it may restrict how high you can go. The panels shown here are 5 feet high, and are designed to sit 9 inches off the ground. Although the post and panel system has a number of small adjustments built into it, it's designed for level ground, not for sloped or hilly terrain.

BUILDING THE FENCE

1 Cut the wood. There is a lot of wood in one fence panel. If you are attempting to fence a considerable distance, it will be worthwhile to figure the total amount of wood you will need and see whether you can't get a quantity deal, either from your regular lumber retailer or from a small local sawmill. To minimize waste, buy 10-foot lengths.

2 Assemble the stiles. The stiles, which anchor the fence panels at the posts, each consist of two overlapped pieces of wood. The overlap is 2½ inches, as shown in the photo below, which creates a long and substantial rabbet. Draw a layout line, spread glue on one stile piece, set the other one place, and screw the two together with six of the 1¼-inch galvanized-screws.

Assemble the stiles. The two stile pieces overlap 2½ inches. Roll glue on both pieces (above). Screw them together with 1¼-inch screws (below).

3 **Join the rails and stiles.** The three rails connect the stiles. They sit on the rabbet you just glued into the stile. The top and bottom rail are inset 2 inches from the ends of the stile, and the third one is centered. Locate and square one end of each rail in turn, glue it and fasten it with three of the 1¼-inch screws. Then fasten the free ends of the rails to the rabbet in the second stile. This completes the structural framework of the fence panel.

4 **Attach the slats.** Screw the decorative slats to the rails. Leave the framework on the worktable the way it was when you finished fastening the rails to the stiles, with the screwheads uppermost. This is the back side of the fence panel. Now you can arrange the decorative slats the way you want them to be. The arrangement of narrow, medium and wide slats, shown in the photo below, is only one of dozens of workable designs. When you settle on an arrangement you like, slip the decorative slats underneath the rails, locate and square each one up, and screw it tight to the three rails. Put two of the 1¼-inch screws into each rail. Start with the center slat and work toward both ends of the panel.

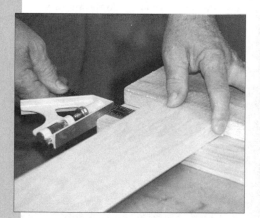

Join the rails and stiles. Fit the three rails into the glued-up rabbet (left). Glue and screw the rails to the stiles. Be sure each rail is square to the stile (above). Glue and screw the free ends of the rails to the second stile (below).

Attach the slats. Screw through the rails into the decorative slats. Start at the center of the fence and work toward the ends (above). Gauge the space between the slats with wooden spacers (below).

Fasten the wide faces to the narrow ones. Glue and nail the wide faces to the edges of the narrow ones. Nail into the stub as well.

Fasten the narrow faces to the stub. Glue and nail the first narrow face to the stub (above). Use a second piece of 4×4 to support the second narrow face, while you align it with the speed square (right).

BUILDING THE POSTS

1 Cut the wood. The posts shown in the photos are made of rough-sawn pine lumber, which is about an inch thick. To minimize waste, buy the wood in 6-foot and 12-foot lengths. You can substitute smooth-planed pine from the home center. You'll have to decide whether to saw the wide faces to width, or to allow any extra width to form a reveal.

2 Fasten the narrow faces to the stub. The narrow post faces match the width of the 4×4 stub. Square a layout line around the stub to represent the top of the cup atop the metal stake. Roll a generous coating of glue on the stub, and spike the first of the two narrow post faces to it with six 3-inch spiral nails. Glue and nail the other post face on the opposite side of the stub. Align the edges of the face with the

stub, drive the first nail and pause to check the alignment at the top end, as shown in the photo above.

3 Fasten the wide faces to the narrow ones. The wide post faces bridge the narrow ones. Roll a generous coating of glue on the edges of the narrow faces and on the stub. Nail the first wide face to one side, then nail the second one to the other side.

Space the 3-inch nails a hand-span apart, and drive six more nails through each wide face into the post stub itself.

4 Cap the post. The decorative cap consists of two layers of wood running at right angles to one another. Each layer is made up of three pieces, a center and two edges. Assemble the cap with glue and siding nails right on the post. Start with the bottom center piece. Center it across the post, glue it, and nail it to the ends of the post faces as shown in the photo at right. Then butt-glue and nail the two bottom edge pieces to the center piece. Hold the three top cap pieces in position to see how they fit, and draw a layout line. Glue and nail them to the post, as shown in the photo at center.

5 Add the panel retainers and ledger. The vertical panel retainers form a groove down the side of the post, into which you can fit the fence panel. The ledger supports the weight of the panel. Glue and nail the panel retainers to the side of the post, but be sure to use a sample of your actual panel material to gauge the width of the groove. Then glue and nail the ledger into the bottom of the slot between the retainers. Nail through the ledger into the post face, and also nail through the retainers into the ledger.

6 Trim the post. The trim pieces run down two faces of the post, as visual extensions of the bottom center cap. Spread glue on each trim piece, center it on the post face, and nail it to the post with the siding nails.

Cap the post. Glue and nail the lower center cap piece to the top of the post (above). Butt the lower cap edges up to the center piece (right). Glue and nail the upper cap to the lower cap (below).

Add the panel retainers and ledger. Glue and nail the panel retainers to one face of the post (above). Fit the ledger into the bottom of the slot between the retainers (right).

INSTALLING YOUR FENCE

There is a general strategy for installing a fence. The method is to establish the line of the fence, then to make the line level, and finally to locate the posts along the level line.

Begin at the end nearest the house and drive a stake in the ground. Tie a string over the top of the first stake and stretch it along the proposed line of the fence. Drive a second stake on the line of the fence, the length of your level away from the original stake. Use the longest level you have. If what you have is short, tape it to the middle of a straight 8-foot 2×4. Set the long level across the top of the two stakes and lift one end up and down to see how far off it is. Drive the second stake until its top is level with the top of the original stake.

Drive a third stake at the other end of the proposed fence. Now you can sight the string from the first stake, across the top of the second stake, to the third stake. Adjust the string and the third stake to create a straight and level line, and tie the string taut.

Finally, locate the posts by measuring along the string. You can mark the posts with wooden stakes, but it's easiest to go directly to the metal stakes themselves. Start with the gate post closest to the middle of the fence. Decide where you want it to be and start the metal stake into the

Drive a stake at one end of the proposed fence.

Tie a string over the top of the first stake (above). Tape it so it can't slip.

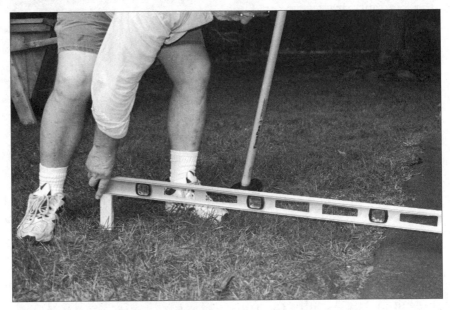

Drive a second stake the level's length away from the first. Adjust it until the two stakes are level.

ground, using a 4×4 stub as an anvil. Drive it down about a foot, then use your level to make it as vertical and plumb as you can as shown in the photos on the facing page. Continue to drive the stake until the base of its cup sits at ground level.

With the first stake in place, note where the level string falls relative to the top of the cup. Measure the width of your fence panel or gate and measure along the string to locate the next metal stake. Be sure to allow for the difference between the width

Measure the width of the gate and drive the second metal stake.

Drive the third stake at the other end of the fence. Adjust the string so it grazes the top of the second or center stake. Tie the string off level.

Locate the first fence post and drive the metal stake into the ground.

Use the level to make sure the metal stake is vertical.

Set the fence post in the metal stake. Make sure it is plumb.

of the wooden post and the width of the metal stake. Drive the stake into the ground, checking carefully for alignment as you go. Drive it down until the string crosses the metal cup in the same place as on the first stake.

Now you can proceed along the line of the fence, driving each stake down level with the string.

If the ground rises a bit, you might have to dig a hole, and if the ground falls, you'll have to mound it up around the stake.

When you install the fence posts in the metal stakes, make sure they are vertical. If one is really off, you might have to uproot it and replant it, as shown in the photo at right.

To adjust a metal stake, you may have to uproot it and reset it. Pry it out of the ground with a 2×4 lever.

GARDEN GATE

This swinger makes a clean break between yard and garden

The garden gate makes a transition from the yard to the vegetable patch or flower garden. It's not a security apparatus so it doesn't have to be massive. It's a visual device, and perhaps a deer barrier. The width of the gate is up to you, and since its function is visual, the arrangement of the slats gives you an opportunity to play. You can vary the number and width of the slats, their spacing, and their height.

Glue and #6 × 1-inch galvanized construction screws hold the gate together. You don't see the screws from the front because they're all driven from the back side. This means you assemble the gate face-down on the worktable. You don't see most of the screws from the back side either, because they're hidden under the hinge rail, which goes on last.

Because this project requires sawing wood lengthwise, and also sawing bevels, it's designed for the table saw. However, the bevels and the variations in width are aesthetic, not structural. You could eliminate them and make a modified gate by cutting the wood to length with a chopsaw, a portable circular saw, or a handsaw.

GARDEN GATE

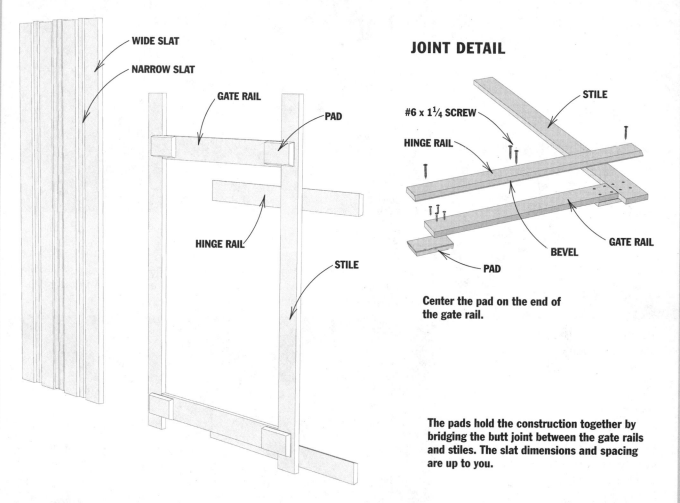

WIDE SLAT

NARROW SLAT

GATE RAIL

PAD

HINGE RAIL

STILE

JOINT DETAIL

#6 x 1¼ SCREW

HINGE RAIL

STILE

BEVEL

GATE RAIL

PAD

Center the pad on the end of the gate rail.

The pads hold the construction together by bridging the butt joint between the gate rails and stiles. The slat dimensions and spacing are up to you.

BUILDING THE GARDEN GATE

1 Saw all the parts. All the material comes out of 1×4 pine lumber. The two hinge rails and the four pads, which hold the gate together, have a 15° bevel on three edges, with the fourth edge left square. To make the hinge rails, start with two 32-inch lengths of clear wood. Tilt your table saw to 15° and bevel one long edge of each piece, then set the saw's fence 3 inches from the blade and bevel the other long edge. To make the beveled pads, start with a 24-inch length of clear wood, and bevel it to match the hinge rails. Leave the table saw blade tilted

YOUR INVESTMENT
<u>Time:</u> One afternoon
<u>Money:</u> $35

SHOPPING LIST
40 feet 1×4 pine
20 feet 1×1 pine
Two galvanized strap hinges
#6 × 1¼-inch galvanized construction screws
#6 × 2-inch galvanized construction screws

PROJECT SPECS
The gate shown is 32 inches wide and 53 inches high.

CUTTING LIST

PART	QTY.	DIMENSIONS	NOTES
Stile	2	¾ × 3½ × 48	1×4
Gate rail	2	¾ × 3½ × 25½	Vary length to gate opening
Pad	4	¾ × 3 × 5	Bevel 15°
Wide slat	4	¾ × 3½ × 52	1×4
Narrow slat	4	1 × 1 × 52	
Hinge rail	2	¾ × 3 × 31½	Bevel 15°

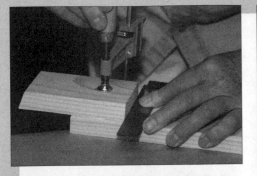

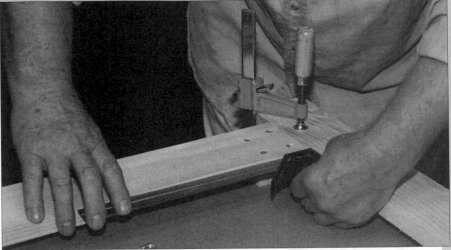

Join the stile and rails. Spread glue on the pad and the end of the gate rails, clamp them to the stile, check for square, then screw the joints together.

Attach the second stile. Clamp the parts together and drive one screw through each joint, then measure the diagonals. When they are equal, the frame is square and you can drive the rest of the screws.

Join the pads and gate rails. Spread glue on the bottom of the pad, then use a square to align it with the end of the rail (top). Clamp it in place. Turn the parts over and make the joint with four screws (bottom).

at 15° and use the saw's miter gauge to crosscut one end of the hinge rail, and also to crosscut the pads blank into four 5½-inch pieces. Finally, square up the saw blade to crosscut the other end of the hinge rails, and of the four pad blanks, to their finished lengths.

2 Join the pads and gate rails. The pads hold the gate together by bridging the butt joint between the horizontal gate rails and the stiles, or vertical posts. The first step is to glue and screw the pads to the ends of the gate rails. Find the center of each pad and square a line across. Align a pad on the end of a gate rail, as shown in the photo above, so it overlaps by half its length with the pad's square end on the gate rail and its beveled end extending into

space. Spread glue on the pad, then screw the two pieces together with four of the 1¼-inch screws. Attach the other three pads in exactly the same way.

3 Join the stile and rails. Choose which sides of the stiles you want to face front, and lay both stiles face-down on the worktable. Begin at the bottom of one stile. The bottom gate rail lands 2 inches up from the ends of the stiles. Align the parts with a square as shown at top right, and draw layout lines. Spread glue on the mating sur-

faces, clamp the assembly to the table, drill pilot holes and drive four screws through the joint from the back side. The top gate rail sits 6 inches down from the end of the stile. Align it, glue it, clamp it, and screw it.

4 Attach the second stile. The remaining stile should drop perfectly into place, making a square frame. Spread glue, clamp the parts together, then drive one screw through each of the two joints. As shown in the bottom photo, check the diagonals of the frame with

Screw the first two slats to the frame. Clamp the slats against the pads. Drive two screws through each gate rail into the slat.

Add two more wide slats. Use a 2-inch spacer block, top right, to align the slats. Draw layout lines, then glue and screw the parts together.

Attach the narrow slats. Slide the narrow slats into the spaces and line them up with the wide slats. Spread glue and screw them to the gate rails.

your tape measure. If they are equal, the frame is square, so drive three more screws through each joint. If they are not equal, push one corner square to the frame, clamp up, and drive the remaining screws.

5 Screw the first two slats to the frame. Four wide slats and four narrow ones fill in the center of the gate. The first two wide slats butt tightly against the square ends of the pads. They're set up 1 inch from the bottom of the stiles. Draw layout lines, then spread glue and screw the slats to the gate rails.

6 Add two more wide slats. To align the remaining two wide slats, use a pair of 2-inch spacer blocks made from scrap wood, as shown in the top middle photo. This will leave a wide center gap between the slats, which you'll fill in the next step. Glue and screw the slats to the gate rails, with two screws through each joint.

7 Attach the narrow slats. Slide the narrow slats into

Add the hinge rails. The square end of the hinge rails goes to the hinge side. Glue and screw the hinge rails to the back of the gate rails.

place and space them however you like. We spaced them ⅝ inch from the wide slats. Draw layout lines, spread glue within the layout lines, and drive a total of four screws through the gate rails into each narrow slat.

8 Add the hinge rails. You have to decide now whether the gate will be hinged right-handed or left-handed, because the square ends of the hinge rails are what supports the

hinges. The square ends fit flush with the edge of the stile. Spread glue all across the gate rails, and screw each hinge rail down with four 2-inch screws.

9 Finish the gate. Once you've installed the gate in its fence, you'll probably want to add a latch and sand off the sharp edges where people will be handling the wood. Then stain the gate to match the fence, or leave it alone to darken in the weather.

POTTING BENCH

Transplanting is a treat with this sturdy companion

Nothing enhances gardening like a sturdy potting bench with a lot of built-in storage. This bench is a real winner. It can go outdoors or in the garden shed, on the deck, or in the greenhouse. Wherever it's located, you'll have a comfortable place to work, with ample room for tools, pots, bags of peat moss and vermiculite, and anything else you might need for working with your potted plants.

The bench in the photographs was built out of 4/4 rough-sawn pine lumber, which you can find for a reasonable price at a rural sawmill. It's generally a full inch thick, often a bit more. None of the dimensions is critical, so it's easy to transpose the design into 5/4 pine from the home center, which usually comes out around 1⅛ inches thick. If you're building the bench for a sunspace, you might use regular 1× pine, which is ¾ inch thick and results in an elegant lightness. The bench shown is unfinished so it will weather. Rough pine can be stained, and regular 1× pine can be varnished or painted.

Of course, you can make the bench any size you like. The height shown here, 36 inches, is about right for gardeners of average height. If you are tall, make the legs longer, and if you are short, make them shorter. If you aren't sure, check the height of your kitchen counters. If the kitchen counter is comfortable for you, that's the height to use. If it isn't, adjust an inch or two up or down. A small adjustment makes a big difference.

The composite legs are three-layer wood sandwiches. The center layer is assembled from three small pieces of wood, which creates support surfaces for the cross rails and aprons.

POTTING BENCH

Assemble the front legs, apron, and cross rails. Then build the back legs and apron onto the cross rails. Nail the worktop and shelves to this structure.

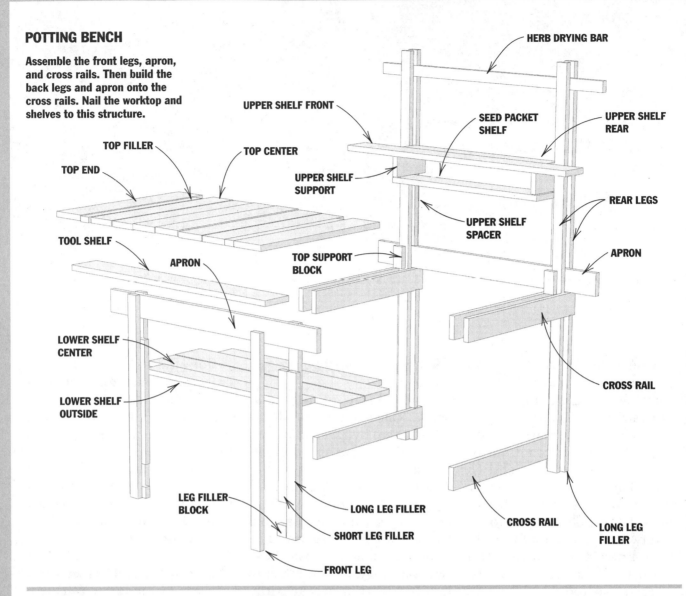

TOP FILLER

TOP END

TOP CENTER

UPPER SHELF FRONT

SEED PACKET SHELF

UPPER SHELF REAR

HERB DRYING BAR

UPPER SHELF SUPPORT

UPPER SHELF SPACER

REAR LEGS

APRON

TOOL SHELF

APRON

TOP SUPPORT BLOCK

LOWER SHELF CENTER

CROSS RAIL

LOWER SHELF OUTSIDE

LEG FILLER BLOCK

LONG LEG FILLER

CROSS RAIL

LONG LEG FILLER

SHORT LEG FILLER

FRONT LEG

YOUR INVESTMENT
<u>Time:</u> One weekend
<u>Money:</u> $95

SHOPPING LIST
96 feet 1×6 rough-sawn pine
#6 × 2-inch galvanized screws
#8 × 3-inch galvanized screws
2½-inch galvanized finishing nails

PROJECT SPECS
The potting bench is 72 inches high, 48 inches wide, and 28 inches deep. The worktop is 36 inches off the floor.

CUTTING LIST

PART	QTY.	DIMENSIONS	NOTES
Front leg	4	1 × 2 × 35	
Rear leg	4	1 × 2 × 72	
Long leg filler	4	1 × 2 × 29	
Short leg filler	8	1 × 2 × 23	Cut to fit
Leg filler block	4	1 × 2 × 2	Cut to fit
Cross rail	6	1 × 4 × 28	
Apron	2	1 × 4 × 48	
Lower shelf outside	2	1 × 4 × 38	
Lower shelf center	2	1 × 6¾ × 48	
Tool shelf	1	1 × 6 × 48	
Top end	2	1 × 6 × 28	Rip width to fit
Top filler	2	1 × 2 × 24¾	
Top center	6	1 × 5¼ × 28	Rip width to fit
Top support block	2	1 × 2 × 6	
Upper shelf spacer	2	1 × 2 × 14	
Upper shelf support	2	1 × 4 × 8	
Upper shelf front	1	1 × 5 × 48	
Upper shelf rear	1	1 × 4 × 31¾	
Seed packet shelf	1	1 × 5 × 31¾	
Herb drying bar	1	1 × 2 × 48	

Join the front legs and apron. Place the two front legs on the bench top and lay the apron flush with the top of the legs. Set the combination square to 6 inches and draw lines to locate the legs on the apron (left). Drill four pilot holes through the apron, inside the layout lines (right). Angle the holes toward the center of the wood.

This useful strategy allows you to construct serviceable wood joints without having to cut intricately shaped parts.

The slats that make the top of the bench run from front to back instead of from end to end. This allows you to saw useful pieces out of cheap material, which is liable to be too twisted and knotty to yield long boards. You'll find the front-to-back slats easy to sweep clean, too.

Other important details include the setback of the lowest shelf, the top overhang, and the upward extension of the back legs to form shelf supports. The low shelf has enough ceiling room for bags of potting soil, while the setback creates shin room. The top overhangs the long rails by a full 2 inches, so you can get a cleanup bucket right in where you need it. The upward leg extension makes the high shelves a stable part of the bench structure, so clay pots won't teeter off.

BUILDING THE POTTING BENCH

1 Join the front legs and apron. Once you've cut all the wood, begin by assembling two front legs to one apron piece, to make a U-shaped assembly. The trick is keeping the legs square to the apron. The front legs are set in 6 inches from the ends of the apron. The photo sequence across these two pages shows the steps of laying out the intersection, drilling pilot holes for screws, spreading glue, and driving the screws home. Use the longest screws that will fit without poking through the other side.

2 Square up the assembly. Drive one screw through the apron into each leg, then measure the width of the top and bottom and both diagonals. If the widths are equal, and the two diagonals are equal, the assembly is square. If it's not square, pull the pieces into position before the glue sets, then drive the remaining screws.

3 Join the front legs and top cross rails. Drill three pilot holes through both ends of four cross rails. Smear a bead of glue on the wood, then clamp the rails to the front legs and apron. Pull the rails up tight to the bottom surface of the apron as shown in the bottom photo on the facing page. Drive three of the 3-inch screws through each joint.

4 Join the bottom cross rails. The top of the lower rails is 6 inches off the floor. Measure 6 inches up the inside face of both legs, then glue and screw the cross rails in position.

5 Assemble the legs. The long leg filler piece fits tight against the top cross rail and extends to the floor. The short leg filler fits tight between the top and bottom cross rails. Hold these pieces in position to mark their length, then saw them so they fit snugly between the rails. Attach each filler to the front legs with glue and four of the 2-inch screws. Finally, saw the leg filler

Square up the assembly. Drive a single screw into each of the two joints. Bury the heads in the wood (left). Measure the width top and bottom, then measure the two diagonals from the outside bottom corner of the leg to the inside corner of the apron (right). Adjust the assembly until the diagonals are equal, then drive the remaining screws.

BELT AND SUSPENDERS

The drawing on page 193 shows neither the many galvanized construction screws that hold the potting bench together, nor the glue.

In general there are at least two, but no more than four, screws through every wood-to-wood intersection. And there's also a fat bead of yellow glue everywhere that two parts lie across one another.

Whether there is room for two screws or three or four screws, always space them as widely apart as possible, and angle them so they're better able to resist stress.

Clamp the mating parts tightly together before driving the construction screws. Four 12-inch clamps, like the ones shown in the photographs at right, are all you need for a construction like this: glue, clamp, and screw each joint before moving on.

Use the longest screws the thickness of the wood will accept, short of the screw point emerging on the other side.

Spread yellow glue where the parts fit together. Spread it on all the mating surfaces. Pine is so soft that you don't need to drill pilot holes, except when you're within a couple of inches of the end of the wood. Clamp up first, then drill just through the top piece, using a regular twist bit that's smaller than the screw's thread diameter.

Surely two or three galvanized construction screws at every intersection would be strong enough to hold a bench together? Well, probably. But, like the gentleman who wears both belt and suspenders, the glue is insurance. It would keep the parts together even if the screws were to work loose.

Spread yellow glue where the parts will fit together.

Clamp the mating parts tightly together so they don't shift while you drive the screws.

ASSEMBLING THE LEGS

Run a bead of glue along both filler pieces, then press the leg into place. The leg fits tightly between the two cross rails.

Clamps hold the leg while you drive pairs of screws into the filler pieces.

COMPOSITE LEG

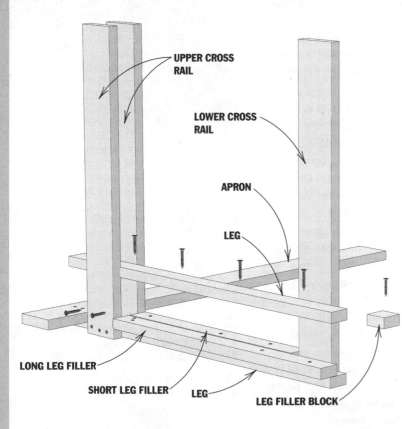

UPPER CROSS RAIL

LOWER CROSS RAIL

APRON

LEG

LONG LEG FILLER

SHORT LEG FILLER

LEG

LEG FILLER BLOCK

Complete the front legs. Driving two more screws through the cross rail and into the leg makes the construction incredibly strong.

The composite leg is a four-piece wood sandwich assembled around the apron and cross rails. The leg filler pieces support the two top cross rails. Trim the short leg filler to a tight fit between the top and bottom cross rails. Glue and screw all the parts as you assemble the leg.

blocks to just fill the space below the bottom cross rails. A little glue and a single screw is enough to hold each filler block in place.

6 **Complete the front legs.** Fit the remaining leg piece between the cross rails and clamp it in place. Screw through it into the apron and leg fillers. Finally, drive a couple of 3-inch screws through the outside face of each cross rail into the side of the leg piece, as shown at bottom left. These screws make the construction very strong.

7 **Construct the rear legs.** Despite their extra length, the rear legs are also composites that go together in exactly the same way as the front legs, as shown at above right. Glue and screw the rear leg parts to the cross rails as you go along. The rear apron slides in last. This completes the structure of the potting bench.

8 **Fit the lower shelves.** Crosscut the four boards for the lower shelf and nail them in place, as shown at right. Don't make the fit too tight. It's better to leave a little space between the boards, so the wood can swell if it gets wet. Screw the narrow tool shelf to the underside of the cross rails. You'll be surprised by how handy this shelf is when you're working.

9 **Make the tabletop.** Screw the two small support blocks to the rear legs, then fit and nail the two top fillers in place. Add the two top end boards, which should fit flush with the ends of the aprons. Fill in the center

Construct the rear legs. Make sure the short leg fillers fit tightly between the top and bottom cross rails. Glue and screw the composite legs together.

Fit the lower shelves. You can get at the tool shelf and at least one of the boards for the lower shelf while the potting table is still on its back on the worktable. Stand it upright to complete nailing the shelf parts in place.

space. If all the boards are not the same width, arrange them in a pattern. Drive galvanized finishing nails through the top boards into the aprons.

10 **Fit the upper shelves.** Fit the upper shelf spacers into the slot between the rear legs. Screw the upper shelf supports to the rear legs. Cut the upper shelf rear to fit between the rear legs and nail it in place. Nail the upper shelf front onto the supports. Nail the seed packet shelf onto the bottom of the shelf supports. Finally, nail the herb drying bar between the rear legs.

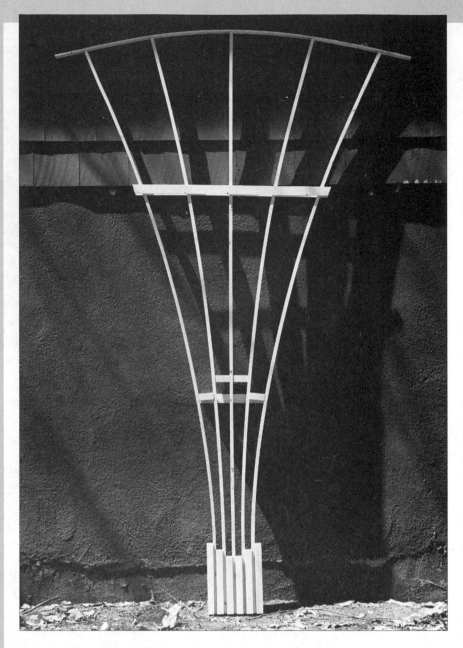

FAN TRELLIS

Here's a curvy way to train your climbing roses

The charm of a trellis arises from its curve, and this is one of the few times in woodworking where the curve comes easily. You control the curve by where you locate the spacers, the cross stringers, and the top stringer. The trellis shown here has five long slats, but you could make a wider trellis with more slats and more spacers.

BUILDING THE TRELLIS

1 Rip the 2×4. Select clear material for making the long trellis slats. It's worth the extra money to buy totally clear wood, because any stray spike knots probably will cause a broken slat. Start with an 8-foot 2×4 and a 4-foot one. Rip, or saw lengthwise, a ¼-inch slice off each side of the 8-footer, then saw the wood into five ½-inch slats. Saw the spacers and support blocks from the other 2×4. Make the stringers from the edge rippings.

2 Start with one slat. There are six support blocks, of three different lengths. The longest ones go to the outside of the trellis. Lay a slat flat on the worktable. Prop it up on a scrap and clamp it. Place an outside support block flush under the end of the long slat, as shown in the top left photo on the facing page. Attach the slat to the block with two 1¼-inch screws.

3 Complete the trellis base. Alternately add support blocks and slats to the assembly. Align the parts at the bottom and back, with the variation thickness and length to the front and top.

Every sort of creeping vine and climbing rose can use a garden trellis. These simple constructions can be staked upright in the garden, or attached to the house or to a fence. They're quick to make, and economical, too, since one trellis comes out of a single 12-foot 2×4. This project does, however, require a table saw, for cutting the 2×4 into lengthwise strips.

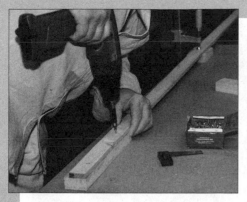

Start with one slat. Clamp the free end of the slat to a block of wood. Attach it with two screws.

Make the curve. Clamp the center slat to the worktable, then insert the center blocks to fan the trellis.

Locate the cross stringer. Tack the stringer to the center slat, then adjust the curves of the outer slats.

4 Make the curve. The four center spacers begin to create the curve. They're about 36 inches up from the base. Insert them where you like them, and tie them to the long slats with a single 1¼-inch screw into each. Leave one side of each spacer free for now.

5 Locate the cross stringer. The cross stringer defines the curve. Tack it to the center slat with a single nail, make it square to the center slat, and lock it in place with a second nail. Now adjust the curve of the other slats and tack them to the cross stringer as well. Nail the second cross stringer to the back of the trellis, right behind the first one.

6 Add the top stringer. The top stringer completes the curve and locks all the slats in place. Begin by screwing the

FAN TRELLIS

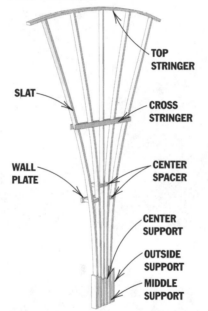

center of the top stringer to the end of the center slat. Then adjust the spacing of the slats until they make a sweeping curve that you like, from one end to the other. Screw the top stringer to the end of each slat.

Add the top stringer. Screw the top stringer to the ends of the slats. Start from the center slat and work outward. Adjust the spacing for curves you like.

7 Complete the trellis. Use a handsaw to trim the ends of the top stringer and center stringer to lengths you like. Go over all the joints and anchor any loose places with nails or screws. The trellis can be tied to a stake in the garden. To attach it to the wall of a building, screw the wall plate to the center spacers, then nail or screw the plate to the wall.

YOUR INVESTMENT
<u>Time:</u> One evening
<u>Money:</u> $6

SHOPPING LIST
12 feet 2×4
#6 × 1¼-inch galvanized screws
2-inch galvanized siding nails

PROJECT SPECS
The trellis is 8 feet high and 4 feet wide.

CUTTING LIST

PART	QTY.	DIMENSIONS	NOTES
Slat	5	½ × 1½ × 96	
Outside support	2	1 × 2 × 11	
Middle support	2	1 × 2 × 10	
Center support	2	1 × 2 × 9	
Center spacer	4	1 × 2½ × 4	
Cross stringer	2	¾ × 1½ × 28	Use 2×4 edge ripping
Top stringer	1	¾ × 1½ × 48	Use 2×4 edge ripping
Wall plate	1	½ × 1½ × 12	

COLD FRAME

Wooden box with glass lid protects tender plants from cold winds

A cold frame is a little green-house without heat. It gives the gardener an early start in the spring, and a place to shelter tender plants that can't handle the local winter. The cold frame sits directly on the ground. The loose-fitting glass lid can be lifted and propped up for ventilation on sunny days, or it can be slid to one side. An additional ventilation slot in the back of the box can be left open, or covered with a slat of wood.

You've probably seen published designs for large cold frames with elaborate and even automated lid-lifting mechanisms. However, cold frames in established gardens are more likely to be wondrous old things tacked together from salvaged storm windows and peeling wood. They're utility construc-tions, not works of art or pieces of furniture. It's OK to make them in a rustic manner.

Grandiose frames actually don't function as well as a small cold frame, like the one shown here. It's easy to work with and to move. You can reach from one side to the other, without having to walk all around. When you need more acreage under glass, simply build more frames.

COLD FRAME

Screw the box fronts and sides together, then screw the sloping side to the box. Trim the ends flush. Make the glass frame from the inside out: Join inner frame rails to inner frame stiles, attach muntins and glazing strips, attach the outer frame to the inner frame.

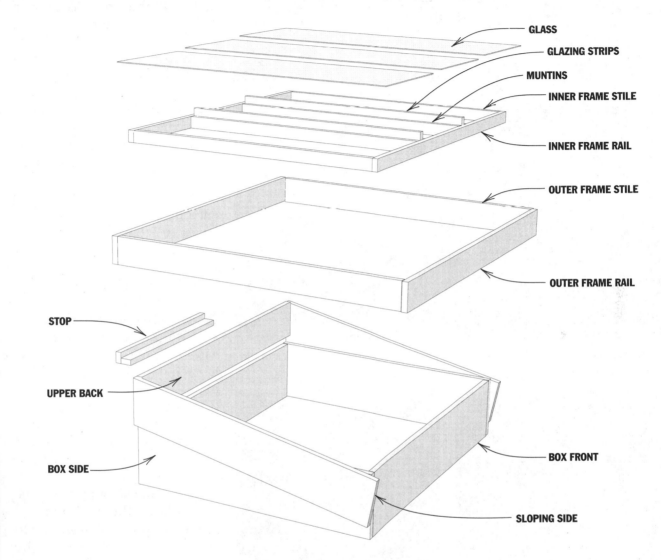

YOUR INVESTMENT

<u>Time:</u> **One afternoon**
<u>Money:</u> **$25 for wood, $12 for glass**

SHOPPING LIST

12 feet 1×8 roughsawn pine
10 feet 1×6 roughsawn pine
24 feet 1×2 pine
6 feet 1×3 pine
16 feet 1×4 pine
#6 × 1½-inch galvanized screws
#6 × 2-inch galvanized screws
#8 × 2½-inch galvanized screws
9 square feet double-strength
    window glass

PROJECT SPECS

The cold frame measures 42 inches wide, 40 inches front to back, and 17 inches high.

CUTTING LIST

PART	QTY.	DIMENSIONS	NOTES
Box side	2	¾ × 8 × 32	
Box front	2	¾ × 8 × 36	
Sloping side	2	¾ × 6 × 34	Trim ends
Upper back	1	¾ × 5 × 38	Trim to fit
Inner frame rail	2	¾ × 1½ × 40½	1×2
Inner frame stile	2	¾ × 1½ × 32¼	1×2
Muntin	2	¾ × 2½ × 32¼	1×3
Glazing strip	4	¾ × 1½ × 32¼	1×2
Outer frame stile	2	¾ × 3½ × 38	1×4
Outer frame rail	2	¾ × 3½ × 42	1×4
Stop	2	¾ × 1½ × 19	
Glass	3	⅜ × 13 × 35	

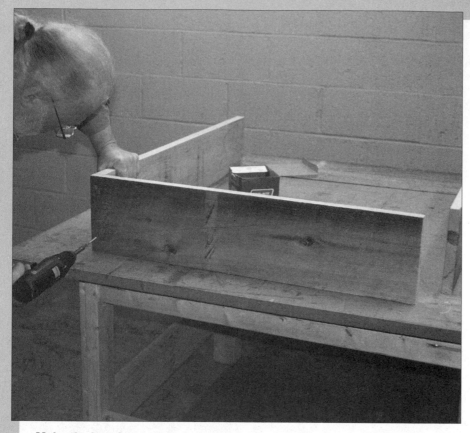

Make the box. Screw through the face of the box sides into the end grain of the box front and back.

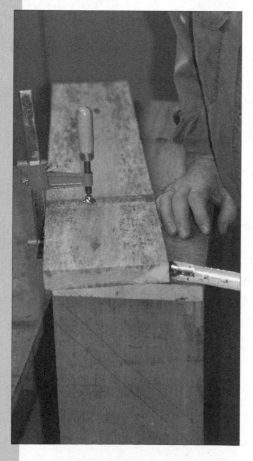

Attach the sloping sides. Position the sloping side 1¾ inches up from the bottom front corner, and crossing the top back corner (left). Clamp the sloping side in place and screw it to the box side (above).

BUILDING THE COLD FRAME

1 Cut all the wood. The box in the photos is made with 4/4 rough-sawn pine lumber, which is cheap and plentiful in our part of New England. You can use the rough lumber that grows in your region, or whatever salvaged wood you might have around, or regular pine boards from the home center. The frame, which holds the glass, can also be made of salvaged material or of smooth pine lumber. Cut all the wood to length at the start of the project, though the upper back piece will have to be trimmed to fit in Step 5.

2 Make the box. Screw the box sides to the box front and back with three of the 2½-inch screws in each corner, as shown in the photo at top left. The screws go through the face of the sides, which are the shorter pieces, into the end grain of the front and back.

3 Attach the sloping sides. The slope allows the cold frame to catch the winter sunlight and to shed rain and snow, but the amount of slope is quite arbitrary. As shown in the photos at left, the slope arises from the way the sloping sides are positioned on the box sides: 1¾ inches up from the bottom front corner, and smack on the top back corner. Fasten the sloping sides from inside the box, using four 1½-inch screws.

4 Trim the ends. The back end of the sloping sides has to be brought into line with the end of the main box. Use a straightedge or a framing square to extend

Trim the ends. Extend the line of the box across the back end of the sloping side (left). Jigsaw the sloping side flush with the box back (above).

the line of the box across the wood, and saw it on the line. Use a jigsaw, as shown in the photos above, or a handsaw.

5 **Make the upper back.** The width of the upper back piece is somewhat arbitrary. It should be less than the rise of the sloping sides, in order to leave a slot for ventilation. How much less depends on what the gardener intends to do with the cold frame, as well as on the available wood. The upper back can be made of two narrow slats of wood, if you prefer. Drive screws through the sloping sides into the end grain of the upper back.

6 **Make the inner glass frame.** The glass frame is a two-layer construction, both for strength and in order to create a rabbet for the glass itself. Begin by making the inner frame, which consists of two rails and two stiles. The longer rails overlap the ends of the stiles, as shown in the photo at right. Hold the first corner together on the worktable and drive two screws through the face of the rail and into the end grain of the stile.

Make the upper back. Fit the upper back between the two sloping sides and screw it in position. The gap ventilates the cold frame.

Make the inner glass frame. Clamp the rails and stiles of the inner glass frame to the worktable, and screw them together. The rails, which are longer than the stiles, overlap the ends of the stiles.

Join the other four corners in the same way.

7 Fit the muntins. The two muntins are the same length as the inner frame stiles in Step 6, but they are an inch wider. This extra width will create the glass rabbets in the center of the frame. Divide the width of the frame in thirds to locate the muntins. Screw through the inner frame rails into the ends of the muntins with the 2-inch screws, as shown below.

8 Make the glazing strips. The four glazing strips are screwed to either side of the center stiles, forming the glass rabbet. Fit the glazing strips in place and clamp them to the stiles.

Screw them to the inner frame rails, and to the center stiles, as shown in the photos at the bottom of the page.

9 Attach the outer frame stiles. The outer frame stiles continue the glass rabbets and form the lip that keeps the glass frame on the box. The outer frame stiles fit flush with the inner frame stiles at one end, with a 4-inch overhang at the other, which will become the front. Center the inner frame on the width of the outer frame rails, as shown in the photo at the top of the facing page, and screw the parts together from the inside, using 1¼-inch screws.

10 Make the outer frame rails. The outer frame rails complete the glass frame. They're screwed to the end grain of the outer frame stiles, as shown in the photos in the center of the facing page. Also screw the rear rail to the inner frame stile.

11 Make the lid stop. The lid stop keeps the lid from skidding

Fit the muntins. Divide the width of the inner frame into thirds and fit the muntins. Screw through the rails into the end grain of the muntins.

Make the glazing strips. Screw a glazing strip to each side of the muntins (above). Drive a screw through the inner frame rails into the ends of the muntins as well (left).

off the frame when it's propped open. It consists of two pieces of 1×2 pine screwed together to the back of the box, as shown in the bottom left photo.

12 **Glaze the cold frame.** When you buy glass, specify panes ¼ inch narrower than the openings in the cold frame, and a full inch shorter. This gap allows the glass to drain. Set the glass in its rabbets, and secure it with a few glazing points. Press the points into the wood with a putty knife, as shown at bottom right.

Attach the outer frame stiles. Center the outer frame stiles on the inner frame, with a 4-inch overhang toward the front (left in the photo above).

Make the outer frame rails. Screw the outer frame rails to the inner frame (left) and to the ends of the outer frame stiles (above).

Make the lid stop. Screw two pieces of 1×2 to the back of the box, to make a lid stop (above).

Glaze the cold frame. Set the glass in its rabbets and anchor it with glazing points (right).

GARDEN CART

This big and useful box on wheels bounces over any terrain

After 20 years of hard service, the axle supports rusted out and the plywood bottom rotted away, and my old garden cart bit the dust. Time to make a new one.

The old cart came out of a kit of metal hardware and plywood. I wanted the new cart to be all wood, except for the wheels and axles. It had to be larger, and perhaps better overall.

The new cart would have to be sturdy enough for every garden chore: moving tools and flats of plants and balled shrubs, loads of earth and compost, bales of hay and peat moss, piles of rocks, firewood, and leaves. It should have soft pneumatic tires, for easy rolling over gravel and uneven ground. The box ends had to be angled, not only for dumping, but also for foot clearance while toiling up a steep grade. Not least, I wanted to use up a leftover sheet of T1-11 siding. T1-11 is tough mat-

erial, and it's not bad looking.

If you're like me, you're liable to leave your garden cart outdoors all summer. Even though the T1-11 is made with waterproof glue, the wood will rot if rain water pools on it. Therefore, I cut the cart's bottom panel a little bit short of the ends, for drainage. If you haul a lot of loose sand, you might consider this detail a bug instead of a valuable feature.

Be sure to use Titebond type

GARDEN CART

Assemble the box by gluing and screwing panels of T1-11 siding to the frame pieces. Then make the axle assembly, and finally add the top trim, handles, and legs.

AXLE DETAIL

Nuts and washers space the wheel on the threaded-rod axle. Two nuts jammed together hold the wheel on the axle.

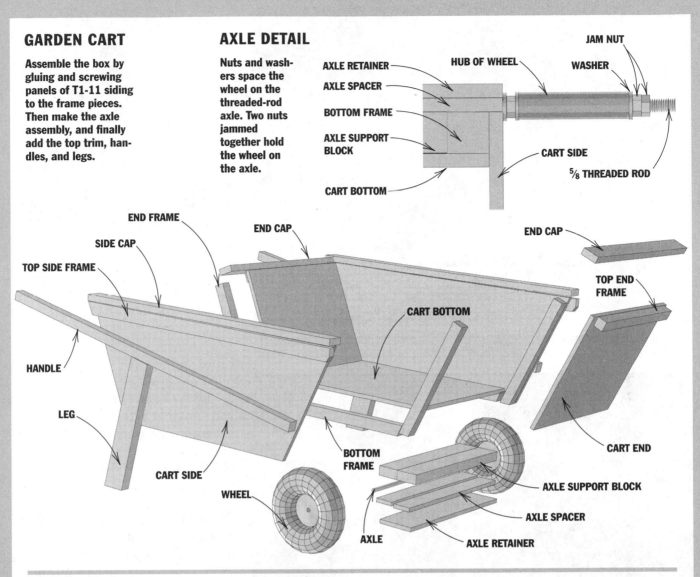

YOUR INVESTMENT

<u>Time:</u> One weekend
<u>Money:</u> $35 for wood; $35 for wheels and hardware

SHOPPING LIST

32 feet 2×4
One sheet ⅝-inch or ¹⁹⁄₃₂-inch
  T1-11 siding
16 feet 1×3 pine
3 feet ⅝ × 16 NC threaded rod
Six ⅝-inch washers and nuts
Two 13-inch pneumatic wheels
  with ⅝-inch ball-bearing hub
#6 × 1⅝-inch galvanized screws
#6 × 2-inch galvanized screws
#8 × 2½-inch galvanized screws

PROJECT SPECS

The cart measures 60 inches from handles to far end, 25 inches high, and 36 inches wide at the axle.

CUTTING LIST

PART	QTY.	DIMENSIONS	NOTES
Cart side	2	¹⁹⁄₃₂ × 18 × 48	T1-11 siding
End frame	4	1½ × 1½ × 22	Rip from 2×4
Bottom frame	2	1½ × 1½ × 29½	Rip from 2×4
Cart end	2	¹⁹⁄₃₂ × 19¼ × 23½	T1-11 siding
Cart bottom	1	¹⁹⁄₃₂ × 23½ × 29⅛	T1-11 siding
Axle support block	2	1½ × 3½ × 20¼	2×4
Axle spacer	2	¹⁹⁄₃₂ × 3 × 24¾	T1-11 siding
Axle retainer	1	¹⁹⁄₃₂ × 6 × 24¾	T1-11 siding
Handle	2	1½ × 1½ × 60	Rip from 2×4
Leg	2	1½ × 3½ × 15	Bevel one end
Top end frame	2	1½ × 1½ × 21	Trim to fit
Top side frame	2	1 × 2 × 52	Trim to fit
End cap	2	1 × 2½ × 46	Trim to fit
Side cap	2	1 × 2½ × 32	Trim to fit

Make the cart sides. Saw the T1-11 diagonally across the first decorative panel on each edge of the sheet. Clamp the siding to the worktable to saw these lines.

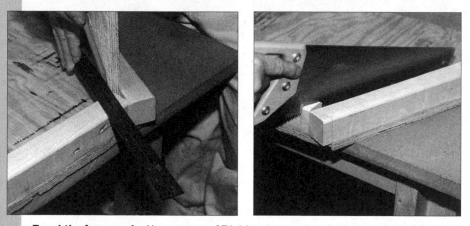

Bevel the frame ends. Use a scrap of T1-11 to lay out the slot between end frame and bottom frame. Saw the slot. Also saw the end frame flush with the cart side.

Add the end frames. Glue and clamp the end frames to the cart sides. Align the bottom of the side with the inside corner of the end frame. Drill pilot holes and screw the parts together.

2 glue, or its equivalent, for water resistance. Spread glue everywhere two wood surfaces fit together. The screws are all galvanized, and you must always drill pilot holes.

If you buy 2×2 wood for the frames and handles, you can saw all the rest of the parts, including the T1-11 siding, with a shark-tooth handsaw like the one shown in the top photo. Otherwise, you'll need access to a table saw to cut these parts lengthwise out of 2×4 studs.

BUILDING THE GARDEN CART

1 Make the cart sides. Saw two pieces of T1-11 measuring 18 inches by 48 inches, with the decorative grooves running across the short dimension. Use the grooves, which are $7\frac{1}{2}$ inches apart, to lay out the slope of the cart ends. As shown at top left, draw a diagonal line from groove to groove across the first panel of siding. Clamp the sheet to the worktable so the layout line is just beyond the

table edge. If you have a portable circular saw, you can fire it up to saw this line, or else you can do it with a handsaw, as shown in the photo at left. Saw both ends of the cart side. Lay out the second side by tracing along the first one.

2 Add the end frames. Saw an 8-foot 2×4 in half lengthwise to make 2×2 material for the cart's structural frame. Crosscut one piece into four 22-inch lengths. Glue and clamp them along the angled cut on the plain face of the cart sides, so the inside corner of the wood comes flush with the bottom of the cart side, as shown above. Screw through the T1-11 into the end frames.

3 Make the bottom frames. Use the other half of the 2×4 you just sawed to make the two $29\frac{1}{4}$-inch bottom frames. The bottom frame pieces should just fit between the end frames, flush with the bottom edge of the T1-11 cart side. Drive eight screws through the T1-11 cart sides into each bottom frame.

Fit the end panels. Fit the end panels into the slots between the frame pieces. Glue and screw both ends to one cart side (above). Glue and clamp the other cart side in place, and screw the assembly together (right).

4 Bevel the frame ends. The ends of the bottom frames need to be beveled parallel to the end frames, leaving a ⅝-inch gap for the T1-11 cart ends. Lay a scrap of T1-11 against the end frames to draw a layout line, as shown at bottom left on the facing page. Cut the bevel with your handsaw as shown at bottom right on the facing page. Similarly, trim the protruding bottom corner off the end frames.

5 Make the cart ends. Two cart ends come out of one 48-inch width of T1-11 that's 19¼ inches long. Saw the siding down the middle of the center groove. Then saw the partial grooves off both edges of each piece, leaving three full panes of siding. Our end panels finished 23½ inches wide.

6 Fit the end panels. The two end panels connect the sides of the cart. Lay one cart side on the worktable and spread glue on the end frames. Fit the first panel into the slot between the end frame and bottom frame. Align the panel with the cart

side. Drill pilot holes and screw through the end panel into the end frame. Attach the second end panel to the cart side in the same way. Finally, spread glue on the end frames of the other cart side, plug it into place, and screw the cart body together.

7 Add the cart bottom. The cart bottom is also T1-11 siding, with the smooth back facing up. It's glued and screwed to the bottom frame. The dimensions given in the cutting list fit tightly from side to side, with ¼-inch of clearance in length. This clearance creates narrow slots at either end, which allow water to drain out of the cart. If you don't want your cart to leak, mark and cut the bottom to a tight fit. If you were to bevel the ends of the bottom to match the slope of the cart ends, you could bring the box within caulking distance of watertight.

8 Make the axle support blocks. The wheel axle is a 36-inch length of ⅝-inch threaded rod. It's supported by two lengths of 2×4 glued and

Make the axle support blocks. Glue and screw two lengths of 2×4 to the cart bottom. These blocks should fit tightly between the bottom frames.

screwed to the cart bottom. If you can't find a single 36-inch length of threaded rod, you can use two shorter lengths instead. Either way, the construction is the same. Saw the two axle support blocks and trim the to a tight fit between the bottom frames. The first axle support block fits 6 inches back from the front end of the cart. The second one fits tightly against it. Spread glue on the cart bottom as well as on the support blocks, and also spread glue in between the two blocks. Tap them into place, clamp them together side to

Cut and fit the axle spacers. Clamp the spacers against the axle. The T1-11 is absorbent, so use plenty of glue and lots of screws.

Complete the frame. Glue and screw reinforcing frame pieces around the top edges of the cart body, then saw the protrusions flush.

Cap the frame. Fit cap pieces onto the top edge of the cart and screw them in place. They'll get dinged up in use, and eventually you'll need to replace them, so don't glue them.

side, and screw them to the T1-11 from inside the cart. Use the 1⅝-inch galvanized screws.

9 Cut and fit the axle spacers. The spacers, which are sawn from scraps of T1-11, trap the axle in place. Fit the wheels on the axle in order to locate the washers and nuts, then remove the wheels. Set the axle into the little valley between the two support blocks. Spread glue on one of the spacers, then fit it tightly against the axle. Drill pilot holes and screw the spacers to the axle support blocks and bottom frame. Spread glue on the second spacer, clamp it tight against the axle, and screw it down in the same way.

10 Cap the axle. The axle retainer, which is another strip of T1-11, caps the axle assembly. This strip has to be strong, so when you saw it from the plywood sheet, avoid the decorative grooves. Spread the glue

and drill pilot holes for 24 of the 2½-inch screws. Drill the pilot holes and drive the screws at various angles, which will strengthen the construction. You may hit a screw in the next layer down. If so, back out the one you were driving, and move it over a half inch or so.

11 Mount the wheels. Slide a washer onto the threaded rod, then a nut, then another washer, then the wheel, then another washer, then two nuts jammed tight together. The first nut and washer keep the tire from rubbing the cart sides.

12 Complete the frame. Reinforce the top of the T1-11 cart body with four frame pieces. These pieces fit on the outside of the T1-11, flush with its top edge. They'll be capped with four more pieces of wood in the next step. The top end frames are pieces of 2×4 sawn in half lengthwise and then cut to

fit between the end frames. The top side frames are 1×2 strips of pine. Glue, clamp, and screw these frame pieces onto the cart. Then trim any protruding pieces flush with their mates, as shown in the top right photo.

13 Cap the frame. Four strips of 1×3 wood cap the cart sides, covering the joints between the T1-11 and the frame pieces. The cap pieces are certain to get banged up, so consider them replaceable parts. Screw them down, but skip the glue.

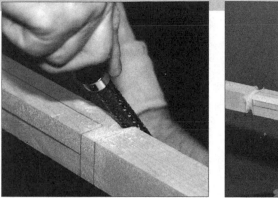

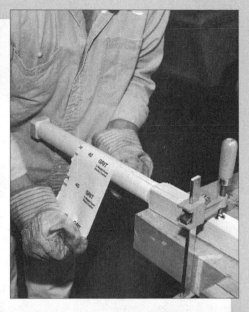

Make the handles. Draw layout lines and use a coarse round file or Surform to make a groove at both ends of the handle section (above left). Rasp off the corners of the handle to make an octagon, then rasp off the octagon's corners (center). This brings you close to round. Sand the handle with 40-grit paper, then move through 80-grit and 120-grit (right).

14 Make the handles. Saw a 5-foot-long 2×4 in half lengthwise to make two handle blanks. Choose knot-free wood with closely spaced annual rings. Shape the 15-inch rounded sections with Surform rasps and sandpaper, as shown in the photos above.

15 Fit the handles. Clamp one handle to the cart and test it. Adjust the angle so the lift is comfortable for you. Draw a layout line, and transfer the layout line to the other side of the cart. Unclamp the handles, drill pilot holes through the cart sides, and countersink the pilot holes on the inside of the cart. Glue and screw the handles to the cart sides. Drive at least six 2-inch screws into each handle.

16 Make the legs. The legs, which are pieces of 2×4, should prop the cart up level. The top of the leg fits against the handle. Hold the 2×4 in place so you can lay out the angle on the bottom of the legs, as shown at right. Saw the legs to length, then glue and screw them in place.

Fit the handles. Clamp one handle to the cart sides so you can check the lift. Adjust the handle to your own height.

17 Finish the cart. You could leave the cart unfinished, or you could paint it. The traditional finish for working tools is boiled linseed oil. Let the oil soak into the wood, then wipe it off with a rag. Let it dry for a week, then coat it again. If you wad up an oily rag, it's liable to ignite spontaneously, so spread the rag outdoors to dry flat. When it's completely dry and stiff, put it in the trash.

Make the legs. The leg fits square against the handle, so it needs to be sawn on an angle at the ground. Hold it in place, then draw a layout line against a block of wood.

Spike the arms onto the uprights. Nail both arms flush with the edge of one upright (above). Drive the nails at an angle to one another, for maximum holding power. Nail the second upright to the free ends of the arms, inset by the thickness of a piece of scrap (below). Fasten the second set of arms to the other side of the uprights (bottom).

HOSE HOLDER

Simple device gets the hose off the ground without tangles

Garden hoses get into a terrible tangle if they're not kept coiled. The devices that the home center sells are lightweight contraptions, when what's needed is something sturdy and substantial, like the hose holder shown here.

This hose holder can be made in either of two variations, a small one that can be fastened to the side of the house, and a larger one that can be staked to the ground. If your house has wooden siding, you probably wouldn't object to screwing the hose holder directly onto it. However, if your house has aluminum or vinyl siding, you may prefer the staked version.

BUILDING THE WALL HOLDER

1 Cut the wood. Make the hose holder parts from regular 2×4 lumber, or from scraps of 2×4 left over from other projects.

2 Spike the arms onto the uprights. The arms are flush with the upright that's going to be fastened to the wall, but they extend an inch beyond the other upright. The uprights extend above and below the arms by 3½ inches. Make layout lines and attach two arms to the same edge of one upright, using three 3-inch spiral nails at each intersection. Nail the second upright to the free ends of the arms, as shown in the photos at left. Then turn the assembly over to add the other two arms.

3 Mount the holder on the wall. Drill clearance holes for six 3-inch screws, two at the top, two at the bottom and two at center. Screw the upright to the side of the house or garage near the water spigot, as shown below. Loop the hose loosely over the hose holder, as shown in the opening photo.

Mount the holder on the wall. Screw the hose holder to the wall near the water spigot. Screw into a wall stud.

WALL-MOUNTED HOSE HOLDER

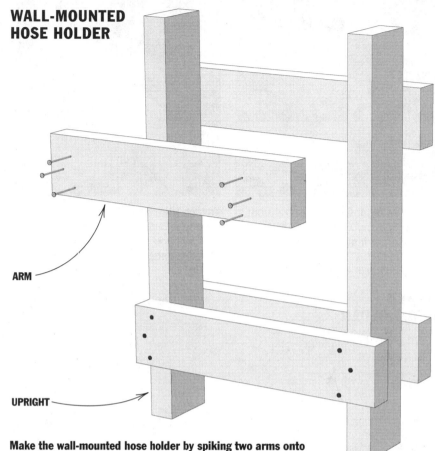

ARM

UPRIGHT

Make the wall-mounted hose holder by spiking two arms onto one side of the two uprights, then add the second pair of arms.

YOUR INVESTMENT
<u>Time:</u> **One hour**
<u>Money:</u> Wall-mounted hose holder, $5; Staked hose holder, $25

SHOPPING LIST
WALL-MOUNTED HOSE HOLDER
10 feet 2×4

STAKED HOSE HOLDER
4 feet 4×4
8 feet 2×3
4 feet 2×4
24-inch metal stake for 4×4 post
3-inch galvanized spiral nails

PROJECT SPECS
The wall-mounted hose holder is 24 inches high and projects 16 inches from the wall. The staked hose holder stands 42 inches high and is 24 inches wide.

CUTTING LIST

PART	QTY.	DIMENSIONS	NOTES
WALL-MOUNTED HOSE HOLDER			
Upright	2	1½ × 3½ × 24	2×4
Arm	4	1½ × 3½ × 16	2×4
STAKED HOSE HOLDER			
Post	1	3½ × 3½ × 42	4×4
Upright	2	1½ × 3½ × 24	2×4
Arm	4	1½ × 2½ × 24	2×3

Cut the wood. Instead of a 4×4 post, you can bulk up a pair of 2×4s with a ½-inch center insert of solid wood or scrap plywood.

Attach the arms. Nail the arms to the post with 3-inch spiral nails. Drive the first nail and start the second, then check for square.

Attach the uprights. Fit the uprights between the arms and nail them in place.

STAKED HOSE HOLDER

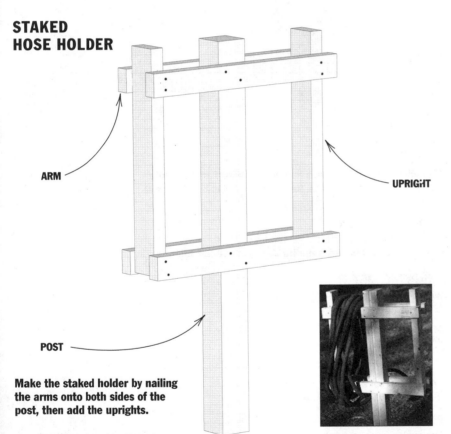

ARM

UPRIGHT

POST

Make the staked holder by nailing the arms onto both sides of the post, then add the uprights.

BUILDING THE STAKED HOLDER

1 Cut the wood. Unless you are willing to use pressure treated lumber, you may have difficulty obtaining a 4×4 post. However, you can assemble the post from two lengths of regular 2×4, with a center insert to bring it up to the thickness that fits the cup atop a commercially made metal stake, as shown at top left. Make the center insert from a scrap strip of ½-inch plywood, or by sawing two ½-inch strips from the edge of a third piece of 2×4.

2 Attach the arms. The 2×3

arms are centered on the face of the post. The upper arms are set down by 3½ inches from the top of the post. The lower arms are set flush with the bottom of the uprights. Attach each arm to the post with two 3-inch spiral nails. Hold the arm in position to drive the first nail and to start the second, then pause and check it for square before driving the second nail home, as shown in the photo at center above. Turn the post over to attach the second set of arms in the same way as the first.

3 Attach the uprights. Fit the uprights between the arms. Make each upright flush with the bottom edge of the lower arms, but inset by about an inch. Fasten the upright to the arms with two 3-inch spiral nails at each intersection, as shown in the top right photo.

4 Drive the stake and set the post. Decide where you want to install the hose holder and drive the stake into the ground, as described for the garden fence on page 186. Connect the hose to your faucet and spray away.

BEAN TEEPEE

Eight climbing poles make a comfy home for French beans

French beans run all over the place, unless you give them a teepee to climb. Then they're perfectly happy and you will be too, because the harvest stays within easy bounds.

This bean teepee consists of a wood-and-nails spider attached to eight 1×2 climbing poles. You can set it wherever you like, then fold it up like an umbrella at the end of the season.

BUILDING THE TEEPEE

1 Cut the wood. The cutting list specifies 1×2 material for the climbing poles, but you can use any wood you've got: narrow rippings, gardening stakes, what-ever. They don't have to all match, and they don't bear any appreciable weight, so knots and defects are not important.

2 Make the spider. The spider is a square block of wood with eight nails coming out of it. Choose a straight-grained scrap of wood, so it's less likely to

BEAN TEEPEE

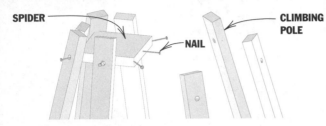

Drive eight nails into a block of wood to make the spider. Drill holes in the eight climbing poles and thread them onto the nails.

YOUR INVESTMENT
Time: One hour
Money: $5

PROJECT SPECS
The bean teepee stands 7 feet high and spreads about 5 feet.

SHOPPING LIST
56 feet 1×2 pine
2½-inch spiral nails

CUTTING LIST

PART	QTY.	DIMENSIONS	NOTES
Spider	1	¾ × 4½ × 4½	
Climbing pole	8	¾ × 1½ × 84	

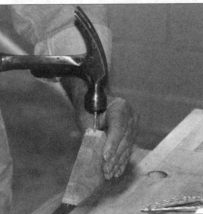

Drill the climbing poles. Make a 5/16-inch hole near the end of each of the eight climbing poles. Drill the poles in groups of two or three.

Make the spider. Mash a flat on the corner of a square block of wood (left). Drive nails into the corners and the centers of the sides (right).

Erect the teepee. Thread the climbing poles onto the spider (above). Spread the poles and bed them into the ground. Then plant the beans (right).

split. Hold the wood in a vise if you have one, or else balance it on the worktable. To make a nailing flat at the corner of the spider, mash the wood with the hammer. Drive a 2½-inch spiral nail into the center of each edge, and into each corner, as shown in the top left photos.

3 Drill the climbing poles. Drill a 5/16-inch hole a couple of inches from the end of each climbing pole. Drill the poles two or three at a time, as shown in the top right photo.

4 Erect the teepee. Slip the climbing poles onto the spider nails. Spread the poles as far apart as the nails permit and push them into the soil.

RASPBERRY POST

Supports put the canes on a manageable path

RASPBERRY POST

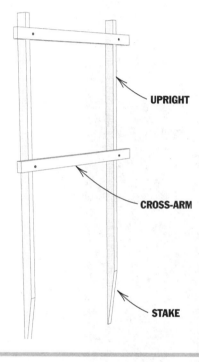

UPRIGHT

CROSS-ARM

STAKE

YOUR INVESTMENT
Time: One hour
Money: $4

SHOPPING LIST
13 feet 1×2
#6 × 2-inch galvanized screws
Gardening twine

PROJECT SPECS
One raspberry post is 48 inches high and 24 inches wide.

CUTTING LIST

PART	QTY.	DIMENSIONS	NOTES
Upright	2	¾ × 1½ × 48	
Cross-arm	2	¾ × 1½ × 24	

Saw the point on the uprights, then screw the cross-arms to them. Install the raspberry posts, then tie twine between the cross-arms to support the raspberry canes.

Sharpen the uprights and stakes. Draw a diagonal line starting from the corner of the stake, and jigsaw a point.

Join the uprights and cross-arms. Screw the uprights to the edges of the cross-arms.

Raspberries make a brambly mess if left to themselves, but unlike beans, they prefer to grow along a horizontal line instead of up a vertical pole. These simple trellises also work for peas and sweetpeas. Make raspberry posts in pairs, one for either end of the row, and connect them with twine, not wire.

BUILDING THE POSTS

1 Cut the wood. You can get one raspberry post out of an 8-foot 1×2, but you can also use scrap wood or garden stakes.

2 Sharpen the uprights. Sharpen the uprights to make it easy to set the raspberry post a few inches into the ground. Draw a diagonal line off one corner of the upright to a point 9 inches up, and jigsaw the point as shown in the top photo.

3 Join the uprights and cross-arms. A single screw makes an adequate connection between each upright and cross-arm. Screw through the face of the cross arm into the edge of the upright. Space the cross-arms about 16 inches apart.

4 Install the raspberry post. Set the raspberry posts in early spring, just as last year's canes begin to sprout new runners. Shove them 6 or 8 inches into the soil. Connect the cross-arms with lengths of twine, at least two and as many as four between each pair of cross-arms. Finally, run diagonal lengths of twine from the top cross-arm back to a 12-inch stake driven into the ground. This not only stabilizes the posts, it also makes an additional line for the raspberry runners to climb.

COMPOST BOX

Sturdy frame opens on one side

Seasoned gardeners develop their own approaches to composting, and their own box designs, but this simple box is a good way to get started. It has slatted sides and ends, so the air can circulate, and the front of the box lifts out, so you can turn the pile. When it's time to move the composted material into the garden, tip the box over and shovel the black gold.

The box shown is big enough for a household's kitchen and garden waste, plus the autumn leaves from a couple of trees. You can refigure the box to any size you like, and if you make several of them, you'll have enough microbial spas to decompose the largest garden.

You could make the compost box with regular pine lumber from the home center. But it is a compost box, not a piece of furniture, so it's the perfect place for using up scrap wood and short ends. The box shown takes advantage of a pile of mangy, roughsawn pine boards that had sat out in the weather. Your scrap material will be different from ours, so you'll have to work out the number of pieces from the widths you have. Just be sure to leave one-inch spaces for air to circulate, and avoid painted wood and pressure-treated lumber.

Ultimately, of course, the compost box goes the way of all organic material. By then, you will have formed your own opinion about how compost should be managed. You will be equipped by experience to design your own compost box.

BUILDING THE COMPOST BOX

1 **Make the corner posts and flanges.** Saw the four 2×3 corner posts to their final length, 36 inches in the box shown here. Make the four flanges the same length as the corner posts.

2 **Nail the front posts.** The flange pieces are nailed to the front corner posts, to make them into U-shaped channels. Align each flange piece with the ends and one edge of the corner post, then attach it with five or six 2½-inch spiral nails, as shown at top left on the next page. Attach two flange pieces to each front corner post.

COMPOST BOX

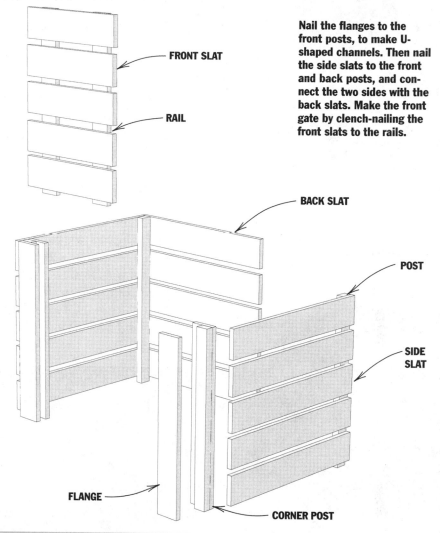

FRONT SLAT

RAIL

Nail the flanges to the front posts, to make U-shaped channels. Then nail the side slats to the front and back posts, and connect the two sides with the back slats. Make the front gate by clench-nailing the front slats to the rails.

BACK SLAT

POST

SIDE SLAT

FLANGE

CORNER POST

YOUR INVESTMENT
Time: One afternoon
Money: $25

SHOPPING LIST
12 feet 2×3 pine
18 feet 1×5 roughsawn pine
54 feet 1×6 roughsawn pine
2½-inch galvanized spiral nails
3-inch galvanized spiral nails

PROJECT SPECS
The compost box is 33 inches wide, 37 inches deep, and 36 inches high.

CUTTING LIST

PART	QTY.	DIMENSIONS	NOTES
Corner post	4	1½ × 2½ × 36	2×3
Flange	4	1 × 5 × 36	
Side slat	10	1 × 6 × 36	
Back slat	5	1 × 6 × 33	
Front slat	5	1 × 6 × 24	
Rail	2	1 × 4 × 36	

Nail the front posts. Make U-shaped channels by nailing two flange pieces to each front post, using spiral nails (above). Align the pieces on the back side (below).

Nail the side slats to the front posts. Make the side panels by nailing the side slats to the closed side of the U-shaped channel formed by the front posts and flanges.

3 Nail the side slats to the front posts. The side slats of the compost box are 36-inch lengths of ¾-inch or 1-inch thick wood, between 4 and 6 inches wide. Starting at the top of one front post, nail each slat to the post as shown in the photo at bottom left. Drive four of the 2½-inch spiral nails into each intersection. Use a length of regular 1×2 lumber to space the slats. Organize the side slats so that when you get to the bottom of the post, there's a space of 2 inches to 4 inches in width. Nail the second set of side slats to the other front post in the same way, but take care to make a right side and a left side.

4 Nail the side slats to the rear posts. Since the rear post is a regular 2×3, you'll have to drape the front flanges over the edge of the worktable, as shown in the photos below. Nail the free ends of the side slats to each rear post. You should end up with two similar side panels, one right-handed and the other left-handed.

5 Nail the back slats to the sides. Stand the two completed side panels up on end, with the flanged front posts on the ground. Space the back slats across the sides. Connect the two sides by squaring and fastening the top back slat in place,

Nail the side slats to the rear posts. Align the free ends of the side slats with the rear post (above). Nail them together (below).

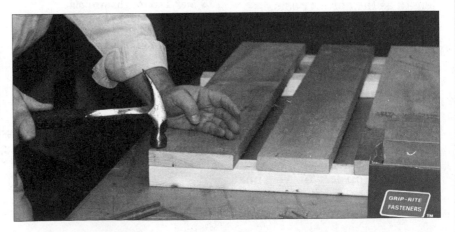

using the 3-inch spiral nails. Nail the bottom back slat, then fill in the space with the remaining slats. Spiral nails are stiff enough, and the nailing surfaces are wide enough, for the box to stand on its own without any bracing across the open front side.

6 Make the front panel. The front slats are clench-nailed to two rails, as discussed in the box below. Make sure the front slats will fit into the U-channeled front posts with ½-inch clearance. Then set the rails far enough in from the ends of the slats so they don't interfere—1¾ inches to 2 inches is about right. Align the top slat with the end of the first rail and drive the first nail. Then check for square, and drive the remaining three nails. Attach the top slat to the other rail in the same way, measuring to be sure the rails remain parallel to one another. Fasten the bottom slat, then fill in with the remaining front slats. Clench all the nails on the back of the panel to ensure that the construction stays together until the wood itself rots.

Nail the back slats to the sides. Stand the two side panels up on end and connect them with the back slats.

Make the front panel. Fasten the front slats to the rails with four nails at each intersection. Drive the nails on an angle and clench them on the back side, as discussed below.

CLENCH-NAILING

Clench-nailing means driving the points of the nails clear through the wood and bending them over on the back side. It is a certain way of holding nailed constructions together. Wooden pallets and stage sets are clench-nailed, and so are farm buildings throughout the Midwest. It's said that a clench-nailed shed can be picked up by a tornado and set down intact.

For a good clench, the nail should protrude about ½ inch on the back side of the wood. Drive the nails at a small angle, say 10 degrees from vertical. Then turn the work over and bend the points down hard into the wood. Do it right, and the nail head won't lift on the front side. Do it with less than full vigor, and the nail head probably will lift, making a secure but wiggly joint.

Clench-nailing. Drive the nails through the two pieces of wood, then bend the protruding points down tight.

den hose, allows you to scrape and brush the muck out of the deepest foot-treads. It's even got a place to lean while you shuck your gumboots and change into dry sneakers. And the duckboard construction makes it a snap to hose clean.

No doubt you could design a smaller and lighter version of the boot scraper. But if you're serious about gardening, then you'll have a serious amount of muck to contend with. You need to kick and bang and stomp on an apparatus built to take it. Likewise, if you enjoy whaling away with your framing hammer, you could knock this scraper together with spiral nails. Otherwise, clamp the pieces and drive galvanized screws, as discussed below.

BUILDING THE BOOT SCRAPER

1 Cut all the wood. You're going to screw the duckboard slats to one rail and then to the other, so it's important to make all the slats the same length. Guarantee equal lengths by setting a stop block on your table saw or chop saw.

2 Start the duckboard. There are two rails and eleven slats in the duckboard. Clamp the first slat to the worktable and butt the first rail up to it. Drill clearance holes and join the two pieces with two of the 3-inch screws. Then insert a couple of scraps of 2×4 as spacers, and screw the next slat to the rail, as shown in the top left photo on page 224. Continue in the same way until you have attached five slats to the first rail.

BOOT SCRAPER

Leave the mud in the garden,
not inside the house

Woe betide the gardener who tracks great clots of spring muck into the clean house. But what is the hapless peasant to do, without a premier boot scraper like the one shown here? This sturdy beast, which you should set up near the gar-

BOOT SCRAPER

Screw the duckboard rails and slats together. Add the posts and scraping bar, then the brush posts and brush bar. Screw the brushes to the slats and brush bar. Add the handrail.

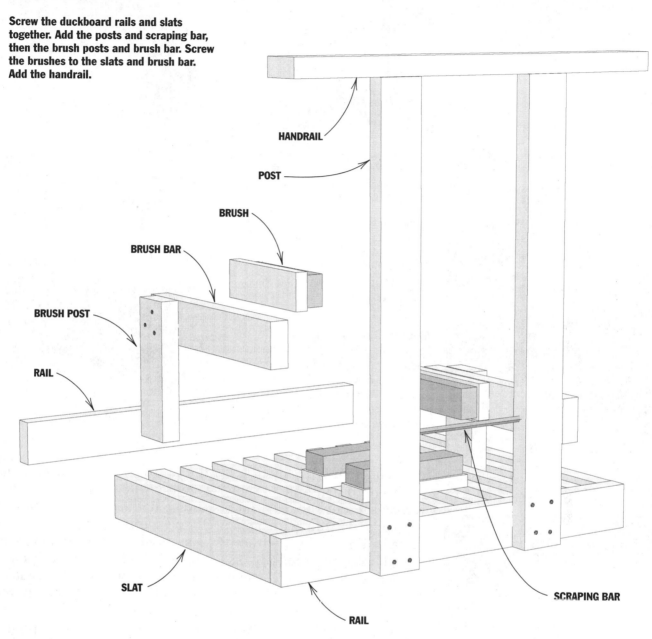

YOUR INVESTMENT

Time: One afternoon
Money: $30

SHOPPING LIST

Six 8-foot 2×4
$\frac{5}{16} \times \frac{5}{16} \times$ **12-inch square** steel bar
Four 10-inch scrub brushes with wooden handles
#8 × 3-inch galvanized screws
#6 × 2-inch galvanized screws

PROJECT SPECS

The boot scraper is 32 inches wide, 36 inches high, and 30 inches front to back.

CUTTING LIST

PART	QTY.	DIMENSIONS	NOTES
Slat	11	$1\frac{1}{2} \times 3\frac{1}{2} \times 24$	2×4
Rail	2	$1\frac{1}{2} \times 3\frac{1}{2} \times 32$	2×4
Post	2	$1\frac{1}{2} \times 3\frac{1}{2} \times 36$	2×4
Brush post	2	$1\frac{1}{2} \times 3\frac{1}{2} \times 11$	2×4
Brush bar	2	$1\frac{1}{2} \times 3\frac{1}{2} \times 18$	2×4
Handrail	1	$1\frac{1}{2} \times 3\frac{1}{2} \times 32$	2×4
Scraping bar	1	$\frac{5}{16} \times \frac{5}{16} \times 12$	Steel

Start the duckboard. Screw the first slat to the rail, then insert scraps of 2×4 to space the next slat (above).

Complete the duckboard. Work from the ends toward the middle, so any uneven spacing turns up between the middle two slats. Then screw the second rail to the free end of the slats (top right).

Mount the scraping bar. Drill a ⁵⁄₁₆-inch hole for the scraping bar in each post, then hammer the bar into one of the holes (left). Make sure to turn the bar corner up. Remove the bar and hammer it into the other post, then fit the two posts together (right).

Screw the posts to the duckboard. Clamp the posts to the rails and make them parallel. Adjust their spacing so that the outside edge of each post lines up with the inside edge of a slat.

3 Complete the duckboard. If you were to continue blithely across the duckboard, you'd probably end up with some extra rail, or worse, without enough rail. You want any discrepancy to show up in the middle space. Therefore, shift now to the other end of the rail and screw the last slat to it. Work back toward the center of the duckboard. Finally, screw the second rail to the free ends of the slats. Screw it to the first and last slats, then to the middle ones, keeping slats parallel with the scrap spacers as shown in the top right photo.

4 Mount the scraping bar. The boot scraping bar is a square rod of steel trapped between the two posts. It's 10 inches up from

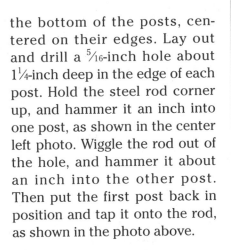

the bottom of the posts, centered on their edges. Lay out and drill a ⁵⁄₁₆-inch hole about 1¼-inch deep in the edge of each post. Hold the steel rod corner up, and hammer it an inch into one post, as shown in the center left photo. Wiggle the rod out of the hole, and hammer it about an inch into the other post. Then put the first post back in position and tap it onto the rod, as shown in the photo above.

5 Screw the posts to the duckboard. Center the posts-and-bar assembly on one rail of the duckboard. The outside edge of each post should line up with the inside edge of a slat, as shown in the lower left photo. Align and square one post and drive four screws into the duck-

Attach the sole brushes. Drill pilot holes and screw the two sole brushes to the duckboards.

Mount the brush posts. Locate the brush posts between the slats and screw them to the slats.

Attach the brush bars. Clamp the brush bars in position and screw them to the posts and to the brush posts.

Attach the side brushes. Screw the side brushes to the brush bars. Let them extend an inch or so beyond the ends of the bars.

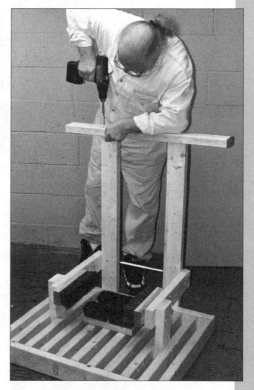

Make the handrail. Screw the handrail to the ends of the posts.

board rail. Then hammer the other post a little further onto the bar, or a little bit off the bar, until it too aligns with the inside edge of a slat, and screw it to the rail in the same way.

6 Attach the sole brushes. Screw the two boot-sole brushes directly to the duckboard slats, centered between the posts. Leave clearance of about 6 inches to the posts, and 3 inches between the brushes, as shown in the photo at top left. Drill clearance holes through the brush backs and fasten them to the slats with 2-inch screws.

7 Mount the brush posts. The two vertical brush posts support the brush bars. Mount them in the second space from

either side of the duckboard, 12 inches from the outside of the back rail. This measurement creates an offset of $1\frac{1}{2}$ inches between the brush post and the end of the brush bar. Screw diagonally down through the duckboard slats into the face of the brush posts, as shown in the photo at top right.

8 Attach the brush bars. The two horizontal brush bars support the brushes that allow you to grind the muck off the sides of your boots. Screw them to the posts and to the brush posts, as shown in the lower left photo.

9 Attach the side brushes. Clamp the side brushes to the brush bars. Keep the brush flush with the top of the bar, but let it

overhang $1\frac{1}{2}$ inches toward the front. Drill clearance holes through the brush bars into the backs of the two side brushes. Screw the brushes to the brush bars, as shown in center photo.

10 Make the handrail. The handrail is a horizontal 2×4 screwed to the tops of the posts. Center it and fasten it with two 3-inch screws into each post, as shown above.

PLANT STAND

Corner tower, nailed together, displays amazing number of potted plants

A plant stand in a flower bed adds an exciting vertical dimension to the garden. On the deck, a tall stand with shelves provides a delightful way to use the corner next to the house. If you make two plant stands and fit them together, you can display an enormous number of plants against a straight wall or in front of a deck railing.

The plant stand relies upon a sturdy corner post, assembled pinwheel-fashion from four identical 1×4 pieces of wood. The remainder of the structure that supports the shelves is made of 1×3 pine lumber. The shelves themselves are sawn from 1×6, 1×8 and 1×10 boards.

The plant stand is held together with galvanized siding nails and glue. Siding nails have a small and unobtrusive head, with a ring shank that really grabs hold. You'll need them 2 inches and 2½ inches long.

Several of the pieces are mitered at 45 degrees, so this project requires a reliable way of sawing a miter. A chop saw or a table saw are ideal, and a jigsaw or portable circular saw are just fine, provided you make the miter jig shown on page 361.

You'll also need a jigsaw for shaping the quarter-circle ends on the shelf pieces. This detail makes an interesting and amusing plant stand, but if you prefer, you can always leave the wood square and straight.

PLANT STAND

To build the plant stand, glue and nail the corner post together, then make and attach the bottom shelf rails and supports. Shape and nail the shelf to its support structure. Continue up the post, attaching rails and ledgers and shelves.

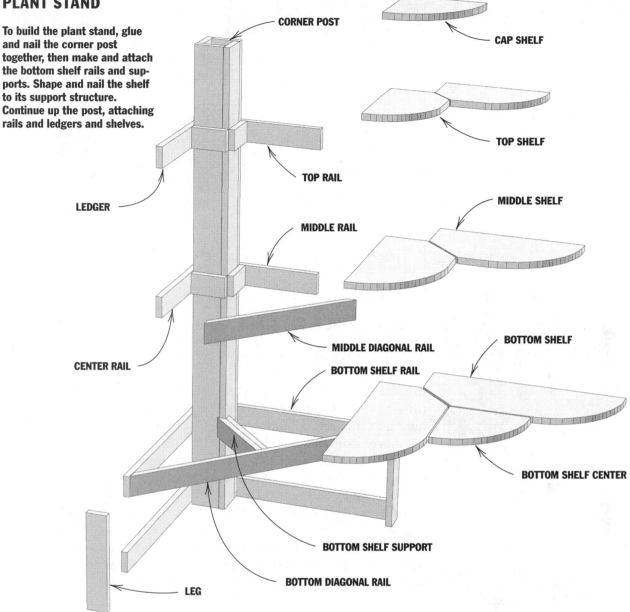

CORNER POST

CAP SHELF

TOP SHELF

TOP RAIL

LEDGER

MIDDLE SHELF

MIDDLE RAIL

CENTER RAIL

MIDDLE DIAGONAL RAIL

BOTTOM SHELF

BOTTOM SHELF RAIL

BOTTOM SHELF CENTER

BOTTOM SHELF SUPPORT

BOTTOM DIAGONAL RAIL

LEG

YOUR INVESTMENT

<u>Time:</u> One afternoon
<u>Money:</u> $36

SHOPPING LIST

32 feet 1×3 pine
24 feet 1×4 pine
4 feet 1×8 pine
12 feet 1×10 pine
2½-inch galvanized siding nails

PROJECT SPECS

The plant stand is 58 inches high, 40 inches wide, and 24 inches deep.

CUTTING LIST

PART	QTY.	DIMENSIONS	NOTES
Corner post	4	$^3/_4 \times 3^1/_2 \times 57$	1×4
Leg	2	$^3/_4 \times 2^1/_2 \times 24$	1×3
Bottom shelf rail	2	$^3/_4 \times 2^1/_2 \times 24$	1×3
Bottom shelf support	2	$^3/_4 \times 2^1/_2 \times 12$	1×3
Bottom diagonal rail	1	$^3/_4 \times 2^1/_2 \times 36$	1×3; miter to fit
Center rail	2	$^3/_4 \times 2^1/_2 \times 12$	1×3; miter to fit
Bottom shelf	2	$^3/_4 \times 9^1/_2 \times 23$	1×10
Bottom shelf center	1	$^3/_4 \times 9^1/_2 \times 9^1/_2$	1×10
Middle rail	2	$^3/_4 \times 2^1/_2 \times 14$	1×3
Middle diagonal rail	1	$^3/_4 \times 2^1/_2 \times 21$	1×3; miter to fit
Ledger	4	$^3/_4 \times 2^1/_2 \times 4^1/_4$	1×3
Middle shelf	2	$^3/_4 \times 9^1/_2 \times 17$	1×10
Top rail	2	$^3/_4 \times 2^1/_2 \times 14$	1×3
Top shelf	2	$^3/_4 \times 7^1/_2 \times 12$	1×8
Cap shelf	1	$^3/_4 \times 9^1/_2 \times 9^1/_2$	1×10

Make the corner post. Spread glue on one edge of each corner post board and nail it to the others, pinwheel fashion.

Make the legs. Glue and nail the legs to the corner post (above). Nail near the edges of the post (below).

BUILDING THE PLANT STAND

1 Saw the wood. You can saw all the legs and rails now, though the diagonal rails and center rails have to be mitered to fit during the construction process. It's more economical to lay out and saw the shelf pieces as you go along. The shelves have miters on one end and quarter-rounds on the other, so the shapes can fit into one another and around defects in the wood. Note that the cap shelf is the same as the bottom shelf center.

2 Make the corner post. The corner post consists of four identical boards glued and nailed together pinwheel fashion to make a square column, as shown in the photo at top right. Roll glue on the edge of each post board and nail into it through the face of the adjacent board, using 2-inch siding nails spaced about a foot apart.

3 Make the legs. The legs and bottom shelf rails are identical horizontal pieces glued and

nailed to the corner post. Start with one of the two legs. Set it in position, square a layout line across the post, and spread glue on the post. Then replace the leg piece and drive the first nail. Check for square and adjust before you drive the remaining nails. Drive six 2½-inch siding nails, and keep them near the edges of the post so they bite through as much wood as possible. Nail the second leg to the post in the same way, as shown at left. Note that the ends of the legs don't overlap.

4 Make the bottom rails. Glue and screw the bottom rails to the post the same way you attached the legs, but make their top edges land 12 inches above the ground.

5 Support the bottom shelf. The two bottom shelf supports are vertical pieces of wood nailed to the ends of the legs and bottom rails, as shown in the top left photo on the facing page. Make each joint with three of the 2½-inch siding nails.

Support the bottom shelf. Nail the two shelf supports across the ends of the legs and rails.

Make the bottom diagonal rail. Mark the length of the bottom diagonal rail and miter it on the chop saw (above). Fit the diagonal rail into the socket formed by the bottom shelf support and bottom rail, and nail it in place (below).

6 **Make the bottom diagonal rail.** The bottom diagonal rail fits in the pocket between the bottom rails and bottom shelf supports, as shown in the drawing on page 227. To fit the diagonal rail, miter one end of the wood as shown in the photo at top right, then hold it in position to mark and cut the other miter. Nail through the bottom shelf supports into the ends of the bottom diagonal rail. Drive the 2½-inch siding nails in line with the diagonal rail.

7 **Make the bottom center rail.** The bottom center rail consists of two 12-inch pieces of wood mitered at one end and then glued together face to face. The two miters make a vee-shaped notch that fits around the corner post. Make the miters first, then hold the wood in position to mark it to final length, and saw it. Draw a layout line on the corner post, and use a stick of wood as a straight edge to help you keep the bottom center rail flush with the bottom shelf rails. As shown in the photo at right, nail

Make the bottom center rail. Glue the two bottom center rail pieces together, then fit them. Nail the center rail to the corner post and to the diagonal rail.

SHELF DETAIL
Make a stick compass to lay out the curves on the shelf pieces.

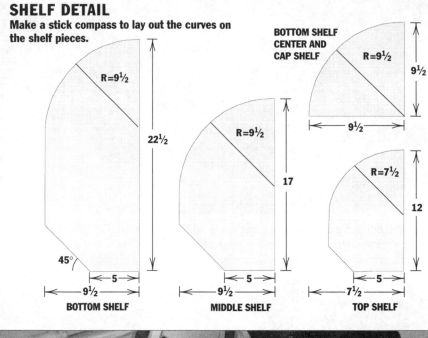

R=9½

22½

45°

5

9½

BOTTOM SHELF

R=9½

17

5

9½

MIDDLE SHELF

BOTTOM SHELF
CENTER AND
CAP SHELF

R=9½

9½

9½

R=7½

12

5

7½

TOP SHELF

Make the bottom shelf. Lay out and saw the miter on both bottom shelf pieces. Make a stick compass to lay out their curved ends. Saw the curves with the jig saw.

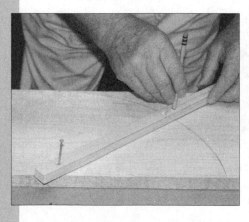

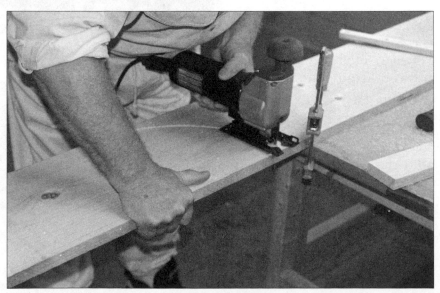

the center rail to the corner post, then nail into it through the diagonal rail.

8 Make the bottom shelf. The bottom shelf consists of three pieces of 1×10 lumber, each with a quarter-circle sawn on one end. The two outside pieces are mitered as shown in the drawing at left, so they fit together at the corner post. The bottom shelf center is a square of wood with the same jigsawn quarter-circle. Saw the miters, then lay out the curves with a compass, as shown in the photos at left below. Saw the curves and sand the sharp edges off the wood.

9 Attach the bottom shelf. Nail the three shelf pieces to the rails. Use a piece of scrap wood to prop up the diagonal rail at the center, as shown at top right, while you nail into it.

10 Attach the middle rails. Glue and nail the two middle rails to the corner post. The top edge of these rails falls 30 inches up from the ground. Draw a layout line, spread glue, clamp the

Attach the bottom shelf. Prop the center rail with a piece of scrap and nail the bottom shelf to the rails. Then attach the bottom shelf center.

Attach the middle rails. Glue, clamp and nail the middle rails to the post. Make sure the parts are square.

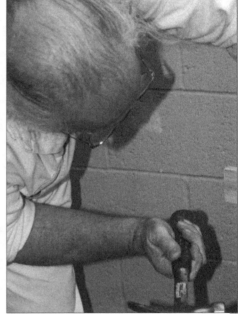

Fit the middle diagonal rail and ledger. Hold the middle diagonal rail in place to lay out and cut the miters, but don't try to attach it yet. Nail the two ledgers to the post alongside the rails.

wood in place, and fasten each rail with six 2½-inch siding nails, as shown in the photo above.

11 Make the middle diagonal rail and ledger. The middle shelf consists of only two pieces of wood, so you can get away without the center rail. You'll still need the middle diagonal rail, which you can make now,

though you can't attach it until Step 13. To lay out the middle diagonal rail, miter one end of the wood, then hold it in place to mark and cut the miter on the other end, as shown in the center photo. Put it aside. Check the fit of the two small ledgers, then glue and nail them onto the face of the corner post, as shown in the photo above.

12 Make the middle shelf. Lay out and saw the two boards of the middle shelf, same as the bottom shelf in Step 8. Nail the middle shelf to its rails and ledgers with the 2½-inch siding nails, as shown in the top left photo on the next page.

13 Fit the middle diagonal rail. The middle diagonal rail sup-

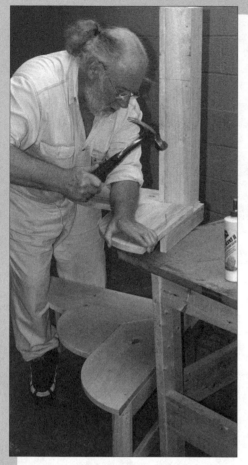

Fit the middle diagonal rail. Clamp the middle diagonal rail underneath the shelf and nail it to the middle rails. Also nail into it through the shelf.

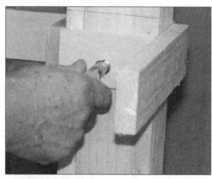

Fit the top ledgers. Glue, clamp and nail the top rails and ledgers to the corner post.

Make the middle shelf. Support the middle rails on the worktable and nail the middle shelf in place.

Make the cap shelf. The cap shelf overhangs the top of the corner post, like the other shelves. Gauge the overhang with a stick of scrap (above). Nail the cap shelf to the post (right).

ports the front of the shelf. You mitered it to length in Step 11. Now lay the plant stand on its side on the worktable so you can nail the diagonal rail to the ends of the middle rails, as shown in the photo at left. Nail the middle shelf boards to the middle diagonal rail.

14 Attach the top rails. Glue and nail the two top rails to the corner post. The top edge of these rails is 47 inches from the base. Draw a layout line, spread glue, clamp and fasten each rail with six 2½-inch siding nails.

15 Fit the top ledgers. The top shelf consists of only two narrow pieces of wood, so you can get away without a diagonal rail, but you still need the ledgers. Glue and nail the ledgers onto the face of the corner post, as shown in the center left photo.

16 Make the top shelf. Lay out and saw the two boards of the top shelf in the same way you made the bottom shelf, in Step 8. Nail the top shelf to the top rails and top ledgers, using the 2½-inch siding nails.

17 Make the cap shelf. The cap shelf is a 1×10 quarter-circle, the same as the bottom shelf center. Jigsaw it and nail it on top of the post. The cap shelf should overhang on the two back sides by the thickness of the wood, as shown in the bottom left photo.

18 Finish the plant stand. Since the plant stand is liable to get wet, paint is a better choice than varnish. But the simplest choice is no finish, as shown in the photo on page 226.

DRYING RACK

A place to hang herbs and flowers

Here is a simple wooden rack for drying herbs and flowers. The rack mounts on a wall. The arms of the rack can be inserted between the bars when you want to dry something, then removed and stowed away atop the rack. It's easy to make the rack any size.

DRYING RACK

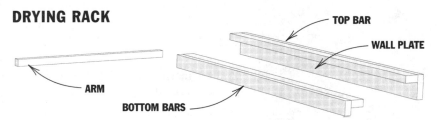

TOP BAR

WALL PLATE

ARM

BOTTOM BARS

Glue and nail the two bottom bars together, glue and nail the top bar to the wall plate, then glue and nail the two assemblies together.

YOUR INVESTMENT
Time: One evening
Money: $5

SHOPPING LIST
10 feet 1×2 pine
6 feet 1×3 pine
2-inch galvanized siding nails
#6 × 2½-inch galvanized screws

PROJECT SPECS
The herb drying rack is 36 inches long, 3 inches high, and protrudes as far into the room as you like.

CUTTING LIST

PART	QTY.	DIMENSIONS	NOTES
Bar	3	¾ × 1½ × 32	1×2
Wall plate	1	¾ × 2½ × 32	1×3
Arm	6	¾ × ¾ × 18	Length to suit

BUILDING THE RACK

1 **Cut the wood.** Make all the pieces at the start of the project. If you don't have a table saw for ripping the arms out of wider boards, buy some ¾-inch square molding instead.

2 **Glue and nail the bottom bars together.** The three bars and the wall plate create a slot into which you can slip the arms, as shown in the drawing. Assemble the pieces in stages, beginning with two of the bars, which you glue and nail into an L-shaped section, using five or six of the 2-inch siding nails.

3 **Glue and nail the top bar and wall plate.** Make an L-shape by gluing and nailing the edge of the top bar to the face of the wider wall plate.

4 **Join the assemblies.** Glue and nail the two L-shaped sub-assemblies as shown in the photo below. Use one of the arms as a spacer.

5 **Mount the drying rack.** Decide where you want to mount the drying rack and drive 2½-inch screws through the wall plate into two wall studs.

Join the assemblies. Use one of the arms to maintain the space between the two L-shaped sections while you nail them together.

PLANT PEDESTAL

This simple stand lifts any potted plant off the deck

Y ou get a lot more mileage out of potted plants when you can arrange them the way you want, and that usually means raising some of them on little stands or pedestals. Here is a plant pedestal you can knock together in a few minutes, using short ends of wood left over from other projects.

The pedestal consists of two wooden right-angles, each made by nailing and gluing two identical pieces of wood together, with square plates of wood top and bottom. The wooden right-angle is an incredibly strong and versatile construction element. Making one of these pedestals is likely to give you all sorts of ideas for other projects that rely on the same idea. For another example, check out the deck tables on page 26.

BUILDING THE PEDESTAL

1 Saw the uprights. Although the cutting list specifies 16-inch uprights, you can make the plant pedestal any height you like. Be sure, however, that all four uprights are the same length.

2 Assemble one right angle. The pedestal base consists of two wooden right-angles glued and nailed together, which you make one at a time. Start by spreading glue on the edge of one upright piece. Nail a second upright onto it, forming the right angle, as shown in the top photo on the next page. Use three or four 2-inch siding nails.

3 Complete the base. Make a second right angle, exactly the same as the first one. Now fit the two right-angles together. You'll find that there is a right and a left, and you might have to turn one of them upside-down to achieve the pinwheel geometry shown in the drawing below.

4 Attach the top and bottom. The top and bottom are square pieces of wood sawn to about the outside dimension of the pedestal—in this case, 7 inches. If what you have on hand is some 1×8 measuring around 7½ inches wide, don't worry. Just cut two squares and everything will be fine. Nail the top and bottom onto the pedestal base, with 2½-inch siding nails.

Assemble one right angle. Use an upright piece as a prop while you nail the two parts together.

Complete the base. Nail two right angles together, forming a pinwheel.

Attach the top and bottom. Nail two square pieces of wood onto the pedestal base.

PLANT PEDESTAL

To make the plant pedestal, make two wooden right angles and nail them together. Then add the top and bottom plates.

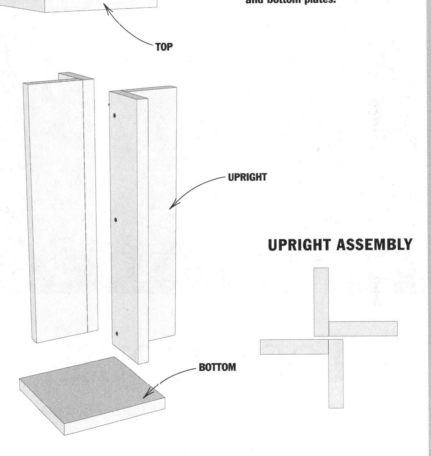

TOP

UPRIGHT

BOTTOM

UPRIGHT ASSEMBLY

YOUR INVESTMENT
Time: An hour
Money: $4

PROJECT SPECS
The pedestal is 17½ inches tall and 7 inches square.

SHOPPING LIST
6 feet 1×4 pine
2 feet 1×8 pine
2-inch galvanized siding nails
2½-inch galvanized siding nails

CUTTING LIST

PART	QTY.	DIMENSIONS	NOTES
Upright	4	¾ × 3½ × 16	1×4
Top and bottom	2	¾ × 7 × 7	

TOOL HOUSE

A handy place to store all your shovels, hoes and rakes

Storage for garden tools is always a problem. The tools you need in the springtime get buried behind the tools you used all winter. With the best of intentions, there's an impenetrable thicket of handles that interferes with doing your chores.

The answer is a special house or cabinet for the garden tools. This tool house is a tall, flat box that stands against the outside wall of your house or garage nearest the garden itself. If you've been thinking that you need a full-scale garden shed,

consider making this simple tool house instead.

The tool house rests on a couple of bricks or blocks on the ground. It's fastened to the building with a couple of nails or screws through the back. The hinged doors open wide so you can easily get at what you need, and they close tight against winter weather. The board-and-rail construction allows you to assemble the back, sides and doors from narrow boards.

The construction of the tool house is straightforward. It's held together with glue and screws. Its sides do have to be sawn at an angle to meet with the pitched roof. The steps below show laying out and cutting the angle with a hand saw, after you assemble the sides. If you've got a power saw, the task is that much easier.

The tool house doors have a Z-shaped rail and brace on the inside. This is a very useful way of making a stiff panel out of narrow boards, one that you can use in other applications.

The inside of this tool house measures 9 inches deep, 34 inches wide, and 6 feet high. Of course the size of the box can be adjusted, though if you make it deeper than about 12 inches or wider than 48 inches, you would need to add rafters to help support the roof. You can make it narrower or shallower without any change in construction, and there is something elegant about keeping cabinets like this down to their minimum useful size. If you like to garden with nothing but your custom-made European hoe, you could make the house exactly big enough to store that one tool.

BUILDING THE TOOL HOUSE

1 Cut the wood. The tool house, as shown, is made of solid wood with a plywood roof. When you buy the 1×6 lumber for the sides, back and doors, choose 6-foot or 12-foot boards, not 8-footers. Begin by sawing all the wood to the sizes given in the cutting list. Since the back is neither structural nor visible, it's a good place to use up knotty and twisted wood. You could substitute a piece of ⅝-inch CDX plywood measuring 33 inches × 70 inches for the six back boards, and T1-11 siding for the plywood roof, but the sides and doors look best as solid wood.

2 Make the first side. Each side of the tool house consists of two 1×6 boards connected by three glued-and-screwed rails. The bottom side rail is 6 inches up from the end of the boards; the middle side rail is 40 inches up, and the top rail, which is discussed in Step 3, establishes

TOOL HOUSE

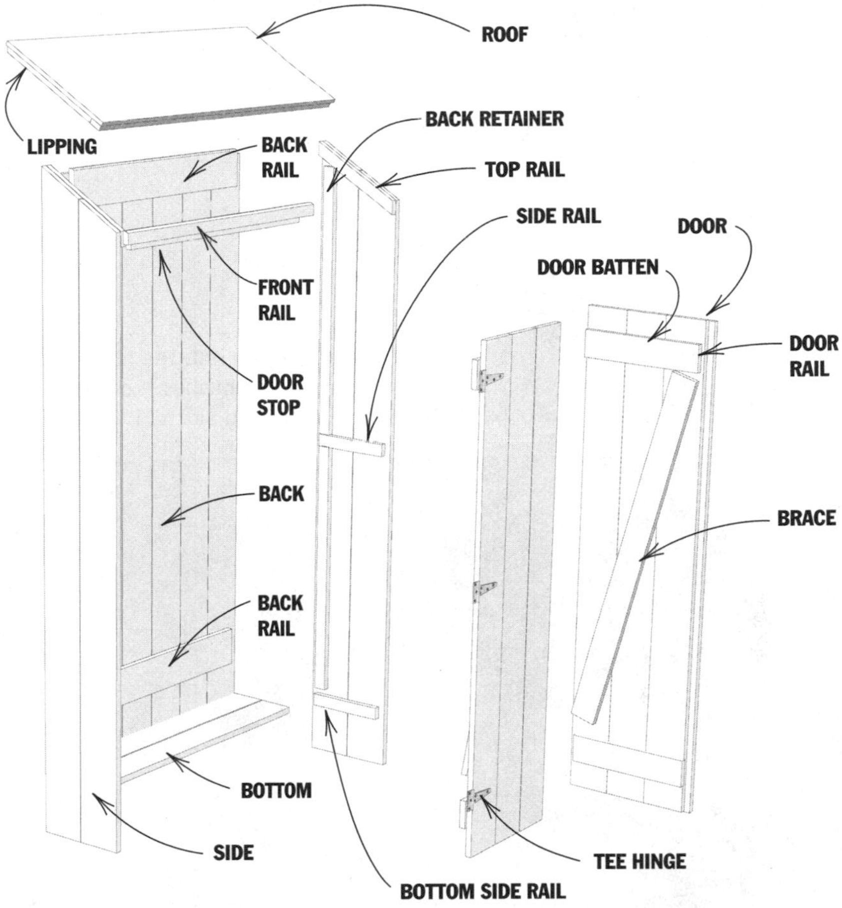

Begin by making the tool house sides and attaching the back retainers. Make the back and screw it to the sides. Add the front rail and the bottom, install the roof, then make the doors. Hang the doors, then install the tool house against your house or garage.

YOUR INVESTMENT

<u>Time:</u> **All day**
<u>Money:</u> **$80**

SHOPPING LIST

32 feet 1×2 pine
16 feet 1×4 pine
16 feet 1×5 pine
96 feet 1×6 pine
⅙ sheet ½-inch CDX plywood
#6 × 1¼-inch galvanized screws
#6 × 1⅝-inch galvanized screws
#6 × 2-inch galvanized screws
Six 4-inch galvanized tee hinges
One 3-inch barrel bolt

PROJECT SPECS

The tool house is 79 inches high, 43 inches wide at the roof, and 15 inches deep at the roof.

CUTTING LIST

PART	QTY.	DIMENSIONS	NOTES
Side	4	¾ × 5½ × 78	1×6
Side rail	4	¾ × 1½ × 9½	1×2
Top rail	2	¾ × 1½ × 15	1×2; cut to fit
Back retainer	4	¾ × 1½ × 36	1×2; cut to fit
Back	6	¾ × 5½ × 70	1×6
Back rail	2	¾ × 4½ × 30	1×5
Bottom	2	¾ × 4½ × 35	1×5; cut to fit
Front rail	1	¾ × 1½ × 36	1×2; cut to fit
Roof	1	½ × 16 × 43	CDX plywood
Lipping		¾ × 1½ × 72	1×2; cut to fit
Door	6	¾ × 5½ × 63	1×6
Door rail	4	¾ × 3½ × 16	1×4
Brace	2	¾ × 3½ × 48	1×4
Door stop	1	¾ × 1½ × 32	1×2; cut to fit
Door batten	1	¾ × 1½ × 63	1×2

Make the first side. Center the bottom side rail on the side boards. Use a piece of scrap to gauge the margins for the back and door.

Attach the top rail. The carpenter's protractor establishes the 30-degree angle of the top side rail.

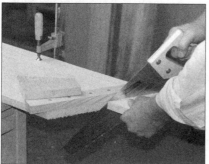

Trim the side and top rail. Saw the side to the angle established by the top side rail (above). Trim the ends of the rail flush with the sides (right).

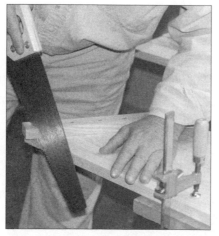

the pitch of the roof. Start with the bottom side rail. Square a line 6 inches up from the end of the side boards, spread glue on the side rail, and clamp it in place. It should be centered from side to side, leaving margins the thickness of the back boards and door, as shown in the photo at top left. Drive four of the 1¼-inch screws through the side rail into the two side boards. Attach the center side rail to the two side boards in the same way.

3 **Attach the top rail.** The top rail establishes the 30-degree pitch of the tool house roof. Use a speed square or a carpenter's protractor, as shown in the photo at left, to locate the top rail on the side. Spread glue on it, clamp it, and screw it to the two side boards with six of the 1¼-inch screws.

4 **Trim the side and top rail.** The top rail is the template for sawing the side boards to match the pitch of the roof. Saw directly along the edge of the top rail, as shown in the photos at left. Then trim the ends of the top rail to match the sides. If you deviate from the line established by the rail, rasp the excess wood off with a Surform.

5 **Make the second side.** The second side of the tool house is the same as the first side, except of opposite handedness. Attach the bottom and middle side rails. Keep the completed side panel close at hand when you attach the top rail, so you can be sure its pitch is opposite, as shown in the photo at the top of the facing page.

6 Attach the back retainers. The back retainers provide a means for attaching the back panel to the tool house sides. Cut them to fit from 1×2 wood. The bottom retainer fits between the two side rails, leaving a gap for the tool house bottom, as shown in the center photo at right. The top retainer fits between the middle side rail and the top rail. While you could cut an angle at its top end, it's not necessary to do so. Glue and screw the back retainers to the side boards. Use a piece of scrap wood as a gauge to set the retainers in from the back edge of the side panels. Drive four of the 1¼-inch screws through each retainer.

7 Make the back. The back consists of six boards held together by two back rails. There should be a little space between the back boards, so the wood can move with changes in the weather. The top back rail becomes the nailer for the roof, so it has to overlap the ends of the boards by 1½ inches, as shown in the photo below at right. The bottom back rail has to clear the bottom of the tool house, so locate it about 6 inches up the back. Center each rail from side to side, leaving a margin of an inch at either side. This margin has to be wide enough to clear the back retainers. Screw the two back rails to the six back boards with two or three 1¼-inch screws through each rail into each board.

8 Attach the back to the sides. Making the initial connection between the back and sides is somewhat awkward, but once

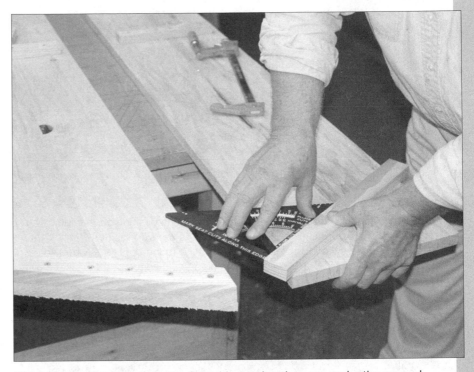

Make the second side. Keep the first side nearby when you make the second side, to be sure one is right-handed and the other left-handed.

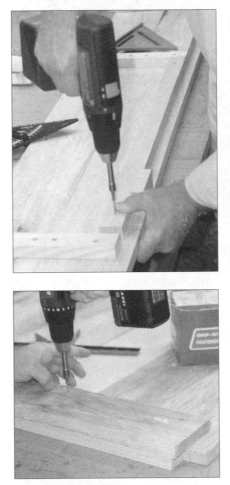

Attach the back retainers. Fit the back retainers between the side rails, leaving a gap for the bottom (left). The gauge block, behind thumb, holds the space for the tool house back.

Make the back. The top back rail extends beyond the six back boards by the width of the 1×2 gauge strip (left). Screw the bottom back rail to the back boards (above).

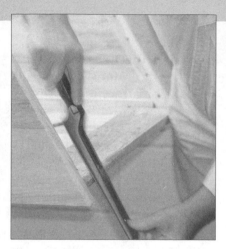

Attach the back to the sides. Stand the first side in position on the back. The top edge of the back rail extends just beyond the top side rail (left). Attach the back with two screws driven from below (center). Turn the assembly over to attach the second side, and drive screws along both edges of the back (below).

Shape the top back rail. Rasp a flat along the edge of the top back rail. The flat makes a nailing surface for the roof.

Make the bottom. Screw the two bottom boards to the bottom side rails.

the first two screws are in, the whole process becomes easy. Stand one side in position on the back, as shown in the photo at top left. The top edge of the top back rail should extend just beyond the top side rails. Draw a layout line on the back, remove the side, and drill two clearance holes through the back where the side will fit, one near the top and the other near the bottom. Then run a bead of glue along the back retainer and

replace the side on the back. Now reach up from below to drive two 2-inch screws through the back and into the back retainer, as shown in the photo at top center. These two screws give the construction enough stability for you to turn it over on the worktable and attach the second side with glue and a couple of screws, as shown in the photo directly above. Then, go all along both edges of the back and screw it to the retainers.

9 Shape the top back rail. The top back rail needs a nailing flat where the roof will fit. In the previous step you let the top back rail extend just beyond the top side rails. Now rasp the corner off the top back rail, to create a flat that is in line with the pitch of the top side rails, as shown in the top right photo.

10 Make the bottom. The bottom of the tool house consists of two 1×5 boards screwed onto the bottom side rails. Since the precise width of the tool house depends on the width of your 1×6 lumber, the length of the bottom boards has to be cut to fit. After you've screwed the bottom boards to the bottom side rails, also screw through the back into the edge of the bottom.

11 Make the front rail. The front rail ties the top of the tool house together, and also allows the door to clear the front edge of the roof. Hold the top rail in place, its bottom edge flush with the tail of the top side rail. Mark and saw it to length, then glue and screw it to the top of the sides and the ends of the top side rails. Finally, rasp its top edge flush with the pitch of the roof, as shown in the photo at right.

12 Install the roof. The roof is a piece of exterior-grade plywood or T1-11 siding. It's screwed to the pitched sides of the tool house, and to the front and top back rails. Since plywood isn't very flat, glue and screw a 1×2 lipping to the exposed three sides of the roof before you attach it to the tool house, as shown in the photo at bottom right. If you set the lipping back ¼ inch from the edge of the plywood, it not only makes a shadow reveal, it also makes a drip edge that sheds water. Center the roof from side to side and fasten it to the tool house with 1¼-inch screws.

13 Make the first door. The doors are made of the same 1×6 lumber as the back of the tool house. Each door consists of

Make the front rail. Screw the front rail to the top side rail, then rasp its edge into line with the pitch of the roof. Use a stick to gauge your progress.

Install the roof. Glue and screw the lipping to the plywood roof, then screw the roof to the tool house.

three boards connected by two rails and a brace. Fit three of the door boards tight together on the worktable. Lay the diagonal brace across the three boards, as shown in the photo at left below. Center the brace from end to end, and bring its corners just inside the edges of the door boards. Attach the brace by driving six of the 1¼-inch screws into each door board. Space the screws as widely apart as possible. Center the two door rails on the door, 3 inches up from either end, and attach them with four screws into each door board, as shown in the photo at bottom left.

14 Make the second door. The doors are strongest when the brace runs down toward the hinge side, as shown in the photo on page 236. This means the two doors should be of opposite handedness. Make the second door with the first door laying on the worktable as reference, so that one brace runs one way and the other runs the other way, as shown in the photo below.

15 Hang the doors. Each door hangs on three tee hinges. Screw the hinges to the doors while they are still on the worktable, then hang the doors on the tool house. Locate the top and bottom hinges so the screws go into the door rails. Screw the narrow leaf of the tee hinges to the edges of the tool house sides, as shown in the top right photo on

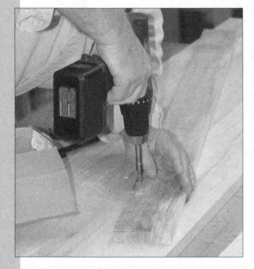

Make the first door. Screw the diagonal door brace across the door boards (above). Center the door rails 3 inches in from the ends of the door (below).

Make the second door. The braces on the two doors should run in opposite directions, with the bottom of each brace on the hinge side of its door.

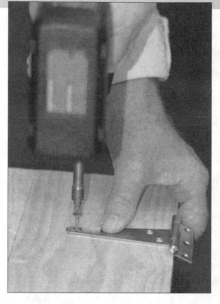

this page. To create clearance, lay a stick of scrap on the bottom of the tool house, then rest the bottom door rail on it.

16 Make the door stop. The door stop creates a surface for mounting the strike of the barrel bolt, and incidentally fills the gap at the top of the doors. It's screwed to the back of the front rail. Cut the length of the door stop to match the distance between the top side rails. Its width depends on the height of your doors, and on how much gap you have to fill.

Hang the doors. Screw the tee hinges to the doors (above), then screw them to the tool house sides (right).

17 Make the door batten. The door batten is a vertical strip attached to the outside edge of one door. When this door is bolted shut, the batten catches and holds the other door closed. It also covers any vertical gap between the doors. Screw the batten to the door from the inside.

Make the door stop. Screw the door stop to the back of the front rail. Make it just wide enough to fill the gap above the doors.

18 Mount the barrel bolt. The barrel bolt mounts vertically at the top of the battened door. Mount the strike on the door stop, as shown in the photo below at right.

19 Install the tool house. To delay rotting, the sides of the tool house should rest on bricks or concrete blocks. Adjust the blocks until the tool house stands vertically against the wall of the building. Then nail or screw through the back into the wall. If the building has board-and-batten siding, shakes, clapboards or shingles, you can add matching trim to the tool house roof and sides. Paint it or stain it to match the building.

Mount the barrel bolt. Attach the batten to one of the doors, then mount the barrel bolt on the same door. Screw the strike to the door stop above the door.

TRUG

Traditional wooden basket helps harvest your tomatoes

Oh, it's so romantic to traipse through the garden with your trug slung over your arm, gathering a bountiful harvest of beans, rhubarb or daisies. The bees buzz and the dewdrops glisten in the morning sunshine. The rustic trug allows you to imagine, just for a moment, that you've been transported to a simpler time with nothing more important to do than harvest your tomatoes.

As a gardening tool, the trug, or wooden basket, has a couple of singular virtues. The base is broad, so it's almost impossible to upset. The loose weave is washable under the garden hose. The high handle is easy to pick up. And the trug is simple to make, despite the apparent complexity of its woven basket.

Trugs are traditional British woodcraft, though the one shown here is not an authentic copy of something traditional, but a contemporary rendition.

The basket is woven from slats sawn lengthwise off the edge of a 2×4, a maneuver that requires a table saw or a band saw. The curve is jigsawn or bandsawn into the edges of regular 1×4 pine boards. Nails and screws hold the trug together.

Weave the basket. Lay the center weft across four long warps (left). Drop the remaining three warps on top, then weave in the second and third wefts, over and under (center). Add the fourth and fifth wefts at either end of the panel (right).

BUILDING THE TRUG

1 Cut the wood. To make the slats, begin with a 24-inch knot-free length of 2×4. Set up the table saw rip fence for a thin cut, $\frac{1}{8}$ inch or a little less. Reduce the entire 2×4 to thin slats—you need 11 total.

2 Weave the basket. The basket of the trug is a wooden weaving that consists of seven long slats, or warps, crossed by five short slats, or wefts. Lay the seven warps flat on the worktable, then remove three of them, as shown in the photo at top left. Center a weft across the four warps, then replace the three warps you just removed. Now weave a pair of wefts over and under on either side of the center warp. This will stabilize the "fabric." Then add another

TRUG

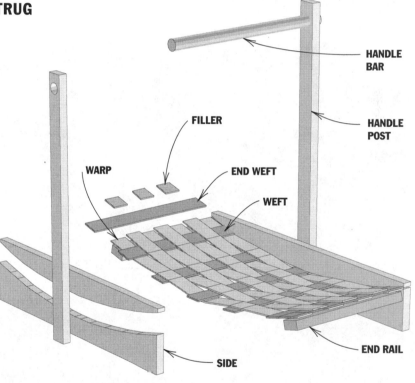

Weave the basket of the trug. Jigsaw the sides, connect them with the end rails, then nail the woven basket to them. Drill the handle posts and screw them to the trug sides. Nail the handle bar to the handle posts.

YOUR INVESTMENT

Time: One evening
Money: $5

SHOPPING LIST

4 feet 1×4 pine
2 feet 2×4 pine or fir
6 feet 1×2 pine
1-inch nails
1-inch brass linoleum nails
2-inch galvanized siding nails
1¼-inch galvanized screws

PROJECT SPECS

The trug is 24 inches long, 12 inches wide, and 24 inches high.

CUTTING LIST

PART	QTY.	DIMENSIONS	NOTES
Warp	7	$\frac{1}{8} \times 1\frac{1}{2} \times 24$	Rip from 2×4
Weft	7	$\frac{1}{8} \times 1\frac{1}{2} \times 12$	Rip from 2×4
Filler	6	$\frac{1}{8} \times 1\frac{1}{2} \times 1\frac{1}{2}$	Rip from 2×4
Side	2	$\frac{3}{4} \times 3\frac{1}{2} \times 24$	1×4
End	2	$\frac{3}{4} \times 1\frac{1}{2} \times 10\frac{5}{8}$	1×2
Handle post	2	$\frac{3}{4} \times 1\frac{1}{2} \times 24$	1×2
Handle bar	1	1 dia. × 18	dowel

pair of wefts, one at either end of the panel. Once all five wefts are interwoven with the seven warps, you can space them any way you like.

3 **Make the curved sides.** Bend one of the long warp slats to lay out the curve in the sides, as shown below. At the center, the curve is 1¾ inches deep. Jigsaw the first side, then trace its shape onto the second one and jigsaw it too. Make these saw-cuts as single sweeps without any back-tracking, and keep the curved scraps, because you'll nail them onto the trug in Step 7 below. Ending up with a one-piece scrap is more important than precision.

4 **Make the ends.** The ends are short pieces of 1×2 nailed between the sides. The top face of the ends comes flush with the jigsawn curve. Hold the ends in place and once you see how they go, nail them to the sides with two of the 2-inch siding nails at each joint, as shown in the photo at bottom left.

5 **Nail the wefts to the sides.** Press the woven wood onto the curved sides. It should fit nicely between them, with the ends of the wefts on the sawn curves, as shown at bottom right. Starting at the center, tack the wefts onto the sides. Drive two 1-inch nails into each weft.

Make the sides. Tap a nail near each end of the side, and bend a long warp slat against the nails. Trace this curve onto the wood (left). Then jigsaw the curve (right).

Make the ends. Nail the ends between the curved sides. The face of the end piece follows the jigsawn curve.

Nail the wefts to the sides. Fit the woven wood into the trug and nail the ends of the wefts to the sides.

Fill in the ends of the warps. Slip the end weft into the basket, and fill the gaps with the filler pieces (above). Nail the warps to the ends (right).

Replace the curved scrap. Fit the curved scrap from whence it came and nail it to the sides, trapping the woven basket.

Make the handle. Center and square the handle posts on the sides of the trug (top). Screw the posts to the sides from underneath (above). Insert the dowel handle and tack it in place (below). Trim the handle ends with a handsaw.

6 **Fill in the ends of the warps.** At the ends of the trug, you'll be able to slip an end weft between the warps without going over and under, leaving a gap beneath every other warp. Fill the gaps with the 1½-inch fillers, as shown in the photo at top left. Support the end rails with scraps of wood and tack the ends of the basket to it with the brass linoleum nails.

7 **Replace the curved scrap.** Fit the curved scraps from the jig-sawing operation in Step 3 back onto the sides, covering the ends of the wefts. Nail the curved scrap onto the sides, using the 2-inch siding nails, as shown in the lower left photo.

8 **Make the handle.** The handle consists of two upright posts spanned by a dowel handle bar. Begin by drilling a 1-inch hole through the two handle posts, 2½ inches from the top of the posts. Next, fasten the handle posts to the sides of the trug with three screws from inside and underneath, plus a fourth screw through the curved scrap. Finally, insert the handle bar and retain it with brass nails, as shown in the photo at right.

VEGETABLE DRYING TABLE

This handy device folds up and stows away for the off-season

At harvest time, the gardener needs a worktable to wash and dry the vegetables, like this wire-mesh table. Root vegetables need to dry off before they can be taken in for storage.

You'll find the mesh table handy when you're cutting flowers, and also for potting. You can use it for washing down as well as for air-drying. The rest of the year, however, the table probably would only be in the way, if it didn't fold flat for storage. But since it does fold flat,

it's easy to hang it on the wall or tuck it away, and bring it out again at the start of the next gardening season.

BUILDING THE TABLE

1 Cut all the wood. The length of the end rails depends on the width of your wire mesh. If the mesh measures 24 inches, make the end rails 22¾ inches long. The length of the cross rails depends on the wood thick-

ness. Trim them to an exact fit in Step 5 below.

2 Make the top frame. Screw the side rails and end rails together to make the rectangular frame. Start at one corner, by clamping one of the end rails up on edge on the worktable. Bring a side rail up to the end rail and clamp it in position, as shown in the photo at far right. Drill clearance holes and make the joint by driving three of the 2-inch screws. Make the other

VEGETABLE DRYING TABLE

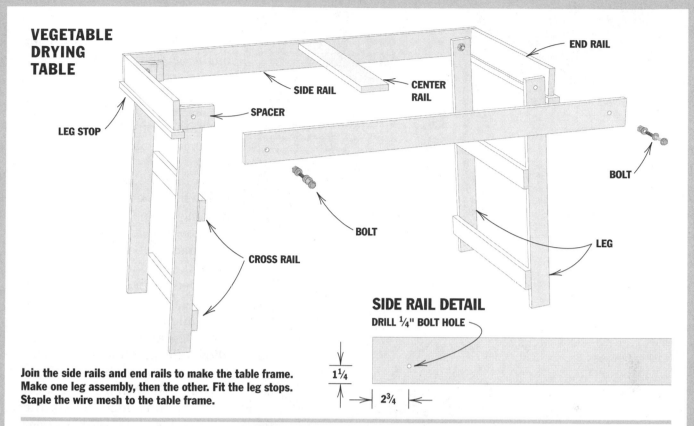

LEG STOP

CROSS RAIL

SIDE RAIL

CENTER RAIL

SPACER

BOLT

END RAIL

BOLT

LEG

Join the side rails and end rails to make the table frame. Make one leg assembly, then the other. Fit the leg stops. Staple the wire mesh to the table frame.

SIDE RAIL DETAIL

DRILL ¼" BOLT HOLE

$1\frac{1}{4}$

$2\frac{3}{4}$

YOUR INVESTMENT

<u>Time:</u> One evening
<u>Money:</u> $20

SHOPPING LIST

8 feet 1×2
24 feet 1×3
16 feet 1×4
#6 × 2-inch galvanized screws
½-inch hardware cloth, 24 × 48
Two ¼ × 3-inch hex-head bolt
Two ¼ × 2-inch hex-head bolt
¾-inch wire staples

PROJECT SPECS

The vegetable drying table is 48 inches long, 24 inches wide, and 30 inches high.

CUTTING LIST

PART	QTY.	DIMENSIONS	NOTES
Side rail	2	¾ × 3½ × 48	1×4
End rail	2	¾ × 3½ × 22¾	1×4
Leg	4	¾ × 2½ × 30	1×3
Cross rail	4	¾ × 2½ × 24	1×3; cut to fit
Spacer	2	¾ × 2½ × 4	1×3
Leg stop	2	¾ × 1½ × 24¼	1×2
Center rail	1	¾ × 3½ × 22¾	1×4

three corners of the frame in the same way. At each corner, screw through the side rail into the end grain of the end rail.

3 **Lay out the holes for the leg bolts.** A single ¼-inch bolt joins each leg to the table frame. The ¼-inch bolt hole must be correctly positioned, or else the leg won't be able to fold up. As shown in the drawing above, the correct position is 1¼ inches up from the bottom of the rail, and 2¾ inches in from the end of the

Make the top frame. Clamp the side rail and end rail to the worktable. Drill clearance holes, and screw the side rails to the end rails.

Fit one pair of legs. Clamp the first pair of legs in position, inside the table frame. Leave ½-inch pivoting clearance at the end of the leg (above). Drill the bolt hole through the side rail and leg (below). Bolt the leg to the side rail, with a clearance washer between the two parts (right).

Connect the legs with the bottom cross rail. Cut the bottom cross rail to length and screw it to the legs. The rail fits 3 inches up from the end of the leg.

rail. Locate and mark this point on the outside of the side rails.

4 Fit one pair of legs. The folding leg assembly at each end of the table consists of two legs and two cross rails. Spacer blocks at one end of the table allow that leg assembly to fold inside the other one. You'll avoid alignment problems if you complete the first leg assembly, without spacer blocks, before going on to the second. Clamp the legs in folded position inside the side rails, leaving ½ inch of pivoting clearance between the end of each leg and the end rail, as shown in the photo at top left. Drill the ¼-inch bolt hole through the rail and leg. Bolt each leg to a side rail with the 2-inch bolts. Put a washer under each bolt head and under the nut, and put one extra washer, for clearance, between each leg and side rail.

5 Connect the legs with the bottom cross rail. Measure the outside distance between the legs at the bolt, and subtract ⅛ inch. Cut the two cross rails to this length. The bottom cross rail fits 3 inches up from the end of the legs. Center the rail across the legs, with ¹⁄₁₆ inch of clearance at either end. Glue and screw the cross rail in position, using two 2-inch screws at either end. Leave the second cross rail aside for now.

6 Fit the second leg assembly. The second leg assembly folds inside the first pair of legs. The spacer blocks create the necessary clearance. Glue the blocks inside the corner of the table frame, as shown in the photo at right. Then drill and assemble the legs and cross rail as in the previous two steps. The only difference is, put two clearance washers between each leg and spacer block.

7 Fit the upper cross rails. The upper cross rails fit 16 inches up from the bottom of each leg assembly. Glue and screw the upper cross rails to the legs, as in the previous steps. Center each cross rail from side to side so there is $\frac{1}{16}$ inch of clearance to the outside of each leg.

8 Make the leg stops. The leg stops are horizontal pieces of 1×2 fastened underneath the end rails. They limit the splay of the legs when the table is unfolded. The amount of splay is up to you, but one method of making it uniform is shown in the photo below. When you get the leg assemblies in the position you want, butt the leg stops tight against them, then glue and screw the stops to the end rail. Use the 2-inch screws.

9 Fit the center rail. Screw the center rail between the side rails. It goes face-up, so it won't interfere with the folding legs.

10 Make the mesh top. Unroll the $\frac{1}{2}$-inch galvanized wire mesh. It's easy to cut with tin snips or side-cutting pliers, but wear gloves because there are sharp ends. Staple the mesh onto the table frame, as shown in the photo at far right. File off any sharp ends, and you're ready to harvest vegetables. The table doesn't need any finish.

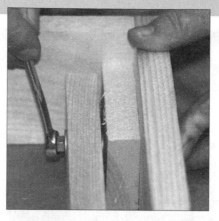

Fit the second leg assembly. Glue the spacer inside the corner of the table frame, then clamp the leg in place, leaving the $\frac{1}{2}$-inch pivot clearance. Drill the bolt hole and bolt the leg in place, with two clearance washers between the leg and spacer (left).

Fit the upper cross rails. Trim the upper cross rails to length and screw them to the leg assemblies.

Make the leg stops. To set the splay of the legs, establish a vertical line with a square and a piece of scrap. Then pull the leg assembly 4 inches off vertical, and butt the leg stop against it (left). Screw the leg stop to the end rail.

Make the mesh top. Staple the $\frac{1}{2}$-inch wire mesh to the table frame. Trim the sharp ends off the mesh, and file off any burrs.

GREENHOUSE CABINET

Extend the growing season with this rollaway glass box

Every gardener dreams of a greenhouse, but few can manage the expenditure of space or money. However, you can extend your growing season on a small scale with this handsome greenhouse cabinet. It offers you most of the virtues of a full-size greenhouse, without all of the expense. It's small enough to park on the corner of your condo deck, backyard patio or apartment balcony. You can roll it around to capture the best light, and it rolls away for the off-season.

The greenhouse cabinet has small panes, so you can use ordinary single-strength glass. Complete the cabinet, and measure the actual openings, before you order the glass. Make sure there's ⅛ inch of clearance, so the glass can expand and contract with temperature changes. You could save money by stapling polyethylene to the framework instead of using glass.

The back is made of ⅜-inch exterior-grade plywood. The bottom uses up the remains of the plywood sheet, screwed to a sturdy 2×4 base. The heavy base permits the cabinet to roll across an uneven deck without flexing, thereby protecting the glass from breaking.

The greenhouse cabinet features a hinged top, which can be propped open at any height for more or less ventilation. The

The greenhouse cabinet features sliding shelves made of wire mesh or hardware cloth, so the light will filter through to the plants below.

shelves, made of wire mesh, slide easily through the double-door opening. You can load a shelf with seedlings, slide it out to work on the plants, then slide it back into the cabinet.

The cabinet sides, doors and skylights are made of ordinary 1×2 pine lumber, which actually measures ¾ inch thick and 1½ inches wide. However, it's important to avoid large knots. Small, tight knots will not cause a problem, but large knots with black edges of bark are liable to fall out, weakening the structure. No. 2 pine will do if you can choose your wood at the home center. If you can't choose, consider paying extra for "select" or "clear" wood.

This is a large project with a lot of pieces of wood, and accu-

racy is important. However, the construction is straightforward and modular, and you can complete each assembly before moving on to the next. The key skill you need is the ability to saw a stick of wood square and to length. You will need to miter the ends of a few of the 1×2s at 12½ degrees, and you can save money by sawing your own glazing strips, as discussed in Step 1 on page 256.

Except for a coat of white paint on the plywood back and bottom, we left our cabinet unfinished. If you want to finish yours, the right material is paint, but you must make the decision before you install the glass. That way you can paint the wood without struggling to keep paint off the glass.

GREENHOUSE CABINET

The greenhouse cabinet looks complex but its construction is simple and modular. Make the base and back, then the two sides, then the doors and skylight, and finally the shelves.

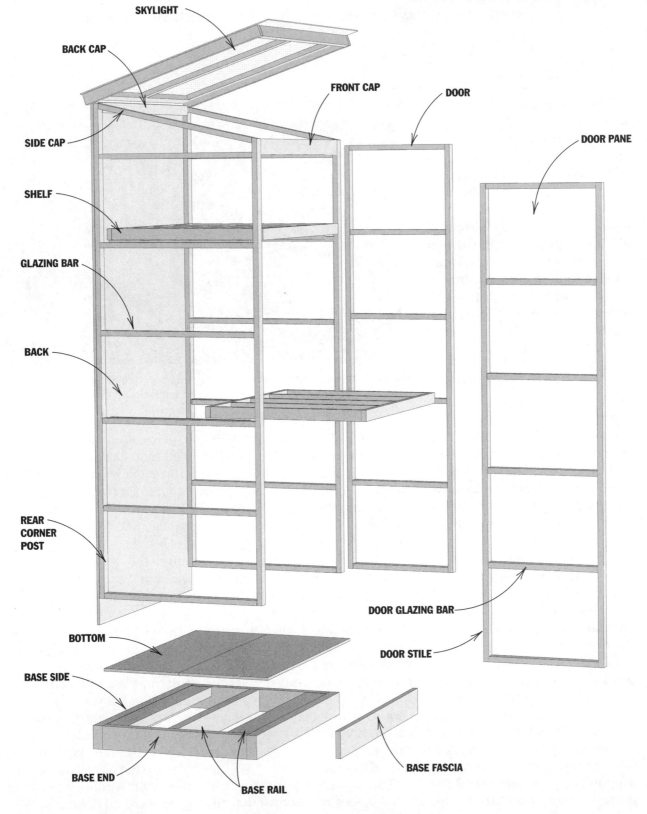

SKYLIGHT

BACK CAP

FRONT CAP

DOOR

DOOR PANE

SIDE CAP

SHELF

GLAZING BAR

BACK

REAR CORNER POST

DOOR GLAZING BAR

DOOR STILE

BOTTOM

BASE SIDE

BASE END

BASE RAIL

BASE FASCIA

YOUR INVESTMENT

Time: One weekend
Money: Glass and acrylic, $85; wood, $75; hardware, $30

SHOPPING LIST

144 feet 1×2 pine
48 feet 1×4 pine
20 feet 2×4
One 4×8 sheet ⅜-inch CDX plywood
Four 2-inch ball-bearing casters
6 pair 1½-inch × 1½-Inch steel hinges
#8 × 3-inch galvanized screws
#6 × 2-inch galvanized screws
#6 × 1-inch galvanized screws
¾-inch wire brads
12 square feet ½-inch mesh hardware cloth
36 square feet single-strength window glass
9 square feet ⅛-inch acrylic sheet

PROJECT SPECS

The greenhouse cabinet measures
27½ inches deep by 35½ inches wide by 76 inches high.

RAIL DETAIL

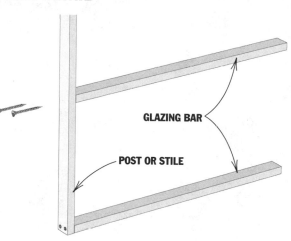

GLAZING BAR

POST OR STILE

Pairs of 2-inch screws hold the cabinet joints together. All the joints in the greenhouse sides and doors are made the same way.

CUTTING LIST

PART	QTY.	DIMENSIONS	NOTES
Base side	2	1½ × 3½ × 36	2×4
Base end	2	1½ × 3½ × 22¾	2×4
Base rail	3	1½ × 3½ × 33	2×4
Back	1	⅜ × 36 × 76	Fir plywood
Bottom	1	⅜ × 25¾ × 36	Piece from plywood offcuts
Base fascia	1	¾ × 4 × 36	
Front corner post	2	¾ × 1½ × 72	Miter one end 12½°
Rear corner post	2	¾ × 1½ × 66¾	Miter one end 12½°
Glazing bar	12	¾ × 1½ × 24	Standard 1×2
Back cap	1	¾ × 1½ × 33	Trim to fit
Side cap	1	¾ × 1½ × 25	Miter both ends 12½°
Front cap	1	¾ × 2¼ × 33	Trim to fit
Door stile	4	¾ × 1½ × 65	Standard 1×2
Door glazing bar	12	¾ × 1½ × 15⅜	Standard 1×2
Glazing strip		¼ × ¾ × 240 feet	Cut to fit
Skylight long rail	3	¾ × 1½ × 37¼	
Skylight side rail	3	¾ × 1½ × 25	
Skylight outer side rail	2	¾ × 1½ × 29	
Shelf stile	4	¾ × 1¾ × 32½	
Shelf rail	6	¾ × 1¾ × 23	
Shelf support	8	¾ × ¾ × 22	
Door stop	1	¾ × ¾ × 9	
Side pane	10	11⅞ × 23⅞	Single-strength window glass
Door pane	10	11⅞ × 15¼	Single-strength window glass
Skylight	1	⅛ × 31 × 39	Acrylic sheet
Vent pane	2	6 × 23⅞	Cut to fit

Build the base. Clamp the base side to the bench, bring the end piece square to it, and clamp it down as well. Then drill pilot holes and screw the pieces together.

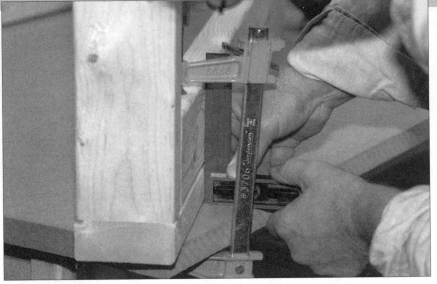

Make the bottom. Spread glue on the wheels base rail, clamp it inside the base frame, then screw it in place (above). Roll glue onto the base frame. Screw the plywood to the frame (below).

BUILDING THE GREENHOUSE CABINET

1 Cut all the wood. The cabinet sides and doors are made from standard 1×2 lumber, which is ¾ inches thick and 1⅝ inches wide. The cabinet base is made from standard 2×4, while the back and bottom come out of a sheet of ⅜-inch exterior plywood. The glass retaining strips measure ¼ inch thick by ¾ inch wide. You can buy stock molding of this dimension, but it's expensive. We sawed the glass retaining strips from 1×4 lumber, with the table saw rip fence set to the finished thickness of ¼ inch. You must use a push stick for this cut. Crosscut the lumber to exact length before you saw it into strips.

2 Build the base. The base has to bear the stress of wheeling the cabinet around your deck or patio, so it should be sturdy. It's made of 2×4s, joined with two

3-inch screws in each corner. Drill pilot holes through the face of the long base side, so the screws go into the end grain of the end piece, as shown in the top left photo.

3 Make the bottom. Arrange two plywood offcuts on the 2×4 base, and trim them to a neat fit. Where they meet locates the

center base rail, so make a layout line on the 2×4 base. The other two base rails support the wheels. They're turned on edge, then glued and screwed to the 2×4 base, with 3-inch screws. Roll glue onto the edge of the wheels rail. Clamp the rail in place as shown in the top right photo, then drill pilot holes into each end and drive a pair of

BUILDING THE CABINET SIDES

To build the cabinet sides, screw the first glazing bar to the back corner post. Use the 12-inch gauge to space the next glazing bar. Join all the glazing bars, then add the front post and the side cap. Build the doors in the same way.

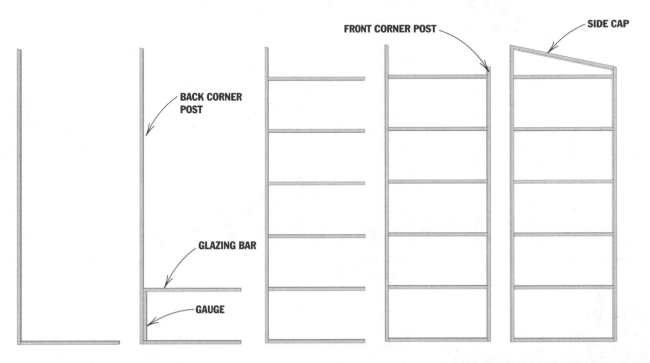

BACK CORNER POST

FRONT CORNER POST

SIDE CAP

GLAZING BAR

GAUGE

screws. Drive three more screws through the side of the base into the edge of the rail. Screw the center rail to the base sides, then attach the plywood with glue and finishing nails.

4 Make the sides. Each side consists of a front and back corner post connected by six glazing bars. The corner posts are screwed to the glazing bars with two 2-inch screws in each joint. The screws go through the posts and into the end grain of the glazing bars. Begin at the bottom corner, but make sure the top miters are correctly oriented, that is, parallel with their long points toward the back of the cabinet, as shown on the next page. Clamp the back post and the first glazing bar to the worktable. Check for square, then drill pilot holes and drive the first two screws. Since all the glass openings are 12 inches

Make the sides. Clamp the corner post to the worktable. Use a gauge to space the glazing bars. Drive two screws into each joint.

high, saw a 12-inch gauge from 1×2 wood. Use the gauge to locate each glazing bar. Attach the front post to the free ends of the glazing bars in the same way. Use the gauge to locate each joint, and check for square before you drill for the screws.

Miter the side cap. Hold the side cap in place to mark and saw the miter. Drill pilot holes and drive two screws through each intersection.

Join the back and base. Support the plywood on the worktable while you screw it to the base.

SIDE DETAIL

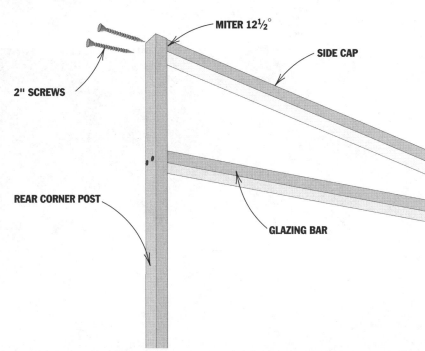

MITER 12½°

SIDE CAP

2" SCREWS

REAR CORNER POST

GLAZING BAR

The side cap fits between the front and rear corner posts. Miter one end and hold the part in position to lay out the other end. Saw the second miter and screw the cap in place.

5 Miter the side cap. The side cap completes the sides. It fits between the corner posts with a matching miter at each end. The length given, 25 inches, is nominal. Miter one end 12½ degrees and hold the cap in position to lay out and cut the second miter.

6 Join the back and base. Glue and screw the plywood back to the 2×4 base. Roll glue onto the base, then position the plywood flush with the bottom edge of the base. Draw a layout line and drive 12 of the 1¼-inch screws through the plywood into the base.

7 Join the sides. Lift the back-and-base assembly onto the worktable and clamp the first side in position. Make sure the side will clamp up square—there's a little room to wiggle in every direction. When it's right, draw a layout line on the plywood, take the side down, and roll glue onto the plywood. Clamp the side to the base and back, and screw it down. Screw down through the bottom glazing bar into the base, making sure to countersink the screwheads, because if they contact the glass, it will break. Screw through the plywood back into the ends of the glazing bars with 2-inch screws, then drive a 1-inch screw at the center of each glass opening.

Join the sides. Roll glue on the plywood, then screw the cabinet together.

Trim the back cap. Rasp the corner off the plywood and back cap to match the slope of the side cap (below).

8 Trim the back cap. Trim the back cap to fit between the corner posts, then glue and screw it to the plywood back. Use a Surform, a rasp or a plane to bevel the top edge of the back cap, so it matches the slope of the sides, as shown at right.

9 Fit the front cap. Trim the front cap to fit between the front corner posts. Take the measurement at the bottom of the door opening, not at the top. Screw the front cap to the top of the door opening. It not only braces the cabinet opening, but it also acts as a stop or kicker for the doors.

10 Complete the base. The cabinet mounts on four ordinary 2-inch utility casters, which fit inside the corners of the base. Lay the cabinet on its back to screw the wheels to the base rails. Make sure the casters have room to pivot freely. Nail the base fascia on the front of the base, covering the edge of the plywood.

Complete the base. Screw the casters to the wheel rail under the base. Set them in from the sides so they can pivot freely.

Build the skylight. Glue and screw the outer side rails to the skylight frame (above). Drill oversized clearance holes for the screws that attach the acrylic to the skylight frame. Drill the acrylic with an ordinary twist bit (below left).

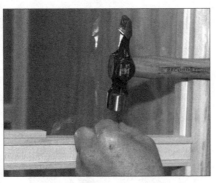

Glaze the cabinet. Nail glazing strips around all of the openings, fit the glass, then nail the second set of glazing strips on the outside of the glass.

BUILDING THE SKYLIGHT

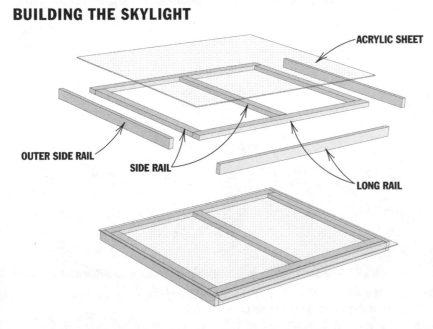

ACRYLIC SHEET

OUTER SIDE RAIL

SIDE RAIL

LONG RAIL

11 Make the doors. The two doors are made in exactly the same way as the cabinet sides, minus the mitered cap strip. Be sure you use the same 12-inch gauge to position each door glazing bar on the door stiles.

12 Build the skylight. The skylight is a square frame hinged to the cabinet. It's got overhanging front and side rails, and it's completely covered with a sheet of acrylic plastic, so it's reasonably weathertight. Lay two of the side rails and two of the long rails flat on the worktable and screw them together with two 3-inch screws through each joint. Glue and screw the outer side rails to the frame, turning them up on edge so they make a flange. Glue and screw the third side rail across the center of the skylight opening and the third long rail across the front between the outer side rails. Fit the skylight onto the cabinet and fasten it with two 1½-inch × 1½-inch galvanized hinges. Finally, screw the acrylic plastic to the top of the skylight frame. The plastic fits flush with the sides, but it overhangs 1½ inches at the front and ½ inch at the back.

13 Glaze the cabinet. The glass is trapped between pairs of glazing strips nailed to the doors and cabinet sides. Fasten the strips with ¾-inch wire brads, four in each horizontal strip and three in each vertical. Begin by nailing the glazing strips all around the inside of all the openings. These strips fit flush with the inside faces of the doors and cabinet sides. Working one opening at a time, set the glass in place, then nail the outside strips into the

GLAZING

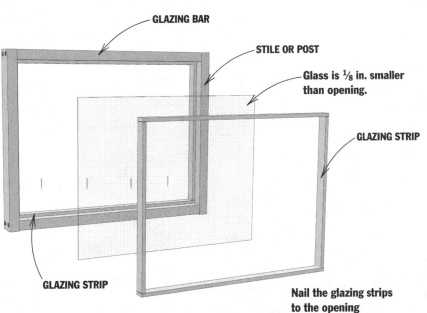

GLAZING BAR

STILE OR POST

Glass is ⅛ in. smaller than opening.

GLAZING STRIP

GLAZING STRIP

Nail the glazing strips to the opening

Hang the doors. Screw the hinges onto the door, then screw them to the corner posts. The hinges will cover the screwheads in the frames.

openings, tight against the glass. The strips will protrude ⅛ inch, creating a shadow reveal around each glass pane, as shown at top right.

14 Hinge the doors. Hinge each door to the front corner post with six 1½-inch × 1½-inch hinges. Locate the hinges at the ends of the glazing strips, flush with the outside edge of the corner post, as shown at top right. This gives the most support to the door, and it also conceals the screws in the cabinet sides.

15 Triangular openings. There are two triangular openings at the top of the cabinet sides. What you do about them depends on your climate and growing plans. We cut triangular pieces of glass, sizing the glass to leave ⅛ inch of clearance. You could fill them with wood or plastic, or you could leave them open for ventilation.

Make the shelves. Staple wire mesh onto the shelves. Rasp the sharp ends off the wire mesh.

16 Make the shelves. The shelves are simple wooden frames screwed together like the cabinet sides and doors. With the doors fully open, they slide straight into the cabinet. They're covered with ½-inch wire mesh or hardware cloth. Cut the mesh with wire cutters, and wear leather gloves because the ends are sharp. Nail it or staple it to the wood. Rasp the

Support the shelves. Center the shelf supports on the inside of the glazing bars and screw them in place.

sharp ends off the wire, as shown in the photo above.

17 Support the shelves. The shelf supports are square sticks of wood screwed to the inside of the glazing bars. They don't go all the way back, so it's possible to brush them clean of debris. Finally, screw a 9-inch scrap to the bottom of the opening, to act as a door stop.

LANDSCAPE PROJECTS

Projects for the landscape tend to be utilitarian constructions designed to improve your outdoor property. Sometimes they're large projects, like steps and bridges, but just as often they're small enhancements, like a birdhouse or a mailbox post.

Unlike lawn and patio projects, landscape projects generally stay outdoors all year around. They have to be built to withstand all kinds of weather. That is why many landscape projects look best when left unfinished. They'll quickly weather to soft brown and gray colors, blending gently with the trees and with the land itself.

GARDEN GATEWAY

Arts-and-Crafts design opens a path between outdoor rooms

A graceful gateway defines the spaces in your outdoor living area. It helps you organize your yard and garden into "rooms." When people pass through a gateway, they expect a change of place: from lawn to flower garden, from playground to patio, from one side of the lawn to the other.

This gateway consists of two archways connected by decorative side panels. The strong vertical lines of the grilles in the side panels suggest Arts-and-Crafts furniture. There are seven grille pieces, and seven rafters. You can change the dimensions of the gateway to suit your own tastes, and you might want to change the number of grille and rafter pieces. However, if you do, keep the number odd, so one piece always falls on center. It looks better that way.

You can set a gateway in a fence or hedge, and you can hang a gate in it. But you can also set a gateway out in your yard without any fence or gate, on a pathway or on the lawn. Like the Arc de Triomphe in Paris, it creates spaces just by being there.

GARDEN GATEWAY

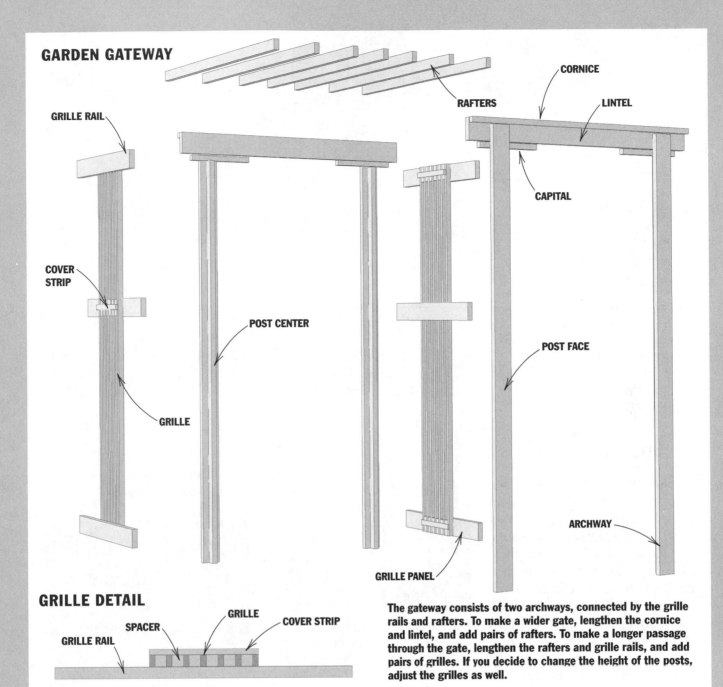

RAFTERS

CORNICE

LINTEL

GRILLE RAIL

CAPITAL

COVER STRIP

POST CENTER

POST FACE

GRILLE

ARCHWAY

GRILLE PANEL

GRILLE DETAIL

GRILLE RAIL

SPACER

GRILLE

COVER STRIP

The gateway consists of two archways, connected by the grille rails and rafters. To make a wider gate, lengthen the cornice and lintel, and add pairs of rafters. To make a longer passage through the gate, lengthen the rafters and grille rails, and add pairs of grilles. If you decide to change the height of the posts, adjust the grilles as well.

YOUR INVESTMENT

Time: One day
Money: $35

SHOPPING LIST

125 feet 1×4 rough-sawn pine
#6 × 1⅝-inch galvanized screws
#6 × 2-inch galvanized screws
1½-inch galvanized finishing nails
1½-inch galvanized spiral nails
2-inch galvanized spiral nails
2½-inch galvanized spiral nails

PROJECT SPECS

The gateway stands 84 inches high, 42 inches wide, and 28 inches deep.

CUTTING LIST

PART	QTY.	DIMENSIONS	NOTES
Post face	4	$1 \times 3\frac{3}{8} \times 81$	
Post center	4	$1 \times 1\frac{1}{2} \times 77$	
Lintel	2	$1 \times 4 \times 48$	
Capital	4	$1 \times 1 \times 12$	
Cornice	2	$1 \times 1 \times 48$	
Grille	14	$\frac{1}{2} \times 1 \times 72$	
Grille spacer	36	$1 \times 1 \times 3$	
Grille rail	6	$1 \times 3\frac{3}{8} \times 26$	
Rafter	7	$1 \times 1\frac{1}{8} \times 46$	
Cover strip	6	$\frac{1}{2} \times 1 \times 12$	Trim to fit

Make the posts. Glue and clamp the post center to the post face. The end offset is the width of the lintel (above). Turn the assembly over and nail through from the back. Angle the nails for the best grip (right).

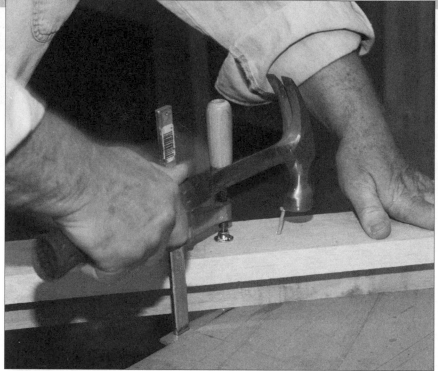

BUILDING THE GATEWAY

1 Saw the parts. Rough-sawn pine, which is available in most parts of the country, not only looks good against green plants, but it's also a full inch in thickness. Thicker looks better, but nowhere is the thickness of the wood a critical dimension. You can substitute lumberyard 1× pine, which is about ¾ inch thick, or the more robust 5/4 pine, which is actually about 1⅛ inches thick. Saw all the parts before you begin construction. The ½-inch grille pieces and the various 1-inch and 2-inch parts can be sawn lengthwise from 1×4 material. If you don't have a table saw for cutting the wood lengthwise, substitute 1×1 and 1×2 lumber for the grilles, cornices, and capitals.

2 Make the posts. The four posts, T-shaped in cross-section, are two-piece assemblies. The

Join the lintel and capitals. Set the capital 2 inches in from the end of the lintel (above). Nail the capitals to the lintels (right).

post center is shorter than the post face by the width of the lintel, or 4 inches. Spread glue on the edge of the post center and clamp the two parts together. Make them fit flush at the bottom, then measure to make sure the offset at the top is the actual width of your lintel. Nail through the post face into the post center with 2½-inch spiral nails. It's easiest to make all four posts at the same time.

3 Join the lintel and capitals. The little capitals make the visual transition between the horizontal lintels and the vertical posts. Glue and nail two capitals to the edge of each lintel. Set them 2 inches in from the ends of the lintel.

Connect the posts. Clamp the lintel to the posts and measure for equal width at top and bottom (left). Screw a scrap strip across the bottom, then measure the diagonals (right). To square the gateway, shift the parts until the diagonals are equal.

4 Connect the posts. Each lintel spans two posts, with its capitals resting on the post center pieces. Lay the two posts on the worktable and clamp them down. Set the lintel-and-capital assembly in place across the posts. Locate the outside edge of the posts 2 inches in from the ends of the capitals. Clamp the assembly together. Check for parallel by measuring the distance between the posts at top and bottom. Cut a scrap stick to the distance between the center pieces and screw it across the bottom of the gateway. Check for square by measuring the diagonals. Now spread glue and screw through the face of the lintel into the posts, with four of the 1⅝-inch screws in each joint.

5 Add the cornice. The cornice is a horizontal strip of wood glued and nailed to the lintel and resting atop the posts. Spread glue on the cornice piece, clamp it in place, and nail into it through the face of the lintel, with the 1⅝-inch nails. Build the second archway in the same way.

POST-TO-LINTEL JOINT

The lintel and capital rest on the post center. The cornice caps the post face and helps the assembly resist racking.

CORNICE

LINTEL

CAPITAL

POST FACE

POST CENTER

Connect the posts. Screw through the lintel into the post face.

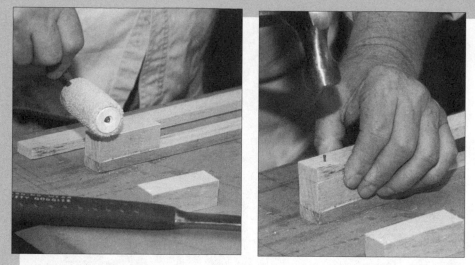

Space the grilles. Roll glue and nail the first set of spacer blocks to the first grille (left). Continue to add grilles and spacers to complete the grille panel (right).

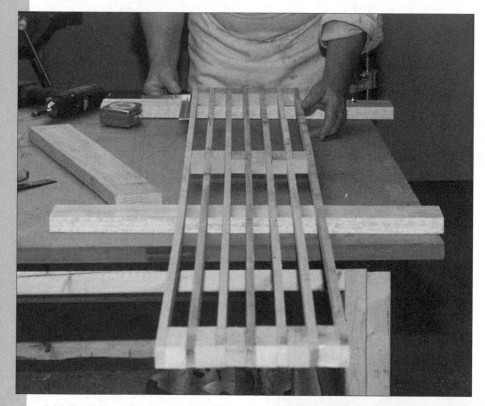

Add the grille rails. Center the grilles on the top grille rail and check for square (above). Screw the spacer blocks to the grille rails (right).

6 Space the grilles. The grille panels fill in the sides of the gateway. Each panel consists of seven grilles separated by three sets of spacer blocks. Glue and nail the first set of three spacers to one grille, using the 1¼-inch finishing nails. The two end spacers fit flush with the ends of the grille. A 24-inch gap separates the top spacer from the center spacer. Add a second grille, then glue and nail the second set of spacers to it, using 2½-inch siding nails, which are extra thin so they don't split the wood. Continue to glue and nail spacers and grilles until you complete both panels.

7 Add the grille rails. The horizontal grille rails will connect the posts, but first, glue and screw them to the grilles themselves. There's a rail at each set of spacer blocks. The top and bottom rails go on one side of the grilles, and the middle rail goes on the other. Center the grilles on the top rail, draw layout lines, and spread glue. Slip the rail into position and drive the first 1⅝-inch screw through a grille spacer into the rail. Check for square, then drive the remaining screws. Attach the bottom rail in the same way, then turn the grille panel over to attach the center rail on the other side.

8 Assemble the gateway. Stand the front and back archways up on edge, with one of them against the wall of the workshop. The grille rails span the post center pieces top, bottom and center. To keep the assembly from flopping around, clamp the grille rails to the posts, then screw them in place, with two 1⅝-inch

Assemble the gateway. Stand the two archways on edge, with one of them against a wall. Fit the grille panel to the posts and screw the rails in place.

Complete the rafters. Attach the outside rafters and the center rafter. Space the remaining rafters in between.

Cover the screws. Glue and nail the cover strips across the grille spacer blocks.

screws at each end. Rotate the assembly to attach the second grille panel.

9 Start the rafters. If you're working indoors, carry the gateway outside before you add the rafters. Afterward, it probably wouldn't fit through the doorway. The seven rafter pieces stand up on edge across the top of the cornices and lintels. The two outside rafters don't fit flush with the end of the cornice and lintel; they're set in an inch. Clamp the first rafter so you can drive $2\frac{1}{2}$-inch screws up into it through the cornice. Rotate the gate to attach the companion rafter on the other side.

10 Complete the rafters. The remaining five rafters march across the top of the gateway. Locate the center rafter by measuring the distance between the two outside rafters. Screw it in place, then divide the remaining spaces into widths of pleasing proportion and screw the rest of the rafters to the cornices. The gateway shown on page 264 has smaller spaces in the center, which emphasizes the opening.

11 Cover the screws. There's an unsightly row of screwheads where you attached the grilles to the grille rails. Trim the cover strips to length, then glue and nail them over the screwheads with several finishing nails.

12 Install the gateway. Set the posts on bricks or flat stones. Level the posts by leveling the supporting bricks. Then drive an 18-inch wooden stake into the ground alongside each post, and tie or screw the bottom of the post to it. Remove the scrap spreaders at the bottom of the gateway, and amble on through.

BIKE RACK

Modular unit can support the neighborhood's two-wheelers

Kids can drop bicycles into a fearful tangle, unless you build them an easy-to-use rack, like this one. The basic rack accommodates two bicycles. After that the rack is totally modular, so you can add parking spaces for as many bicycles as you like.

The rack is made of standard 1×4 and 2×4 lumber, held together with glue and galvanized screws. This method is

accurate and relatively easy, but it does require you to clamp each joint together. As an alternative to screws, if you consider it therapeutic to hammer on spiral nails, you can use them instead. You'll still find it very helpful to clamp each joint, so it's less likely to swim around under the force of nailing.

The slot for the bicycle wheel is 2¼ inches wide, the result of making the posts by

face-gluing three pieces of 1×4. This fits regular mountain bikes. If your bikes have skinny racing wheels, you can get away with a 1½-inch two-layer post.

This is an interesting construction project because it goes together virtually without measuring. Once you've cut all the wood, you can use the various pieces as gauge blocks to space and align the parts of the rack, as shown in the photos.

BIKE RACK

Make the two posts, then screw four rails to each post.
Attach the front legs to the free ends of the rails.
Connect these assemblies with the three cross rails.

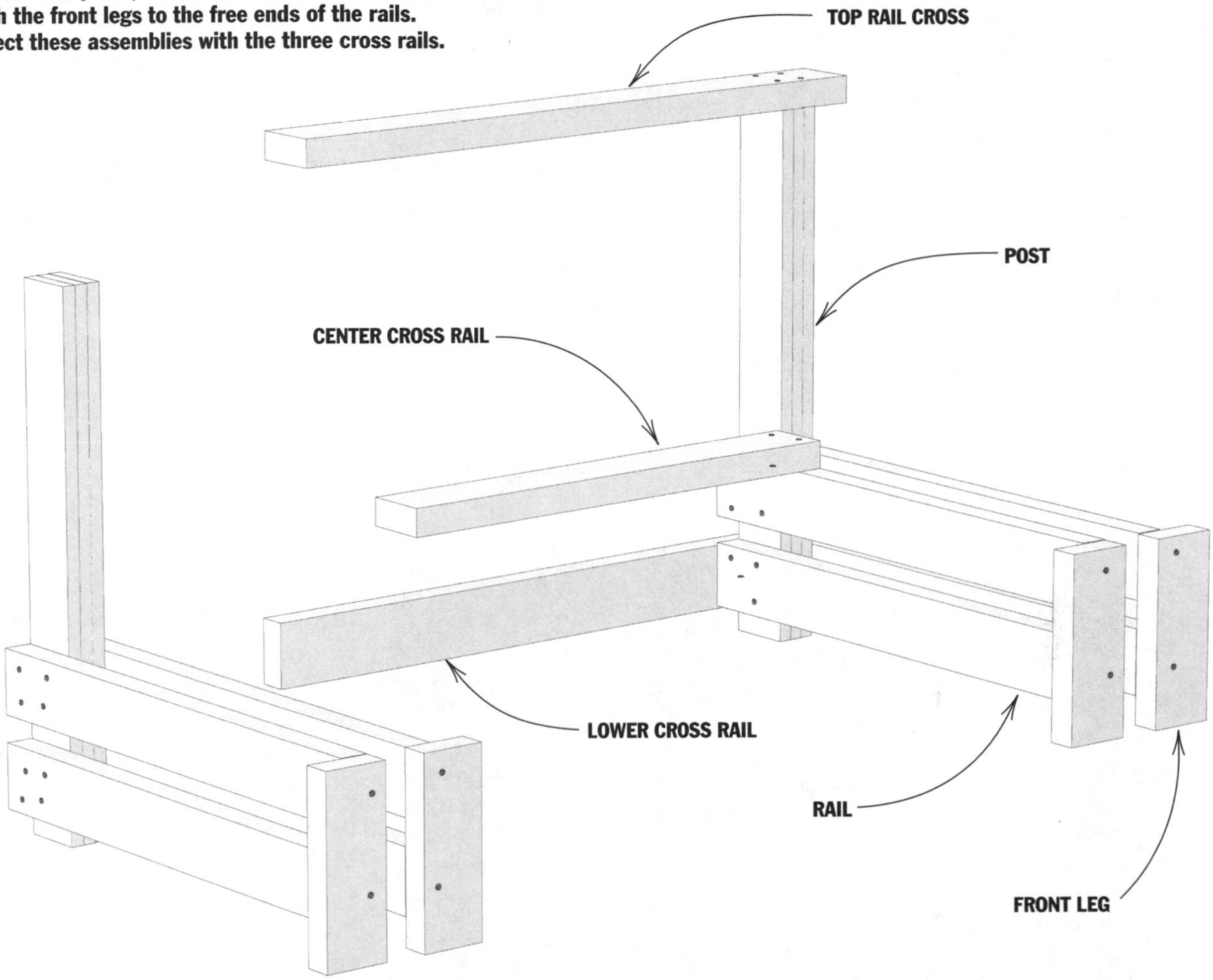

TOP RAIL CROSS

POST

CENTER CROSS RAIL

LOWER CROSS RAIL

RAIL

FRONT LEG

YOUR INVESTMENT
<u>Time:</u> One afternoon
<u>Money:</u> $15

SHOPPING LIST
2 8-foot 1×4
3 8-foot 2×4
#6 × 2-inch galvanized screws
#8 × 3-inch galvanized screws

PROJECT SPECS
The bike rack stands 39 inches wide, 30½ inches high, and 32 inches deep.

CUTTING LIST

PART	QTY.	DIMENSIONS	NOTES
Post	6	³⁄₄ × 3½ × 29	2×4
Rail	4	1½ × 3½ × 29	2×4
Front leg	4	1½ × 3½ × 10	2×4
Top cross rail	1	1½ × 3½ × 36	2×4
Center cross rail	1	1½ × 3½ × 27	2×4
Lower cross rail	1	1½ × 3½ × 35	2×4

BUILDING THE BIKE RACK

1 Cut all the wood. The basic bike rack modules contain just two lengths of wood, 29 inches and 10 inches. For the basic two-bike rack, you'll need 6 of the 29-inch 1×4s, 8 of the 29-inch 2×4s and 4 of the 10-inch 2×4s. For each additional module, you'll need 3 of the 29-inch 1×4s, 4 of the 29-inch 2×4s and 2 of the 10-inch 2×4s. You need one each of the three cross rails for the basic rack, and another set if three for each additional module. Cut them all at the start.

Make the posts. Roll glue onto the 1×4 post pieces and clamp them together. To keep the three pieces in line, clamp them edge-up under a block (above). Screw them together from both sides.

Screw the first upper rail to the post. Clamp a stop block 10 inches from the end of the post and screw the rail to the wide face of the post (above). Drill clearance holes and drive the screws at an angle to one another (below).

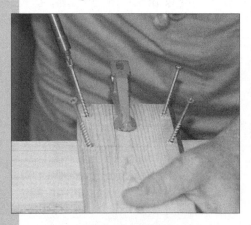

2 Make the posts. The basic rack has two posts, and after that you need to make one post for each additional bike. Each post consists of three pieces of 1×4 pine, joined face-to-face with glue and 2-inch screws. Roll glue on all the mating surfaces for one post and clamp the three pieces together. It's important to keep the edges flush, so clamp the wood as shown in the photo at left. Then drive 8 or 10 screws through from each side into the center piece. For maximum strength, stagger the screws from side to side and drive them at various angles. Scrape any squeezed-out glue off the side of the post with a chunk of scrap wood.

3 Screw the first upper rail to the post. The top of the upper 2×4 rails cross the posts 10 inches up from the ground. Make sure the rails cross the wide face of the post, not the narrow one. The ends of the rails come flush with the back edge of the post. Clamp one of

Screw the second upper rail to the post. Use a square to align the second rail on the other side of the post. The spacer blocks keep the parts parallel.

the 10-inch legs to the post as a gauge block, as shown in the center photo at left. Clamp the first upper rail to the post and make it square, then drill pilot holes and attach it with four 3-inch screws. The bottom left photo on the previous page shows how to angle the screws for maximum strength.

4 **Screw the second upper rail to the post.** Turn the assembled post and rail over on the worktable and lightly clamp the second rail in position. Use the speed square to align the rail, as shown in the photo at bottom left, then clamp it tight. Drive four 3-inch screws.

5 **Screw the lower rails to the post.** The lower rails are parallel to the upper ones, spaced the thickness of a 2×4 away, as shown in the photo at right. This creates about 1½ inches of ground clearance. Align and clamp each rail in turn, and screw it to the post with four of the 3-inch screws. Now make the

second rail-and-post assembly in the same way.

6 **Screw the front legs to the rails.** The 10-inch front legs span the free ends of the rails, as shown in the photo at right below. Join each leg to the rails with two 3-inch screws.

7 **Install the cross rails.** The three cross rails tie the two bike

racks together at a safe separation for handlebars, as shown in the three bottom photos. The 27-inch center cross rail connects the two inside top rails, just forward of the post. Drill pilot holes and screw it to the rails. The top cross rail spans the top of the posts. The lower cross rail is screwed into the ends of the lower rails. It can be screwed to the post as well.

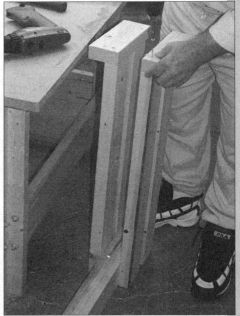

Screw the lower rails to the post. Space the lower rails the thickness of a 2×4 away from the upper ones, and align them at both ends. Then screw them to the post (above).

Screw the front legs to the rails. Stand the assembly up on end to fasten the legs to the free ends of the rails (right).

Install the cross rails. The center cross rail spans the upper rails just forward of the posts (above). The upper cross rail connects the tops of the posts (right). The lower cross rail completes the bicycle rack (far right).

DELIVERY BOX

Simple, tidy and weather-tight shelter for packages

These days everyone buys things from catalogs with 800-numbers, and everyone goes to work. That's why every household can use this simple delivery box. It's a sheltered outdoor house where delivery drivers can leave cartons, packages and envelopes, and pick them up too.

The box features a sloping, hinged lid with small blocks near its front edge. This allows you to leave outgoing packages on top of the box, provided weather is fair. It won't take long for the people who regularly deliver to your home to figure out that inside the box is the best place for both outgoing and incoming.

The box is made from regular 1× lumber, joined together with glue, screws and nails. It does require you to lay out and saw a consistent miter on one end of the six side pieces. The miters are specified at 25 degrees, but angular accuracy is much less important than consistency.

As shown here, the box can accept ledger-sized document boxes as well as small cartons of clothing, books or electronics. The shelf underneath can shelter medium-sized boxes. If all you ever receive is envelopes and small packages, you can tailor a smaller box that follows the same construction method.

DELIVERY BOX

Make the sides of the delivery box, then connect them with the box bottom, shelf and rails. Attach the front and back boards to the bottom and rails. Make and hinge the lid.

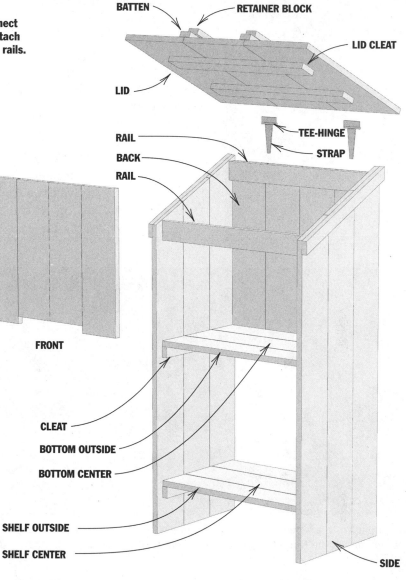

The commodious box has plenty of room for deliveries.

YOUR INVESTMENT

Time: One day
Money: $50

SHOPPING LIST

8 feet 1×10 pine
48 feet 1×6 pine
12 feet 1×5 pine
4 feet 1×3 pine
16 feet 1×2 pine
1¼-inch galvanized screws
2-inch galvanized siding nails
Two 4-inch galvanized tee-hinges

PROJECT SPECS

The delivery box stands 48 inches high, 25½ inches wide, and 16½ inches deep.

CUTTING LIST

PART	QTY.	DIMENSIONS	NOTES
Side	6	¾ × 5½ × 48	1×6
Cleat	4	¾ × 1½ × 14½	1×2
Bottom outside	2	¾ × 4½ × 22	1×4
Bottom center	1	¾ × 5½ × 22	1×6
Shelf outside	2	¾ × 4½ × 22	1×4
Shelf center	1	¾ × 5½ × 22	1×6
Rails	2	¾ × 2½ × 22	1×3
Front	4	¾ × 5½ × 18½	1×6
Back	4	¾ × 5½ × 25	1×6
Lid	3	¾ × 9½ × 22	1×10
Lid cleat	2	¾ × 2½ × 21	1×3
Batten	2	¾ × 1½ × 22	1×2
Strap	2	¾ × 1½ × 19	1×2
Retainer block	2	¾ × 1½ × 3	1×2

BUILDING THE BOX

1 Saw the wood. The delivery box is made entirely with standard 1× pine. There's no cut-and-fit, so it's safe to begin by sawing all the wood to the lengths given in the cutting list.

2 Lay out and miter the sides. The sides of the box are mitered 25 degrees, which gives the lid its weather-shedding slope. Place the three boards for each side flat on the worktable and align them at the bottom end. Use the speed square and a 1×2 stick to draw the 25-degree angle across all three boards for each side, as shown in the photo at left. Saw the miters with the chop saw, or with a jigsaw and the mitering jig shown on page 361. Worry about making the same angle on all six boards, not about how many degrees it is.

3 Join the sides with the cleats. The three boards in each side panel are joined by two glued-and-screwed cleats. The bottom edge of the lower cleat is $4\frac{1}{2}$ inches up from the end of the sides, or the width of a 1×5 board. The top edge of the upper cleat is $23\frac{1}{4}$ inches up. The cleats also support the shelf and box bottom, so it's important to get them in the same place on each side panel. It's also important to make a right side and a left side, as shown in the bottom left photo. Roll glue on each cleat, center it, and attach it to the sides with two $1\frac{1}{4}$-inch screws into each board.

Lay out and miter the sides. Use the speed square and a stick to draw a line at 25 degrees across the three boards for each side (top). Cut the sides on the chop saw (above).

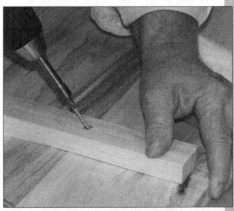

Join the sides with the cleats. Roll glue on each cleat and screw it to the side (left). Drive the screws on an angle to pull the boards tight together (right).

Nail the bottom and shelf to one side. Glue and clamp each bottom board to the cleat and fasten it with siding nails (left). Nail the shelf to the second cleat (right).

4 **Nail the bottom and shelf to one side.** The bottom boards connect the two sides of the delivery box. They must be inset from the edges of the sides by the thickness of the wood; the inset creates the space for the back and front boards. Attach the bottom boards first to one side of the box, and then to the other in Step 5. Spread glue on the ends of the two outside bottom boards, position them as shown in the photo above, and nail them to the upper cleat with four 2-inch siding nails. Glue and nail the bottom center board to the cleat, and attach the three shelf boards to the lower cleat in the same way.

5 **Nail the other side to the shelf and bottom.** Stand the completed box side, with the bottom and shelf attached, upright on the worktable. Fit the other side of the box in position, with its cleats under the free ends of the shelf and bottom boards. When you see how it goes, take the side away to

Nail the other side to the shelf and bottom. Spread glue where the shelf and box bottom will fit on the cleats (left). Nail the free ends of the boards to the cleats (right).

spread glue where the boards intersect, as shown in the photo above, then put it back in position. Make sure you maintain the board-thick inset of the box bottom. Nail the bottom and sides to the cleat.

6 **Join the front and back rails.** Turn the box onto its side on the worktable to attach the front and back rails. The rails

create anchoring surfaces for the front and back boards. They fit between the box sides right at the top, but they must be inset by the thickness of the wood, which you can make automatic by clamping a piece of scrap to the box side, as shown in the top photo on the next page. Nail through the box side into the end grain of the front rail. Nail the back rail in the correspond-

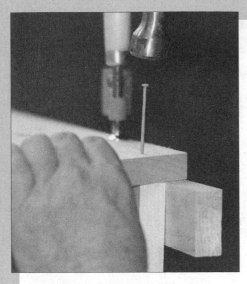

Join the front and back rails. Use a piece of scrap to inset each rail, and nail it to the sides.

ing location at the top back of the box. Then turn the assembly onto its other side to nail into the free end of both rails.

7 Attach the front and back. The front and back of the box each consist of four boards, attached to the front and back rails, and to the edges of the box bottom. Sand the sharp corners off the edges of the front boards before you fit them in place. If you like, you can add a decorative touch by shortening two of

the front boards by about an inch, as shown in the photo on page 274. Nail the front boards to the edges of the box bottom, then screw into them through the rails, from inside the box. Use the 1¼-inch screws. Nail the back boards to the box bottom, and screw them to the back rail from outside the box. Make the top of the back boards flush with the top edge of the back rail, as shown in the photo at bottom left.

8 Make the lid. The hinged lid consists of three 1×10 boards, connected by two lid cleats and sealed from the weather by two battens. Choose the most attractive face of the 1×10 for the top side of the lid. Turn the boards underside up on the worktable and locate the cleats: they go 5 inches in from either end of the top boards. Draw layout lines. Spread glue on the lid cleats, center them from side to side, and fasten them to the lid with 1¼-inch screws, as shown in the top left photo on the facing page. Now glue and clamp the battens along the joints between the boards, on the top side of the lid.

Add the straps. The straps tie **9** the top ends of the side boards together. They're 1×2s mitered to fit. Spread glue, then screw into the straps through the box sides from the inside, as shown in the bottom left photo on the facing page.

10 Hinge the lid. Two 4-inch tee-hinges connect the lid to the box. Begin by setting the lid in position and holding one of the hinges up to it, with the long leaf

Attach the front and back. Nail the front boards to the box bottom (above). Screw the front boards to the front rail from inside the box (below left). Screw the back boards to the box bottom and back rail (below right).

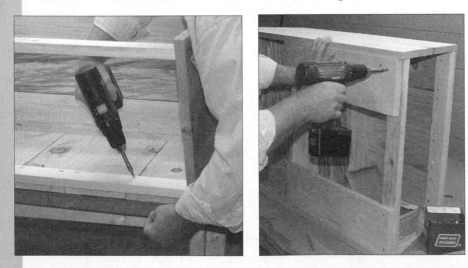

Make the lid. Glue and screw the lid cleats to the three lid boards. Then cover the cracks with battens.

Add the straps. Miter the straps to match the box sides and screw them to the outside of the box.

Hinge the lid. Clamp the tee hinge to a scrap of wood and drill an extra screw hole in it (above). Fasten the short leaves to the box lid (below). Then screw the long leaves to the back of the box (bottom).

extending down the back of the box. You'll quickly see which way around the hinge has to go, and where its knuckle falls. You'll also be able to see whether the standard holes will be OK. If one of them falls over air instead of wood, you'll have to drill a new hole, as shown in the top right photo. Screw the hinges to the lid, then set the lid in position on the box and screw them to the box.

11 Attach the retainer blocks. Two retainer blocks glued and nailed to the lid battens create a good-weather ledge for outgoing envelopes and packages.

12 Finish the box. Sand and paint the box to match the siding on your house. Or leave it alone, and it will weather gray.

LOG BENCH

Here's a quick seat made with two rounds and a plank

The log bench is among the simplest of landscape projects, provided you've got a couple of short logs to work with. It's just a pair of round logs with a pair of planks nailed on top. The big decision is where to put the bench, because once you spike the seat planks onto the logs, it won't be easy to move.

The logs in the photos are about 17 inches long and 13 inches in diameter. They came from land clearing. If you have firewood delivered, you should be able to ask for a couple of unsplit rounds, stove length.

Any diameter over 12 inches will make a good bench. Length variations are no problem. The bench will be fine down to about 12 inches high. If the logs are too long and you don't have a chainsaw, you can always dig them a couple of inches into the ground.

As an alternative to the bench shown in the photos, you can lay the logs on their sides, like the wheels of Fred Flintstone's car. You have to choose logs of equal diameter. Drive three spikes through each plank, in a triangular pattern.

BUILDING THE BENCH

1 Prepare the wood. For the seat, select clean, knot-free construction lumber; Douglas fir is best. Avoid pitch pockets, which will ooze sticky pitch until the end of time. Cut your seat material into two planks of equal length. Select or saw logs whose ends are flat and parallel.

2 Spike the seat onto the logs. Drive one or two of the spikes into each end of each plank, as shown in the photos on the facing page.

Spike the seat onto the logs. Set the first seat plank in place and nail through it into the end of the round log. Spike the second seat plank in the same way.

LOG BENCH

Spike the 2×8 seat planks onto the ends of the round logs. As an alternative, spike the planks onto the sides of the logs.

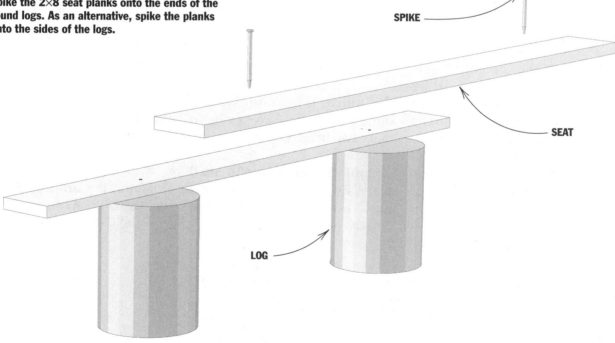

SPIKE

SEAT

LOG

YOUR INVESTMENT

<u>Time:</u> **10 minutes**
<u>Money:</u> **$10**

SHOPPING LIST

14 feet 2×8
6-inch galvanized spiral-shank timber spikes

PROJECT SPECS

The slab bench is 18 inches high, 15 inches wide, and 7 feet long.

CUTTING LIST

PART	QTY.	DIMENSIONS	NOTES
Log	2	13 × 13 × 17	
Seat	2	1½ × 7½ × 84	2×8

Attach the brace. Clamp the brace to the arm and nail into it through both the wall plate and arm.

Mount the bracket. Screw the bracket to a stud, through the wall of the garage.

WALL BRACKET

How to get heavy stuff off the ground

A pair of these handy brackets, which you nail together from scraps of 2×4, will support as many as three ladders on the wall of the garage. You can use the brackets for whatever you want to organize and store: lumber, pipes, bicycles, hoses. However, don't make the arm longer than about 12 inches.

BUILDING THE BRACKET

1 Choose the wood. Gather enough 2×4 or 2×6 scrap to make two brackets at a time.

2 Nail the arm to the wall plate. Begin by spiking the arm onto the wall plate with three 3½-inch galvanized spiral nails.

3 Attach the brace. Clamp the brace in position, as shown in the top photo. Drive three spiral nails into the brace through the wall plate, and three more through the arm.

4 Mount the bracket. Screw or nail the brackets to the wall. Be sure the fasteners go into studs.

YOUR INVESTMENT
Time: One hour
Money: $3

SHOPPING LIST
6 feet 2×4 stud
3½-inch galvanized spiral nails

PROJECT SPECS
The wall bracket extends 11½ inches out from the wall, and 16 inches down the wall.

CUTTING LIST

PART	QTY.	DIMENSIONS
Wall plate	2	1½ × 3½ × 16
Arm	2	1½ × 3½ × 10
Brace	2	1½ × 3½ × 6

WALL BRACKET

Nail the arm to the wall plate, then nail the brace into position between the arm and wall plate. Make the wall brackets in pairs.

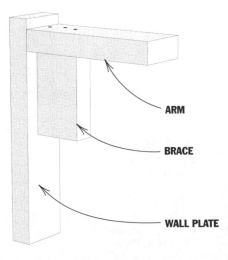

ARM

BRACE

WALL PLATE

LITTLE DECK

Build this flat spot in an afternoon

A little deck gives you a place to park your lawn chair while you watch the kids, or a level barbecue platform on an uneven lawn. You could pitch a tent on it, or put up a screen house. There's lots of places to use a little deck in the yard, provided you've got an easy way to make it.

The project results in a 6-foot × 6-foot deck. You can make it larger or smaller, as suits you. It can sit easily on level land, and it's not difficult to stake into a slope. You can build and install this deck in an afternoon.

The deck framework is made of 2×4s spiked together with 4-inch galvanized nails. Although you drill clearance holes, these nails nevertheless require a substantial amount of hammering. As an alternative, you can connect the joists with metal joist hangers, like the ones in the bridge on page 288. The little deck is small enough to construct inside the workshop, but if there's a large deck attached to your house, that may be a more convenient place to build.

The platform is an assembly of four 24-inch × 48-inch pieces of ¾-inch exterior grade plywood, with one 24-inch square of plywood in the center. This not only makes an interesting pattern, it liberates you from wrestling with a 4×8 sheet. Home centers these days sell half-sheets and quarter-sheets that are accurately cut and easy to carry, for no significant price premium.

BUILDING THE DECK

1 Cut the wood. Saw the joists to length at the start of the project. Don't trim the headers to length until you've nailed the joists to the rim joist and can measure the actual spans. The fit should be snug, and it's affected not only by centering the plywood decking, but also by the thickness of the wood.

2 Lay out the rim joists. The four joists run between the two rim joists, which therefore have to be marked out to match one another. Start with two 8-foot studs for rim joists; you'll be able to use the overhang to help you install the deck, and you can saw the excess off at the end, or leave it if you like. Clamp the two rim joists together face-to-face and locate the four joists, as

shown in the top right photo on the facing page. The layout dimension is the width of the 2-foot × 4-foot pieces of plywood. The two outside joists need to be 6 feet apart from outside edge to outside edge. Space the two inside ones 24 inches from outer edge to joist center.

3 Nail the joists to one rim joist. Two of the 4-inch nails, dri-

LITTLE DECK

To make the little deck, spike the joists to the rim joists. Then add the headers. Locate the deck, stake it to the ground, and fit the posts. Deck it with ³⁄₄-inch plywood.

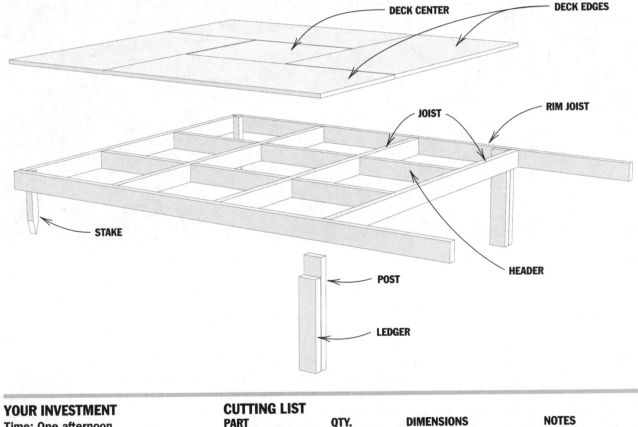

YOUR INVESTMENT

Time: One afternoon
Money: $50

SHOPPING LIST

Seven 8-foot 2×4
4-inch galvanized nails
#8 × 3-inch galvanized screws
2½-inch siding nails

PROJECT SPECS

The little deck is 6 feet square.

CUTTING LIST

PART	QTY.	DIMENSIONS	NOTES
Rim joist	2	1½ × 3½ × 96	2×4
Joist	4	1½ × 3½ × 69	2×4
Header	6	1½ × 3½ × 24	2×4; trim to fit
Stake	2	1½ × 1½ × 12	From 2×4
Post	2	1½ × 3½ × 24	Cut to fit
Ledger	2	1½ × 3½ × 24	Cut to fit
Deck center	1	³⁄₄ × 24 × 24	CDX plywood
Deck edge	4	³⁄₄ × 24 × 48	CDX plywood

Lay out the rim joists. Clamp the rim joists together and locate the four joists. Space them so the plywood decking falls on the joist center lines.

Nail the joists to one rim joist. Drill clearance holes and nail the four joists to one of the rim joists. Drill and nail on an angle to strengthen the joint.

ven through the rim joist into the end grain of each joist, will make a strong connection. Clamp the first joist in position on the worktable and drill two $3/16$-inch clearance holes through the rim joist. Drill the clearance holes so they toe in a few degrees, as shown in the photo above right. Swing the heaviest hammer you can manage to drive the 4-inch nails home. Attach the other three joists to the rim joist in the same way.

4 Attach the other rim joist. The second rim joist traps the free ends of the joists. Unless you're working on the floor, by now you will have overflowed the bounds of your worktable. You can support the structure on the table by clamping scrap props to the overhang, as shown in the center photo. Drill the $3/16$-inch clearance holes and nail the rim joist to the free ends of all four joists.

5 Make the headers. The six headers make the deck frame into a tic-tac-toe pattern, creating solid support for the plywood. The headers should fit tightly into the joist bays, so measure and cut each pair to fit.

Attach the other rim joist. Clamp props to the construction to support it while you nail the other rim joist to the free ends of the joists (center). Measure the diagonals to make sure the frame is square (above).

Make the headers. Cut the two center headers and fit them in place, using the center square of plywood as a gauge (above). Nail the headers to the joists (below left). Toenail the outside headers where they meet the center headers. Toenail through the face of the joist, not through the edge, on the angle indicated by the bit that will drill the clearance hole (below right).

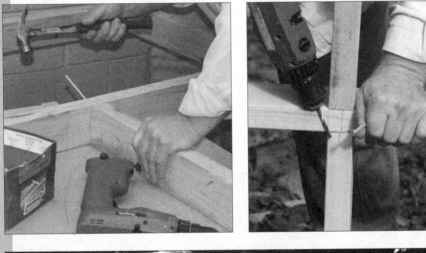

Start with the two headers between the two center joists. Use the actual plywood as a gauge to locate and nail the headers in place, as shown in the photo at left. Then nail the remaining headers across the outside joist bays. Make the center connections by toe-nailing, as shown in the center photos.

6 Locate the deck. It's much easier to locate and stake the deck to the ground without the plywood decking in place. The best site is dead-level grass, and the next best is a gentle slope. Carry the frame to where you want it and arrange it so one edge, or at least one corner, sits firmly on the ground. With this edge staked, you can raise the other edge onto 2×4 posts, as discussed in Steps 8 and 9.

7 Stake the deck. Drive a 12-inch stake inside the grounded corner of the deck frame. Drive the stake down below the top of the joists. Drill two clearance holes through the stake, and fas-

Stake the deck. Carry the frame to the site and drive a stake at the high corner (left). Drill clearance holes and drive two screws through the stake into the joists (above).

ten it to the joists with 3-inch screws, as shown in the bottom left photo on the previous page. Move to the next highest corner and block it up level on rocks or bricks. Drive the second stake into the pocket formed by the joists and attach it with two screws. Tamp the supporting rocks firmly under the joist.

8 **Pitch the deck.** Now move to the free edge of the deck and block it up to about an inch from dead level. This pitch allows it to drain. You can pitch it on stacks of rocks or scrap, or you can clamp props to it, as shown in the photo at top right.

9 **Make the posts.** A post resting on a flat rock supports each of the two remaining corners of the deck. Make the posts one at a time. First, choose your flat rock. Next, hammer out a rock-sized depression under one corner of the deck. Tamp the rock into the depression. Hold the post in place and mark it at the top and where it crosses the bottom of the joist. Saw off the top, then saw a ledger the length from the bottom of the joist down to the rock. Screw the two pieces of wood together as shown at center right, creating a rabbet. Plant the post on the rock and tuck the rim joist into the rabbet. Screw the joists to the post, as shown in the photo at far right. Make and fit the last post in the same way.

10 **Deck the deck.** Arrange the plywood pieces on the deck frame and fasten them with 2½-inch spiral deck nails, spaced 8 inches apart. Paint the deck, or leave it to weather naturally.

Pitch the deck. Bring the low side of the deck to within an inch of level and block it up or clamp it to temporary props.

Make the posts. Plant a flat rock under the corner of the deck and set a post on it (top left). Mark the height of the joist on the post and trim it to length (top right). Nail the ledger to the post (left), then screw the post to the joists (right).

Deck the deck. Arrange the plywood decking and nail it to the frame.

BRIDGE

Joist hangers help make a span that's strong and safe

The usual reason for building a bridge is to get across a gully or stream. However, like the gateway on page 264, a bridge doesn't have to go anywhere. It can stretch from point to point across perfectly level ground. It's reasonable to make a bridge just for fun, especially a bridge like the one shown here. This bridge is extremely strong, it's good looking, yet it's not difficult to build.

A bridge is an exercise in wood engineering, because the last thing you want is uncertainty about its strength. Every piece of wood in this bridge contributes its share of support. Even the spacers between the balusters and the main beams are structural. They not only support the balusters while allowing the deck to extend beyond the width of the bridge frame, they also help keep the main beams from twisting.

The spine of the bridge is a ladder made from standard 2×6 construction lumber, held together with nails and joist hangers. The bridge shown is just over 8 feet long, so the two main beams and the four cross beams can come out of a pair of 12-foot planks. These dimensions put the cross beams on 24-inch centers. If you decide to make a longer bridge, make the beams deeper by switching from 2×6 to 2×8 lumber. You'll also need more cross beams, but keep the spacing between 16 inches minimum and 24 inches maximum.

The deck, handrails, and balusters, or handrail supports, are made from 4/4 rough-sawn pine, which is readily obtainable from small sawmills in most parts of the country, and which measures about an inch thick. You could substitute any 4/4 rough-sawn lumber that's available in your locale; for a really tough bridge, use white oak. If you can't find rough-sawn material, you can use regular 5/4 pine lumber from the home center. It's generally about 1⅛ inches thick. Making this change will require that you make the bridge decking about ¼ inch longer. You might also want to increase the width of the handrail cap by ¼ inch. The dimension given is wide enough to cover the pieces underneath, plus a shadow reveal. While you don't need the shadow reveal for any structural reason, it does help the bridge look good.

Whether you use rough-sawn lumber or 5/4 pine, you will have to saw some pieces lengthwise in

BRIDGE

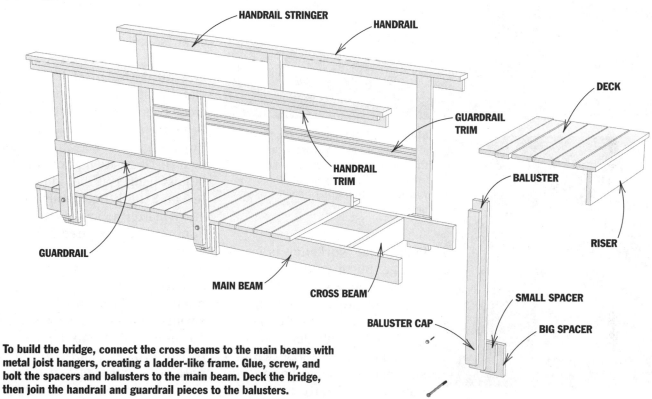

To build the bridge, connect the cross beams to the main beams with metal joist hangers, creating a ladder-like frame. Glue, screw, and bolt the spacers and balusters to the main beam. Deck the bridge, then join the handrail and guardrail pieces to the balusters.

YOUR INVESTMENT

Time: All weekend
Money: $75

SHOPPING LIST

Two 12-foot 2×6 planks
150 linear feet (75 board feet) 1×6 rough-sawn pine
Six joist hangers
1½-inch galvanized joist-hanger nails
Six ⁵⁄₁₆ × 3½-inch lag bolts with washers
Six ⁵⁄₁₆ × 5½-inch hex-head machine bolts with nuts and washers
#6 × 2-inch galvanized screws
3-inch galvanized spiral nails
2-inch galvanized siding nails

PROJECT SPECS

The bridge spans a gorge up to 6 feet wide.

CUTTING LIST

PART	QTY.	DIMENSIONS	NOTES
Main beam	2	1½ × 5½ × 98	2×6
Cross beam	4	1½ × 5½ × 23	2×6
Big spacer	6	1 × 5½ × 7½	
Small spacer	6	1 × 4½ × 6½	
Baluster	6	1 × 3½ × 38	
Baluster cap	6	1 × 2½ × 34½	
Riser	2	1 × 5½ × 30	
Deck	18	1 × 5½ × 30½	Random widths
Handrail stringer	2	1 × 2½ × 96	
Handrail	2	1 × 3½ × 96	
Handrail trim	2	1 × ⅞ × 93	
Guardrail	2	1 × 2½ × 81	
Guardrail trim	4	1 × 1 × 38	Trim length to fit

Mount the joist hangers. Clamp the joist hangers to the cross beams so they won't move while you nail them. Make sure the hangers are the same way up at either end of each cross beam.

Lay out the main beams. Lay out the location of the cross beams on both main beams at the same time. Making the beams match is more critical than precise spacing.

order to complete the bridge. The table saw is the tool of choice for sawing lengthwise, but as an alternative you can clamp a straight piece of wood to the workpiece to guide the cut with a portable circular saw, as shown on page 361.

If you build the bridge in the workshop, be sure you can get it out the door. It's no problem when your workshop is in the garage, but if your shop has a regular doorway, you probably won't be able to mount the balusters before you carry the construction outside.

To install the bridge across a stream or ravine, make sure you have an adequate footing on both sides. If there's any kind of a footing in place already, use it. Otherwise, the simplest footing would be a landscaping tie set into the ground at either end of the bridge. Dig shallow trenches for the ties and bed them in gravel so their top surfaces come just above the ground. Sight across the gully from one tie to the other, and rearrange the gravel to level them as best you can. Hump the bridge into position on the ties, then spike it to them with several 3-inch nails driven on an angle.

BUILDING THE BRIDGE

1 Make the beams. The main beams and cross beams can be sawn out of two 12-foot 2×6 planks, or else from three 8-foot 2×6 planks. When you buy the wood, look for clean material with square edges. Small, tight knots are no problem, but be sure to avoid large knots, bark-covered edges, and splits. You might have to pay extra for clean, sound wood.

2 Mount the joist hangers. Metal joist hangers connect the cross beams to the main beams. Begin by nailing joist hangers on both ends of all the cross beams. There are many varieties of joist hanger at the home center, and the little details don't much matter, so long as the type you get are designed for connecting 2×6 planks at right angles. Joist hangers are strong and forgiving, but the hanger part does have to fit tightly against the piece it's supporting. To get it right, clamp the hanger to the cross beam while you nail, as shown in the photo above. Be sure you get the hangers the same way up at either end of the cross beam.

3 Lay out the main beams. There's a cross beam 12 inches from either end of the main beams, and the cross beams are spaced 24 inches apart. Make layout marks as shown in the photo at left, and pencil an X on the main beams where you want the cross beams to fit. Lay out both main beams at the same time, because having them match is more important than precise spacing.

Join the cross beams to one main beam. Place the main beam on the worktable and stand the cross beams in position. Drive one nail through the joist hanger and check for square before driving the remaining nails (left). A good fit: The joist hanger pulls the cross beam tight (above).

4 Join the cross beams to one main beam. Lay a main beam on the worktable and stand the first cross beam in position. The joist hangers have little metal positioning tabs you can hammer into the wood. Drive one nail through the joist hanger into the main beam, then check that the construction is square, and if it is not, tap it into place. Drive the rest of the nails. Join the other three cross beams to the main beam in the same way.

5 Complete the bridge frame. Lay the second main beam flat on the worktable, and stand the assembled main beam and cross beams on it. Pay attention to your layout marks, and also to keeping the top surface of the beams flush. The construction will be precarious until you nail one of the center joist hangers to the second main beam. Once one cross beam is attached at both ends, it's easy to square up

Complete the bridge frame. Lay the second main beam flat on the worktable and stand the assembled section on top of it. Nail one of the center joist hangers first, to stabilize the construction.

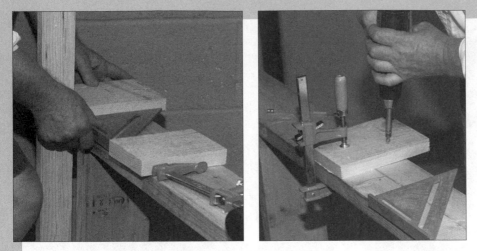

Make the first baluster support. Stand the bridge frame on edge and locate three big spacers on the main beam. Align the end spacers with the edge of the cross beams and put the third spacer in the center of the bridge frame (top left). Glue, clamp and screw the big spacers to the main beam (top right). Center the small spacer on the big spacer, flush at the top edge, and trace a layout line (below).

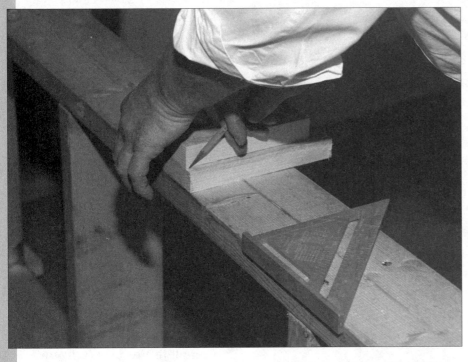

BALUSTER SQUARE

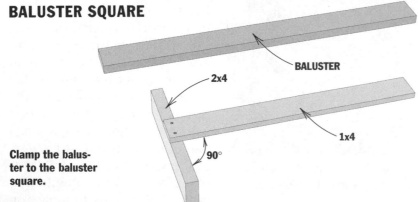

BALUSTER

2x4

1x4

90°

Clamp the baluster to the baluster square.

and nail the remaining joist hangers. This completes the frame of the bridge.

6 Make the first baluster support. The balusters are the vertical assemblies that hold up the handrails. The baluster supports connect the balusters to the main beams. Each baluster support consists of two wooden spacers glued and screwed together. Begin by standing the bridge frame on edge on the floor, so you can locate three of the big spacers on the main beam. The big spacers at the ends of the bridge line up with the edge of the cross beams. The third big spacer sits at the center of the bridge frame. Spread glue on the first big spacer, clamp it in place, and screw it to the main beam with four 2½-inch screws. Be sure the top edge of the the spacer is flush with the top edge of the main beam. Center the small spacer on the big spacer, also flush with the top edge of the main beam. Draw a layout line around the small spacer, spread glue within the layout line, clamp it, and screw it down. Use one of the balusters to lay out the four screws on the small spacer. If you keep the screws within the width of the baluster, they will be concealed.

7 Complete the baluster supports. Create the remaining five baluster supports in exactly the same way as you made the first one. It's a small point, but it's worth the trouble to examine each spacer before you spread glue on it. If it's cupped, spread the glue on the hollow side. This way, the edges are more likely to

Mount the balusters. Clamp the baluster square to the baluster (left). Plant the 2×4 arm of the baluster square onto the main beam, and the attached baluster will be correctly positioned (right).

Bolt the balusters. Drill a ⅜-inch bolt hole ⅝ inch from the bottom of the baluster. Angle the hole a few degrees to make sure you catch the main beam.

Add the baluster caps. A lag screw driven through the baluster cap makes the construction strong and rigid. Tighten the lag screw with a wrench.

remain tight and rainproof. In a rough softwood construction, when you clamp the parts together, you can get away without drilling clearance holes. However, if you decide not to bother with clamps, then you must drill clearance holes through the spacers. Otherwise, the screws can't pull them tight.

8 Mount the balusters. The balusters should rise vertically from the bridge deck, which means they should be at right angles to the main beams. However, since they're spaced outward by the baluster supports and offset as shown in the photo at right, there's no convenient place to fit a square. So, unless you want to measure laboriously for each of the six balusters, make a baluster square by nailing a 31½-inch length of 1×4 to the edge of a 2×4. When you clamp the 1×4 arm to the baluster, and plant the 2×4 on the main beam, the baluster ends up in the correct place, as shown in the photo at top right. Spread glue on the baluster, clamp it to the spacer, and screw it in place with four

2½-inch screws. Mount the other five balusters in the same way.

9 Bolt the balusters. To make sure the balusters stay put, bolt them to the main beams. The 5½-inch bolt goes through the baluster, both spacers, and the main beam itself. Locate the bolt ⅝ inch from the bottom of the baluster. Drill a ⅜-inch hole, but angle it a few degrees in order to make sure the bolt catches the

main beam, as shown in the photo above left. Tighten the bolt with a wrench, and bolt the rest of the balusters to the main beams in the same way.

10 Add the baluster caps. The baluster caps stiffen the baluster assemblies. They're glued and screwed to the outside of the balusters, then insured with a 3½-inch lag screw. Make sure the baluster caps end 2½ inches

Make the risers. Center and nail the vertical risers at both ends of the bridge. The top edge of the riser fits flush with the top of the beams.

Deck the bridge. Measure the actual distance between the balusters for the length of the deck boards and use whatever widths of wood you have on hand. Space the deck boards with a pair of ¼-inch slats, which are visible angling up behind the board being nailed.

Mount the handrail stringers. Center the handrail stringers from end to end, then glue and screw them to the balusters.

from the top of the balusters themselves. This space is for the handrail stringer, which comes in Step 13. Drill a ¼-inch hole for the lag screw, located as far up the baluster cap as possible while still penetrating the baluster spacers. Drive the lag screw with a socket wrench, as shown on the previous page.

11 Make the risers. There's a vertical riser at each end of the bridge, nailed to the ends of the main beams. Center the risers from side to side, their top edges flush with the top of the beams. Nail them in place with 3-inch spiral nails.

12 Deck the bridge. The cutting list gives a nominal width for the bridge deck, but the boards can come from whatever widths of lumber you have. For the length of the deck boards, measure the actual distance between the balusters. Start decking from one end of the bridge. The first deck board overhangs the riser by about ½ inch. Use a pair of ¼-inch slats of wood to space the deck boards, as shown in the photo at top right. Attach the deck to the main beams with two 3-inch spiral nails in each end of each board. When you come to the end of the bridge, nail the last deck board to the riser before you install the next-to-last board, which you will have to saw to fit the remaining space.

13 Mount the handrail stringer. In Step 10, you constructed a ledge at the top of the balusters, for the handrail stringer. Center each handrail stringer from end to end; they should sit on the

Make the guardrails. Mark a line 18 inches up from the bottom of the baluster caps for the guardrail trim. Screw the trim to the baluster (left). Roll glue onto the outside face of the guardrail trim, then clamp the guardrail to it. Screw the guardrail into the baluster caps and nail it to the guardrail trim (below).

Make the handrail. Nail the handrail into the ends of the balusters as well as into the stringers.

ends of the baluster caps and come flush with the tops of the balusters themselves. Mark where the handrail stringers fit, spread glue, clamp them in place and screw them to the balusters. Drive three 2-inch screws into each joint.

14 Make the handrails. The handrails are centered on the handrail stringers, then glued and nailed. Use the 3-inch spiral nails. Nail into the ends of the balusters as well as into the stringers. Space the nails about 9 inches apart.

15 Make the guardrails. The guardrails help keep small children from falling off the bridge. The guardrail trim stiffens the guardrails. Begin by marking a line 18 inches up from the bottom of the baluster caps. Cut the four pieces of guardrail trim to fit between the baluster caps. Drive a single $1\frac{5}{8}$-inch screw through each end of the trim, into the baluster itself. Roll glue onto the outside face of the guardrail trim and clamp the guardrail to it. Center the guardrail up and down, and also

from end to end. It should fit about $\frac{1}{2}$ inch inside the end baluster caps. Screw through the guardrail into the baluster caps, then nail through the guardrail trim into the guardrail itself, using 2-inch siding nails.

16 Trim the handrails. Glue and screw the handrail trim under the outside lip of the handrail. Clamp the trim in place while you drive the 2-inch screws up into the handrail itself. The trim not only stiffens the handrail, it also creates a shadow reveal that defines the architecture of the construction.

Trim the handrails. Glue and clamp the handrail trim under the outside lip of the handrail. Screw it to the handrail.

LANDSCAPE STEPS

Simple structure is flexible and adaptable to many landscape situations

Rustic steps make a handsome addition to your yard. Shallow slopes are somewhat easier to manage than steep ones, but in most situations the basic procedure is the same.

The steps can be made of logs, of landscape timbers, or of lumber. The steps shown are made of lumber, which has a lifespan of between 5 and 10 years before it will need repair. Fortunately, steps are not difficult to refurbish.

To tailor the steps to your landscape, you'll need to make a sketch and do a few calculations, as discussed in the sidebar on page 298. As shown in the diagram at right, each step consists of a riser and a tread. People will stumble unless all the steps in a flight have the same height (rise) and width (run). As discussed in the sidebar, steps with a low riser need wide treads, while high steps can get away with narrow

treads. In the landscape you can make wider treads than you could use inside a building.

The strategy is to start at the bottom, level and stake the first riser, dig out the first tread and bed it in gravel, then spike the two together. Bedding in gravel helps the steps drain, increasing the lifespan of the wood. Then level and stake the second tread and riser, and so on. Once all the steps are in place, fill in any voids with gravel, and replant.

BUILDING THE STEPS

1 Stake the four corners. Decide where you want the steps to run, and drive a wooden stake at each corner. The steps shown in the photos are 3 feet wide, with a rise of just under 5 feet. In the steps shown, the bottom step is out of line with the top by about two feet. This misalignment not only looks good on the land, but also creates solid attachment points for handrail balusters, which you might decide to add later on.

2 Clear the site. Spade through the vegetation within the rough rectangle marked by the stakes, and remove the plant cover down to bare soil. You can establish the edges of

Stake the four corners. Walk the land and figure out where the steps should be. Drive a stake at each corner.

LANDSCAPE STEPS

Assemble each tread to the riser above it. Set each tread-and-riser in place, drive two stakes and screw the riser to them, and nail the tread to the riser below. Stagger the steps to fit the land.

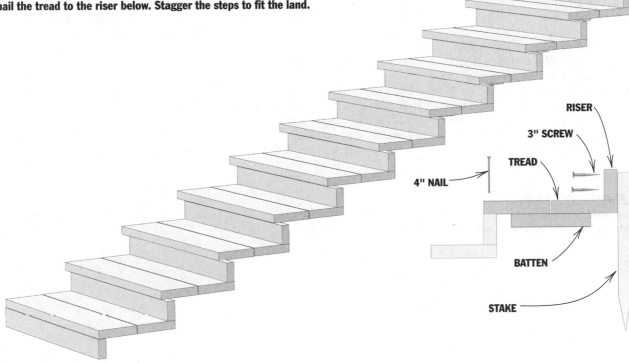

RISER

3" SCREW

TREAD

4" NAIL

BATTEN

STAKE

YOUR INVESTMENT

Time: One weekend
Money: $50

SHOPPING LIST

Eight 8-foot 2×8
Six 8-foot 2×4
#8 × 3-inch galvanized screws
4-inch galvanized nails

PROJECT SPECS

The steps have a 5-foot rise and an 11-foot run, and are 3 feet wide.

CUTTING LIST

This cutting list is for the steps shown in the photos and drawings. Each situation is different, so each builder must develop his own cutting list and shopping list, following the general discussion on the next page.

PART	QTY.	DIMENSIONS	NOTES
Riser	10	$1\frac{1}{2} \times 3\frac{1}{2} \times 36$	2×4
Tread	18	$1\frac{1}{2} \times 7\frac{1}{2} \times 36$	2×8
Stake	20	$1\frac{1}{2} \times 1\frac{1}{2} \times 12$	From 2×4
Batten	18	$1\frac{1}{2} \times 1\frac{1}{2} \times 9$	From 2×4
Last riser	1	$1\frac{1}{2} \times 7\frac{1}{2} \times 36$	Width to fit
Last stake	2	$1\frac{1}{2} \times 1\frac{1}{2} \times 36$	From 2×4

DESIGNING STEPS

You can't purchase materials until you make a sketch of your steps, and work out the dimensions of each step. Use your tape measure and a couple of long sticks to establish the total rise and the total run of the steps, as shown in the photo at far right.

In these steps, the rise is 58 inches and the run is 135 inches, or a little more than 11 feet. The first decision is the height of the riser—in the steps shown, it's a 2×4 on edge, plus the thickness of the tread on top, for a total of 5 inches. This is a shallow step; you could use a 2×6 on edge to make a deeper 7-inch riser.

To find the number of risers you need, divide the total rise by the height of one riser. In the steps shown, it's 58 inches divided by 5 inches, for eleven risers with a few inches left over. This is not a building, it's the landscape. Nevertheless, unequal risers are dangerous, so

plan to dig or fill to eliminate any discrepancies.

The number of treads is always one fewer than the number of risers. To find the width of each tread, divide the total run by the number of treads. In the steps shown, the calculation is 135 inches of run divided by 10 treads, or $13\frac{1}{2}$ inches per tread.

The last step in the calculation is to figure out how you will achieve the tread width using standard widths of lumber. Since each riser sits on top of the tread below it, you have to allow for the thickness of the risers. In the steps shown, the total tread width is $13\frac{1}{2}$ inches for the run plus $1\frac{1}{2}$ inches for the next riser, a total of 15 inches.

The stairbuilder's rule of thumb is that the rise of one step, plus the width of one tread, must be at least 17 inches and shouldn't be more than about 21 inches. A 5-inch riser

with a $13\frac{1}{2}$-inch tread is a total of $18\frac{1}{2}$ inches, within the rule of thumb. In landscape steps you can go to a riser-plus-tread total of 24 inches without tripping anyone.

There is wiggle room in these calculations. In the landscape it's easy to fudge the height of the risers or the width of the treads to match the wood you can get. These risers are planted on the treads, but they could be wider boards nailed to the back of the treads instead of between their faces. You could make up the tread with three boards instead of two, there is no reason for all the boards in a tread to be the same width, and you could leave gaps between the boards.

The width of the steps is up to you, but once you decide what it is to be, you can figure out how much wood to buy. If you want a handrail also, screw balusters to the risers and screw a 2×4 to them.

DESIGNING STEPS

To calculate the number of treads, measure the total run and divide by the width of one tread. There is always one more riser than treads. To calculate the rise of one step, divide the total rise by the number of risers.

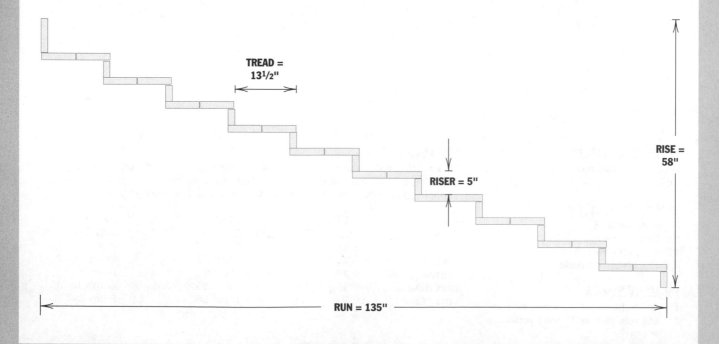

TREAD = $13\frac{1}{2}$"

RISER = 5"

RISE = 58"

RUN = 135"

the steps by running a string between the stakes, or you can do it by eye.

3 **Calculate the rise and run.** Measure the total height or rise and the total length or run of your steps. Use this information to sketch the steps you propose to build, as discussed in the box on the facing page. This sketch yields the cutting list, and your shopping list.

4 **Cut the wood for the steps.** The steps shown in the photos are 3 feet wide, with eleven risers and ten treads. Thus there are ten 36-inch 2×4 risers plus one 2×6 riser at the top. Since each tread consists of two 2×8 planks, there are twenty 36-inch treads. There are also twenty 12-inch stakes, two 36-inch stakes, and twenty 9-inch battens.

5 **Join the treads and risers.** Each tread consists of two planks joined together by a pair of battens. The riser sits on top of the tread. These pieces are all joined together by galvanized screws. You can assemble treads and risers as you go, or you can assemble them all now, at the beginning of the construction. Drive four of the 2½-inch screws through each batten. Drive four of the 3-inch screws through the bottom of the tread into the edge of the riser, as shown in the center right photo.

6 **Level the first riser.** Begin at the bottom of the steps. Locate the first riser and level it from end to end. Drive a pair of 12-inch stakes in the ground, tight against the riser. Ordinarily the stakes would go inside the riser,

Calculate the rise and run. These steps will be 3 feet wide, with a total rise of almost 5 feet. You can survey with the aid of a 6-foot level, but you can get close enough with nothing but a tape measure.

Join the treads and risers. Screw the battens to the treads. Then screw the assembled tread to the riser.

Level the first riser. Set the first riser at the foot of the steps and drive a stake behind it or in front of it, as shown. Screw the riser to the stake, then level it and drive the second stake.

Attach the first tread assembly. Dig out the first step (left), and lay a bed of gravel (right).

Stake the second riser. Set the first tread and second riser in place, level them, and drive stakes behind the riser (above). Screw the riser to the stakes (below).

but in the situation shown in the photo at left, the first tread jumps a curbstone. Now screw the stakes to the riser, with two 3-inch screws at each end.

7 Attach the first tread assembly. The general procedure is to excavate for each tread in turn, to lay a shallow bed of gravel, and then to fit the assembled tread and riser to the staked riser below, as shown in the photos on this page. This way, when you excavate for the next tread, you can back-fill the one below with the loosened earth. Nail through the front edge of each tread into the riser below, with four of the 4-inch spikes.

8 Stake the second riser. With the tread-and-riser assembly nailed to the riser below, drive two of the 12-inch stakes into the ground behind the top riser and hard against it. Screw through the riser into each stake, with two of the 3-inch galvanized screws, as shown in the photo at left.

9 Stairway to heaven. Once you've established the basic method of setting each tread

Stairway to heaven. Continue upward by digging out each step, then level the tread, nail it to the riser below, drive stakes and screw them to the riser.

and riser, keep doing more of the same until you reach the top, as shown in the photos above. One way to make the work less than endless is to keep the jobsite reasonably tidy. Cover the built steps with a tarp while you back-fill, and sweep the clods of dirt off the wood, so you don't grind it into your knees.

10 The last riser. At some point the stairway has to end. It normally ends with a riser, which should not differ in height from the risers below it. In the step shown in the photos, the riser is a piece of 2×8 tread, spiked to the back of the last tread. Once the last tread and riser are in place and level, drive two 3-foot stakes into the hillside behind the riser. Drive them down as far as you can, as shown in the photo at right, and saw them off flush with the top of the riser. Finally, screw through the riser into each stake with two 3-inch screws.

11 Complete the step. Fill in any gaps with earth, gravel and plants. If you wish, make a landing following the same method as the little deck on page 283.

The last riser. Complete the steps with a riser. Drive stakes as deep as possible behind the last riser (above). Saw the stakes off flush (below).

TREE SEAT

You can construct this modular seat for many different locations

Trees are inherently big, so a seat that embraces one also has to be big. This tree seat, however, relies upon a modular seat unit, three of which make the seat shown here, and eight of which would neatly surround almost any tree. Once you know how to make one of the seat modules, it's straightforward to make as many as you like.

Two of these modular seats make a right angle, so a two-seat bench plugs perfectly into an inside corner on your deck or patio. Three together look great against a straight wall, with room at either end for a planter or a little table. You probably wouldn't make four or five, but with six seats, or two sets of three, you've almost completed all eight.

The three-seat assembly is the heart of the system, so it's what these instructions show you how to make. You make three seats by building two iden-

tical freestanding chairs, then you connect them with additional rails and slats. You would build the full octagon in the same way: Make two identical three-seaters, then join them with additional slats and rails. If you make these last parts extra long, the octagon would surround an oval space instead of a circular one.

The tree seat is made of standard 1× and 2× pine lumber. This is not a beginner project,

TREE SEAT

The tree seat is a modular construction you can make any size you want. To build the three-module seat shown here, make four h-shaped seat sides, then add connecting rails to make two complete seats, then connect the seats with a third set of rails.

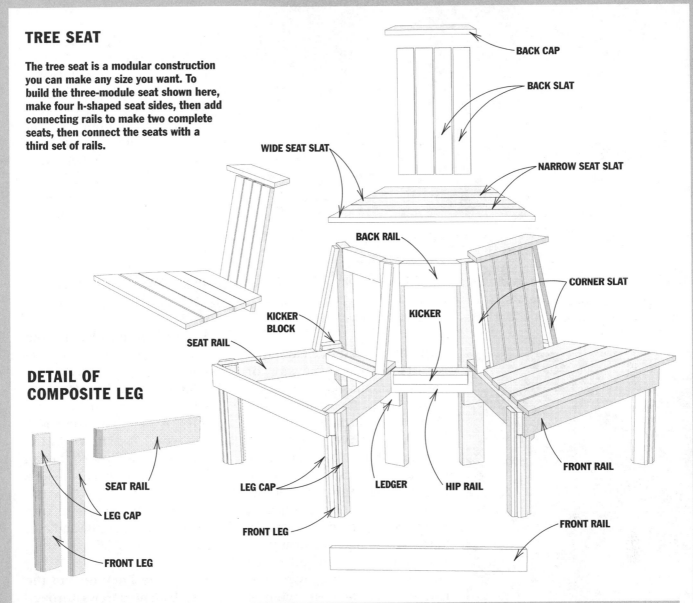

BACK CAP

BACK SLAT

WIDE SEAT SLAT

NARROW SEAT SLAT

BACK RAIL

CORNER SLAT

KICKER BLOCK

KICKER

SEAT RAIL

FRONT RAIL

DETAIL OF COMPOSITE LEG

SEAT RAIL

LEG CAP

FRONT LEG

LEG CAP

LEDGER

HIP RAIL

FRONT LEG

FRONT RAIL

YOUR INVESTMENT

<u>Time:</u> All weekend
<u>Money:</u> $50

SHOPPING LIST

4 feet 2×2 pine
32 feet 2×4 pine
8 feet 1×2 pine
48 feet 1×3 pine
40 feet 1×4 pine
#6 × 2-inch galvanized screws
#8 × 2½-inch galvanized screws
#8 × 3-inch galvanized screws
2-inch galvanized siding nails
2-inch galvanized finishing nails

PROJECT SPECS

The three-unit tree seat is 72 inches wide, 34 inches high, and 34 inches front to back. It will embrace trees up to 3 feet in diameter.

CUTTING LIST

PART	QTY.	DIMENSIONS	NOTES
Back leg	4	1½ × 3½ × 33	2×4
Seat rail	4	1½ × 3½ × 20½	1×4; miter 22½°
Ledger	4	1 × 2½ × 3½	From scrap
Front leg	4	1½ × 3½ × 13	2×4; round edges
Leg cap	8	¾ × 2 ½ × 16½	1×3; round edges
Front rail	3	¾ × 3½ × 28½	1×4; double-miter 22½°
Back rail	3	1½ × 3½ × 9⅛	2×4; miter 22½°
Hip rail	3	1½ × 3½ × 12¼	1×4; miter 22½°
Kicker	3	1½ × 1½ × 11¼	2×2
Kicker block	4	¾ × 1½ × 3¼	1×2
Corner slat	4	¾ × 1½ × 16¾	1×2
Wide seat slat	As needed	¾ × 3½ × 288	Miter 12 slats to fit
Narrow seat slat	As needed	¾ × 2½ × 72	Miter 8 slats to fit
Back slat	12	¾ × 2½ × 19	1×3; round edges
Back cap	3	¾ × 3½ × 14	1×4; miter 22½°

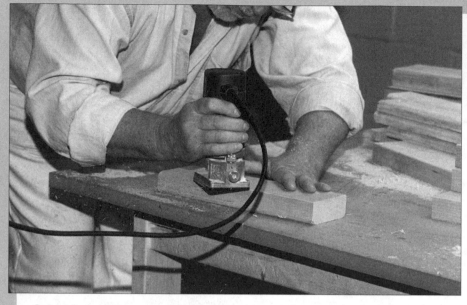

Cut and round the parts. Saw everything except the seat slats to length, miter the ends, and round over the long edges of the front legs, front leg caps and back slats.

Attach the ledgers. Use a front leg to mark the height of the ledger on the back leg. You can see an assembled leg-and-ledger in the foreground of the photo.

though even beginners will succeed by following the steps. There are a lot of parts, many of them are sawn at an angle, and some of them have to be cut to fit. The angled, or mitered, parts are all sawn at the same setting, 22½°. The chop saw is the tool of choice for sawing angles,

though you can get excellent results with a table saw or portable circular saw.

You may also want to rout the corners off the wood with a ⅜-inch roundover cutter. The tree seat shown has a soft look because all its edges were rounded over. You can omit this step if you like, though as a result your project will have a harder, more linear appearance. Paint tends to crawl off sharp corners, so the roundover alternative makes the best technical sense if you plan to paint.

BUILDING THE SEAT

1 Cut and round the parts. The cutting list gives actual full, square dimensions. Each of the mitered pieces can be sawn out of the square size specified. Cut everything except the seat slats at the start of the project. If you intend to roundover the front leg, front leg caps, and back slats, do so now. Don't cut the seat slats until you need them. Then miter the slats to fit, as discussed in Step 17.

2 Attach the ledgers. The construction depends upon a strong, square joint between the back leg and the seat rail. However, there's no easy way to position the rail, until you glue and nail a positioning ledger to each leg. The ledger also resists downward thrust. Since the top of the ledger is at the height of the front leg, use the front leg as a gauge piece to position it, as shown in the photo at left below. Make the joint by driving screws through the back leg into the end of the seat rail.

3 Miter the seat rails. The four seat rails each have one double-mitered end, in order to create flat surfaces for attaching the front rails. The miters, which are 22½°, run the width of the wood, as shown in the drawing on page 306, so the rail comes to a point when you look straight down on it. Saw the miters on the chop saw, or with a portable circular saw and a jig as shown on page 361.

4 Screw the back legs to the seat rails. The screws through the back leg must pull tight on the seat rail. Center the end of the seat rail on the ledger you attached in Step 2, and draw a layout line around it. Drill three ³⁄₁₆-inch clearance holes through each back leg. The ³⁄₁₆-inch drill matches the threads of the #8 screws. Angle the holes as shown in the photo at the top of the next page. Then spread glue on the end grain of the seat rail and on the edge of the ledger, and clamp the parts together. Now drive the screws into the end grain of the seat rails, pulling the parts together.

5 **Make the composite legs.** A composite leg allows you to construct woodworking joints without having to cut intricately shaped parts. The tree seat has composite front legs, which are three-piece sandwiches consisting of one front leg and two leg caps. Positioning the parts as shown in the illustrations at right not only builds a socket for the seat rail, but also creates two little ledges that support the front rails. Spread a light coat of glue on the face of a leg cap and center it on on the front leg, as shown in the photo at top right. Then clamp the parts to the worktable, nail them together with 2-inch finishing nails, and set the nailheads. Make the other three composite legs in the same way.

6 **Join the legs to the seat rails.** When you're done with this step, you'll have four h-shaped seat sides. Slip the seat rails into the sockets of the composite legs. To gauge how far forward the rails should come, hold a straight edge against the mitered end of each rail. Shift the parts by tapping with a hammer. When the straight edge also bears against the round corner of the leg cap, as shown in the photos at right, the parts are in the correct place. Take them apart to spread glue, then reassemble the construction and clamp it together. Drill pilot holes and drive three 2-inch screws through each leg cap into the seat rail.

7 **Miter the front, back and hip rails.** The front, back and hip rails connect the four seat

Screw the back legs to the seat rails. Glue and clamp the seat rail to the leg and ledger. Drill clearance holes and drive the screws on an angle. Bury the screwheads in the wood.

Make the composite legs. Roll glue onto the inside face of the leg cap. Use a square to position the leg cap on the front leg. Screw the parts together.

Join the legs to the seat rails. Fit the seat rail into the slot of the composite front leg. Tap the parts into place with a hammer (left). When the mitered end of the seat rail lines up with the rounded corner of the leg cap, the parts are in the right location. The front rail will rest on the little ledge below the miter (right).

H-SHAPED SEAT SIDE

The three-piece front leg assembly allows you to assemble a wooden joint without cutting intricate parts.

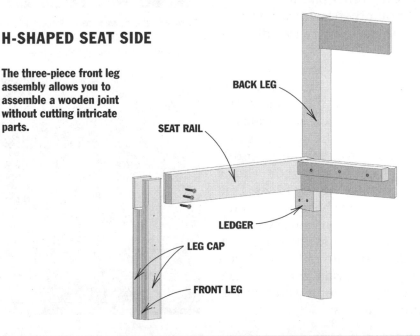

BACK LEG

SEAT RAIL

LEDGER

LEG CAP

FRONT LEG

sides you joined in the previous step. They're all mitered both ends at $22\frac{1}{2}°$, as shown in the drawing at right. Saw the miters the same way you mitered the seat rails in Step 3.

8 **Connect the seat sides.** Stand two seat sides upright on the worktable, and hold the front rail in place. It should rest on the little ledges on the composite legs, it should fit flat on the mitered ends of the seat rails, and it should bear against the corners of the leg caps. Get the rail into position on both side assemblies and hold it with a clamp, then check that the legs are vertical. The photo at right shows how the front rail fits. When you see how the assembly has to go, take it apart so you can spread glue on the mating surfaces, then clamp it back together. Drill pilot holes for four 2-inch screws in each end of the front rail, two into each seat rail and two into each leg cap, and drive these screws. Repeat this step to connect the other pair of seat sides with another front rail, leaving the third front rail aside until Step 15.

9 **Join the hip rail.** The mitered hip rail makes the fourth side of the seat frame. It fits between the seat rails and against the back legs, and it rests on the ledger that's attached to the back legs. Drill two clearance holes through the seat rails so you can drive 3-inch screws straight into the end-grain of the hip rail. There's not much long-grain gluing surface in this joint, but it won't hurt to glue it anyway.

MITER DETAIL

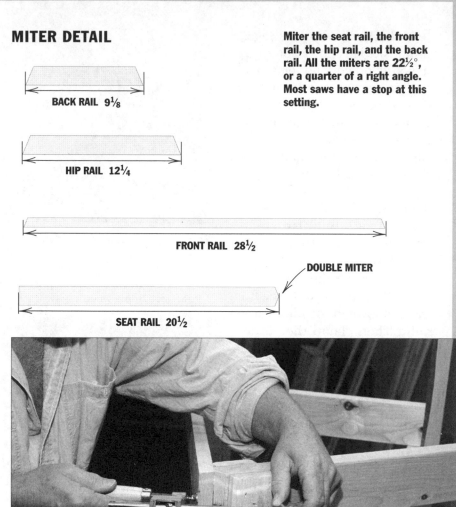

BACK RAIL 9⅛

HIP RAIL 12¼

FRONT RAIL 28½

DOUBLE MITER

SEAT RAIL 20½

Miter the seat rail, the front rail, the hip rail, and the back rail. All the miters are $22\frac{1}{2}°$, or a quarter of a right angle. Most saws have a stop at this setting.

Connect the seat sides. Stand the two seat sides upright on the worktable and fit the front rail in place. Clamp it as shown (above). Make sure the front legs are vertical before you attach the front rail (below left).

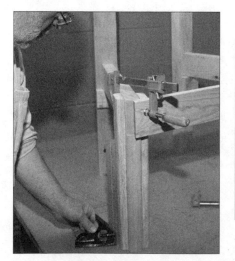

Join the hip rail. Fit the hip rail on the back legs and screw it to the seat rails.

10 Add the back rail. The mitered back rail fits between the back legs at the top, flush with the front face of the legs. It will be locked in place by the back cap you make in Step 19. For now, toenail a pair of 3-inch screws through the top edge of the back rail and into the legs, as shown in the photo at right, plus a similar pair of screws through the face of the rail. When you have screwed the back and hip rails into both seat modules, you'll have completed the basic structure of two sturdy chairs.

11 Make the kicker. The kickers are auxiliary rails screwed on to the hip rails, in order to give a comfortable slope to the seat back. Fit the kicker flush with the top of the hip rail, and center it from side to side. The easy way to do this is to mark a centerline on the kicker and on the hip rail. Then align these centerlines. Glue and screw the kickers to the hip rails, using the 2½-inch screws.

12 Add the kicker blocks. The kicker blocks give the corner slats the same slope as the rest of the seat back. They're just blocks of wood glued and nailed onto the seat rails, tight against the back legs.

13 Fit the corner slats. The corner slats define the seat backs, and they help the back slats turn the corner. Sand the sharp edges off the corner slats. Rest them on the seat rail and center them on the back legs and the kicker blocks, and fasten them in place with the 2-inch siding nails.

Add the back rail. Join the back rail to the back legs by driving 3-inch screws on an angle through the top of the rail and also through its face.

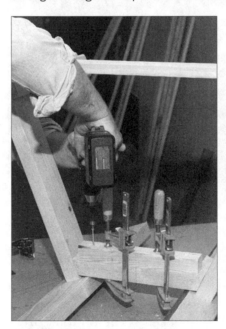

Make the kicker. The kicker creates the slope of the seat back. Center it on the hip rail, then glue it and screw it.

14 Fit the back slats. There are four back slats in each seat module. Nail the outer two in place first. The back slat should touch the corner slat at the top, and it

Add the kicker blocks. Nail a kicker block to each seat rail. The kicker block fits tightly against the back leg.

Fit the back slats. The corner slat rests against the kicker block and the back leg. Nail it in place with 2-inch siding nails. Nail the outer two back slats alongside the corner slats. Then space the remaining two slats across the opening.

Connect the two seats. Space the two seat units with the hip rail, and clamp the front rail in place. Glue and screw the front rail to the composite legs (above). Join the hip rail to the back legs (left).

should line up with the end of the kicker at the bottom. Drive three 2-inch siding nails through the top and bottom of each back slat. Once you've attached the two outer slats, space the remaining two slats evenly between them.

15 Connect the two seats. Place the two seat units on the floor as

if there was an imaginary third seat in between them. When you add the three connecting rails— that is, the front rail, hip rail and back rail—the imaginary seat will be made real, as shown in the photo below. First, space the seat units by dropping the hip rail into position on the ledgers, then fit the front rail. Clamp it tightly against the front-rail miters on the two completed seats. Spread glue on the front rail and screw it to the seat rail and leg caps, the same way you did in Step 8. In Step 9, you were able to screw through the back legs into the hip rail, but now you can't get the same access. You have to screw through the face of the hip rail into the back legs. Fit the back rail at the top of the back legs, the same as in Step 10. Use 2½-inch screws for all these joints.

16 Make the middle back. The middle seat shares the existing legs and corner slats, but it does need its own kicker. Screw the kicker to the hip rail, as you did in Step 11. Now you can space and nail the four back slats, the same as in Step 14.

17 Make the center seat. The seats consist of alternating wide and narrow strips of wood, mitered 22½° and nailed to the seat rails. The cutting list does not give individual sizes for these parts, because you have to cut and fit your way along. This way, you can compensate for variations in construction, and you can work around knots to get the most out of your wood budget. Rounding over the top edges and mitered ends of the seat slats also helps dis-

Make the middle back. Fill in the middle back with four back slats.

Make the center seat. Draw a centerline on the seat rails, and clamp a scrap of wood on one center line, as shown at the top left of the photo. Fit the seat slat against the scrap and mark where it crosses the center line. Miter the slat and nail it in place. Use a narrow stick to space the slats front to back.

guise variations. To fit the slats, draw centerlines on the seat rails and clamp a scrap of wood on one centerline. Butt the mitered end of the slat stock against the scrap, in order to locate and mark the other miter. Space the seat slats with $\frac{3}{16}$-inch scraps of wood, as shown in the photo at top right. Nail them to the seat rails with 2-inch siding nails.

18 Fit the end seats. Once you have established one seat, you can fit the adjacent seats to it. You no longer need the clamped piece of scrap. If you're making a three-seat unit, make the slats of the end seats long enough to overhang the seat rail and cover the outside leg caps. To make the full octagon, just continue to cut and fit seat slats from center line to center line until all the openings have been filled in.

19 Fit the back caps. The back caps trim out the seat and hide the top ends of the legs. The back caps are mitered 22½° and

Fit the back caps. Miter and fit the back caps to cover any irregularities in your project. Glue and nail the caps onto the back rails.

Trim the back caps. Go over the tree seat and look for objectionable points of wood to saw off.

have to be trimmed to fit. Begin with the center piece. Miter one end, fit the front of the cap flush with the face of the back slats, and mark where to miter the other end. Where the miters fall is not critical, so you can fudge them to cover construction goofs. Round over three long edges, leaving square the edge that fits onto the back slats. Glue the back cap onto the back rail, and anchor it with 2-inch

siding nails. Fit the other back caps the same way.

20 Trim the back caps. There are a couple of places where the protruding corners of the back caps could bruise the paying customers. Mark them and saw them off, as shown in the photo above right. Trim the protruding miters off the seat slats too, unless you prefer their crisp appearance.

MAILBOX POST

Assembled construction puts the post beyond snowplow's reach

Post office regulations govern the height of mail box posts, but in winter regions of the country, the snowplow imposes its own requirements. The post office wants the box to be 4 feet off the asphalt, level with the window of the mail van. The snowplow uproots anything in its path. A cantilevered construction allows the post to be set back from the road, out of the blade's path.

This mailbox post is nailed together from two chunks of 4×4 post and eight lengths of 2×4 stud. While you could glue and screw it, it's not necessary—the nails are more than strong enough. The post is set in the ground with a metal stake.

BUILDING THE POST

1 Cut the wood. You can get all of the 2×4 pieces out of two 10-foot lengths of wood, or from two 8-foot studs plus a 3-foot scrap. The arrangement in the post shown here is not the only way to go. It's easy to clamp the pieces together and fiddle around with them.

2 Nail the uprights to the stub. The stub makes the connection with the metal post stake. Fit it into the stake to test the fit, and make a layout line ½ inch above the top of the stake. Clamp the uprights to the stub on the layout line, and drive one 4-inch spike through each upright into the stub, as shown in the photo above left.

3 Align the uprights. Check the alignment of the uprights with a speed square, as shown in the photo above right. With only

Nail the uprights to the stub. Drive a single 4-inch nail through each upright into the stub, which will fit into the metal stake.

Align the uprights. Use the speed square to bring the uprights into line, then drive three more nails through each.

MAILBOX POST

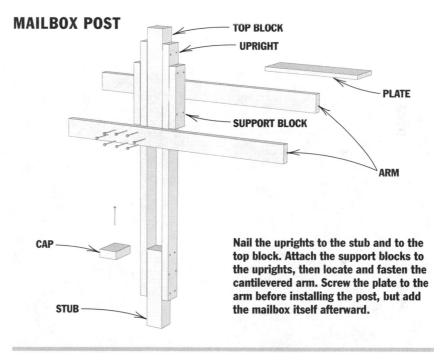

TOP BLOCK

UPRIGHT

PLATE

SUPPORT BLOCK

ARM

CAP

STUB

Nail the uprights to the stub and to the top block. Attach the support blocks to the uprights, then locate and fasten the cantilevered arm. Screw the plate to the arm before installing the post, but add the mailbox itself afterward.

YOUR INVESTMENT
Time: One afternoon
Money: $25

SHOPPING LIST
3 feet 4×4
18 feet 2×4
24-inch metal post stake
3-inch galvanized spiral nails
4-inch galvanized spikes

PROJECT SPECS
The mailbox post is 5 feet high, with the box itself 4 feet above the roadway. The box is cantilevered 30 inches beyond the center of the post.

CUTTING LIST

PART	QTY.	DIMENSIONS	NOTES
Stub	1	$3\frac{1}{2} \times 3\frac{1}{2} \times 16$	4×4
Top block	1	$3\frac{1}{2} \times 3\frac{1}{2} \times 20$	4×4
Upright	2	$1\frac{1}{2} \times 3\frac{1}{2} \times 51$	2×4
Arm	2	$1\frac{1}{2} \times 3\frac{1}{2} \times 47$	2×4
Support block	2	$1\frac{1}{2} \times 3\frac{1}{2} \times 12$	2×4
Cap	1	$1\frac{1}{2} \times 3\frac{1}{2} \times 5$	2×4
Plate	1	$\frac{3}{4} \times 6\frac{3}{8} \times 18\frac{3}{8}$	To fit mailbox

Fit the top block. Adjust the top block so it protrudes 3 inches beyond the uprights (above). Nail it in place with a half-dozen spiral nails from each side.

Cap the stub. Protect the stub from water by nailing a cap of wood onto its end grain (right).

Attach the support blocks. Set the support blocks 4 inches down from the top of the uprights, and nail them in place.

6 Attach the support blocks. Since the mailbox will be cantilevered almost 3 feet out from the uprights, the arms need a broad attachment surface. The support blocks give the assembly the necessary breadth, and also contribute visual interest. Clamp them 4 inches down from the top of the uprights, and fasten them by driving four of the 3-inch nails into each block.

7 Attach the arms. Locate the first arm as shown in the photo at top left on the facing page: square to the uprights, 13 inches down from the top of the top block, 10 inches extension on the back side. Clamp it to the assembly and nail it in place. Drive two of the 3-inch spiral nails through the center of the arm into the top block. Then drive a 4-inch spike into each of the support blocks, on center, with another pair of spikes into each of the uprights. Attach the second arm to the other side of the post in the same way, making sure that the two arms align with one another.

one nail in each upright, it's still possible to move them into line with each other. Spike each upright to the stub with three more of the 4-inch nails.

4 Fit the top block. Fit the top block into the space between the uprights so it protrudes 3 inches, as shown in the top left photo. Clamp the assembly, then nail the uprights to the block

with six of the 3-inch spiral nails. Nail at the top and bottom of the block, then remove the clamp to nail the center of the block.

5 Cap the stub. Water soaking into the end-grain ultimately will cause the stub to rot. Delay it by nailing a little roof onto the stub, a 5-inch scrap of 2×4 held by one 3-inch spiral nail, as shown in the photo at top right.

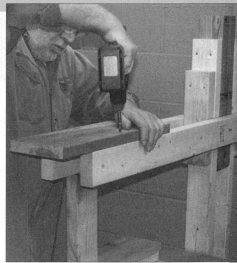

Attach the arms. The arms extend 10 inches beyond the back of the support blocks, and cross the top block 13 inches down. Align the second arm with the first before driving the nails home.

Attach the plate. Make a plate to match the base of your mailbox, and screw it to the ends of the arms.

8 Attach the plate. The plate supports the mailbox itself, so its dimensions depend on the box you have. Prop the post up against the worktable, as shown in the photo at top right, and screw the plate to the arms. Let it extend 4 or 5 inches beyond the ends of the arms, to increase the cantilever.

9 Install the post. Decide where you want to install the post and drive the metal stake into the ground, as shown in the photo at near right. Pay attention to the orientation of the stake, so the mailbox approaches the road at the angle you want. With the stake driven down to the turf, set the stub into the metal cup and bolt it tight, as shown in the photo at far right. If necessary, add shims or wedges to make the post vertical.

10 Attach the mailbox to the plate. Set the mailbox on the plate and fasten it with 1-inch galvanized screws, as shown at right. Use the holes in the bottom flange of the box.

Install the post. Use a scrap of 4x4 to drive the metal stake into the ground. Make sure it is oriented the way you want it (left). Then set the post in the cup atop the stake and tighten the bolts (above).

Attach the mailbox to the plate. Set the mailbox on the plate. Screw through the holes in the mailbox into the plate.

Wooden Swing

Fly safely through the air on this sturdy structure

Bolt the braces to the posts. Clamp the braces to the posts and drill through holes for the four ⁵⁄₁₆-inch bolts (left). The 1½-inch overhang at the lower left of the photo will be the bottom of the post. Put a washer under the head, tap a bolt into the hole and use a socket wrench to tighten a nut against a second washer (right).

Awooden swing brings on sweet nostalgia for childhood in a way that no metal swing-set ever could. A wooden swing speaks of small towns and simpler times, and of coming as close to flying through the air as ordinary mortals can.

Because the swinger does almost fly, it's critically important that the swing not fail. While one could calculate the stresses and engineer it with precision, the practical answer is to overbuild it. A side benefit of overbuilding is, you get a lot of visual interest from the various pieces of wood.

The wooden swing shown here is a 2×4 construction, held together by sturdy bolts and lag screws. The posts have a T-shaped cross section, which makes them enormously stiff. The posts are braced with 2×4 triangles. This is a simple way of achieving incredible strength. You can apply this method to other structural problems around the homestead. For example, shorter posts and a wider crossbeam would make an excellent hoist for lifting engines out of cars, or for moving machinery into a loft.

Lag screws connect 2×4 parts the same way wood screws connect 1× parts. There has to be a clearance hole the full diameter of the lag screw completely through one piece, with a pilot hole no larger than the root diameter of the screw thread into the other piece. Otherwise, the screw cannot draw the two pieces tightly together. Since this project uses ⁵⁄₁₆-inch lag screws, all the clearance holes will be ⁵⁄₁₆ inch. Drill the pilot holes with a ³⁄₁₆- or ¼-inch bit, for half the length of the thread, and let the lag screw make its own hole the rest of the way. The screws will be a tight fit in their clearance holes, so tap them through with a hammer.

All the bolts and lag screws should be galvanized, to resist rust. However, when you shop for hardware you may find not all sizes available in the galvanized section. In that case, it's better to use regular zinc-plated hardware of the correct size, instead of oversized or undersized galvanized hardware.

BUILDING THE SWING

1 Cut all the wood. It's not easy to manage 10-foot and 12-foot 2×4s, so it's best to set up for crosscutting and saw all the material to length at one time. The mitered braces all can be trimmed out of the lengths given in the cutting list.

2 Bolt the braces to the posts. Four bolts hold each post and brace together, creating a T-shaped cross section. This makes an extraordinarily strong and stiff structure. Lay the post flat on the worktable and center the brace on it. Make the two pieces flush at the top end, with an inset of 1½ inches at the bottom, and clamp them together. Lay out and drill holes for four ⁵⁄₁₆-inch bolts, as shown in the photos above. Locate the first two holes 6 inches from either end of the brace. The other two holes will be 30 inches away, and 30 inches apart. Slip a washer onto each bolt, tap it into its hole, slip a second washer and a nut onto the other side, and tighten the nut with a wrench.

WOODEN SWING

Make the swing as five subassemblies: two posts, beam with yokes, and two bases. Begin by bolting the two posts to the post braces. Make the beam and fasten the yokes to it. Make the two base assemblies. Attach the outriggers to the posts. Assemble the swing on level ground.

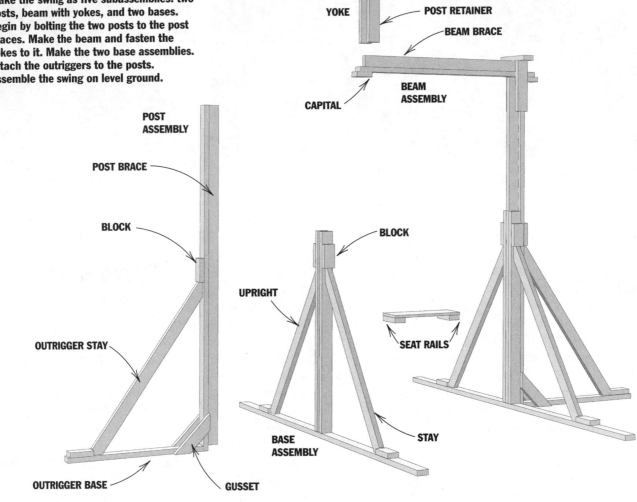

YOUR INVESTMENT

<u>Time:</u> All weekend
<u>Money:</u> $60 wood, $60 hardware

SHOPPING LIST

15 10-foot 2×4, Douglas fir
17 $5/16 × 5^1/2$-inch hex-head bolts with washers and nuts (posts and beam)
2 $1/2 × 8$-inch eye bolts with washers and nuts (chain)
4 $5/16 × 8$-inch hex-head bolts with washers and nuts (yoke)
22 $5/16 × 5$-inch galvanized lag screws
12 $5/16 × 3$-inch galvanized lag screws
6 12-inch galvanized landscape spikes
16 feet $3/8$-inch steel chain
4 $5/16 × 5$-inch eye bolts
4 $1/4$-inch U bolts
2 $5/16$-inch U bolts

PROJECT SPECS

The wooden swing is 9 feet 2 inches high, 10 feet front to back at the base, and 12 feet wide at the outriggers. The swing space is 4 feet wide.

CUTTING LIST

PART	QTY.	DIMENSIONS	NOTES
Post	2	$1^1/2 × 3^1/2 × 103^1/2$	2×4
Post brace	2	$1^1/2 × 3^1/2 × 102$	2×4
Beam	1	$1^1/2 × 3^1/2 × 62$	2×4
Beam brace	1	$1^1/2 × 3^1/2 × 58$	2×4
Capital	2	$1^1/2 × 3^1/2 × 5$	2×4
Tie	2	$1^1/2 × 3^1/2 × 13$	2×4
Post retainer	4	$1^1/2 × 3^1/2 × 16$	2×4
Stay	4	$1^1/2 × 3^1/2 × 60$	2×4; miter
Base	2	$1^1/2 × 3^1/2 × 120$	2×4
Upright	4	$1^1/2 × 3^1/2 × 60$	2×4
Outrigger stay	2	$1^1/2 × 3^1/2 × 60$	2×4; miter
Outrigger base	2	$1^1/2 × 3^1/2 × 42$	2×4
Block	12	$1^1/2 × 3^1/2 × 7$	2×4
Gusset	4	$1^1/2 × 3^1/2 × 16$	2×4; miter 45°
Seat	1	$3/4 × 7^1/2 × 22$	1×8
Seat rail	2	$1^1/2 × 3^1/2 × 7$	2×4

Brace the second post in the same way.

3 Make the beam. The beam and beam brace make a T-shaped section, same as the posts, and they are held together in the same way, except with only three bolts instead of four. Two of the bolts fall 8 inches in from either end, with the third bolt on center. Clamp the two parts together, with the beam brace centered from end to end and side to side. Block the beam parts up on scraps of 2×4, for drilling clearance.

4 Install the eye bolts. Two substantial ½-inch eye bolts support the chains and the swing. While you have the beam on the worktable, drill the holes and install the eye bolts. The holes should be 12 inches from either end of the beam brace. To avoid a splintered exit hole, drill through the edge of the brace until the point of the spade bit just emerges through the bottom face of the beam. Then turn the beam over and complete the hole from the other side. Slip a ½-inch washer onto the eye bolt, tap it into the hole, then add a second washer against the nut, as shown in the photos above.

5 Attach the capitals. The capitals locate the beam atop the posts. The post retainers and ties make a yoke which will connect the beam to the posts, in Step 7. While you have the beam on the worktable, lag-screw a capital at each end. The 5-inch capitals overhang the end of the beam by 1 inch. Drill clearance holes for a 3-inch lag screw down through the capital into

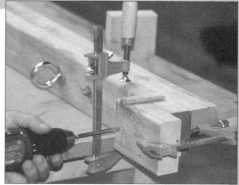

Attach the capitals. Clamp the capitals to the ends of the beam and fasten them with lag screws (above).

Install the eye bolts. Drill ½-inch holes through the beam and install the eye bolts. Put a washer under the eye as well as under the nut (left).

Make the yokes. Clamp the two retainers together and drill a ⁵⁄₁₆-inch bolt hole through them both (left). Space the retainers with a 2×4 scrap and lag-screw the tie piece to them (right).

the beam, and for a second 3-inch lag screw up through the beam into the capital.

6 Make the yokes. The yokes are U-shaped assemblies consisting of two post retainers connected by a tie piece. They guarantee the connection between the swing beam and the posts. You have to drill the holes and assemble the pieces in order, or you will have alignment problems. Begin by clamping the two

retainers together face to face, and square a layout line across them, 4¼ inches from one end. Drill a centered ⁵⁄₁₆-inch clearance hole through both pieces. Now unclamp them and set them up on the worktable with a 2×4 spacer, as shown in the photo above. This spacer represents the swing beam, allowing you to locate and two drill clearance holes in the tie. Fasten the tie to the retainers with two of the 5-inch lag screws.

7 Join the yokes and beam. Fit the completed yokes onto the beam as shown in the photo at left. The yokes should embrace the beam and overlap the edge of the capitals by about ¼ inch. Use the clearance hole you already drilled in the retainers as a guide for drilling completely through the edge of the beam. Attach each yoke to the beam with an 8-inch hex-head bolt. This bolt will be too long, but you probably can't find a 7-inch one, so make it tight by packing the bolt head and nut with extra washers.

8 Make the stays. The two base assemblies each consist of two 2×4 triangles which, when lag-screwed to the posts, keep the swing vertical in the front and back direction. When the stays are joined to the base and uprights, they become the long sides or hypotenuses of right-angle triangles. To make a neat joint, the ends of the stays must be mitered at 35 degrees and 55 degrees, as shown in the drawing below. If you have a chop saw, use it to cut these angles. Otherwise, jigsaw one stay, then use it as a pattern to lay out the others. Make the long cut at either end first. The short cut is at 90 degrees to the long cut, so it can be laid out with a square. Make six identical stays: four for the base assembly, and two for the outriggers.

Join the yokes and beam. Extend the holes in the retainers through the beam, and bolt the parts together.

STAY DETAIL

LAY OUT THE ANGLED ENDS OF THE STAYS BY DIRECT MEASUREMENT, OR WITH A PROTRACTOR.

60 | 1⅜ | 1¾ | 1
1 | 90° | 90° | 2½
2½ | 55° | 35° |
1¾ | STAY | 3½

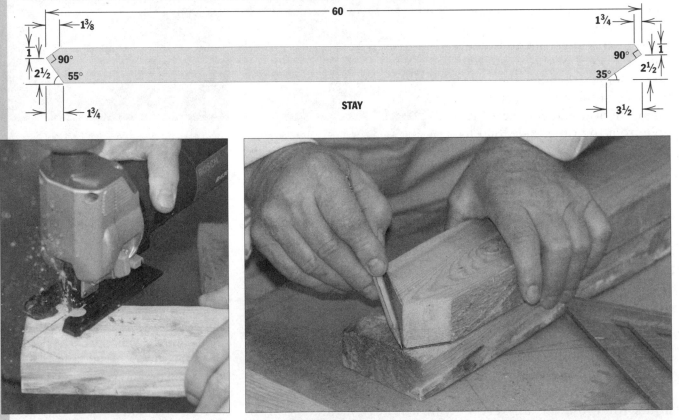

Make the stays. Jigsaw the angled ends of the first stay (left). Use it as a pattern to make the other five stays (right).

9 Screw the uprights to the base. The two base assemblies each consist of a 10-foot base, two uprights and two diagonal stays. Complete one base assembly, then make the other. The two uprights are lag-screwed to the base piece at its center. The uprights ultimately will be bolted to the posts, so they need to be spaced the thickness of the 2×4 post apart, by clamping them to a gauge piece, as shown in the photo at right. Drill $\frac{5}{16}$-inch clearance holes through the base, then change bits and drill $\frac{1}{4}$-inch pilot holes several inches into the end of each upright.

10 Attach the stays. Clamp the assembled base and uprights to the worktable, making sure they're at right angles to one another. The stays must now be lag-screwed to the upright and base. Fit the first stay in position, blocked up on scrap so it's centered in the width of the wood. Be sure you get it right way up: the top of the stay should be about 48 inches from the base. Measure $2\frac{1}{4}$ inches down from the top end of the stay and square a line, as shown in the photo at center left. Drill a $\frac{5}{16}$-inch clearance hole through the stay on this line, as shown in the photo at center right. Put the stay back in position, drill a pilot hole, and drive the 5-inch lag screw into the upright. At the base, push the stay toward the upright and clamp a block to anchor it. Then drill a clearance hole through the base, a pilot hole into the upright, and drive a 5-inch lag screw. Join the second stay to the other end of the base in the same way. And now

Screw the uprights to the base. Clamp the two uprights to a 2×4 spacer and lag-screw them in the center of the 10-foot base piece.

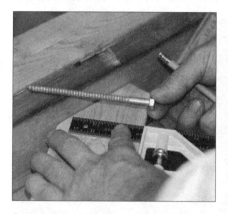

Attach the stays. Square a line across the top of the stay where the lag screw will fit (above). Drill a clearance hole (right) and fasten the stay to the upright. At the bottom end, drill up through the base into the stay (below).

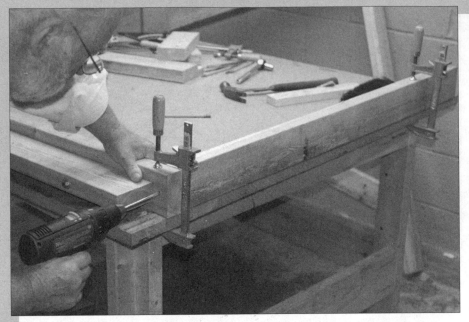

Make the outrigger base. Clamp the post and outrigger base in position, and drill through the post into the end of the base (above). Drive a lag screw (below).

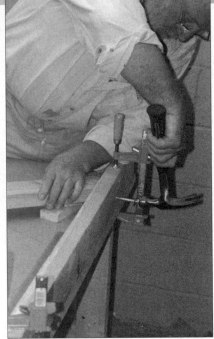

Attach the outrigger stay. Lag-screw the outrigger stay to the base and post.

Reinforce the stays with blocks. Glue and screw a block against each end of all the stays.

that you have completed one base assembly, make the other in exactly the same way.

11 Make the outrigger base. The outrigger stay and outrigger base attach directly to the post, with 5-inch lag screws. Clamp the post to the worktable as shown in the photo above, and

bring the outrigger base up to the bottom of the post. It will be screwed to the bit of post that overhangs the post brace, on the opposite side from the post brace. Clamp the outrigger base in position, square to the post. Drill a $5/16$-inch clearance hole through the post overhang, and a $1/4$-inch pilot hole about 2

inches into the end-grain of the outrigger base. Complete the joint with a 5-inch lag screw.

12 Attach the outrigger stay. The outrigger stay completes the triangle described by the post and outrigger base. Fit it in position the same way you positioned the base stays. Drill clearance holes and pilot holes, and fasten it to the post and to the outrigger base with a 5-inch lag screw at each end, as shown at left. Attach the other outrigger base and stay to the other post in the same way.

13 Reinforce the stays with blocks.

Blocks, glued and screwed at both ends of each diagonal stay, guarantee the integrity of the construction. Spread glue on each block, clamp it tight against the end of the stay, and screw it to the face of the post, upright or base piece with two of the 3-inch wood screws, as shown at left.

14 Drill two clearance holes.

When you assemble the swing, you'll find that the head of the lag screw joining the outrigger base to the post has nowhere to go. It needs a shallow clearance hole. Drill a 1¼-inch hole ½-inch deep in the center of the edge of the base, as shown in the photo at right. Drill this shallow clearance hole on one side of each base assembly.

15 Make the swing seat.

The seat is a 1×8 pine board with two rails screwed cross-grain beneath it. An eye bolt and shackle at each corner connects the seat to the chain. Attach the seat to each rail with four 2-inch screws. Drill ⁵⁄₁₆-inch holes for the eye bolts, 1½ inches in from the edges of the seat and 2 inches in from either end. Put a washer under the eye and also under the nut on each bolt, as shown in the photo at top right. Then cover the exposed thread with a second nut jammed tight against the first one.

16 Position the posts and beam.

The first step in assembling the swing is to position and connect the posts and the beam. This means finding a large place to work, which can be an empty garage, outdoors on a deck, or on sawhorses in the yard, as shown in the photo below. The posts fit into the yoke, between the retainers. They stop against the capitals. Get them square with a framing square, then measure the distance between the posts at the beam end. Make a piece of scrap

Drill two clearance holes. The shallow clearance hole in the center of the base fits over the lag screw in the outrigger.

Make the swing seat. Screw the seat to the rails, then fit an eye bolt at each corner.

Position the posts and beam. Fit the parts together, with the top of the posts trapped between the retainers and tight against the capitals. Tack a spacer across the bottom of the swing and measure the diagonals to check for square.

this same length and screw it across the post braces near the other end. This ensures that the posts are parallel. Now measure the diagonals and nudge the parts until they are equal, whereupon the swing is square. Clamp it to the sawhorses.

17 **Join the posts to the retainers.** Drill two ⁵⁄₁₆-inch clearance holes through each retainer, for two of the 3-inch lag screws. Drive them into the edge of the posts. Before you turn the assembly over to do the other side, screw a gusset at the bot-

tom of each post, spanning the edges of the post and of the outrigger base, as shown in the photo below. The gusset makes sure the outrigger never loses its grip on the post. Now enlist a friend to help you turn the assembly over, so you can screw

Join the posts to the retainers. Drill clearance holes and lag-screw the retainers to the posts (above). Screw gussets between the posts and outrigger base pieces (right).

Raise the contraption. Stand the swing subassemblies upright and fit them together (left). Clamp each post into its slot in the base, then drill clearance holes and bolt the pieces together (right).

Level and stake the swing to the ground. Drill and drive a 12-inch landscape spike at the end of each base piece.

Hang the swing. Three shackles connect the swing seat to each chain (right). Larger shackles join the chain to the eye bolt in the swing beam (below).

the retainers and gussets to the other side of the swing. Don't let the friend escape, because you will need more help in Step 18.

18 Raise the contraption. Find level ground and lug the two base assemblies and the posts-and-beam assembly there. Stand the post assembly up vertical. Have your helper hold it up while you slide the base assemblies onto the post braces. You might have to lift each post to slide the base under the brace. Tug the pieces tight together with clamps, as shown in the photos at bottom left. Drill a $\frac{5}{16}$-inch bolt hole clear through the uprights and brace at the top, center and bottom. Install a $5\frac{1}{2}$-inch hex-head bolt in each hole.

19 Level and stake the swing to the ground. Go around the base of the swing and see what you can do to bring the ends of each base piece into firm contact with the ground. You may need to dig some earth away, and you may need to install

some wooden wedges. Once everything is as solid as you can make it, drill a $\frac{3}{8}$-inch hole through each base piece, near the ends farthest from the posts. Angle these holes toward the posts and drive a 12-inch landscape spike into the ground, as shown in the top left photo.

20 Hang the swing. Iron shackles connect the chain to the eye

bolts in the beam and seat. The chains make a short Y about 6 inches above the seat itself, as shown in the photo above. The height of the seat above the ground is entirely up to you. Cut the chain with a chain-cutting tool, or clamp it in a vise and hacksaw it. Tighten all of the screw pins in the shackles. Now the swing is ready for a test flight.

BASIC BIRDHOUSE

Homeless little birds will sing your praises

A birdhouse is a great warm-up project for woodworkers. Every yard needs one, even in the city. The investment in material is trivial, and the rewards, when the birds move in, are large and rich.

Make the birdhouse by nailing four pieces of wood together pinwheel fashion, as shown in the illustrations. This method produces a square birdhouse from four equal-width pieces of wood.

This birdhouse features a tricky bentwood pole. You might think you would need to be an advanced woodworker to bend a piece of wood, but these gentle curves are easy and anyone can do it. The secret is to select clear, knot-free wood with straight grain.

In case you don't like the bentwood pole, the instructions on pages 326 and 327 also show how to mount a birdhouse atop a straight length of 2×3. Install either pole by digging a hole about a foot deep. Set the birdhouse post in the hole and tamp some gravel in around it. As an alternative, drive a sharpened stake into the ground, then screw the birdhouse pole to it.

BUILDING THE BIRDHOUSE

1 Cut the wood. It's always most efficient to begin a project

BIRDHOUSE

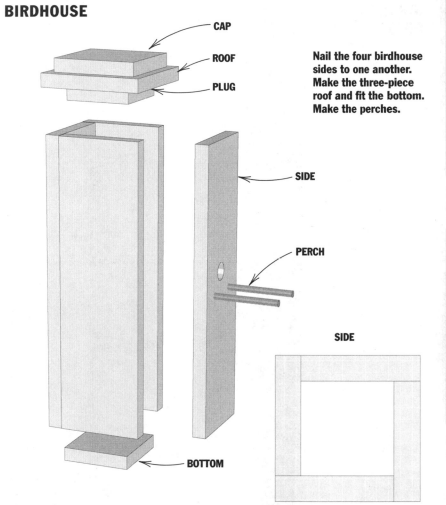

CAP
ROOF
PLUG
SIDE
PERCH
SIDE
BOTTOM

Nail the four birdhouse sides to one another. Make the three-piece roof and fit the bottom. Make the perches.

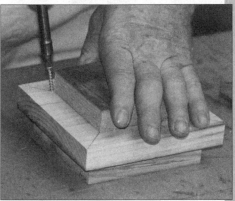

Drill the bird entrance. Drill a 1-inch hole in the center of one side piece.

Make the roof. Screw the plug and the cap to the center of the roof piece.

YOUR INVESTMENT
<u>Time:</u> **One evening**
<u>Money:</u> **$8**

SHOPPING LIST
2 feet 1×4 pine
4 feet 1×5 pine
1 foot 1×6 pine
1 foot ³⁄₈-inch dowel
#6 × 1¼-inch galvanized screws
2-inch galvanized siding nails
Bentwood post: 24 feet 1×2 pine
Straight post: 8 feet 2×3 pine

PROJECT SPECS
The birdhouse is 5 inches on a side and sits on an 8-foot pole.

CUTTING LIST

PART	QTY.	DIMENSIONS	NOTES
Side	4	¾ × 4½ × 16	1×5
Plug	1	¾ × 3½ × 3½	1×4
Roof	1	¾ × 5½ × 5½	1×6
Cap	1	¾ × 4½ × 4½	1×5
Bottom	1	¾ × 3¾ × 3¾	Trim 1×5
Perch	2	⅜ dia. × 4½	dowel
Bentwood post	3	¾ × 1½ × 96	1×2
Straight post	1	1½ × 2½ × 98	2×3
Plate	1	¾ × 5½ × 5½	1×6

by sawing all the wood to the sizes given in the cutting list.

2 Drill the bird entrance. To attract nuthatches and other nondescript little birds, drill a 1-inch hole in one side piece. Offset the hole an inch toward one edge of the wood, as shown in the top photo.

3 Nail the sides together. Join the four sides of the birdhouse with 2-inch siding nails. Make the sides into a square section by joining them pinwheel fashion, as shown in the drawing.

4 Make the roof. As shown in the bottom photo, the birdhouse roof is a three-layer sandwich of wood, screwed together.

Plug the bottom. Saw a piece of wood so it fits inside the birdhouse, and nail it in place.

Make the perches. Drill two ³⁄₈-inch holes below the bird entrance. Glue the dowel perches into the holes.

5 Plug the bottom. Nail the bottom plug between the sides of the birdhouse, as shown in the top photo.

6 Make the perches. The perches are short pieces of ³⁄₈-inch dowel set into the front of the birdhouse, about an inch down from the bird entrance. Drill a hole for each perch and glue it in, as shown in the bottom photo.

7 Make the bentwood post. The bentwood post consists of three lengths of 1×2 pine. Begin with the two side pieces, then add the third piece. Clamp the two 1×2s to the sides of the house. Offset them 1¹⁄₂ inches

BIRDHOUSE POSTS

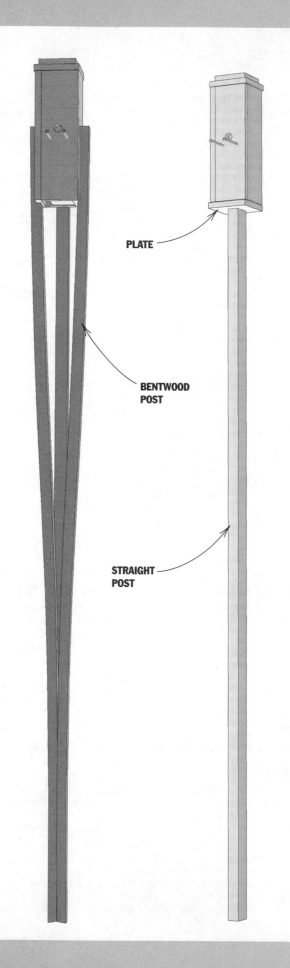

PLATE

BENTWOOD POST

STRAIGHT POST

from the front of the house, as shown in the photo at left, and 3½ inches down from the top. Screw the wood to the sides of the birdhouse with three 1¼-inch screws in each piece. Then clamp the two 1×2s together about halfway along their length. Tighten the clamp until the pieces bend and touch, as shown in the center photo at left. Lock them together with six 1¼-inch screws from either side. Clamp and screw the third post piece to the back of the birdhouse and bend it to touch the first two pieces, as shown in the bottom photo at left. Screw the third post to the other two.

8 **Install the birdhouse.** The birdhouse doesn't need any finish, though you can paint the outside. Dig a hole about a foot deep in the garden. Set the birdhouse post in the hole and tamp some gravel around it.

Make the bentwood post. Position the two side pieces of 1×2 on the birdhouse, offset 1½ inches from the front edge. Screw the side pieces to the birdhouse (top). Clamp the two side pieces together in the middle (above). Screw them together. Drive screws from both sides. Screw the third 1×2 to the back of the birdhouse, and to the first two pieces (below).

THE STRAIGHT POST

The straight post consists of a single length of 2×3 with a square plate screwed to the top. Center the plate on the post, then screw through the plate into the bottom of the birdhouse, as shown below.

BAT HOUSE

Board box beckons backyard bug-bombers

Bats are the nocturnal equivalent of birds, and they play a similar role in the managed ecology of the suburban yard: they eat insects. Better yet, they're especially fond of mosquitoes. Best of all, unlike electric bug zappers, they're totally silent within the sonic range that humans can hear.

You can encourage bats to live and dine in your backyard by building a bat house. It's a broad, flat birdhouse nailed high on the outside wall of a building, with the bat entrance at the bottom. A wooden baffle divides the interior space, which creates the close spaces that bats seem to enjoy. An inch or a bit less of separation between baffles is about right.

A bat house is a summer roost. Your colony of flying mammals is likely to hibernate elsewhere during the winter. If you get the bat house up late in the winter, you might be lucky enough to attract bats the first season, but don't despair. If you build it, they will come.

BUILDING THE BAT HOUSE

1 Cut the wood. The bat house as shown is made from rough-sawn pine. The front, back and baffles can be assembled from whatever widths of wood you have, using as many pieces as necessary. Bats hang upside-down to roost, so they need a rough surface for their little toe-claws to dig into. If you don't have rough-sawn wood, saw grooves across the interior surfaces. Make the grooves about $\frac{1}{16}$ inch deep and $\frac{1}{2}$ inch apart.

2 Make the inner sanctum. The central section of the bat house consists of the two baffles separated by two spacers. Make the baffles flush with one end of the spacers, leaving a 1-inch overhang at the other end. Nail the baffles to the spacers as shown in the top photo on the facing page, with 2½-inch siding nails. Nail from both sides.

3 Add the inner roof. The inner roof closes off the top of the bat spaces. Center the roof board on the top edge of the

baffles and nail it in place, using the 2½-inch siding nails, as shown in the center photo on the facing page.

4 Make the sides. To create the roof slope, saw the sides at an angle of about 15 degrees on one end. Lay out the angle by measuring 1⅜ inches down from the corner of the wood. Saw the sides, then nail them to the baffles and inner roof.

5 Make the front. Nail the front of the bat house to the

BAT HOUSE

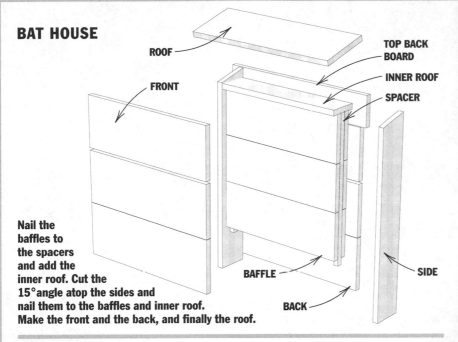

ROOF

FRONT

TOP BACK BOARD

INNER ROOF

SPACER

Nail the baffles to the spacers and add the inner roof. Cut the 15°angle atop the sides and nail them to the baffles and inner roof. Make the front and the back, and finally the roof.

BAFFLE

SIDE

BACK

Make the inner sanctum. Nail the baffles to the spacers. Nail through all three thicknesses of wood at once.

YOUR INVESTMENT
Time: **One evening**
Money: **$18**

SHOPPING LIST
24 board feet roughsawn pine
2½-inch galvanized siding nails

PROJECT SPECS
The bat house is 26 inches wide, 34 inches high, and 7 inches deep.

CUTTING LIST

PART	QTY.	DIMENSIONS	NOTES
Spacer	2	$\frac{3}{4} \times \frac{7}{8} \times 24$	
Baffle	6	$1 \times 8 \times 21\frac{1}{2}$	Rough-sawn pine
Inner roof	1	$1 \times 21\frac{1}{2} \times 5$	Rough-sawn pine
Side	2	$1 \times 5 \times 32$	Rough-sawn pine
Front	3	$1 \times 8\frac{1}{2} \times 24$	Rough-sawn pine
Top back board	1	$1 \times 5 \times 26$	Rough-sawn pine
Back	3	$1 \times 8 \times 24$	Rough-sawn pine
Roof	1	$1 \times 8\frac{1}{2} \times 26$	Rough-sawn pine

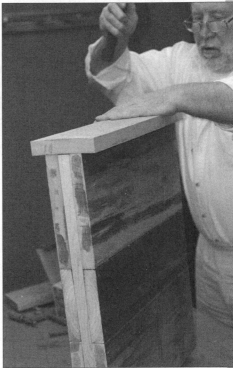

Add the inner roof. Center the inner roof atop the baffles and nail it in place.

sides and inner roof. Check with a square, as shown in the bottom photo at right, to make sure the top edge of the top front board won't interfere with the roof. Leave a ventilation gap of about ½ inch between two of the boards in the front of the house.

6 Make the back. Nail the back of the bat house to the sides and inner roof. The top back board extends an inch on either side, creating a nailing flange for attaching the bat

house to your house. Leave a ½-inch ventilation gap between two of the back boards.

7 Make the roof. Nail the roof to the top of the bat house. It should be flush at the back of the house.

8 Mount the bat house. Choose a high sunny spot on an outside wall. The bat house should be 10 to 15 feet off the ground. Nail it to the building through the top back board and the bottom back board.

Make the front. Align the first front board with the slope atop the sides. Nail the front boards to the sides, leaving one ½-inch ventilation space.

BIRD FEEDER

Hopper-style feeder can be made large or long

Here is a design for bird feeders that contain a reasonable supply of seed, and have ample feeding tables for your feathered friends. It consists of a rectangular hopper with a slot along one corner, through which the feed emerges. There's a horizontal bar under the slot to retain the feed, and a wide table under the bar where the birds can congregate. The lid lifts off for refilling.

Paradoxically, a larger bird feeder is more suitable for smaller birds, while a smaller one is more likely to attract larger birds. That's because of the way the hopper sides slope, limiting access to the feeding bar. The cutting list and instructions that follow include the details for the large feeder, as well as for a longer feeder with a smaller cross-section.

Like all bird feeders, these should be mounted on a pole or suspended from an eave or a tree limb, and not set out on the deck. Otherwise you risk opening a deadly cafeteria for predatory cats.

BUILDING THE FEEDER

1 Cut the wood. Begin the project by cutting all of the wood to length. The pieces are small, so if you have been building other projects around the yard and garden, you'll probably have some suitable scrap. You can tailor the dimensions of the feeder to suit whatever scrap you have.

2 Chamfer the hopper sides. The birdseed emerges through a substantial chamfer on the bot-

BIRD FEEDER
LARGE FEEDER for small birds

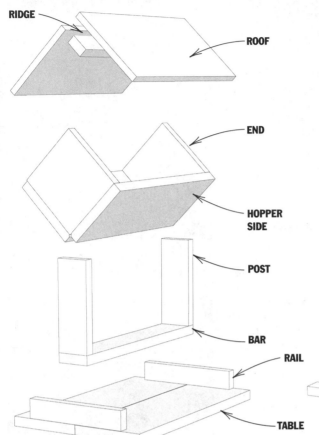

LONG FEEDER for large birds

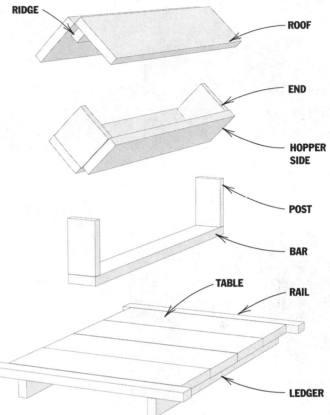

YOUR INVESTMENT
<u>Time:</u> One evening
<u>Money:</u> Large feeder, $8;
Long feeder, $12

SHOPPING LIST
LARGE FEEDER
8 feet 1×6 pine
3 feet 1×3 pine
4 feet 1×2 pine
$\frac{1}{2}$ × 18 × 18 CDX plywood
LONG FEEDER
8 feet 1×2 pine
4 feet 1×3 pine
6 feet 1×4 pine
4 feet 1×5 pine
6 feet 1×6 pine
BOTH FEEDERS
2-inch galvanized siding nails
$1\frac{1}{2}$-inch finishing nails

PROJECT SPECS
The large bird feeder measures 11 inches wide, 17 inches long, and 11 inches high. The long bird feeder measures 18 inches wide, 25 inches long, and 10 inches high.

CUTTING LIST

PART	QTY.	DIMENSIONS	NOTES
LARGE FEEDER for small birds			
End	2	$\frac{3}{4} \times 5\frac{1}{2} \times 5\frac{1}{2}$	
Hopper side	2	$\frac{3}{4} \times 5\frac{1}{2} \times 14$	
Post	2	$\frac{3}{4} \times 2\frac{1}{2} \times 7$	
Bar	1	$\frac{3}{4} \times 2\frac{1}{2} \times 15\frac{1}{2}$	
Table	2	$\frac{3}{4} \times 5\frac{1}{2} \times 17$	
Rail	2	$\frac{3}{4} \times 1\frac{1}{2} \times 8$	
Roof	2	$\frac{1}{2} \times 6\frac{3}{4} \times 15$	CDX plywood
Ridge	1	$\frac{3}{4} \times 1\frac{1}{2} \times 12$	
LONG FEEDER for large birds			
End	2	$\frac{3}{4} \times 3\frac{1}{2} \times 3\frac{1}{2}$	
Hopper side	2	$\frac{3}{4} \times 3\frac{1}{2} \times 23$	
Post	2	$\frac{3}{4} \times 2\frac{1}{2} \times 4\frac{1}{2}$	
Bar	1	$\frac{3}{4} \times 2\frac{1}{2} \times 24\frac{1}{2}$	
Table	4	$\frac{3}{4} \times 5\frac{1}{2} \times 16$	
Rail	2	$\frac{3}{4} \times 1\frac{1}{2} \times 18$	
Ledger	2	$\frac{3}{4} \times 1\frac{1}{2} \times 25$	
Roof	2	$\frac{3}{4} \times 4\frac{1}{2} \times 24$	
Ridge	1	$\frac{3}{4} \times 1\frac{1}{2} \times 21$	

Chamfer the hopper sides. Rasp a ¼-inch chamfer or bevel on one edge of each hopper piece, to make a slot where the birdseed can dribble out.

Nail the hopper sides to the ends. Fit the hopper sides flush with the end pieces and nail them together with galvanized siding nails (right).

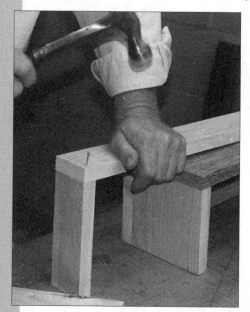

Nail the bar to the posts. Drive siding nails through the bar into the end grain of the posts. To make the first joint, prop the free end of the bar up on the completed hopper (left).

Attach the posts to the hopper. Center the posts on the ends of the hopper, leaving a gap of ½ inch to the bar. Nail through the edges of the ends, into the hopper sides (right).

tom inside corner of the two hopper sides. Lay the wood flat on the worktable and rasp a flat about ¼-inch wide on one edge of each piece, as shown in the photo at top left.

3 Nail the hopper sides to the ends. Fit the hopper sides onto the two end pieces as shown in the photo at top right, leaving a gap of ¼ inch between the chamfered corners. Fasten the sides to the ends with several of the 2-inch siding nails.

4 Nail the bar to the posts. The bar and the two posts make a U-shape. The bar under the slot keeps the feed from gushing out of the hopper. Nail the bar onto the ends of the posts, as shown in the lower left photo.

5 Attach the posts to the hopper. Center the posts on the ends of the hopper, so there's a gap of about ½ inch below the birdseed slot. Nail the posts to the ends of the hopper sides, as shown in the lower right photo.

6 Make the table. Connect the two table pieces with the rails, as shown in the photos at the top of the facing page. Then fit the rails onto the ends of the bar and nail them together.

7 Make the roof. The roof is made of two pieces of ½-inch plywood connected by a 1×2 ridge. Glue and nail the ridge to one of the pieces of plywood, flush with its edge. Use the 1½-inch finishing nails, driven through from the outside and clenched on the inside. See page 221 for information on clenching nails. Then glue and nail the second piece of plywood to the ridge and the first piece, as shown in the center right photo.

8 Suspend the feeder. Suspend the feeder with wires or cords attached to four nails in the corner of the feeding table.

9 Making the long feeder. The long feeder for larger birds follows the same construction sequence given above. There are a couple of alternatives, which you can incorporate if you wish. Instead of rasping or jigsawing the chamfer that makes the slot, simply set the hopper sides $1/8$ inch back from the corners of the end pieces, as shown in the photo below. To make a broader feeding table, nail crosswise boards to a couple of ledgers, as shown in the bottom right photo. And with a hopper of smaller cross-section, you can make the roof from solid wood.

Make the table. Connect the two table pieces by nailing them to the rails (left). Then fit the bar between the rails and nail it in place (right).

Make the roof. Nail the two pieces of plywood to the ridge. Make the joint with six siding nails through each piece of plywood.

Making the long feeder. The long feeder goes together the same way as the large feeder. The birdseed slot can be made by setting the hopper sides back from the corner of the ends (left). A broader table can be made by nailing several boards to a pair of ledgers (above).

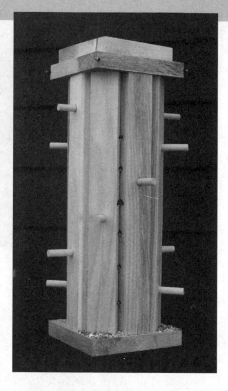

OCTAGONAL BIRD FEEDER

Standard lumber generates interesting shape

The octagonal bird feeder is a symmetrical column that hangs from a single string. It attracts flocks of small birds. The birds alight on the little perches, and peck their meal from the holes drilled into the sides of the octagon.

You can make the octagonal feeder without measuring angles or doing any mathematical calculation. The geometry relies on standard lumber sizes. It's easy to get it to come out right.

BUILDING THE BIRD FEEDER

1 Cut the wood. Begin the project by cutting the top and bottom squares, and the eight side pieces. Make sure that all the side pieces are the same length.

2 Lay out the top and bottom. Although the octagon arises naturally from stock lumber sizes, you do need to make layout lines. First, connect the corners of the square bottom end. This locates its center. Next, draw square lines through the center, as shown in the top left photo on the facing page. Finally, draw lines around the perimeter of the bottom end, ⅛ inch in from the edges of the wood. Lay out the top end the same way.

3 Make the square. Make the octagon in two stages, first by attaching the four sides of a square to the bottom end, then by filling in with the four diagonal pieces. Mark a center line on the end of four of the side pieces. Stand the first piece on one of the centered layout lines, along the ⅛-inch mark. When you see where it goes, start a 2-

YOUR INVESTMENT
Time: One evening
Money: $5

SHOPPING LIST
10 feet 1×2 pine
1 foot 1×5 pine
1 foot 1×6 pine
4 feet ⅜ dowel
2-inch galvanized siding nails

PROJECT SPECS
The octagonal bird feeder is 16 inches high and 5½ inches square.

CUTTING LIST

PART	QTY.	DIMENSIONS	NOTES
End	2	¾ × 5½ × 5½	1×6 pine
Side	8	¾ × 1½ × 14	1×2 pine
Cap	1	¾ × 4½ × 4½	1×5 pine

OCTAGONAL BIRD FEEDER

Make the octagon by nailing the side pieces to the bottom end. Drill the top, then nail it onto the side pieces. Attach the plug to the cap. Drill holes for the perches and for the feed to emerge.

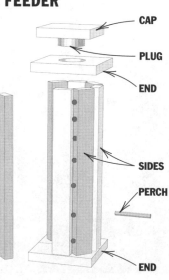

CAP

PLUG

END

SIDES

PERCH

END

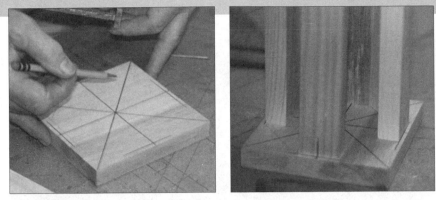

Lay out the top and bottom. Draw center lines and diagonal lines on the wood, then make layout lines ⅛ inch in from the edges (left). Centering the sides on these marks creates the octagon (right).

Make the square. Nail four of the side pieces to the bottom end, to make a square. Brace the wood on the wall.

Attach the top end. Nail the top onto the free ends of the sides. Reach through the hole to align the wood.

Make the cap. Nail the holesaw plug to the cap. Clench the nails on the top side of the cap.

Drill the seed holes. Drill holes in the valley between the side pieces so the birds can peck at the seed.

inch siding nail through the bottom and drive it into the end of the side piece. Anchor it with two more siding nails. Then attach the other three sides of the square in the same way, as shown in the top right photo.

4 Make the octagon. The remaining four side pieces will fill in the sides of the octagon. You might have to sand the corners off the wood to get a tight fit. Nail into each side through the bottom end, as in the previous step.

5 Drill the top end. The top end of the feeder has a large hole, through which you can add birdseed. Drill the hole with a 2-inch or 2¼-inch holesaw. Keep the circular plug of waste

for making the cap in Step 7.

6 Attach the top end. Nail the top piece onto the free ends of the side pieces. You'll be able to reach in through the drilled hole to position each piece on the layout lines. Drive one centered nail into the end of each side piece. This leaves you some wiggle room to adjust the pieces as you drive the remaining two nails into each one. Use the 2-inch siding nails, same as for the bottom end.

7 Make the cap. The cap is a square of 1×5 wood with the holesaw plug attached to it. Attach the plug with two of the siding nails, clenched on the top side. Nail-clenching is discussed on page 221.

8 Make the perches. The little birds that will frequent this feeder like to park on perches, which you can make from 2-inch lengths of ⅜-inch dowel set into the center of the side pieces.

9 Drill the seed holes. Once you've located the perches, drill a couple of feed holes for each. Drill the ¼-inch holes into the corners of the octagon.

10 Hang the feeder. Suspend the feeder from a cord. Tap a cord-anchoring nail into each corner of the top and bring the four short cords together to a single cord about a foot above the feeder. Loop the cord over a branch or through an eye screwed into an eave, so you can lower the feeder to refill it.

ARBOR WITH SEAT

Charming construction improves with age

An arbor with a seat is one of those garden accessories that can only improve with age. The vines creep up the side trellis, the tree branches poke through, the posts become buried in leaves. The arbor becomes part of the landscape, inviting you to rest, listen to the breeze, and renew yourself.

This arbor features a semicircular arch, which you jigsaw and assemble from small pieces of wood. Because rectangular keys join the circular segments, there are no critical angles or difficult joints. Horizontal pieces called capitals connect the arched top to the upright posts. This allows you to tailor the width of the arbor by changing the length of the capitals.

The arbor consists of five discrete assemblies: the arched top, the two side panels, the seat, and the back. These assemblies bolt together, which allows you to make them in the workshop, then carry the parts outdoors to reassemble in their final location. It also allows you to disassemble your arbor for winter storage or for moving.

The upright posts are threepiece composites, and so is the front seat beam. This method of construction is very strong, simple and light. The arch top, the back and the bench seat work together to keep the assembly square.

DETAIL OF ARCHED TOP

The six arch segments are identical segments of a circular ring.

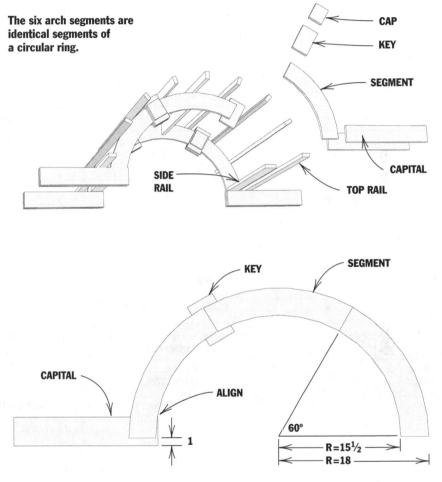

CAP

KEY

SEGMENT

CAPITAL

TOP RAIL

SIDE RAIL

KEY

SEGMENT

CAPITAL

ALIGN

1

60°

R=15½

R=18

BUILDING THE ARBOR

1 Cut the wood. Begin by sawing all of the wood to length. This way you can work around knots and defects, and get the most mileage out of your materials budget. It's important to make all the pieces of the arbor in clear wood, with small knots or no knots.

2 Lay out the arch. Each semicircular arch consists of three segments, connected by two rectangular keys. You must lay out the arch full-size, either on a big piece of paper, or directly on the top of the worktable, as shown in the photo on page 339. Then lay out each segment on the full-

ARBOR WITH SEAT

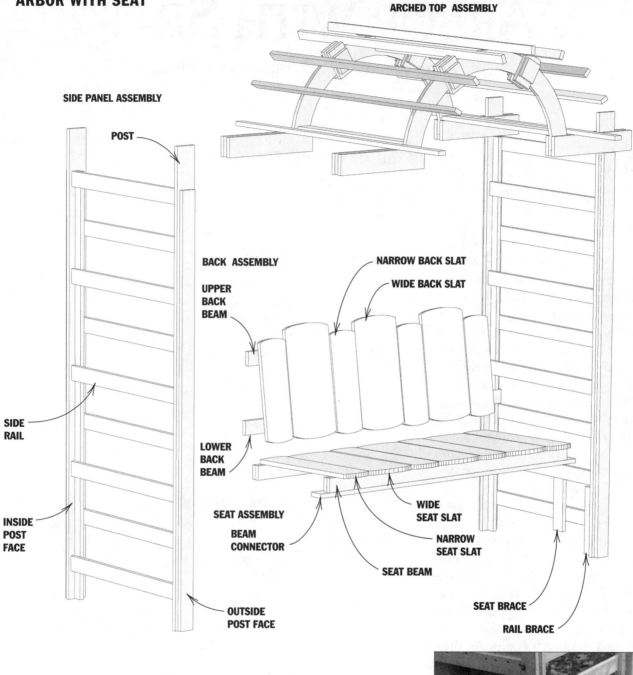

SIDE PANEL ASSEMBLY

ARCHED TOP ASSEMBLY

POST

BACK ASSEMBLY

UPPER
BACK
BEAM

NARROW BACK SLAT

WIDE BACK SLAT

SIDE
RAIL

INSIDE
POST
FACE

LOWER
BACK
BEAM

SEAT ASSEMBLY

BEAM
CONNECTOR

SEAT BEAM

WIDE
SEAT SLAT

NARROW
SEAT SLAT

OUTSIDE
POST FACE

SEAT BRACE

RAIL BRACE

Construct the arbor in five sections: arched top, two side panels, seat, and back. Begin by assembling two arches from the segments, keys and capitals, then connect the arches with the top rails to complete the arched top. Make the four post assemblies and connect them with the side rails, making the two side panels. Screw the seat slats to the seat beams, and the back slats to the back beams. Then assemble the arbor, drill the bolt holes, and bolt the sections together.

Hex-head bolts join the seat and back to the posts.

YOUR INVESTMENT

<u>Time:</u> One weekend
<u>Money:</u> $110

SHOPPING LIST

24 feet 1×10 pine
24 feet 1×6 pine
48 feet 1×4 pine
96 feet 1×3 pine
72 feet 1×2 pine
#6 × 1¼-inch galvanized screws
#6 × 2-inch galvanized screws
2½-inch galvanized siding nails
2-inch galvanized siding nails
12¼ × 3-inch galvanized bolts
10¼ × 4-inch galvanized bolts

PROJECT SPECS

The arbor stands 78 inches high, 32 inches front to back, and 58 inches wide at the ground.

CUTTING LIST

PART	QTY.	DIMENSIONS	NOTES
ARCHED TOP			
Segment	6	¾ × 5½ × 22	1×6
Key	6	¾ × 5½ × 3½	1×6
Capital	8	¾ × 3½ × 18	1×4
Cap	8	¾ × 3½ × 3	1×4
Top rail	9	¾ × 1½ × 55	1×3
SIDE PANEL			
Post	4	¾ × 3½ × 78	1×4
Outside post face	4	¾ × 2½ × 71	1×3
Inside post face	4	¾ × 1½ × 71	1×2
Side rail	21	¾ × 2½ × 29	1×3
SEAT			
Wide seat slat	3	¾ × 9½ × 24	1×10
Narrow seat slat	4	¾ × 5½ × 24	1×6
Seat beam	4	¾ × 2½ × 54	1×3
Beam connector	1	¾ × 2½ × 54	1×3
Seat brace	2	¾ × 2½ × 12	1×3
Rail brace	2	¾ × 1½ × 12	1×2
BACK			
Wide back slat	3	¾ × 9½ × 20	1×10
Narrow back slat	4	¾ × 9½ × 18	1×6
Upper back beam	1	¾ × 2½ × 54³⁄₈	1×3
Lower back beam	1	¾ × 2½ × 58	1×3

size drawing. After you've drawn the semicircular arch itself, divide it into 60-degree sectors with the protractor. You'll be able to lay out and jigsaw each of the six segments within a 22-inch board, as shown in the photo at right.

3 Saw the segments. While it's possible to tether the jigsaw to a center point in order to saw mechanically perfect arcs, it's hardly necessary. You can saw the segments freehand without worrying, because nothing is critical. Clamp each segment to the worktable and saw the outside curve, reclamp it to saw the inside curve, then saw both ends. Be careful you don't clamp

Lay out the arch. Make a stick compass to draw the semicircular arch full-size. Divide the semicircle into 60-degree segments, then transfer the drawing onto six pieces of 1×6 wood.

the line of the cut over the work-table itself, as shown below, or you might saw into it. Keep the curved scrap to use as a template in Step 13.

4 **Join the arch.** The keys join the segments of the arch. Assemble three of the segments on the full-size drawing. Draw a layout line down the center of the keys, as shown below left, then locate the first key on a joint line. It should extend an inch beyond each side of the curve. Spread glue as shown below right, drill four clearance holes and screw the key to the segments with 1¼-inch screws. Make the second joint in the same way, then turn the assembly over to glue and screw a sec-ond key on the back side of each joint, using the 2-inch screws. Make the second arch now too.

5 **Add the capitals.** The four capitals attached to each arch will make the bridge to the uprights. Set the parts in position on the worktable. The bottom edge of each capital should overhang the arch by 1 inch, with the top corner of the capitals meeting the inside curve of the arch, as shown in the photo at right. Use the edge of the worktable to keep the capitals in line. Spread glue on the intersections and drive three 1¼-inch screws through the arch and into each of the first two capitals. Turn the assembly over to attach the second pair of capitals on the other side, using the 2-inch screws. Join the remaining four capitals to the other arch in the same way.

6 **Cap the keys.** The caps are small blocks of 1×3 glued and nailed cross-grain on the keys. They reinforce the joints, and

Saw the segments. Steer the jigsaw around the curved layout lines, then saw the 60-degree mitered ends.

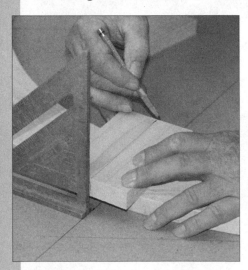

Join the arch. Draw a centerline on the key (above). Roll glue on the joint, and screw the pieces together (right).

Add the capitals. The straight capitals overhang the arch by an inch, but they are flush at the inside top.

Cap the keys. Spread glue on the caps, center them atop the keys, and nail them in place.

they cover the screw holes. Spread glue on each cap in turn and center it on its key, as shown in the top center photo. Attach each cap with two or three of the 2-inch siding nails.

7 Connect the arches. Three side rails connect the two arch assemblies. Two of these pieces fit tight between the arches themselves, flat on the inside ends of the capitals, as shown in the photo at right. Drill clearance holes and drive two of the 2½-inch screws through the face of the arch into each end of the rails, then toenail a third screw through the rail into the capital below. The third rail fits between the arches at the top.

8 Top rails complete the arches. The nine 1×2 top rails make an open pattern against the sky. The top rails stand on edge atop the arches, attached with a 2½-inch screw at each intersection. Each top rail extends 12 inches beyond the outside face of the arch. One top rail goes on center atop the arches, four of them go one rail thickness on either side of the keys, two more sit at the midpoint between the keys and the

Connect the arches. Fit the two side rails on top of the capitals, tight against the inside of the arch. Screw through the segments, then screw down into the capitals. The last rail fits between the summits of the arches.

capitals, and two sit a rail thickness outside the base of the arches, atop the capitals. Use a 6½-inch spacer block to locate the midpoint rail, as shown in the photo at right.

9 Nail the inside post faces to the posts. The composite post assemblies each consist of a 1×4 post, a 1×2 inside post face and a 1×3 outside post face. The height of the posts is somewhat arbitrary; if you deviate from the cutting list, make your post faces 7 inches shorter than your posts. Begin by rolling glue on

Top rails complete the arches. Arrange the top rails around the outside of the arches, using a scrap of wood to make uniform spaces.

Nail the inside post faces to the posts. Glue and clamp the inside post face to the post, then nail the parts together.

Attach the side rails to the posts. The side rails alternate from one side of the post faces to the other. A scrap of wood helps to maintain the uniform spacing between the side rails.

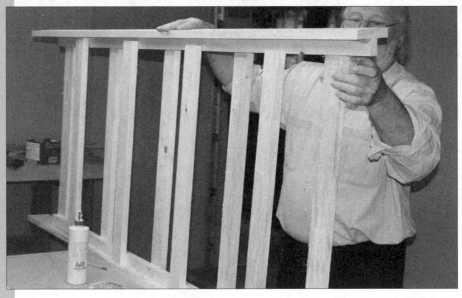

Complete the side panels. Dab glue onto the free ends of the rails, then wiggle the second post assembly into place. Square each rail before you screw it to the inside post face. Nail through the posts into the end-grain of each side rail.

of the first rail and fit it flush with the top of the inside post face. Tack it in place with one 1¼-inch screw. Use a 5½-inch block of wood as a gauge to space the next rail down the post. Glue and screw it to the other side of the inside post face. Continue in this manner to the bottom of the post, where you'll have a space of about 4 inches to the ground. Attach the nine remaining side rails to another of the post assemblies in exactly the same way.

11 Complete the side panels. Now you can plug the remaining two post assemblies onto the free ends of the side rails. Spread glue on the side rails, then wiggle each post assembly into place, as shown at left. Use a framing square to adjust the position of each rail, then screw it to the inside post face. Finally, drive two 2½-inch siding nails through the outside of the posts into the end grain of each side rail. Complete the second side panel in the same way.

one edge of an inside post face. Center it on the post by eye, with one end flush with what will be the bottom of the post, and clamp the two pieces together. Then nail through the post into the inside post face with 2-inch siding nails spaced about 12 inches apart, as shown in the photo at top left. Assemble the other three posts

and inside post faces in the same way.

10 Attach the side rails to the posts. Nine side rails connect each pair of posts, forming the two ladder-like side panels. The side rails alternate from one side of the inside post face to the other, as shown in the photo at top right. Spread glue on the end

12 Nail the outside post faces to the posts. Whereas the inside post faces fit the posts edge-on, the outside post faces fit face-on. Roll glue onto the broad side of an outside post face. Center it on the post by eye, flush at the bottom end. Nail through the outside post face into the post with the 2-inch siding nails spaced about a foot apart. Attach the other outside post faces in the same way.

13 Shape the seat and back slats. The seat and back slats have a jigsawn curve on both ends, as shown in the drawing below right. These curves are the same on all the slats, wide or narrow. As a template for laying out the curves, choose a regular piece of scrap left over from when you sawed the arch segments. Sand the template smooth. Trace the template onto both ends of all the seat and back slats. Since the template is a circular segment, the curve will be symmetrical if you square its straight edge with the edge of the slat, as shown in the photo at right. Jigsaw the curves, and use 80-grit sandpaper to remove any stray splinters of wood. Sand the sharp edges off the slats as well.

14 Make the seat beams. The front and rear seat beams each consist of two pieces of seat-beam material glued and screwed together. Make the joint with six 1¼-inch screws. The front seat beam has a beam connector piece glued and screwed onto its edge, as shown in the photo at far right. Center the seat beam from end to end on the beam connector, but make it

flush along one edge. Join these pieces with six 2-inch screws.

15 Assemble the seat. The seat slats alternate wide-narrow across the seat beams. There's clearance for the posts of 1⅝ inch at either end of the beams. The slats overhang the front beam by 3 inches. At the other end, they're flush with the edge of the rear seat beam. Square the two end slats across

the beams and clamp them in position, as shown in the top photo on the next page. Nail them to the beams with three 2½-inch siding nails at each end. Center and nail the middle seat slat, then fill in the remaining spaces with the remaining slats. There should be a space of about ⅛ inch between the slats.

16 Bolt the seat to the side panels. Stand the side panels

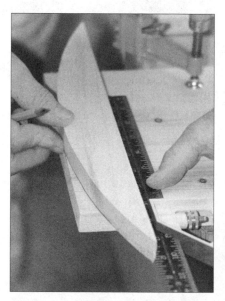

Shape the seat and back slats. Square the scrap template across the end of the slat, then trace its shape.

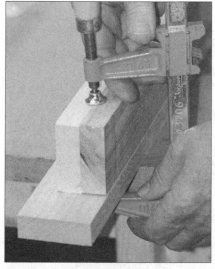

Make the seat beams. Glue and screw the seat beams together, then attach the front seat beam to the beam connector. Center the beam end to end.

SLAT DETAIL

Use the scrap from sawing the arch as a template for the seat and back slats.

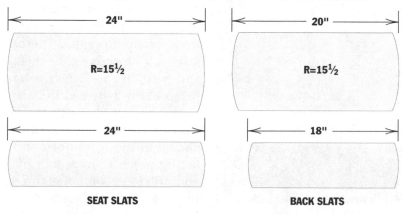

← 24" →	← 20" →
R=15½	R=15½
← 24" →	← 18" →
SEAT SLATS	**BACK SLATS**

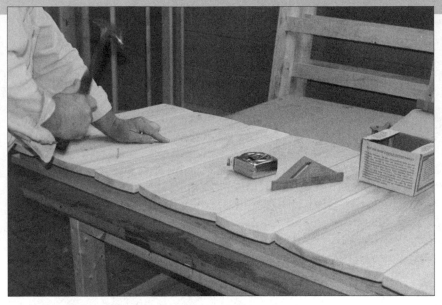

Assemble the seat. Clamp two narrow seat slats at the ends of the seat beams, leaving clearance for the posts. The front overhang is 3 inches (above). Nail the seat slats to the seat beams (right).

Bolt the seat to the side panels. Drill through the beam connector and side rail (above), then bolt the parts together (below).

upright and drop the seat into position. The seat beams rest on the second side rail up from the floor, with the rear seat beam tight in the pocket formed by the upright and side rail. Drill two ¼-inch bolt holes through each rear outside post face and post, and through the rear seat beams, as shown in the photo at left. It's important to bolt through as much wood as possible, which means you must drill the bolt holes on a slight angle. Drill another pair of ¼-inch bolt holes down through the ends of the beam connector and the side rail on which it rests. Fit 4-inch galvanized bolts through all the bolt holes, and thread them with nuts and washers.

17 Fit the back beams. The upper and lower back beams fit between the uprights. The back slats will be screwed to them in the next step. The top back beam fits in between the inside post faces, in line with the bottom of the fifth side rail, as shown in the top photo on the facing page. Clamp it in place and drill four bolt holes through the outside post face and post,

as in the previous step. Bolt the upper back beam in position. The lower back beam rests on top of the third side rail. It can be bolted right through all three components of the uprights, with two bolts in each end.

18 Attach the back slats. The seven back slats span the two back beams and are screwed to the beams from behind. There's a space between the bottom of the back slats and the seat, as shown in the top right photo on the facing page. Align each back slat with the corresponding seat slat. Drive the first 1¼-inch screw through the upper back beam, then square the slat to the beams before driving the second screw through the lower back beam. The two back beams are not in the same plane, which gives the back slats their comfortable slope. Lay out all the screws so they fall near the edges of the beams that bear against the slats.

19 Support the seat. The seat rests on the second side rail up from the ground. The seat brace and rail brace guarantee solid

Fit the back beams. Fit top back beam flush with the bottom of the fifth side rail, and bolt it (above). Bolt the lower back beam to the post assembly (right).

Attach the back slats. Block the back slats up on scrap (above). Screw them to the back beams from behind (below).

support. Glue and screw a rail brace under the front end of the side rails, in the vertical pocket formed by the post and inside post face. Then screw a seat brace vertically under each end of the front seat beam, as shown in the bottom left photo.

20 Assemble the arbor. Begin final assembly by fitting the seat and back between the side panels. Tap all the bolts home and tighten the nuts with a socket wrench. Enlist a helper to support the arched top while you wiggle the top ends of the post in between the four pairs of capitals. Fit one end, then fit the other end. Center the arched top from side to side, and pull the capitals down tight on the ledges atop the the post faces. Drill two ¼-inch holes through each intersection, as shown in the bottom right photo, and bolt the arbor together.

21 Install the arbor. Choose a lovely spot for your arbor, where you have vines and trees. Level the posts with bricks or flat rocks. Relax and contemplate the marvels of nature.

Support the seat. Glue and screw a brace under the front end of the rail that supports the seat. Fasten a second brace directly under the front seat beam.

Assemble the arbor. Drill holes for two bolts through the capitals and posts. Put a washer under the hex head and also under the nut.

TECHNIQUES

Woodworking is an interesting, enjoyable hobby, and if you follow the techniques presented in this book, you'll achieve excellent results. Our emphasis is on quick, direct construction using ordinary materials. You don't need a lot of tools, nor an elaborate workspace.

For best results, however, you do need to acquire a few basic skills: how to measure and make a layout line, how to saw the wood, how to glue and clamp the parts together, and how to drive nails and screws. These skills not only take you through the projects in this book, but also equip you to design and build your own projects around the home and yard.

It might be wonderful to have a workshop in which to build and putter. But if you don't have the ideal workspace, you must not let that stop you from making things. No matter where you live, you can find enough space someplace. All you really need is a worktable, some shelves or a cabinet for tools, and some storage for screws, nails, glue, and paint.

Space

Most homeowners set up shop in an unfinished portion of the basement, or in the space alongside or in front of the car. It's difficult to share shop space with other activities because you may need to leave your project until you can get back to it. An 8 × 8 space is about the minimum—that's the size of a prefab garden shed, or one-sixth of a single-car garage, or an extra room too small for a bedroom. The workspace doesn't have to be any particular shape. An unused storm porch, a few feet wide but running the full length of the house, can be an extraordinarily pleasant place to work, because it's flooded with light.

Another way to get natural light is to store your tools and

WORKTABLE

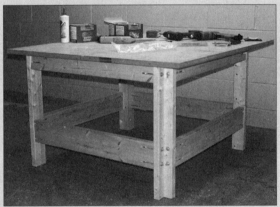

The worktable features a knock-down joint based on a dowel and an eye bolt. It's most likely that once you've made the table you won't want to take it apart again, but it's nice to know that you could. You also could use the joint for many of the outdoor projects in this book. It's strong, it can be tightened, and it's not difficult to make.

BUILDING THE TABLE

1. Cut the wood. The table shown is 48 inches on each side, and 29 inches high. You could make one 24 × 48 by shortening half of the rails from 35 inches to 17 inches.

2. Make the legs. Each leg is an angle assembled from a leg piece and a brace piece. Glue and clamp the pieces together, drill four clearance holes, and drive the #8 × 3-inch galvanized screws. Assemble the other three legs in the same way.

3. Lay out the joints. Lay out the slots and the dowel holes, as shown in the drawing. Verify the layout with the eye bolts themselves, as shown in the photo at right.

4. Drill the dowel holes. Drill the holes for the dowels before you saw the slots, otherwise the drill will splinter the wood. Drill about 2½ inches deep.

5. Jigsaw the slots. Saw both sides of the slots, then work the saw back and forth to nibble the ends square.

6. Install the dowels and bolts. Saw a 3-inch length of ¾-inch dowel for each joint. Spread glue on the dowels, set the eye bolt in the slot, and tap the dowel into the hole. Make sure it catches the eye and enters the wood below.

7. Drill holes in the legs. Position the rails against the legs to transfer the location of the slots, as shown in the photo at bottom right. Drill the ⁵⁄₁₆-inch holes to match the shanks of the eye bolts.

8. Assemble the table. Fit the parts together, slip a washer onto each eye bolt, and tighten the nuts with a socket wrench. Drop the top in place. A top of medium-density fiberboard is heavy enough to stay put.

worktable alongside the car. When you open the garage door to remove the car, leave it open and move your worktable right into the opening. If your only alternative is a windowless cellar, you'll be better off to carry your equipment onto the deck. Don't overlook the spare bedroom, either. You won't make that much noise, and with a good shop vacuum, you can keep the sawdust and debris out of the carpets.

Worktable

For projects like the ones in this book, you need a low assembly table more than you need a regular woodworking bench. Most benches are counter height, 34 to 36 inches, but you'll find it very convenient to work at 28 to 30 inches, or table height, as shown in the project below. To get started, buy a worktable top of 1-inch MDF or two layers of plywood, and drop it across a pair of sawhorses like the ones shown on page 357. The most important thing about the worktable is being able to clear it and sweep it off. This means all your tools and materials need homes of their own.

Lay out the joints. Verify the layout by referring to the actual eye bolts and dowels you plan to use.

Drill holes in the legs. Transfer the hole centers from the slots in the rails.

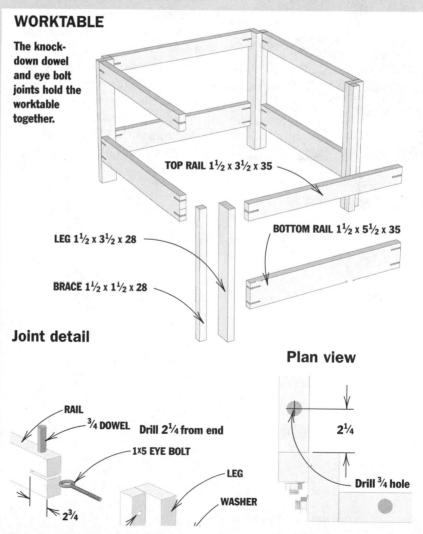

WORKTABLE

The knock-down dowel and eye bolt joints hold the worktable together.

TOP RAIL 1½ x 3½ x 35

BOTTOM RAIL 1½ x 5½ x 35

LEG 1½ x 3½ x 28

BRACE 1½ x 1½ x 28

Joint detail

RAIL

¾ DOWEL   Drill 2¼ from end

1X5 EYE BOLT

LEG

WASHER

2¾

Plan view

2¼

Drill ¾ hole

UTILITY SHELVES

Shelving can be made in almost any size. However, don't make units wider than 30 inches. When you want more width, make two units and stand them side by side. Wide shelves are awkward to move and liable to twist or sag under the weight of motorcycle parts and bowling balls.

To build the unit, make two ladder-like side panels and connect them with the long rails and shelves. Each side panel consists of two uprights joined at the floor by a short rail, then by the ledgers. Ledger construction allows you to make each shelf from two or three narrow pieces of wood. Glue and screw the uprights to the rails, and the ledgers to the uprights. Nail the shelves onto the ledgers with 2-inch siding nails. There's no need to glue.

Tool and material storage

Open shelves work best for tools and materials, such as the ones shown at left. You can glue and screw shelf units together as you need them. Make the shelves 10 inches to 13 inches apart, and make the shelf units 24 inches to 30 inches wide. Any wider than that, and the unit will be awkward to move and liable to sag. It's tempting to make adjustable shelves, but it's rarely worth the trouble. It's more important to gain the rigidity that comes from securely joining every shelf to the ledgers.

To anchor the shelves to a wall, screw a rail between the uprights, directly beneath the top shelf. Then nail through it into a wall stud.

Wood storage

Wood and plywood take a lot of space to store and they are difficult to store correctly. They have to be stored dry and flat. They're heavy and awkward. The pieces you want are always on the bottom of the pile. And you rarely have enough of anything on hand for your next project, so you'll have to go shopping anyway. It's better not to attempt storing a lot of lumber or plywood. You won't be able to avoid accumulating some short ends and extra pieces. Stand them around the walls of the shop and use them freely for general repairs around the house. When you want to start a new project, go to the home center or lumberyard to buy the materials you need.

UTILITY SHELVES

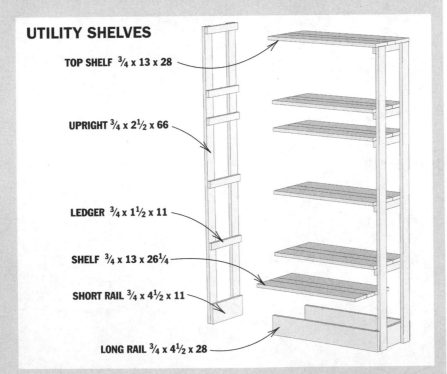

TOP SHELF ¾ x 13 x 28

UPRIGHT ¾ x 2½ x 66

LEDGER ¾ x 1½ x 11

SHELF ¾ x 13 x 26¼

SHORT RAIL ¾ x 4½ x 11

LONG RAIL ¾ x 4½ x 28

All the projects in this book can be made of softwood lumber from the home center or local lumberyard. Most of them use nothing more exotic than ordinary 1× and 2× pine boards. Although a few originally were made with rough-sawn pine from a local sawmill, you can substitute regular lumberyard materials. You could also substitute a durable hardwood such as white oak if you prefer.

There is no need for pressure-treated or chemically preserved lumber. None of the available treatments make environmental sense, and wooden constructions are not particularly vulnerable to water damage, as long as they can drain and dry. Most of the time, when a wooden structure finally does give up to the elements, it's past time for it to go. Let it sink gently into the earth, while you build something new.

Buying enough wood

The cutting lists in this book give the actual size of the pieces of wood you need. If there's a round end or a miter, it will fit within the rectangular dimensions given.

The project shopping lists have been inflated by 15% to 20%. You need to buy that much extra in order to work around knots and other defects, and to give yourself a margin for error. At the end of most of these projects, you'll be left with a box of resinous scrap for starting the barbecue, a stack of short ends, and perhaps an extra board.

How to speak board feet

Lumber sizes are mysterious and the guy at the lumberyard is not about to explain. The first thing to know is, you paid for more wood than you actually got. The reason is, what they sawed out of the log was rough, and what you bought was smooth. In order to make it smooth, they had to shave some wood off the width and the thickness. You're paying not only for the wood you got, but also for what they planed off. When you buy beef it's the other way around, so go figure.

Lumber thickness is measured in quarters of an inch, width is measured in inches, and length is measured in feet. The width and thickness measurements are the rough-sawn size, even if you are buying smooth lumber. The difference between rough and smooth is about ¼ inch in thickness, and ½ inch in width. You generally can buy any length you want, as long as you're willing to round up to the next 2-foot increment.

In an attempt to make sense of lumber measure, the marketplace restates thickness measurements in inches. Thus, what the wholesale trade knows as 4/4 lumber (pronounced "four-quarter") will be sold to you as 1× (pronounced "one-by") lumber. It started out about an inch thick, but after drying and smooth-planing, it's about ¾ inch thick. This is what you commonly find at the lumberyard and home center. You can also buy a 5/4 board, which started out 1¼ inches thick and will be about 1⅛ inches when planed smooth.

The usual sizes of lumber are 1×2, 1×3, 1×4, 1×5, 1×6, 1×8, 1×10 and 1×12. The actual widths are about a half-inch less, a little wider in narrow boards, but somewhat narrower in wide boards. Most 1×2 lumber comes in at 1⅝ inches wide, but 1×12 lumber will be closer to 11¼ inches.

You don't often find solid wood wider than 12 inches. But wide panels glued up from narrow 4/4 or 5/4 boards are increasingly available. Common widths are 17½ inches and 23½ inches, in 4-foot and 6-foot lengths. While not ideal for outdoor construction, these panels are generally made of sound material and are very useful for indoor projects.

Construction lumber, which starts out 8/4 or two inches thick, is sold as 2× or "two-by", and it actually measures 1½ inches thick. Common sizes are 2×2, 2×4, 2×6 and 2×8.

Home centers and lumberyards sell wood by linear feet, or running feet. It's easy for the customer to understand, but it requires them to maintain a menu of prices covering every width and thickness. If you go to a small sawmill and buy rough-sawn lumber, you'll find yourself in the world of board feet, with a single board-foot price for each species and grade in the yard, regardless of width or thickness.

A board foot is an imaginary piece of wood that's 1 inch thick, 12 inches wide, and 1 foot long. When you buy wood at a sawmill, they convert its actual dimensions to the equivalent number of board feet, then charge you for the board-foot total. If board feet make sense to you, go ahead and check the calculation. If board feet don't make sense to you, don't worry about it. The lumber trade customarily avoids arguments by always rounding calculations in the customer's favor.

Wood species

Most of the 1× lumber you can buy in North America is pine. "Pine," however, can refer to a large number of tree species, which may even include hemlock, spruce, larch, and fir. What all these woods have in common is their origin, from needle-bearing trees, their general white or yellow color, and their relative softness.

Other wood species you'll encounter at the home center include cedar, generally in the form of shingles and shakes, redwood or sequoia, a brown, rot-resistant and expensive softwood, and Douglas fir, North America's preeminent 2× construction timber. Douglas fir is pink in color, and it is heavier and stiffer than pine.

Cross-grain construction in softwood is no problem when the pieces are relatively narrow. Plastic-resin glues, such as ordinary yellow wood glue, have some give. However, a wide cross-grain construction (right) is liable to break apart.

Wood movement

Wood ain't plastic; it comes off living trees, which have a cellular structure. It's the nature of wood cells to respond to moisture: They swell in width and thickness when wet, and they shrink when dry. Wet or dry, they hardly change in length. Harvesting and drying the wood doesn't change its moisture response. When the air gets wet, boards swell. When the air gets dry, boards shrink. Paint or varnish slow down the exchange of moisture between the wood and the air, but nothing stops it.

The problem with wood movement is cross-grain construction, as shown in the drawing above. If you glue and screw two pieces of wood in the shape of a cross, the central overlap is cross-grain. Both pieces of wood move in width, but neither changes its length. Too much movement, and the glue gives up.

A piece of wood will be at its smallest indoors in the extreme dryness of wintertime heating. It will be at its largest in muggy summer weather. The amount of wood movement depends on the species as well as on the severity of the moisture cycle. In most softwoods, the maximum potential swing is between ¼ inch and ½ inch per foot of width. If the wood stays outdoors, never experiencing the indoor dryness of winter, the swing is less than half as great.

This is why you can generally ignore wood movement when you build outdoor projects. Movement on the order of 1⁄16 inch to 1⁄8 inch is within the plastic tolerance of softwood and modern glues. And anyway, outdoor woodworking projects are not fine antiques. They are going to change under the onslaught of the elements. Even when a piece of wood does split, if you have followed the construction details given in this book, the project itself is not likely to come apart.

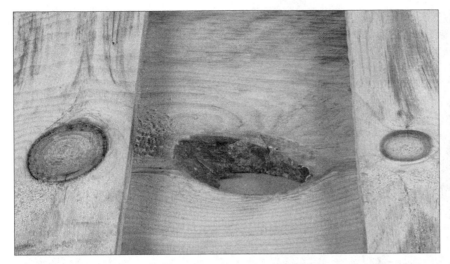

Knots with a black ring of bark (left) are loose and will fall out, leaving a knot-hole (center). Red knots and brown knots (right) are tight. They won't fall out.

All knots point toward the center of the tree. A spike knot (above) may indicate serious weakness.

Knots and defects

Most pine lumber is No. 2 grade, which means it has its share of knots and other defects. You could find clear pine, but you wouldn't like its premium price. Nevertheless, you can get virtually clear wood for your projects by selecting your No. 2 lumber with care, and by managing or eliminating the defects you find in it. For this reason the self-service home center may be a better source than the full-service lumberyard: You can choose your wood yourself. On the other hand, the boards might be so picked over that you're better off with what rises off the pile at the lumberyard.

Always take your cutting list and your tape measure when you go to buy wood. Try to have the major pieces of your project in mind, so you can select wood specifically for them.

Begin by looking at both surfaces of each board. If it runs out to bark at one edge, or it has gross splits or sawmill dings, reject it. Next, look at the knots. Each knot represents a branch, and all softwood branches origi-

Defects such as waney, or bark covered, edges and splits should be sawn out of the wood. The split in the top board was caused by a spike knot.

nate in the center, or pith, of the tree. There are two kinds of knots, black or loose knots, and red or tight knots, as shown in the photo at top left.

Black knots usually include a ring of bark, indicating that after the branch died, the tree trunk grew around it. They'll become loose and fall out, leaving a knot-hole. Red knots, which have no ring of bark, represent living branches. They may crack but they won't fall out. You can work with red knots but you should avoid black knots, or if you can't

avoid them, knock them out. Otherwise, the saw may throw the loose knot into your face.

In pine, the branches tend to grow in whorls, so there may be rows of knots separated by clear wood. You may be able to saw totally clear wood in between rows of knots. However, if you look closely you'll see that the wood's figure is distorted for several inches around the knot itself. While you can incorporate knots and distorted grain in the center of a board, you can't nail it or cut joints in it.

The end grain tells where the board grew in the tree and how it may behave. The 2×4 at left is quartersawn, stable in size and not likely to distort. The flatsawn board next to it is liable to cup. In the middle, tight annual rings indicate strong, slow-grown wood (center left) while wide rings indicate weaker, fast-grown wood (center right). At right, the center 2×4 contains the unstable pith of the tree and you can see that it is not flat. It may also twist. The bottom 2×4, sawn just off the pith, will be more stable, while the top one is rift-sawn and the most stable among this trio. But the most desirable piece of wood in the photo is the quartersawn 2×4 at left.

Now look at the end of the boards. You'll see curved lines, each one representing a year of growth, as shown in the photo above. The spacing of the annual rings tells you how fast the tree grew, and their curvature tells you where the board was inside the tree trunk, which indicates how the wood will behave. Fast-grown softwood, with fewer than five rings to the inch, is weaker than slow-grown softwood, though it's strong enough for most purposes. Boards cut just off the center of the tree are more likely to cup than boards cut from dead center or from farther out. The very center of the tree, called the pith, is unstable wood and should be sawn out of 1× boards and discarded.

Other common defects include pitch pockets, blue or brown stain, and insect holes. When a board oozes gooey pitch, it will continue to do so forever, no matter how many coats of finish you put on it. You can use the board in some unobtrusive place, but not for the seat of a bench. Blue stain and brown stain, caused by fungi and microbes, are harmless discolorations. They don't affect the strength of the wood or its ability to take a finish. Insect holes are no problem, because the culprits will have been killed by the lumber-drying process.

Plywood

There's all kinds of plywood at the home center, but what you want for outdoor projects is exterior grade with one reasonably good face. Buy plywood according to the three-letter grade stamped on each sheet. The most common grade is CDX, where the C and the D refer to the quality of the surfaces, and the X means waterproof glue for exterior use. For projects like the ones in this book, where you're likely to get up close to the finished piece, BDX plywood is generally better than CDX.

Although plywood is stable in length and width, it's rarely flat. This doesn't matter because in most applications you'll nail it onto a structure.

Another useful plywood-type of material is T1-11 siding. Despite its X rating, most plywood ends up covered by other materials. T1-11 is a plywood that's designed to be on show, and also to shed whatever the weather throws at it. It's cheap, strong and durable—an excellent all-around material for utility and garden projects.

You can't make anything nice without measuring tools. You'll use them all the time, every time you cut and connect two pieces of wood. Measuring tools for woodworking commonly measure distance and angles. While you might have a protractor for measuring angles, most of the time the angle of interest is 90 degrees, or square. Distance, of course, is a totally variable number, but a corner or intersection is either 90 degrees or it isn't.

Straightedges and squares are also invaluable for aligning parts. The parts line up or they don't, and if they're off, they have to be wiggled and shoved until they finally do align.

Combination square

The combination square combines a 12-inch straightedge with a 90-degree sliding stock. Thus it can measure both distance and squareness. It's especially useful as a gauge for locating two parts relative to one another, as shown in the photos at top. The sliding stock also has a 45-degree fence for miters.

Speed square

The plastic speed square is a recent addition to the measuring arsenal. Most builders use it instead of the larger and more cumbersome rafter square. The speed square is extremely useful for squaring and aligning parts, as shown in the photos at right.

Tape measure

Splurge for a 25-foot metal tape with a 1-inch blade. Notice that the little metal hook that keeps the blade from disappearing into the case isn't a tight fit. It wiggles back and forth by its own thickness. This allows you to use the same tape for inside and outside measurements.

The metal hook on the end of a tape measure is loose by its own thickness. This permits accurately taking inside and outside measurements.

A combination square helps center one piece on the other (above). The square aligns the parts, and establishes a vertical plane (right).

The speed square makes it easy to align two parts (left) and to make them square to one another (right).

There are four basic kinds of sawing: Crosscutting, or sawing to length; ripping, or sawing to width lengthwise; mitering, or sawing at an angle, and sawing curves. Most of the time you want the sawn piece of wood to end up at some particular size, with its surfaces reasonably flat and smooth. And you often want more than one piece sawn to the same size.

For outdoor projects and general woodworking around the house, perhaps 90% of saw work is crosscutting to length.

Mitering the wood is just crosscutting at an angle other than 90 degrees. While it is handy to be able to rip to width, it's usually not absolutely necessary because you can buy wood in 1-inch increments of width. Most of the projects in this book have been designed around standard widths of lumber.

For making straight cuts, there are six basic types of saw: handsaw, jigsaw, portable circular saw, chop saw, bandsaw, and table saw. Which ones you choose depend upon your bud-

get, your skill level, and how involved in woodworking you intend to become. You can take care of all your sawing needs with a $20 handsaw, along with sandpaper to knock the splinters off the cut. Or you could spend more than $1,000 for a cabinetmaker's table saw.

In terms of safety and skill, the important distinction is whether you move the saw over stationary wood, or move the wood over a stationary saw. It's generally safer to clamp the wood in one place and to move

SAWHORSE

If you're just starting out, a pair of sawhorses can be the foundation of your workshop: Throw a sheet of plywood across them, and you've got your first worktable. Carry them out onto the deck, and you've got a beautiful open-air workshop.

These sawhorses are made of standard 1× lumber, held together with glue and screws. The dimensions given in the drawing make a horse that's 24 inches high, about right to use with a portable circular saw or jigsaw. For handsawing, change the length of the legs to about 18 inches. To support a worktable, make 28-inch legs. The length of the sawhorse top is up to you.

The only angled cut in the sawhorse is the gusset. The angle is about 20 degrees, but the precise measurement mat-

ters less than making all four gussets the same.

Begin by gluing and screwing a gusset onto each pair of legs. Then set the leg-and-gusset assemblies upside-down on a flat surface in order to connect them with the rail. This ensures that their top surfaces will all be in the same plane. Next, glue and screw the top of the sawhorse to the rail and gussets, allowing it to overlap at the ends. Screw right down through the top and bury the screwheads in the wood. The second set of gussets, glued and screwed outside the legs, stiffens the construction.

Sawhorses give you a beachhead in the struggle to build up a workshop. They're extremely strong, yet they're direct and quick to make. Since they stack, you can make a herd as easily as a single pair, and they won't take up any more room in the shop.

Join gussets to legs. Align the top corner of the leg with the outside corner of the gusset. Glue and screw the parts together.

The rail connects the gussets. Center the rail on the leg-and-gusset assembly. Connect the parts with #6 × 2½-inch screws.

the saw, as you do with the handsaw, portable circular saw, chop saw, and jigsaw. It's more accurate, too. When you move the wood over a stationary blade, such as a table saw, you're always at risk of losing control. It takes more skill to make safe and accurate cuts.

It might surprise you to hear that most people can quickly learn how to cut accurately with a handsaw. Even if you have a complete machine setup, you'll find a handsaw the only answer to some sawing

A handsaw is the only way to trim parts after they've been joined together.

problems—trimming parts after they've become part of a larger construction, for example. It's also the easiest way to saw small notches and cutouts.

If you are beginning to woodwork around your house, you

do not need to make a major investment in sawing machinery. If you already have a table saw, fine, but if not, you can do very well with a handsaw or with a jigsaw. If you want a little more machine, consider a sliding-arm chop saw. It will handle all of your crosscutting and miter sawing, it's safe, and it's extremely accurate. The chop saw can't rip, so for the occasional lengthwise cut, and for breaking down sheets of plywood, you'll need a jigsaw or a portable circular saw as well.

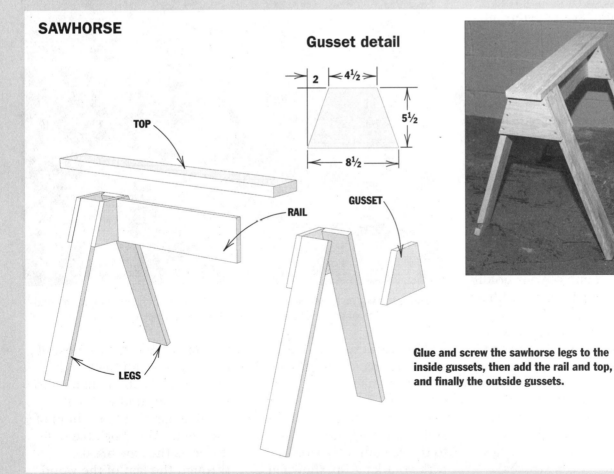

SAWHORSE

Gusset detail

TOP

RAIL

GUSSET

LEGS

Glue and screw the sawhorse legs to the inside gussets, then add the rail and top, and finally the outside gussets.

HANDSAW

There's been a real change in handsaw technology in the last few years. Both Stanley and Sandvik now make a short tool-box saw with a new tooth pro-file derived from Japanese saws. The teeth are long and sharp, with a little triangular facet at the tip. They cut much more effectively than tradi-tional handsaws, they're easier to start, and easier to control. If you have a choice, get the coarser saw, with eight or nine teeth to the inch.

Grip and stance are the keys to learning how to saw by hand. Wrap three fingers through the saw handle, with your index finger pointing along the blade, as shown in the photo at right. Tighten your thumb against your mid-dle finger. Use a low saw horse, 18 inches is about right. This allows you to take a marching stance and to get your body over the work. The sawing motion comes from your shoul-der, not your wrist or elbow. Align the saw with your wrist, arm and shoulder joint.

Hold the workpiece on the sawhorse with your left hand. If you can't easily keep it still, use your knee or a small clamp. Brace the sawblade with the thumb of your holding hand and start the cut with a couple of light backward strokes. This breaks the corner of the wood, and it also gets your body into alignment with the proposed cut. Then push, but don't force the saw. The saw's own weight is almost enough. If the saw jams, it may bend but it won't break. Saw with steady, even strokes.

Handsaw grip and stance. Wrap three fingers around the saw's handle and point your index finger along the blade. Sight straight down on the saw. Align the saw with your wrist, forearm and shoulder joint. To start the cut, brace the sawblade against the thumb of your holding hand. The sawing motion comes from the shoulder, not from the elbow or wrist.

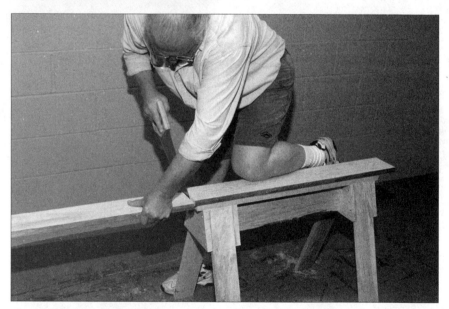

Crosscutting with a handsaw. To keep a long board from splintering at the end of the cut, reach over the saw and support it with your holding hand.

Handsaw crosscut. When you want to cut a long board in half, you'll need to support the offcut and keep it from falling, because otherwise it's liable to splinter. Clamp the workpiece to the sawhorse, or hold it with your knee, as shown in the photo above. Saw most of the way through the wood. When there's about an inch to go, reach around with your holding hand and take hold of the offcut. You'll be able to lift it free as the saw breaks through the last of the wood.

Handsaw rip. Unlike traditional saws, the new handsaws don't come in rip and crosscut versions. The same tooth profile works either way. To rip a board, draw a layout line on the wood. Clamp the workpiece to the sawhorse, stand beside it, and start to saw. When you come to the sawhorse, you'll have to unclamp the workpiece, move it along, and reclamp.

Handsaw miter. Mitering with a handsaw is the same as crosscutting. Draw a line, clamp the workpiece to the sawhorse, and start with short, backward strokes. Brace the saw with the thumb of your holding hand.

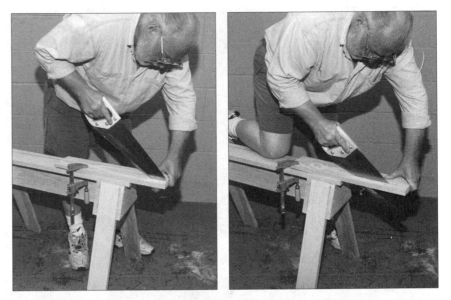

Ripping with a handsaw. Draw a layout line on the wood and clamp it to the sawhorse. Stand beside the sawhorse. Move and reclamp the wood as you progress. You may find it helpful to plant your knee on the sawhorse, so you can get your shoulder right over the saw.

JIGSAW

If you are beginning to woodwork in order to improve your home, a jigsaw is the least startling and most versatile saw you can buy. It's light, it's capable of reasonable accuracy, and it can saw everything, including curves. The blade is little and it goes up and down with a whirring noise, unlike circular saws which go around with a roar and a lot of wind. The jigsaw's disadvantage is the time it takes to set up each cut. There's no ready way to set up once and cut many parts.

If you're only going to have one power saw and you want to limit your investment, the jigsaw is your only choice. A good machine will cost about $150; look for a saw with a blade-guide bearing right above its sole plate. Low-priced saws have sloppy mechanisms and no guide bearings, so they do less accurate work. Be sure to use blades for cutting wood. Blades for metal

and plastic are also available, and they're often sold as a set.

Portable saws require cord management. You do not want to saw through the cord, nor do you want to be pulled up short in the middle of the cut. Always rehearse your cutting path before you turn on the saw. If you start the cut and the tool gets hung up, let go of the trigger and back up a half-inch, and look at

your setup to figure out what's causing the problem. Don't blindly push onward.

As with any other portable power tool or woodworking machine, always wear safety glasses with side shields whenever you use a jigsaw.

Jigsaw rip. While you can freehand the cut, you'll have much better results if you

You can make a rip jig for the jigsaw, as shown on page 361. Here the rip jig is clamped to a diagonal line, so it will make two tapered pieces of wood.

Mitering with a jigsaw. The crosscut jig clamped to the layout line guides the jigsaw. This cut will not have a splintered edge because it is "with the grain." The end of the board was cut from the opposite direction, with visible splintering.

Ripping with a jigsaw. Make a gauge stick, like the stick at the bottom right of the photo, whose width matches the distance from the edge of the jigsaw's sole to its blade. Use the gauge stick to locate and clamp a fence to the workpiece. Cut by pressing the saw against the fence.

clamp a fence to the workpiece. You have to offset the fence by the distance from the edge of the saw's sole to its blade, which you can do by direct measurement, or with a gauge. The gauge is a straight stick of wood whose width matches the jigsaw's sole-to-blade offset distance.

Begin by drawing the layout line on the workpiece. Then use the gauge to position the fence the offset distance away from the layout line. Clamp the fence to the workpiece. The jigsaw is a light tool, it's easy to control, so it's not necessary to clamp the workpiece to the sawhorse or worktable.

Always start the jigsaw before the blade contacts the workpiece, and ease it into the cut. Let the saw cut at its own

Crosscutting with a jigsaw. Use a gauge stick to position and clamp a fence to the workpiece, offset from the layout line. Make the cut by pressing the saw's sole against the fence.

speed. If you force it, you'll flex the blade and send it off the line. You can stop the saw at any time, but don't try to lift it out of the cut while it's running. Let it stop first.

Jigsaw crosscut and miter. The jigsaw is forgiving of grain direction, so crosscutting can be approached the same way as ripping. Position the fence with the gauge, clamp, and go.

Jigs for Portable Saws

A couple of simple jigs take all the guesswork out of ripping and crosscutting with jigsaws and portable circular saws. The basic jig consists of a fence attached to a baseplate. The saw rides on the baseplate, guided by the fence. The first time you use one of these jigs, the saw cuts through the baseplate. Every time thereafter, the saw automatically cuts right along the edge of the baseplate.

Jigs for jigsaws are the same as jigs for the portable circular saw. The only difference is the distance from the jig's fence to the edge of the baseplate, which has to match the distance from the saw blade to the edge of the jigsaw's sole. If you use the saw to trim the jig, it comes out right.

It's tempting to imagine a universal jig for portable saws, one that would make every cut. But in any specific situation, such a jig would never be the right size. It's better to make more than one jig. Make a rip jig for pieces up to 4 feet long. The first time you need to rip a longer piece of wood, you might make an 8-foot jig, but you might go for years without ever getting to that point. Make a 16-inch crosscut jig for ordinary sizes of 1× and 2× lumber. You can also use the crosscut jig for sawing miters.

The rip jig consists of a 4-foot fence made from 1×3 or 1×4 pine, glued and screwed to a baseplate, which is a 4-foot by 6-inch strip of ¼-inch Masonite. Glue and screw the pine fence to the baseplate with ¾-inch screws; Masonite soaks up glue,

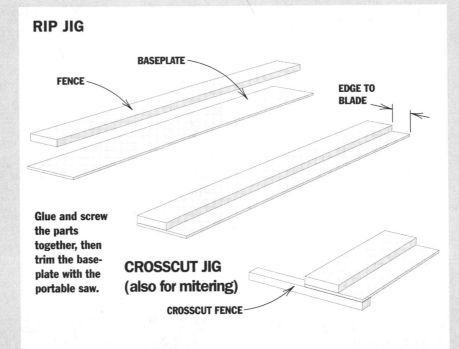

RIP JIG

FENCE

BASEPLATE

EDGE TO BLADE

Glue and screw the parts together, then trim the baseplate with the portable saw.

CROSSCUT JIG (also for mitering)

CROSSCUT FENCE

Trim the baseplate. Clamp the jig to a piece of wood atop the sawhorse. Saw the baseplate with the portable circular saw or the jigsaw.

so roll two wet coats onto it.

To trim the baseplate to the exact width of the saw's sole, clamp the jig to a piece of wood so the cut is supported, and with the saw's sole riding against the pine fence, saw the baseplate from one end to the other. Now the jig is ready to use.

Make the crosscut jig in exactly the same way as you made the rip jig, but make the

Make the crosscut fence. Glue and screw the crosscut fence to the bottom of the jig's baseplate. Align the parts with a square, drive the first screw, then align them again before driving the second screw.

pine fence and the Masonite baseplate 16 inches long. The crosscut fence is a 9-inch length of 1×2 pine. Glue and screw it to the bottom of the jig. The trick is making the crosscut fence square to the edge of the baseplate. To do that, spread the glue and align the parts with your square, as shown in the photo above. Drill a pilot hole and drive one screw. Then square up the parts again, before you drill and drive the second screw.

PORTABLE CIRCULAR SAW

The portable circular saw is an inexpensive way to get started in power-tool woodworking. However, you can't get far with the bare saw. You need to invest time in making jigs.

There are several styles of saw. The main choice is whether the motor is to the right of the blade or to the left. Left-mounted saws are new on the market, and they are easier to use because a right-handed person has a better view of the line of cut. Expect to spend about $150. Cheap saws may not be well engineered and won't be sturdy. If you spend much more than $150, you're into professional grade, worm-drive machines that are liable to be too heavy. Be sure to get a carbide blade.

Like routers and jigsaws, portable circular saws require cord management. Drape the cord so you won't saw through it, and so it won't catch someplace in the middle of the cut.

All portable circular saws have a spring-loaded blade guard. The guard has a hand lever that allows you to lift it out of the way to start the cut. It snaps back into place as soon as the saw leaves the workpiece. However, there is no guard underneath the workpiece, where the blade breaks through. This is why it is critically important always to clamp the workpiece to the sawhorse or worktable, and to keep both hands on the saw. If you try to hand-hold the workpiece, you are liable to curl your fingers into the path of the whirling blade.

Ripping with a portable circular saw. Make a rip jig and clamp it to the workpiece, with the edge of its Masonite baseplate on your layout line. Run the sole of the saw along the jig's fence. Here the saw is ripping a 2×2 from the edge of a 2×6.

Crosscutting with a portable circular saw. Make a crosscut jig and clamp it to the workpiece. The jig's crosscut fence keeps the cut square.

Portable circular saw rip. To rip, or saw the wood lengthwise, clamp a fence to the workpiece so that the edge of the fence guides the portable circular saw along the line you wish to cut. This means offsetting the fence by the distance from the saw blade to the edge of its sole. You can do it by measurement, with a gauge as discussed on page 360, or with the jig shown above.

Note, that you have to allow for the width of the saw blade itself, which is called the saw kerf. If the workpiece is the part of the wood that's clamped under the jig, it's no problem. If the workpiece is the falling board, be sure to offset the jig ⅛ inch to compensate for the kerf.

It takes a little practice to get good results with a portable circular saw. Pay attention to keeping the saw level, with its sole pressed down flat on the workpiece or jig, and tight against the fence. The usual error is to inadvertently tilt the saw, but if you pay attention and make a few practice cuts, you'll soon learn how to get it right.

Portable circular saw crosscut. While it's possible to freehand a crosscut with the portable circular saw, you'll have much better results if you make the jig described on page 361. The jig has a crosscut fence, in addition to the fence that actually guides the saw. The crosscut fence aligns the jig square to the edge of the workpiece. Clamp the edge of the jig's base right on the layout line.

Portable circular saw miter. Mitering, or sawing angles, is essentially the same as crosscutting and uses the same jig. Use the corner of the crosscut fence to position the jig on the layout line. Saw slowly and carefully.

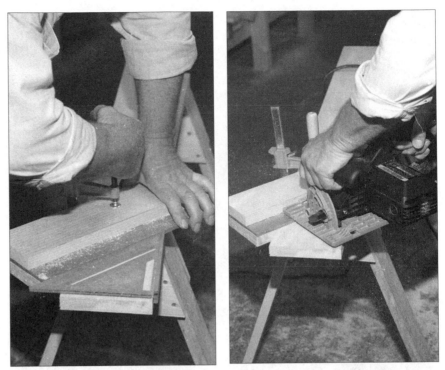

Mitering with a portable circular saw. Clamp the crosscut jig to the layout line. A carpenter's speed square can help you clamp the jig at 45 degrees (left). Guide the sole of the saw along the fence of the jig. Press the saw down level on the jig's baseplate (right).

CHOP SAW

Since most sawing for household projects is crosscutting to length, the chop saw is an excellent choice of machine. With a carbide-tipped saw blade, it makes a superb cut, accurate and clean. Since the saw moves while the wood remains stationary, the chop saw is a relatively safe machine, provided you don't attempt to disable its built-in blade guard. Crosscutting and mitering is all the chop saw can do, so you'll need another way to rip wood to width, such as a jigsaw.

There are two kinds of chop saw, pivoting, and sliding arm. With either type of saw, always cut with the workpiece extending to the left of the blade, and the waste to the right. Hold the

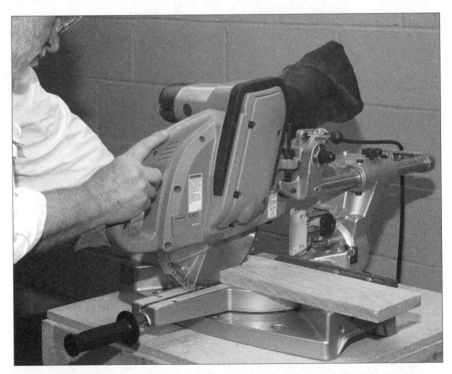

Crosscutting with a chop saw. Hold the workpiece on the left side of the saw blade, with the offcut to the right. With a sliding-arm chop saw, pull the blade forward of the workpiece, then lower it and push it to the back.

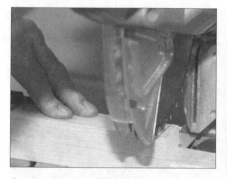

Crosscutting multiples. To saw two pieces the same length, align one piece of wood on top of the second piece. With the saw off, bring the layout line over to the blade (above). Chop through both pieces at once (center). To saw many pieces to an exact length, clamp an auxiliary fence to the chop saw's fence, and clamp a stop block to it. Butt each workpiece against the stop block (below).

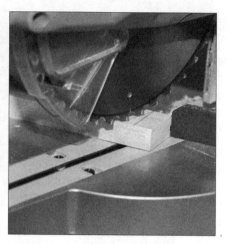

Mitering with a chop saw. Rotate the saw table to the miter angle. To miter at a precise length, make a layout line on the workpiece (above) and make a shallow cut to the right of it. This shows you where the saw is cutting, so you can shift the work to it and chop through (below).

work with your left hand and drive the saw with your right hand. This method gives you the best view of the layout line. With a pivoting saw, the blade pulls down into the wood. With a sliding-arm saw, the blade pivots down and moves forward and backward. Always bring the blade forward of the work and push it through the wood to the back. This takes advantage of the saw's cutting force to push the work into the saw fence.

Always wear a face shield, safety goggles, or safety glasses with side shields whenever you use a chop saw.

Chop saw crosscut. The chop saw is designed to crosscut. Make your layout line on the wood and press it against the fence. With your fingers carefully away from the ON trigger, lower the saw and align the edge of one sawtooth with the layout line. Move the work along the

fence until the layout line is exactly to the left of the saw blade. Make sure none of your fingers are near the line of the cut before you pull the trigger on the saw. Pull it down and push it through the wood.

Chop saw multiples. To make two pieces the same size, saw one end of both pieces, but make sure both are still oversize. Draw a layout line on one piece and put it on top of the other piece, with their cut ends to the left of the saw blade. Align the cut ends with your left hand, while you bring the layout mark up to the saw blade as shown in the photos at left. Then crosscut both pieces at once.

To crosscut multiple pieces to an exact size, make an auxiliary fence with a stop block, and clamp it to the regular chop saw fence, as shown in the bottom left photo on the previous page. However, saw the first end on all the workpiece wood before you attach the auxiliary fence to the saw. Then butt the sawn end against the stop block and go.

Chop saw miter. The chop saw is ideal for mitering. Most models have a rotating saw table.

Whenever possible, rotate the saw table to keep the workpiece on the left of the blade. To miter to a given length, mark the length on the wood and begin the cut ¼ inch to the right of the mark. Cut part-way through the wood, just far enough to see the cut against the layout line. Now you can sneak up on the line by moving the workpiece to the right.

TABLE SAW

You can do an amazing number of operations with a table saw. However, what it does best is rip wood to width, and with a suitable jig or miter fence it can also crosscut it to length or to a given angle.

If you are shopping for a table saw, look at a mid-priced contractor-style machine with a 10-inch blade, about $750. It will be more accurate than an 8-inch benchtop saw. The motor of a contractor-style saw hangs off the back of the machine and drives the blade by means of a vee belt. On a benchtop saw, the blade mounts directly on the saw motor. This arrangement limits the thickness of wood the saw can cut.

All new table saws come with some kind of blade guard. Some guards work beautifully, but some are unwieldy. If your saw has an awkward guard, it is a serious mistake to remove it and work without it. The right answer is to look for an after-market guard that suits you, or to design and make one that really does work well. Take the problem of guarding your saw as a challenge, not as a nuisance. Likewise, always wear a face

PUSH STICK

A pair of push sticks allows you to propel wood past the table saw blade without risking your fingers. Always make push sticks in pairs, and keep one on the left side of the saw table, and one on the right, where they're easy to grab. It's important to make simple push sticks, because there can't be anything in the way of making new ones whenever you need them. If the saw chews one up, it has served its purpose well—chuck it and make another. The push stick

Make the notch with a handsaw.

shown here is made from a 12-inch cutoff of 1×2 pine. You can handsaw the notch, or saw it with a jigsaw.

PUSH STICK ½ |←——— 12 ———→| 90° 1½

shield, safety goggles or safety glasses with side shields.

Table saw rip. Ripping, or sawing the wood lengthwise in order to make it narrower, is a safe and straightforward operation. The fence should be parallel to the saw blade, and on its

right-hand side. The workpiece is the portion of the wood between the fence and the blade; the falling board or offcut is the piece of wood to the left of the blade.

Raise the blade so the bottom of the gullets between the sawteeth clear the top surface

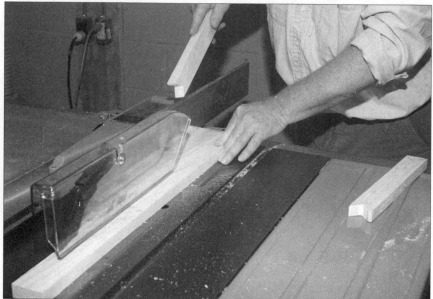

Ripping with a table saw. Stand alongside the wood, not directly behind it. The right hand propels the wood forward into the blade. The left hand holds it down on the table (above). When the back end of the wood reaches the saw table, pause and pick up your push sticks (top right). The splitter, behind the sawblade, keeps the cut from closing and kicking back. Complete the cut with the push sticks. Push the workpiece and the falling board completely past the blade (right).

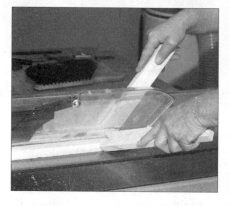

Crosscutting with a table saw. Hold the wood tight against the miter gauge and push the gauge past the saw blade.

of the wood. Set the width before you switch on the power. Make a pair of push sticks, as shown in the drawing on the previous page, and keep them handy, one on the left side of the saw table, one on the right. If the board is longer than about 6 feet, set up an outfeed support to catch it.

For safe ripping, regardless of the style of blade guard your saw has, you must use a splitter. The splitter is a metal plate attached to the saw structure on the back side of the blade. If the wood were to distort, it would keep the sawblade from kicking the wood back at the operator.

To feed the wood, stand in front of the saw, but to the left of

the blade. Make sure the wood is not touching the blade when you turn on the power. Lift the back of the board so its leading end is down tight on the saw table. Feed steadily and evenly, and pay attention to the contact between the fence and the workpiece. When the back end of the board reaches the saw table, pick up one push stick and then the other, both of which you left conveniently placed before you turned on the saw. Propel the tail of the board past the blade with a push stick in each hand, not with your fingers.

Table saw crosscut. Crosscut with the aid of the miter gauge, a T-shaped tool that rides in

grooves in the saw table. Move the rip fence completely out of the way to the right of the blade. The head of the miter gauge is only about 7 inches wide, but you can extend it by bolting an auxiliary fence of wood onto it.

Set the gauge to 90 degrees on its scale, but don't rely on it. Crosscut a piece of wood and

check it with your try square.
Adjust the gauge accordingly.
Make sure the locking knob is
tight before you cut. At the end
of the cut, as soon as the wood
has been severed, pull it away
from the blade to the left, before
you pull the miter gauge back.
Remove the cutoff with your
push stick. Don't reach over the
blade with your hand.

Table saw multiples. To
crosscut multiple pieces, set up
a stop block to the right of the
blade. Make sure the workpiece
entirely clears the stop block
before it touches the blade.
Otherwise, the wood can get
trapped between the blade and
stop block, and it will be thrown
back at you. One safe way to do
this is to clamp a block of wood
to the rip fence, as shown in the
photo above right. The block
must be big enough to keep the
workpiece from being trapped
between the rip fence and the
blade, even if the workpiece
were to pivot diagonally. This is
the only time you can use the
rip fence in conjunction with the
miter gauge.

Another way to saw multiples
is to clamp a stop block onto an
auxiliary fence attached to the
miter gauge, as shown in the
center photo. The workpiece is
to the left of the blade, and the
offcut is to the right. Move the
rip fence entirely out of the way.

Table saw miter. Table saw
mitering is like crosscutting,
except the wood tends to creep
along the miter gauge. Prevent it
from creeping by clamping it to
an auxiliary fence attached to
the miter gauge, as shown in the
photo at right.

Crosscutting multiples. A stop block clamped to the rip fence allows you to
crosscut multiple parts to the same length. The stop block must be at the front
of the saw table, not near the sawblade. It must be wide enough that the workpiece cannot become trapped between the sawblade and the rip fence (top).
The stop block can be clamped to an auxiliary fence that is screwed to the miter
gauge. In this setup, move the rip fence entirely out of the way (above).

Mitering on a table saw. Miter with an auxiliary fence screwed or bolted to the
miter gauge. To keep the workpiece from creeping, clamp it to the auxiliary fence.

Most of the projects in this book are held together with glue and screws, or glue and nails. The glue is more than insurance. It locks the parts and gives the construction tremendous resistance to becoming loose and wobbly. Gluing technique, however, is important.

Use Titebond II glue, or equivalent. This is a yellow polyvinyl acetate (PVA) emulsion formulated for water resistance. You can't build boats with the stuff, but you can expect it to remain intact rain and shine. This kind of glue remains tacky for about 10 minutes after you spread it, giving you plenty of time to bring parts together and install the metal fasteners. The only drawback to PVA glue is cold weather. It can't be allowed to freeze in the bottle, and it doesn't set properly at temperatures lower than 40 degrees.

The best tool for spreading glue is a 3-inch disposable paint roller, the $2 variety sold for painting trim. The roller's plastic package is a small paint tray. Squirt some glue into the paint tray and keep the roller wet with glue. Store the roller in its tray, inside a plastic zip-lock freezer bag. If you always put the roller back in the bag and keep the bag sealed, the glue will remain soft and usable almost indefinitely. Glue doesn't get hard in the bottle, and it won't get hard inside the bag either.

Before spreading any glue, draw a layout line. Then squirt or roll glue on both of the mat-

A small paint roller is the best way to spread a uniform film of glue. Squirt glue into the roller's plastic tray, and store the whole business in a zip-lock freezer bag.

A small amount of glue squeezes out of a good joint.

ing parts, inside the layout lines. Roll the glue out smooth with the paint roller. Be sure to spread a thin film of glue on both mating parts.

How much glue? It depends. The glue will fill small gaps, and you want enough so it squeezes out of the joint in a little bead. You don't want so much that it drips and runs. A little experimenting will show you how to meter the stuff. Glue is expensive and it's messy to clean up, so it's worthwhile learning how to spread just the right amount.

Beginning woodworkers often consider clamps to be optional accessories, but they are not. Because nobody has enough hands, clamps are essential tools. They hold pieces together and in the right place, while you drill holes and drive screws, or pound nails.

The most useful clamps are the quick-action style shown in the photo at right. They're inexpensive, easy to set, robust enough to hold tight, and easy to release.

Clamps are measured by their maximum opening. To begin, buy two 6-inch clamps and two 12-inch clamps. Then build your clamp collection by buying more clamps two at a time—once you discover how helpful they are, you'll find that you can't have too many clamps. Don't, however, start out buying long clamps with the idea of covering every eventuality. Most of the time they'll be too awkward to use. Stick with small and medium clamps, and add a couple of long ones the first time you really need them.

You don't need a lot of pressure to hold parts in line and to glue up, though if you were making hardwood furniture, you would need protective blocks under your clamp jaws. But the projects in this book are all softwood, and all outdoor. Clamp the wood directly to itself and to the worktable. Don't worry about denting the wood, because the first brush-load of paint, or the first rainstorm, will

Set a clamp by holding the fixed jaw against the workpiece (above). Then slide the movable jaw up to the wood and tighten it (left).

If you start clamping with the movable jaw, it will be more difficult to keep the parts in line (below).

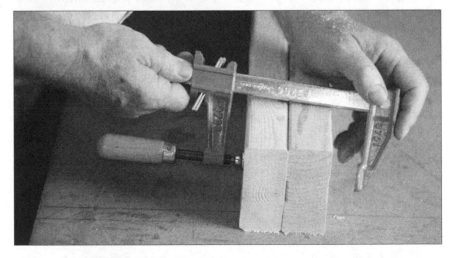

swell the dented fibers.

You'll see clamps in use throughout the projects in this book. If you've been working without clamps, buy yourself a

pair and force yourself to use them. You'll find that you work better and you'll enjoy it more, because it's a whole lot easier with extra hands.

Drills and Screws

The electric drill is everyone's first power tool, and it's amazing how much drill you can buy for $30 or $40—they're genuine bargains. Reasonably good drills are so cheap and common that there is no reason to limit yourself to owning just one. For the kind of glue-and-screw construction you'll find throughout this book, it's most efficient to have two drills. Keep one tool set up for drilling pilot holes and clearance holes. Mount a screwdriver bit in the other.

Drills are sold by chuck size. The most useful general-purpose drill has a ⅜-inch chuck. A ¼-inch chuck is too small for many common attachments, while a ½-inch chuck will be mounted on a tool that's too large and too heavy for household use. The new keyless chucks are much better than the older keyed ones, plus there is no key to lose. Variable speed is

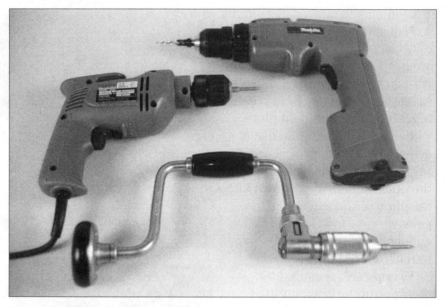

Cordless drills have rechargeable batteries in the handle (right). The corded drill has a screwdriver bit in its keyless chuck (left). An old-style brace is a low-cost alternative to electric drills.

necessary for driving screws, and so is reverse, for removing screws.

Cordless drills are more expensive, but once you've used one you won't want to go back to the copper tether. Modern rechargeable batteries pack plenty of power for woodworking projects. Ask your family to get you a ⅜-inch cordless drill for Christmas. You'll never regret it.

Poor Man's Driver

If you want more exercise from your woodworking projects, or if the luxury of having two electric drills offends you, try driving screws with an old-style bit brace. You can find a good brace at the flea market for between $5 and $10. Look for one with a free-turning ball-bearing in the knob, and make sure the chuck and its ratchet mechanism both operate. Mount a regular Phillips-head driver in the

chuck. You'll find you can generate more than enough force to spin a screw down tight in no time flat. In fact you'll probably need to lighten up at the end, to avoid snapping the head off the screw. The ratchet mechanism allows you to drive and remove screws in tight spots.

A bit brace exerts plenty of screwdriving torque.

SCREWS

There are dozens of types of wood screw at the home center. They can generally be distinguished by size, head style, driver style, and finish, as shown in the photo at right. A typical screw size is #6 × 2, where the #6 refers to the size of wire from which it was cut, and the 2 refers to its total length in inches.

The projects in this book were made with the same basic kind of outdoor construction screw that's sold by every home center in North America. They're typically #6 and #8 screws, ranging from ¾ inch to 3 inches in length, bugle-shaped head for sinking into the surface of the wood, cross-slot (Phillips) style driver, and galvanized for resistance to rust.

What size screw to use? Stick with #6 and #8 screws, and choose the longest you can fit before the point comes through the other side. The sizes we use are #6 × ¾, #6 × 1, #6 × 1⅝, #6 × 2, #8 × 2½, and #8 × 3. We buy them in 2-pound and 5-pound boxes. Bugle-head construction screws are endlessly useful indoors and out, and eventually you will use the whole box, so don't be seduced by expensive little packets of 10 or 12 screws.

In addition to Phillips-head screws, you may find regular single-slot screws, and square-drive Robertson screws. Slotted screws are difficult to drive with a drill. The Robertson square-

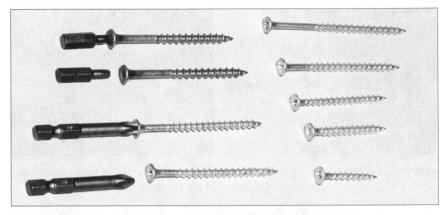

Phillips, or cross-slot, screws are easy to power-drive (bottom). Robertson, or square-drive, screws are standard in Canada and increasingly available in the States (top). The #6 screws at right range from 1 inch to 2½ inches in length.

drive style, which is standard in Canada, is an excellent alternative to the Phillips style and they are increasingly available in the U.S. market.

Pilot Holes, Clearance Holes

Clearance holes and pilot holes remove wood for screws and nails, so the wood pulls tight without splitting. A clearance hole should be the same size as or even a hair larger than the outside diameter of a screw's threads. A pilot hole can be no larger than the core diameter of a screw or nail, and ideally it should be a little smaller.

"A hair larger." "A little smaller." "No larger than." What can you do with such vague specifications? In softwood, "close" is close enough. For a #6 screw, the clearance hole should be ⁹⁄₆₄ inch, but ⅛ inch will do, and the pilot hole should be ⁵⁄₆₄ inch, but ¹⁄₁₆ will do. For a #8

screw, the clearance hole should be ¹¹⁄₆₄ inch but ³⁄₁₆ inch will do, and the pilot hole should be ⁵⁄₃₂ inch. You will never have enough drill bits to match every screw and nail, but you can make do as long as you understand what you are trying to accomplish.

Wood screws pull one piece of wood tight against the other. The pressure is exerted between the underside of the screwhead in one piece of wood, and the top face of the screw thread in the other piece of wood. This is why if you allow the screw threads to cut into the first piece of wood on their way to the second, there's no squeeze. The screw doesn't pull the way it's meant to, and the two pieces won't come tight together.

This is why it is important to drill a clearance hole through the first piece of wood. The clearance hole allows the screw threads to pass cleanly through. The clearance hole should not penetrate the second piece of

Drill clearance holes through the first piece of wood, then drive the screws down tight. The glue squeeze-out indicates a tight joint (right).

Check the squareness of the assembly before driving the second screw.

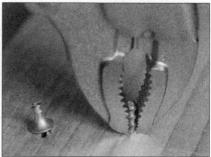

Grab a broken screw with vise-grip pliers, and twist it out of the wood.

3. Put the two pieces back together and clamp them.

4. Drill clearance holes through the top piece of wood.

5. Drive the first screw. Drive it tight enough to bury the head beneath the surface.

6. Check the alignment of the parts and if they have shifted, realign them. Then drive the remainder of the screws.

Troubleshooting

It's always possible to drive a screw so hard that the head twists off. You'll feel it let go and the head will spin freely. You will be able to tease it out of the wood with the point of a knife. When you're joining two pieces of wood face to face with a half-dozen or more screws, you can ignore the broken one. However, when you are making a joint with two or three screws in small pieces of wood, you have to remove and replace it.

Disassemble the joint before the glue sets. Remove any good screws and twist the pieces apart, exposing the broken stub. Grab it with vise-grip pliers, as shown in the photo above, and twist it out of the wood. Then scrape the semi-congealed glue off the wood and start over.

wood, though it's fine to make a pilot hole to steer the screw, and to eliminate any possibility of splitting the wood.

Combination bits for drilling clearance holes for screws typically have three different sections: A conical countersink for the screw head, a clearance section, and a pilot section. Some styles can be adjusted to suit different lengths of screw, and some can't.

Yellow glue and screws will make a permanent joint between two pieces of wood. Such a joint is stronger than the wood itself, which you can check for yourself by making a test joint and trying to break it apart. The general routine for joining wood with screws and glue has six basic steps:

1. Hold the two parts in position and draw layout lines around their intersection.

2. Take the two pieces apart so you can roll glue onto the mating surfaces, within the layout lines.

Nails with glue, and screws with glue, are interchangeable methods of joining softwood. Some people find screws easier to control, while others prefer the controlled violence of driving nails. You can substitute nails for screws, and vice versa, in most of the projects throughout this book.

For accurately made projects, the basic routine is the same for nails as for screws. It goes like this:

1. Fit the mating parts together and draw a layout line.

2. Start a couple of nails in one of the parts, then roll glue onto the mating surfaces.

3. Hold the parts together with your hand or with clamps and drive the first nail.

4. Check the alignment of the parts before you drive the second nail.

5. Drive the rest of the nails at various angles to one another, as shown in the photo at right. This dovetail effect greatly increases their holding power.

Hold the nail in position and start it into the wood with a couple of light hammer taps. Then take your holding hand out of the way and deliver four or five solid blows to drive the nail head down to the surface of the wood. Swing the hammer from your shoulder and elbow, as shown in the top photo. Aim for the surface of the wood, not for the top of the nail.

If you are new to hammers and nails, you'll probably find

Swing the hammer from your shoulder and elbow, not from your wrist. Aim for the surface of the wood, not for the head of the nail.

yourself holding the hammer handle too close to the head. This may improve your aim, but it also delivers a weak blow. Try shifting your grip back on the handle, so you can swing freely and vigorously. If you can't control the hammer when you shift your grip, try changing to a heavier hammer. Perfect your technique by driving practice nails into a scrap 2×4.

HAMMERS

There is a bewildering variety of hammers at the home center or hardware store. The choices include head weight in ounces, face shape, handle type, and claw style. The other key vari-

For greater holding power, drive the nails at an angle to one another, dovetail-fashion.

able is price. You don't need a professional carpenter's hammer, which can cost $100 or more, but you shouldn't make do with the cheapest hammer you can find, either. Expect to

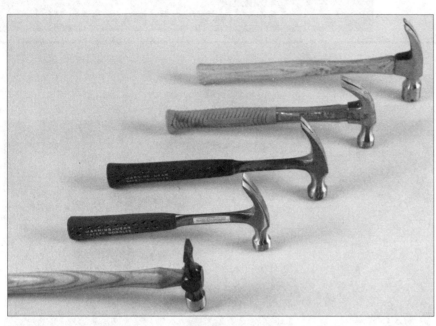

Hammers: choose the one you like. From the top: 24-ounce wooden-handled framing hammer; 16-ounce curved-claw hammer with fiberglass handle; 16-ounce framing hammer with rubber-covered steel handle; 10-ounce tack hammer; 10-ounce cross-peen cabinetmaker's hammer.

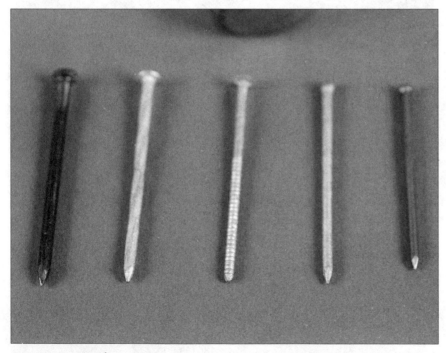

All of these are 2½ inch nails. From the left: common nail, galvanized spiral nail; siding or Maze nail; galvanized finishing nail; bright finishing nail.

pay between $15 and $20 for a good hammer. If you're using an old hammer, make sure the head and handle are securely mated to one another.

Weight: Most people are comfortable with a medium-weight hammer, 14 oz. or 16 oz. The weight should be stamped on the head itself. If you are new to driving nails, consider buying two hammers, a 10-oz. lightweight, and a 16-oz. or 18-oz. heavyweight.

Face shape: The business end of the hammer is called the face. It should be almost flat, with a very small crown, and the edges should be beveled. A hammer with a pronounced crown is liable to strike a glancing blow, bending the nail.

Claw style: The choices are a curved claw or a flat claw. The flat claw works like a pry-bar and is good for rough carpentry and demolition work. The curved claw does a good job of pulling errant nails, so it's the better choice for a general-purpose hammer.

Handle: The alternatives are wood, fiberglass, or stainless steel. They're all good, so choose what feels right in your hand.

Nail-sets: Along with your hammer, buy a set of three nail-sets for driving the heads of finishing nails below the surface of the wood. The nail-set has to be at least as big as the head of the nail, which is why you need three of them.

NAILS

For outdoor projects, choose galvanized nails. They're zinc-coated so they resist rust, and their rough surface also grips the wood better than uncoated nails. In general, use regular wire nails with flat heads for construction projects, use siding nails for furniture details, and use finishing nails when you want to conceal the nailheads. For extra strength, use spiral nails, often sold as screw flooring nails.

Siding nails, or Maze nails, are especially useful for outdoor projects. These galvanized nails were designed for holding clapboard on houses. They're long and slender, with a small head and a grooved section toward the point. The point itself is blunt, which reduces the likelihood of splitting the wood. Whenever you're tempted to use a finishing nail, see whether a Maze nail would not do instead, because it will almost always do a better job.

Like a screw, the nail has to go through the first piece of wood and into the second piece. It must go at least as deep into the second piece as the thickness of the first piece. Ideally, it should go that far again, so to nail a ¾-inch piece of wood onto a 2×4, use a 2½-inch (8d or 8-penny) nail.

When you are nailing pieces of wood together, more isn't necessarily better. When the grain of the wood runs the same way, drive nails 6 inches to 9 inches apart. When you're making a cross-grain joint, use a minimum of three nails, but never so many that the wood starts to split. As with screws, the antidote to splitting is to drill a pilot hole of about half the diameter of the nail itself.

Pulling nails

Catch the head of the nail in the claw of the hammer and lever the nail out of the wood. To protect the surface of the wood, slip

To gain leverage for pulling a nail, slip a block under the hammer head.

a scrap of wood or a shingle under the hammer claw. If the nail is too high for good leverage, slip a thick block of wood under the hammer head, as shown in the photo above. If it's buried in the surface of the wood, see whether you can insert the hammer claw or a pry-bar between the pieces.

Troubleshooting

Lotsa swats: When it takes a lot of blows—more than six—to drive a nail, you aren't delivering enough energy. Extend your swing by holding the hammer farther away from its head. If you're already holding the end of the handle, switch to a heavier hammer, even if you have to choke up on its handle.

Elephant tracks: The hammer skids off the nail head and dings the wood. Check the hammer face for dirt and clean it.

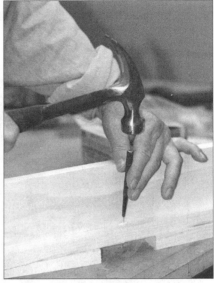

When a nail goes completely wrong, you may be able to drive it out from the back by tapping a nailset against its point.

Most projects can stand a few dents, but you can make one go away if you wet the dent, then steam the wood dry with a regular clothes iron.

The nail bends: Pull it out and start over with a new nail. Don't try to re-use a bent nail. If you were trying to nail into a knot, don't. You can't nail into knots.

Bad angle: If the nail is at the wrong angle, pull it out and try again. You can't change a nail's direction by pushing and pulling the portion that's still sticking out of the wood.

Bad aim: The point of the nail wanders out through the side of the wood, but you don't notice until after setting the nail head. Tap the point of the nail with the nail-set and drive it back, until you can catch the head with the hammer claw.

For edge-trimming, choose a lightweight trim router, such as the corded model, center, or the battery-powered one, right. A standard router, left, also will do the job, but the two plunge routers in the background are too heavy.

Most weekend project builders have electric routers, but there's no reason to buy more machine than you need. Your choices are to buy a plunge-router for $300 or more, a fixed-base router for $150, or a trim router for $50 to $75.

Some of the projects in this book can be enhanced by the straightforward edge treatments a trim router makes possible: Roundover, chamfer, cove. Trim routers are lightweight and low-powered, so you can freehand one around the edges of a project without risking yourself or your work. A fixed-base router is heavier and more powerful, so it's more difficult to maneuver freehand,

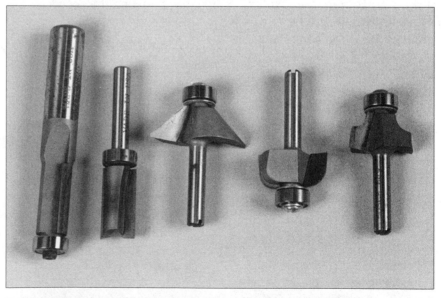

Here is a basic set of bearing-guided router cutters for edge trimming. The profiles are, from left, straight (2), chamfer or bevel, cove, and roundover.

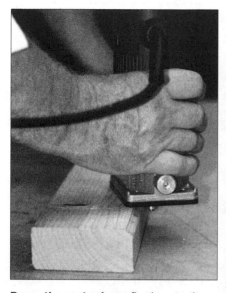

Press the router base firmly onto the workpiece and guide the bearing against the edge of the work. A trim router is light enough to be driven one-handed.

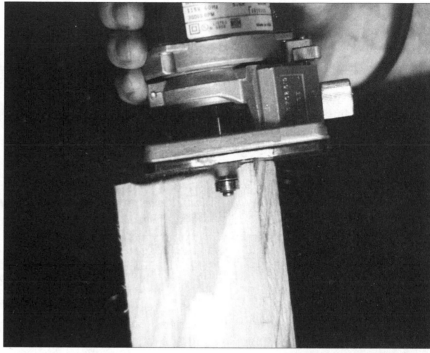

and most woodworkers mount them under tables, like wood shapers. A plunge router can make stopped cuts and other elements of joints.

When you rout the edges of the wood, you'll reduce splintering if you rout cross-grain before you rout long grain. There are several good reasons for routing edges. A smooth edge profile removes sharp corners, reduces the risk of splinters, and makes your projects more comfortable to the hand, body and eye. Furthermore, paint and varnish tend to crawl off sharp corners, which softening the edges will prevent. Even when you leave the edges square, it's always wise to round or chamfer the feet of

chairs and tables that might be dragged across a deck or patio, as shown in the photo above. This trick prevents splintering.

Choose router cutters with ball-bearing pilots, as shown in the photo at bottom left. These bits are designed to be used freehand, without a guide fence. They're guided by the ball-bearing pilot running along the surface of the wood. They cost a little more than bits with solid steel pilots, but they're easier to track and they won't burn a line into the work.

Troubleshooting

When the router cutter itself chars the work, it's either dull and in need of sharpening, or

Burnt wood indicates a dull router cutter or else moving too slowly.

you're going too slow. Move the router more quickly, and if that doesn't stop the burning, send the cutter out to be sharpened.

You've got a lot of choices for finishing outdoor woodworking projects. Each choice has advantages and disadvantages, and they all require some degree of preparation.

The basic preparation is an all-over sanding with 80-grit or 100-grit sandpaper. The goal of finish sanding is not to change the shape of the wood, but to remove sharp edges, splinters and rough spots. While you can continue sanding beyond 100 grit, except for varnish there's not much to be gained. It's more important to be thorough.

Paint and varnish tend to crawl off sharp corners, so preparation should include knocking the corners off the wood. You can do it by sanding, which retains the rectangular form and crisp look of the individual pieces of wood. You can also do it by routing a bevel or chamfer, or a roundover profile. A bevel or chamfer gives the project a more refined appearance without changing its basic lines. However, a roundover has a dramatic effect, and may totally change the appearance of the project.

Varnish

A varnish is a clear coating. Varnishes can be water-based or oil-based; both are equally good, and either may be formulated for outdoor use. All varnishes ultimately degrade in direct sun. Outdoor formulas generally include compounds for blocking ultraviolet light, increasing the resistance of the coating. Some manufacturers call outdoor preparations "spar varnish." A century ago, spar varnish was a boatbuilder's mixture that resisted deterioration by never quite drying. Nowadays it generally means a tough coating with extra ultra-violet inhibitors.

A varnish finish requires careful preparation, because any defect in the wood will show through the film. The main preparation is to sand the wood thoroughly with 150-grit paper, finer than would be necessary for paint or stain. Some varnishes require a self-primer, that is, a first coat thinned with 5% to 10% of the material's solvent. Follow the label's advice.

Whereas nothing looks better than newly varnished wood, few things look worse than varnish that has begun to deteriorate and peel. Consequently, finishing outdoor projects with varnish means making a commitment to renew the varnish more or less annually. Once varnish begins to deteriorate, there is no quick fix. You have to sand it off and start over.

Oil

An oil finish is an excellent alternative to varnish. You can buy oil-based deck finishes, or you can simply apply several coats of a brand-name oil mixture. Slop the oil onto the wood with a brush or rag, let it soak in, then wipe off the excess. Let it dry and repeat this treatment two more times. Oil dries hard, sheds water, and is easy to

Before painting, mix two-part wood filler in a disposable container and putty it onto the screw heads and into any other dings or holes. When the putty dries, which takes only minutes, sand it flush with the wood.

renew. Unlike varnish, oil does not build to a surface film.

Stain

Many outdoor projects look best when they are stained to match the siding on the house. Stains are like thin paints that color the wood without building up to a thick coating. Some stains are translucent while others are opaque. Some recent stain-type products are thicker than regular stains, and do build up a paint-like film. In fact, they are paints being sold under a different name.

Stains are not particularly tough or durable, but they are forgiving materials. They don't require primers or other elaborate surface preparations. Before refreshing a stain finish, the only essential preparation is a thorough cleaning with soap and water.

Paint

Paint is the most durable outdoor finish and in many ways the most versatile. You get control of color and degree of gloss, and modern paints are durable.

More than any other finish, paint covers the mishaps of construction, including fillers and patches. Paint preparation should include filling screw holes and nail holes with some variety of wood putty. The new two-part putties, which are very similar to auto-body filler, stick better than one-part putties, and are less

Paint a coat of primer onto the wood before moving to the color coat. Brush the primer well into the corners and onto the ends of the wood.

liable to shrink. The routine is to mix the putty, butter it over screwheads and defects in the wood, let it set, then sand it level with the surrounding surface.

Paint looks best and sticks best when it's applied over a coat of primer, which penetrates the wood and creates a surface the paint itself can adhere to. Check the label for the manufacturer's advice. In general, oil-based paints need oil-based primers, and water-based paints need water-based primers.

Basic paint maintenance is washing with soap and water. You generally cannot touch up a paint film, because the color will change in sunlight, and the new paint won't quite match the old coating. Instead, you have to

clean the surface and sand any loose areas, then recoat it completely. Unlike varnish, there's no need to go right down to bare wood.

No finish

Wood left out in the sun and rain ultimately weathers to a soft gray color. On the way, it goes through various stages of splotchy brown, and it may be a couple of years before it settles down. The advantage of no finish is no maintenance other than cleaning. The disadvantages are the way it looks on the way to weathered silvery gray, and the lack of protection for the wood. But as long as the wood can drain, it won't rot.

You don't need a lot of tools to build the projects in this book. Here are a few you will find useful, not only for project-building, but also for general handiness around your homestead.

Surform rasp

This hardened steel cheese grater removes wood quickly and cleanly. It's more useful and versatile than the clumsy file-type rasps it replaces. The tool comes in the form of a long round blade, a 10-inch flat and half-round, and a 5-inch flat and half-round. The blades are disposable, and interchangeable. For knocking the corners off pieces of wood, start with the 10-inch handle with a flat and a half-round blade. Add the other styles as you need them.

You'll get best results with the Surform if you clamp the wood to the table and grasp the tool two-handed. Move it around until you find the angle at which it cuts best.

Sandpaper and sanders

Sandpaper is your best defense against rough wood, splinters, and sharp corners. Any project will be improved by a diligent sanding, whether or not you intend to apply a finish.

Sandpaper is sold by grit size, from 36 up though 220 and even finer. Which grits you use is less important than progressing through a series of grits.

The **Surform rasp** makes short work of square corners. Experiment to find the best angle of attack.

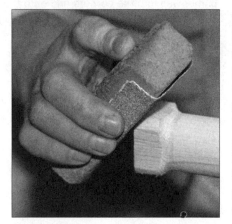

Wrap sandpaper around a cork or rubber block. Use it to refine shapes, clean up surfaces, and knock sharp corners off the wood.

If the wood is really scabrous you might have to start sanding with coarse 60-grit or 80-grit sandpaper. If it's not bad, start at 100 grit. Work over the whole project and sand out everything you want to improve. Don't leave any torn grain or deep scratches for the finer grits of paper, because sanding doesn't work that way. Progress to the next larger grit size, 100-grit or 120-grit, and sand the whole piece to remove the scratches left by the coarser paper. If you intend to paint, you can stop now. If you're going for a perfect varnish finish, proceed to 150-grit or 220-grit, and sand the whole piece yet again. If you discover that you have forgotten to sand some hideous ding, drop right back to coarse paper. Confine your touch-up sanding to the area of the ding, but be sure to work through the whole grit sequence again.

Always sand with a sanding block. While you can grab any

convenient chunk of scrap, it's wasteful because overhanging edges of paper don't do any work. Instead, buy a ¼-sheet cork sanding block from a wood-working supply house, or a ⅓-sheet hard rubber block from the hardware store.

To get high sandpaper mileage, tap the debris out of the grit, and frequently brush the dust off the work. Clogged, torn and bare sandpaper doesn't work.

For power sanding, consider a new random-orbit sander for about $100. It will see you through every finishing chore except grinding off old enamel paint, for which a chemical stripper is better anyway. A cheap vibrating sander is virtually worthless, as is a rotating disk sander; the new detail sanders, which accept pads of various shapes, are excellent; a belt sander takes skill and is more machine than you need for weekend project-building.

Pocket knife

With a sharp pocket knife, you can sidestep many woodworking and home repair problems simply by whittling a piece to fit. The same knife can be used for scribing layout lines, sharpening pencils and puttying holes in the wood. Also for clipping tubes of glue, opening bubble-packs, peeling oranges, and cleaning fingernails. Don't leave home without it.

Pry bar

When you join two pieces in the wrong way, or want to remove the trim from around a window or door, you'll need a pry bar. An old-style crowbar or cat's paw is too thick. The hammer won't do because the handle interferes with the claw. Hardware stores sell a thin steel bar with a sharp bend near one end; one common brand is Wonder-Bar. They come in various handy sizes. Get a little one and a big one.

Bench brush

Back in 7th grade shop class, Mr. Mitchell made sure there was a bench brush in the tool well of every four-boy worktable. It was the only tool you were allowed to leave out, and trying to escape without cleaning up would see you hauled up by the shirt collar.

A pry bar pulls nails and shifts whatever is stuck together or in the wrong place.

Well, Old Man Mitchell was right. Start every project with a clean deck, brush the debris off the worktable as you go, brush it off the project, brush it off yourself. You'll feel better, your project will go better, and perhaps most important, the wood dust won't adulterate the glue.

Sweeping the sawdust and debris off the worktable has the helpful side-effect of clearing the mind for the next step in the project.

INDEX

If you've enjoyed this book, you may be interested in these other titles from Rodale Press.

ACCENTS FOR THE COUNTRY HOME
by Nick Engler
14 projects that are easy to build in a short amount of time—miniatures, candlestands, toys, bowls. Plus techniques for drawing an oval and turning small parts on the drill press.
124 pages; paperback $14.95. ISBN 0–87857–842–0

COUNTRY PINE: Furniture You Can Make with the Table Saw and Router
by Bill Hylton
30 first-class country furniture projects (benches, hutches, tables, chests), each one based on a real antique but redrawn and built with modern tools and techniques. Measured drawings and meticulous step-by-step instructions show you how to make them using primarily a table saw and router.
314 pages; hardcover $27.95. ISBN 0–87596–650–0

DECKS: How to Design and Build the Perfect Deck for Your Home
by Tim Snyder
This book gives you all the know-how you'll need to build any deck, plus 12 deck designs with step-by-step instructions for building them, and a color gallery of decks to inspire you with your own design.
244 pages; paperback $14.95. ISBN 0–87857–955–9

THE GREAT ALL-AMERICAN WOODEN TOY BOOK
by Norm Marshall
Give the kids and grandkids something special! Toys, toys, and more toys—50 projects in all—boats, planes, trucks, tractors, animals—with scaled patterns for all the parts.
212 pages; paperback $13.95. ISBN 0–87857–628–2

OUTDOOR FURNITURE FOR THE BACKYARD BUILDER: Easy-to-Build Projects for the Yard and Deck
by Bill Hylton with Fred Matlack and Phil Gehret
Don't settle for store-bought junk! Make your own glider, picnic table and benches, adirondack chairs, and porch rockers—well-designed projects that will last a lifetime.
120 pages; paperback $12.95. ISBN 0–87596–728–0

OUTDOOR FURNITURE FOR THE WEEKEND WOODWORKER: Stylish Projects for the Yard and Deck
by Bill Hylton with Fred Matlack and Phil Gehret
You can't buy outdoor furniture that's this well made. Or better looking. With this book, you'll make sturdy, attractive tables, chairs, and loungers out of solid wood, using detailed step-by-step instructions.
120 pages; paperback $12.95. ISBN 0–87596–727–2

SHELVING AND STORAGE
by Nick Engler
All 16 of these projects are designed to help bring order to the chaos of "stuff" you live with. And they're good-looking as well. Your books, bikes, blankets, stereo equipment, closets, and knickknacks can all be better organized with the projects here.
124 pages; paperback $14.95. ISBN 0–87857–851–X

SHOP TIPS: Expert Advice on Making the Most of Your Shop Time and Tools from America's Best Woodworkers
Over 600 tips direct from the shops of 200 professional woodworkers! Plus 33 longer entries detailing essential woodworking techniques and machines, and a whole chapter on designing and building a workbench.
312 pages; hardcover $27.95. ISBN 0–87596–591–1

THE WORKSHOP COMPANION: Using the Scroll Saw
by Nick Engler
A full-service owner's manual, this book shows you everything you need to know about setting up and using a scroll saw, including how to make your own from a saber saw. Four scroll-saw projects.
124 pages; hardcover $19.95. ISBN 0–87596–654–3

THE WORKSHOP COMPANION: Using the Table Saw
by Nick Engler
Get more from your table saw! More accuracy, more safety. Better crosscuts, smoother rips. Dead-on miters, perfect dadoes. Cut coves and tapers. More than a dozen jigs, and three furniture projects.
124 pages; hardcover $19.95. ISBN 0–87596–127–4

 For more information or to order any of these books, call 1-800-848-4735 or fax us anytime at 1-800-813-6627. Or visit our World Wide Web site at: http://www.woodforum.com